The Drum and the Hoe

THE DRUM
AND THE HOE

Life and Lore of the Haitian People

BY HAROLD COURLANDER

UNIVERSITY OF CALIFORNIA PRESS

Berkeley, Los Angeles, London

University of California Press
Berkeley and Los Angeles

University of California Press, Ltd.
London, England

© *1960 by Harold Courlander*

California Library Reprint Series Edition 1973

Published with the assistance of
grants from the Ford Foundation and
the John Simon Guggenheim Foundation

ISBN: 0-520-02364-1
Library of Congress Catalog Card Number: 72-95299

Designed by Adrian Wilson

Printed in the United States of America

For Emma

Preface

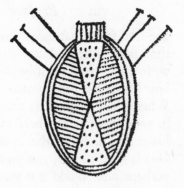

Every student of Haitian life is soon impressed by the richness of the materials spread out before him and the necessity of limiting his field of investigation. A study of Haitian religious practices, for example, draws one deeper and deeper into profusion, variation, and contradiction. One finds little difficulty in drawing a generalized picture with swift, bold lines; but when he descends into detail he discovers that the broad generalizations of the religious system contain within them many shifting and even warring motifs, and that what in one region is held to be true is not so regarded in another. The gods of *Vodoun* that are revered in one village are given only perfunctory treatment in another. Rites for the dead have a common denominator everywhere in the country, but each community brings to them something of its own or emphasizes traditions that elsewhere are forgotten. So it is also with music and dancing. A traditional drum rhythm may have one name in the north and another in the south, or a certain rhythm may be called by different names. There are diverse opinions about which dances are preferred by certain deities. The meaning of a song can be interpreted differently by different people. It is therefore no wonder that competent works on Haiti do not completely agree with one another in many respects, or that they seem, now and then, to be saying different or even contradictory things. Yet in many instances the seeming inconsistencies are in reality only minor variants within an overall scheme.

The purpose of this book is to present a broad view of certain aspects of Haitian culture and wherever possible to extract some of the flavor of Haitian thinking as well as its sense. It is easy to be fooled in regard to both. I remember seeing an old bearded man in the mountains beyond Furcy walking around his freshly hoed garden breaking a ripe tomato into small juicy bits which he scattered on the ground. It was about as primitive a method of planting as I had ever seen, and I wondered if even one seed from that tomato would ever take root under the hot sun. Some time later, when I knew this man well, I talked to him about the care with which seeds must be planted if they are to grow properly. I told him how *we* grew *our* tomatoes. He listened carefully, nodding his head. When I had finished he said: "Yes, that must be a good way to do things in your country. But here in this valley God is good. He does not forget his children. From the broken tomato many plants will sprout. When God is good to you, you do not have to count the seeds." I suggested that perhaps one should not waste any of the precious seeds that God had provided; and to this he replied: "How is there waste? My garden is made to flourish by Zaka [the country man's special deity]. Some people give Zaka a feast every year, but between times they forget. Zaka helps me in my work, and I don't forget him. When I break the tomato and put it on the ground that way, it is a little taste for Zaka. Whatever I plant, I give him some. He is good to me, I am good to him."

What I learned from many incidents like this one was that the eye does not always see correctly. The old man was not just planting tomatoes, nor was he performing a conventionalized ritual act. It was a highly personalized act of faith in nature and confidence in the deity who shared his work.

A large part of this book deals with Vodoun, the religious practices based on West African traditions. One soon discovers that the songs and dances of Vodoun ritual are not merely music and motion supplementing and decorating more serious affairs. Virtually every aspect of Vodoun ritual is placative or invocational. The songs that are sung and the dances that are danced are direct supplication of various supernatural forces.

Undoubtedly, a number of principles which are put forward in this study do not apply equally to every region of Haiti; but they are, I think, true in general terms. Not until one has accepted the fact that different explanations exist for given phenomena, that the same rites are performed in different fashion in different places, and that the cult priests themselves do not agree on many details, may one begin to work toward a general view of the Haitian scene.

All of Haitian life is not Vodoun. And there are of course some Haitians who are relatively outside the central circle of its influence. But the inner meanings of Vodoun and its relationship to the total view of life permeate the entire scene. Music, too, binds together practically the entire fabric of Haitian existence. It is essential not only to the cult temple but to countless workaday activities. Agrarian work groups often perform their tasks to the accompaniment of a drum. And in the cult temple, the iron hoe of the fields often serves as a percussion instrument.

The Drum and the Hoe is the result of studies made over a period of

years. Several short sections of this book have appeared in substance in
Haiti Singing (1939), the *Musical Quarterly,* the *Journal of Negro History,* and other journals. The song and story texts presented in several
chapters were taken on disc and tape recorders during nine separate field
trips to Haiti, between 1937 and 1955. They have been selected from more
than six hundred examples recorded by this method.

Support for work on these recorded materials was received from the
American Council of Learned Societies and the American Philosophical
Society. Research on African survivals in the New World was aided by a
Guggenheim fellowship. Originals or copies of some of the tape and disc
recordings are now in the archives of Indiana University and Northwestern University.

The persons who helped me gather songs, stories, legends, and lore
were innumerable. Many of them I did not know by name, but I want to
thank them as well as the following friends for their open-hearted assistance in many ways:

Voluska Saintvil (Ti Goave), Joseph Dérosier (Cap Haitien), Julia
Immacula (Southwest Haiti), Sigbrien Bellis (Port-au-Prince), Vénéise
Macélise (Léogane), André Jean (Morne l'Hôpital), Christophe Oxilas
(Ti Goave), Edgar Dérosier (Port-au-Prince), Isnardé Din (Léogane),
Wilfred Beauchamp (Port-de-Paix), Lydia Augustin (l'Asile), Louise
Joseph (Port-au-Prince), St. Élia Alsandor (Jérémie), Georgette Alcède
(Southwest Haiti), Élizia Moron (Anse-à-Veau), Prosper Louis (Port-au-Prince), Télisman Charles (Morne l'Hôpital), André Charles (Morne
l'Hôpital), Daïs Charles (Anse-à-Veau), Simon Jean (Pétionville), Tonton Cabrit (Morne l'Hôpital), Micano Cassis (Cap Haitien), Louis Desbornes (Port-au-Prince), André Coyotte (Port-au-Prince), Innomine
Pierre (Morne l'Hôpital), George Gabriel (Port-au-Prince), Simeon Benjamin (Port-au-Prince), Romain St. Aude (Port-de-Paix), Jean Ravel
Pintro (Jérémie), La France Belvue (Anse-à-Veau), Morgina La Vache
(Jacmel), Alten St. Ville (Morne l'Hôpital), Abner Juslin (Port-au-Prince), Jean Louis La Rivière (Dondon), St. Jean Nago (La Gonave),
Jean Pierre Marigot (Terrier-Rouge), Libera Borderau (Morne Mardi
Gras), Charles Hector (Anse-à-Veau), Immacula Lorival (Southwest
Haiti), Aléanne François (Port-au-Prince), Felix Charlotin (Southwest
Haiti), Julie Gentil (Port-au-Prince), Lena Hibbert (Anse-à-Veau), Ti
Yogan Borderau (Léogane), César Jeanbaptiste (Southwest Haiti) and
Idamente Joseph (Ti Rivière de Nippes). Special thanks are due Aléis
Conrolé, a *houngan* of the region of Morne Mardi Gras, who was generous
in many ways in explaining the workings of the cult temple.

I am of course indebted to the work of a number of scholars, cited herein, who have reported on various aspects of the Haitian scene. And to Dr. Melville J. Herskovits, Dr. William Bascom, Dr. George Eaton Simpson, and Dr. George Herzog I wish to express my appreciation for their many acts of encouragement and support of this study. For permission to reproduce some of their photographs, my thanks go to Dr. George Eaton Simpson, Roger Coster, and Mme Odette Mennesson Rigaud. The music transcriptions in chapter 19 were prepared by Dr. Mieczyslaw Kolinski.

HAROLD COURLANDER

Contents

xii   *Contents*

Illustrations

PICTURE CREDITS

1. The Making of the Haitian

If you come to Haiti by sea, a way that is old-fashioned but full of magic, you are first aware of the island as a range of hills rising out of the water, and then, as you sail closer, new ranges come into view behind the first, and eventually you see that everything is mountains. The ranges pile up in the distance and finally lose themselves in the white morning mists that the country people call "snow." A Haitian proverb says, "Behind the mountains are mountains," and that is a true picture of the island.

In the summer after the rains have come, the hills and mountain slopes are green; but later they turn brown, and it is then that one notices the deep gashes where the earth has eroded and washed away into the valleys below and into the sea.

From the top of the range called La Selle ("The Saddle"), when the heavy mists form and settle across the highland valleys one sees nothing but the great rounded sugar-loaf peaks, which appear as floating islands in a vast sea of white.

From a distant ship in the Caribbean in the full glare of daylight it is hard to imagine that millions of people have made a home of these mountains. But at night it is different. The mountains are alive then with twinkling spots of light made by cooking fires, torches, and electric bulbs. For the hillsides as well as the coastal lowlands are dotted with tiny huts and homesteads, and the trails from one village to another crisscross and lie on the land like a woven net. They lead from the high-up places down to the seacoast towns, through the waterless mesa of the frontier, through the pine forests of the southern range, through dense blankets of wild strawberries, wild-bamboo groves, and plantations of coffee. They find their way to the salt marches, the rice fields of the Artibonite Valley, and the cities.

In the lowlands the days are hot and tropical. It is there the sugar cane, bananas, and plantains grow so lushly. In the mountains the people have fires in their houses at night to keep out the damp cold that sweeps through the passes. And a man on the trail before dawn may wear a blanket over his head and carry a glowing ember with him for warmth.

On the south coast there are sometimes hurricanes and tidal waves, and many a small fishing boat and grass-covered house has been washed away in these storms. But the great mountains of the southern range deflect the winds, so that to the north their full fury is never known.

In the great Bay of Gonaïves the fishing boats sail out at night with the friendly winds that carry them to the fishing grounds of the island of La Gonave, and they return to the shore with their catches in the morning, or in the afternoon with the setting sun. The sailing boats from the tiny fishing village called Ville Matelot each day pass the deserted islet named Isle à Cabrit, where four Indian camps once stood. Today Isle à Cabrit is only a waterless, denuded place, a hunting ground for Carib and Arawak pottery and carved stone images.

In the frontier lakes of the Cul-de-Sac Plain there are wild ducks and alligators. Here the villagers fish with nets from rafts and dugout canoes. Now and then an iguana is seen, but there is little other game, because the edible wildlife of the country was long ago eaten by hungry people.

For the things that grow wild the Haitian is grateful—the avocado, the mango, the cashew, and the cotton which once planted produces again and again each year. He is grateful for the coconut palms, the calabash tree, the gourd vines, and the medicinal herbs that grow on every side. But the gifts of nature are not prolific. Most of the great stands of timber— lignum vitae, mahogany, dyewood and pine—have been cut away. Once fertile garden spots have dried up, and the soil that produces the yams, the pumpkins, the kaffir, and the rice is tired.

But the Haitian himself is not tired. He has suffered from malaria, yaws, and chronic hunger; yet out of the great old mountains of Haiti he has fashioned a way of life and a nation.

The Haitian of today was created out of the fabric of three continents— Africa, America, and Europe. He was shaped out of the plains and hills of Nigeria, Dahomey, and the Congo; the summers and winters of Europe; and the mountains and mountain mists of Haiti itself. He is the synthesis of the folk beliefs of the French and Spanish peasants, the Yoruba and the Arada of West Africa, and perhaps of the Carib Indians with whom he had close contact during his first days in the New World. He has brought into affinity the religious practices of Africa and the beliefs of the Church of Rome. He is outwardly simple and poor, but inwardly he is a complicated and rich man. He is rich in music, in the capacity for spiritual expression, in tradition, in folklore, and in memories. He has been able to marry work to play, drudgery to singing, and despair to hope. In his complicated world, life and death are simply different aspects of the same thing. Those who die live as long as people remember them. And those who are alive in the physical sense are receptacles for the spiritual forces that exist on all sides—the echoes of the dead, the multitude of spirit beings, good and evil, and dancing and music.

What are the origins of this simple and complicated man?

The beginnings of the Haitian came with the discovery of America and the establishment of slavery in the New World. When the Spanish colonizers first began to organize the economy of the new colony of Hispaniola, as they called it, they attempted to enslave the indigenous Caribs to work the fields. But the Indians of Haiti found no sense and no comfort in the new system. It violated their views of life and destroyed their culture. They were proud, and they were not resilient. They did not care to pan gold for the Spaniards or to grow sugar for them. They died under the conditions of slavery, or fled into the mountains, or took to the sea in their canoes, looking for sanctuary on other islands where the Europeans had not yet settled. They left the rich earth of the Haitian valleys to the conquistadores. In less than eighteen years the new Spanish colony was dying on the vine for lack of laborers. It was then that Spain, like France, England, and Portugal, turned its eyes to Africa. There were old precedents. The Spanish and Portuguese had for many years used the African for labor. They had had intimate contact with Africans during the Moorish invasion of Iberia. And the slave trade had been an old and familiar thing even before the discovery of America.

The first Africans sent to Haiti arrived there in 1510. The precise origins of these first African immigrants to the New World are not known, but they came from somewhere along that long stretch of African coast between Senegal and Angola. It was a great crossroads in world history. As much as any other ethnic group, these Africans and those who came after them built America. They, as much as any other, turned the West Indies into a prize over which the nations of Europe fought for three hundred years. And in Haiti, as in Brazil, the United States, and other American nations, they raised moral and ethical issues for the peoples of European stock which have not been solved to our own day.

The acquisition and transportation of slaves is an old and familiar story. Slavery was an ancient institution in some parts of Africa. Some of the wars between kingdoms were, in part at least, huge slave raids. In other wars, the taking of slaves was only incidental. But the selling of these human chattels to European merchants came as easily to African chieftains as it did to Arab entrepreneurs. Often they were merely selling off "surplus" stock. The African's motives sometimes were political rather then mercenary—to weaken and disperse unfriendly neighboring tribes. Occasionally, members of a royal family, possible contenders for tribal power and all the prerogatives that went along with it, were "exiled" in this extremely effective and final way. Although Africans were the victims of this monstrous commerce, it is clear that without the participation and coöperation of other Africans the slave trade as it existed in the sixteenth, seventeenth, and eighteenth centuries would not have been possible. The African, along with the Asian and the European, shares the guilt for the indecencies and degradation that grow out of human barter.

The voyage to the New World was at best horrible and inhuman. Nothing that can be said about the manner in which the captains of the slavers attempted to care for their cargoes can change the picture. The slaves suffered from thirst, disease, hunger, seasickness, and impersonal brutality. The anxiety and dread which these captives must have suffered in anticipation of things to come are difficult to imagine. A strange, unfamiliar world awaited them across an ocean larger than Africa itself. Some slaves killed themselves. Others who had survived long overland marches died of exhaustion or disease aboard the slave vessels. And many a slaver had to report in its log that a number of chained males, taking advantage of a brief spell on the upper decks, had leaped into the sea.

But among those who reached port in the New World there was a fierce determination to survive. The history of African slavery in the Americas is full of accounts of resistance and revolt against the European masters. The shipwrecked slaves who took over the Island of St. Vincent and came to be known as the Black Caribs, the Ashanti who revolted and vanquished the Dutch armed forces in Surinam, the Maroons of Jamaica, and the ex-slaves of Haiti who destroyed Napoleon's armies, all bear witness to the unquenched spirit of those millions of Africans exiled from their own land.

Whereas the Indians of Haiti were not resilient, the Africans were. More and more slaves were poured into Hispaniola. By the eighteenth century the slave population represented countless tribes and kingdoms of West Africa. There were Senegalese, Foulas, Poulards, Sosos, Bambarras, Kiambaras, Mandingos, and Yolofs from northwest Africa. There were Aradas, Mahis, Haoussas, Ibos, Anagos or Yorubas, Bini, Takwas, Fidas, Amines, Fantis, Agouas, Sobos, Limbas, and Adjas from the coast and interior of the great bulge of Africa. From Angola and the Congo basin came the Solongos, the Mayombés, the Mousombés, the Moundongues, the Bumbas, the Kangas, and others. Although there is no official record, Haitians themselves say that there were also those tall people known as the Jangheys, or Dinkas, from the region of the Upper Nile, and Bagandas from Uganda.[1] A few proper names that have survived, such as Ras Médé, suggest that there may have been men from Ethiopia among them. Old slavers' records show that numerous shipments were made from Madagascar and Mozambique on the East African coast.[2]

These transplanted people came from all classes and stations of life. Some were criminals condemned and sold by their own tribesmen; others were prisoners captured in intertribal raids or by Arab slave hunts. There were men of royal blood among them, as well as artisans and tribal scholars. The slave cargoes included leaf doctors, bards, musicians, wood carvers, metalworkers, drum makers, boatbuilders, hunters, and farmers.

In Haiti they were thrown together into a common mold. Shoulder to shoulder in the plantation fields were Bambarras, Anagos, Takwas, and Bumbas—peoples with different backgrounds, different languages, different legends, and different traditions. There were Moslems and so-called pagans, herdsmen and river-boatmen. Each of them brought something of his past and unwittingly poured it into the new amalgam that was to be the Haitian.

And into this amalgam flowed some of the literature, the traditions, the religious thoughts, and the superstitions of Europe. Under Spanish, French, and English rulers the slaves were constantly subjected to ways and ideas that were new to them. They absorbed and digested, and out of the diverse and even contradictory elements they worked out new patterns of life and thinking. This was the strength and resiliency of the West African in the New World. His capacity for adaptation and for remembering what was valuable to him and forgetting what had ceased to be useful preserved his spirit and his pride.

Among the things that were lost in this vast process of adaptation were the traditions of wood carving, bronze and brass casting, and weaving. Remembered, however, were music, dancing, games, religious beliefs, concepts of nature and the supernatural, folk tales, and legends. It was the outward, material things that were abandoned, and the inward, nonmaterial things that tended to survive.

The slave system itself was largely responsible for the loss of special arts and skills. Craftsmen with specialized knowledge in metalwork were set to repairing wagons and hoes, or they simply wielded hoes in the fields. Wood carvers found no patrons to encourage them to carve images and stools. The colonial emphasis was on mass production of sugar. Other things were valueless. There was little leisure or incentive for the slave to follow his artistic aptitudes.

And yet the things that survived were able to do so, in certain respects, because of the particular brand of thinking of the colonial masters. Why has so much of the African past survived in Haiti when it has been all but obliterated in the United States? The answer lies primarily in the Catholic background of the Europeans who controlled the colony—first the Spanish, and then the French. The Catholic Church regarded every slave as a soul to be saved, as a complete and finished man except for salvation. And though it was an official of the Church who is alleged to have suggested African slavery in the New World,[3] the Church itself took the view that the differences between the slave owner and the slave were only worldly and transient things. The Church did not insist on washing out of the African mind everything that was there. It regarded its mission as that of supplying the single quality that was lacking—salvation. Its attitudes during the past four hundred years in Haiti have been vacillating and erratic; it has often pressed for destruction of the African cults; but on the whole it has been satisfied with conversion.

The Protestant churches in Haiti, on the contrary, have demanded that their converts become new people. They have forbidden their adherents to take any part in non-Christian rituals or other activities—including even the dance. They have presented them with a simple and painful choice.

These were the essential attitudes that prevailed during slavery days in the United States. In the beginning, while plantation owners fought against church activities among the Negroes, the church and the plantation owners were largely united in their war against "heathen" practices. Africanisms which might have either died in due course or persisted were stamped out with Puritan fervor. Significantly, it was in French-Catholic Louisiana that African-style drumming, singing, and dancing survived in the United States to the beginning of this present century.

The Catholic attitude of tolerance-by-necessity in Haiti won for it most of the country's four million souls. Today, many a Haitian who participates in the rites of Vodoun on Saturday worships in a Catholic chapel on Sunday.

Such sporadic efforts as were made to wipe out African memories in Haiti were unsuccessful. Slowly the uprooted slaves found a common denominator. The peoples of different origins developed a common language based on the French spoken by the masters. Their different religious systems merged one into another.

The necessity for adaptation and amalgamation produced a cultural hybrid of an energetic and vital kind. By the beginning of the nineteenth century the people of African descent in Haiti were a cultural alloy, fired and hardened and ready to deal with the French, the Spanish, and the English in battle or in politics. They were no longer slaves struggling to cope with a new and strange system. Little by little, imperceptibly they had become true Haitians.

2. Man and the Universe: Vodoun

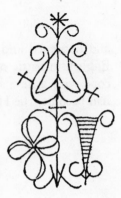

When the African slaves stepped ashore in the New World they brought with them highly developed religious beliefs and attitudes toward life. But Africa was a continent of many cultures and nations, and its belief systems varied. The Congo African did not have the same view of the natural and supernatural as the Senegalese, for example; and even neighboring peoples such as the Ibos, the Yorubas, and the Mahis did not have common religious traditions. Yet in the strange new land that was Haiti, the common elements in their religious beliefs were accented. In time a new composite religious system emerged. It was called Vodoun.

The preponderance of Africans in Haiti came from the region of Dahomey, Togoland, Nigeria, and the Congo River basin. Among them the Dahomeans were the most numerous, and it was they who provided the framework for the Afro-Haitian religious system.

The word Vodoun itself is Dahomean in origin. Among the Fon-speaking people of West Africa it signified "spirit," or "deity." In Haiti the word came to be applied in a general sense to all the activities of cult life, from the ritual of the "temple" to the songs and dances, though in some old songs it still applies specifically to the idea of a supernatural spirit. However, the Congo word *loa* came to be used to designate the deities.[1]

In a literal sense, Vodoun in Haiti consists of the rites, beliefs, and practices of the Vodoun cult, built around the similar religious systems of the Dahomeans and the Nagos. In a wider sense it applies to similar but distinct ritual activities of other cults. The Ibo-Kanga rites and dances are in a specific sense "not quite" Vodoun. The rites in the Congo-Guinée cult group—made up of Congo, Bambarra, "Guinée," and miscellaneous elements—have separate practices and deities of their own, and are often regarded as not Vodoun at all. Yet the term Vodoun is used in a generic sense to include all these rites, and examination of the beliefs and activities of these cult groups shows that they have drawn in considerable measure upon a common inheritance.

Vodoun is clearly more than ritual of the cult temple. It is an integrated system of concepts concerning human behavior, the relation of mankind to those who have lived before, and to the natural and supernatural forces of the universe. It relates the living to the dead and to those not yet born. It "explains" unpredictable events by showing them to be consistent with established principles. In short, it is a true religion which attempts to tie the unknown to the known and thus create order where chaos existed before.

As in Dahomey, it is not a system imposed from above but one which pushes out from below. It is bred and nurtured in the family, in the towns, and in the fields. It is common law, with deep roots in an unbroken and continuous past. The priests of Vodoun do not control it and direct its course. They, like the least fortunate peasant, simply move about within it and make use of its resources. They are its servants and its interpreters. In their cult centers, the principles of Vodoun are brought into sharp focus and dramatized. Vodoun is democratic in concept. Any man or woman may have direct contact with the deities or dead ancestors without the intervention of the cult priest. There is no place or situation beyond the influence of the loa or beyond the limits of Vodoun. At every crossroads is the spirit of the crossroads guardian, Legba, and on every long trail is the spirit of the Master of the Highway.

The cult priest nevertheless plays a significant and essential role. He translates beliefs that otherwise might tend to become amorphous into formalized action. He is a teacher, a repository of cult learning, and a vital catalyst. He gives form to abstraction, and practical meaning to symbols. He is the intellectualizing agency of a tremendous emotional force. Through his knowledge of the substance and forms of Vodoun, his experience in dealing with the loa, and in some instances his capacity to set magical forces into action, the cult priest is a dynamic power within his community.

Though the making of *pouins* and *magie* (ritual magic) and *ouangas* (aggressive magic directed against individuals) is within the realm of the cult priest's activities, these things are part of Vodoun only in a subsidiary sense. Magic lurks on the periphery of Vodoun. It has little or no place in the placating of the deities or the dead. It concerns the relationship of the living with each other and with *lou-garos* (*loups-garous*) and *baka* (demons). Although cult rituals include various pouin and magie ceremonies, the cult priest draws upon magic as he draws upon other mystic arts and fields of learning—leaf doctoring, divination, Catholic ritual, and Masonic symbolism. He attempts to bring together all thinking that widens the scope of Vodoun, in order to strengthen his hand to deal with all aspects of the natural and supernatural. But the reputable cult priest does not dabble in "black" magic—the kind that maims or destroys human beings. One who does so is said to "work with two hands": one for the loa and one for evil. (The expression *servi dé main*—"serving with two hands"—is also applied to a cult chief who deals with deities of more than one "nation.") Many a cult priest in making his ritual flour drawings on the earth holds his left hand behind his back and draws with his right, giving testimony that he "works with one hand" only.

Each cult priest maintains his own cult temple, or *hounfor*. There are no cult officials above him, as there is no formal religious organization beyond the hounfor itself. Within his own special community he is therefore the chief religious functionary, the apex of an intratemple social organization. Under the cult priest, ordinarily, there are two grades of assistants, and below them two classes of servitors.

The cult priest is usually referred to as a *houngan*, a Fon (Dahomean) title signifying "spirit chief." Sometimes he is called *gangan* (a Bantu word meaning "conjuror" or "doctor") [2] or *capla*. He also is known by the title *bocô* or *bocor*, which seems to be derived from *bocono*, the diviner or priest of the Dahomean Fa cult. [3] The bocor is, in fact, sometimes referred to as a *divineur*, and he is regarded by some Haitians as a clairvoyant and a practitioner of magic. As in Dahomey, the bocor in Haiti foretells fate through the throwing of shells or chips, much in the manner of the secular game *mayamba*. He also reads destiny with small sticks or ashes. In earlier days the cult priest was sometimes known by the Yoruba name *babalao*, a title which has been corrupted to *papaloi*. A female cult leader is known as a *mambo*. She is presumed to have, in a general way, the same powers as the houngan, though in some quarters her *connaissance*, or "understanding," is not regarded so highly, and her status is believed to be somewhat lower.

Directly under the houngan is his chief assistant, the *laplace*, and perhaps a little below him on the ladder, the *mambo caille*. The laplace is regarded as the vice-houngan, and he assumes responsibility for running the hounfor in the absence of his chief. The mambo caille, a woman, runs the cult center in the absence of both the houngan and the laplace. One step farther down the ladder is the *houngénicon*, who acts as a sort of chief of the main body of devotees. These high-ranking assistants to the houngan are sometimes called *badjicans*, or keepers of the altar.

The servitors of the cult are known as *hounsi*, or "spirit wives," a name that was given to certain categories of cult servants in Dahomey. [4] There are two main groups of hounsi: *kanzo* (those who have passed through a ritual fire test) and *bossale* (those whose loa are wild or untamed). The loa makes his appearance in Vodoun ritual by possessing ("mounting") one or more of the participants. When these possessions first occur, the possessed persons lapse into a kind of frenzy without controls or direction. They may stagger, fall, and go into convulsions. The deity must be controlled so that he will not harm the person whose body he takes over. The houngan eventually establishes a conditioned, formalized response to possession; and once this is achieved, the loa is regarded as having been tamed. The *hounsi bossale* then becomes eligible for elevation to the status of kanzo. The term *kanzo* means "to tie fire"; that is, to conquer or show mastery over fire. Demonstrations of supremacy of possessed persons over flames, hot coals, and red-hot metal characterize many Vodoun rituals. In the kanzo ritual the initiate must undergo the test of boiling oil.

The hierarchy of the cult temple, in general, looks like this:

> *Houngan* (or *Mambo*)—chief of the hounfor
> *Laplace*—first assistant to the houngan
> *Mambo caille*—"mistress of the house"
> *Houngénicon*—topmost of all the hounsi
> *Hounsi kanzo*—the highest grade of hounsi
> *Hounsi bossale*—the lowest grade of hounsi

Among the hounsi there are some who have special duties or functions. There is the *reine silence,* for example, whose job is to maintain order. The one assigned to cook the various sacrifices is called the *hounsi cuisinière,* and so on.

There is no single, clear-cut process for becoming a Vodoun priest. A man with special talents may rise from the rank of hounsi and eventually become a houngan by succession. Or a person with a strong *connaissance* may simply feel the call—sometimes in a dream—and establish himself as a houngan or bocor. If such a man demonstrates that he is "strong," a following will gather around him to constitute his *société.*

When a houngan dies, his cult center may be abandoned, or it may be taken over by another established houngan or by the deceased man's protégé. Frequently the laplace will inherit the cult temple and all that goes with it. Acquisition of a cult center by inheritance is looked upon as a means of keeping an established hounfor intact. The man who wishes to achieve the rank of houngan applies to the oldest and most venerable cult priest in the district and announces that he wishes to receive the *asson* (the ritual rattle) that is, to become a houngan. If the elder priest approves and wishes to sponsor the younger man's elevation, he consults other reputable houngans and arranges for a *grand service* for purification and investiture. The elder cult priest conducts the ceremonies. He is regarded as especially wise because of his age and long experience in dealing with the loa, whose approval of the candidate's elevation is needed. He is also regarded as being on more intimate terms with the family ancestors who, likewise, must be in accord with the proceedings. The candidate for the asson is confined within the hounfor for a number of days, during which he takes purification baths and participates in other rituals. The rites that take place during this period are prescribed by the elder priest who has assumed responsibility. When the purification is ended, the candidate emerges into the *peristyle* (roofed court) to participate in the general service, and to undergo further tests.

Present during the ceremonies are all the principal houngans of the region—men who will be friendly associates of the new priest or, possibly, unfriendly competitors. The candidate is tested on his knowledge of how to use the asson and the tiny hand bell, and in the course of the service he is mounted by the loa who is the chief protector of the cult temple. Animals are sacrificed, and all the loa sacred to the hounfor are invoked and asked for their approval and support. But it is not only the loa and the dead who must indicate their approval. The elder houngan polls the hounsi kanzo on whether they will accept their new cult chief and follow him. He also asks the chief drummer, who polls his assistant drummers. It is taken for granted that the decision is in the hands of the hounsi. The consensus is known before the actual service, but the formality of asking the question is observed. Should the hounsi refuse to accept the candidate for the asson, the elevation cannot take place.

The city and the countryside contain many self-styled houngans and bocors who are not recognized as bona fide by the community, regardless of the route by which they claim to have achieved their station. Sometimes they are regarded as *pas fort* (not strong); that is, they do not have profound knowledge and understanding. The Haitian is quick to detect the difference between a houngan who knows and one who does not know. Many are stated to be outright fakes. One man who attempted to hold a service in Port-au-Prince aroused such contempt and disgust that a number of persons who had been drawn by genuine interest walked out with remarks that the man should be punished. In fact, his failure to show any essential qualifications for the houngan's role was commented upon in a song of ridicule that made its appearance at a secular dance that same night. The song noted some of the humorous aspects of the service, such as when the "impostor" struck himself vigorously on the head with the flat of a machete to show his "strength" and virtually incapacitated himself for the rest of the evening.

It is easily observed that no two hounfors are exactly alike. They differ in many details. But, in general, the cult establishment consists of a central building of one or more rooms with an adjoining court, or peristyle, over which there is a covering—usually a straw roof. The covering, called the *tonnelle,* is supported by a number of poles, one of which is placed squarely in the center of the court. This center pole—the *po'teau mitan* or *po'teau planté*—is the focus of most of the ritual activities. The loa who descend upon the service enter by way of this pole. The ritual *vèvès,* or flour paintings, are made at its foot. Around it all the dancing takes place. On certain rare occasions when rituals are held in the open, a carefully selected tree becomes the center post—though it is by no means certain that the po'teau mitan is not, in fact, a symbolic tree.

The building adjoining the peristyle contains the inner sanctum. Here are deposited the paraphernalia of the cult, such as ritual bottles and jars, flags of the société, and the iron kettles used in various ceremonies. On the walls there may be primitive paintings of the special loa of the hounfor, or perhaps of his symbol. The loa of the sea, Agwé, may be represented by a ship. Damballa, the serpent-rainbow loa, may be represented by a snake or a rainbow. Usually there are colored lithographs of Catholic saints, who have both Catholic and African names. And there are hand-beaten iron crosses, dishes containing Indian celts in which loa are believed to reside, gourd bowls, and carved wooden double and triple bowls used for services to dead twins and triplets. Upon the altar place, called *badji,* there are the *criches* or *govis,* earthen jars or bottles in which rest the loa removed from the heads of people who have died. Sometimes special niches are built on the hounfor grounds for the deities. Each cult priest designs his hounfor in his own way.

A hounfor belonging to a mambo near the town of Croix des Missions gave the appearance of having a large and prosperous société. Under the tonnelle eight beautifully carved Arada drums were suspended from a single peg. At a respectable distance hung a Martinique drum used only for dances on the occasion of a Nine Night. Inside the hounfor was an impressive display of sacred objects and decorations. One corner of the room was reserved for Symbi Yendézo, a patron loa of drinking water and rainfall. He was portrayed on the wall as a long, thin snake crawling in a maze of crosses. On the ground beneath the picture was a small concrete pool, in which two water snakes swam. Another corner was reserved for Agwé, and on his wall was a picture of a steamship. Along the back of the altar was an impressive array of govis, containing the spirits removed from the heads of deceased persons. There was a large plate of loa stones, and various protective charms stood near by. Flags and sabres were stacked against the wall, and set about in various places were several assons, iron crosses, Catholic lithographs, chains and iron bars for the loa Ogoun, candles set in bottles, and an old forged double bell of African design.

Some of the hounfors found elsewhere are more elaborate and reflect the richer resources of the immediate community, or the creative impulses of the houngan and his helpers, or the pressure of competition. Some cult temples are prolific with painted designs and symbolic representations of the deities. Others are unpretentious, simple, and even Spartan.

In his book *En Haiti,* written approximately fifty years ago, Eugene Aubin describes a hounfor in the Cul-de-Sac Plain, a few miles from Port-au-Prince, as he saw it in 1906:

[The] *hounfor* is fronted by a *peristyle,* which is used for the Vodoun dances and services; it is a large area, with a floor of beaten earth, covered with a straw roof. On three sides the walls rise to support the roof; on the fourth there is the inscription:

*Société la Fleur de Guinée
Roi d'Engole
[Flower of Africa Society
King of Angola]*

indicating the name of the patron of the society [the loa Roi Angole, or Wangol], over which the *houngan* presides. The *hounfor* is an ordinary house, a little larger than average. The sanctuary contains a principal *pé* [altar], running the whole length of the room on one side, and another altar, a little smaller, in one of the corners. These *pés* are altars largely made of brick, in which the under part is decorated with hearts and stars in relief; above, draperies hang from the ceiling. The lateral *pé* is divided into three compartments. There are, therefore, four sections in all, consecrated to each of the *loa* served in the *hounfor:* Aguay Aoyo [Agwé Woyo], Damballa, Ogoun Badagry, and Loco [Loko], Nago King. Maître Aguay is represented by the customary little boat; a medallion is consecrated to Monsieur Damballa, shown holding two snakes in his hand; a figure on horseback represents Ogoun Badagry, with a woman at one side holding a flag; Papa Loco is pictured in full uniform, smoking a pipe and fanning himself. The walls are covered with religious paintings [Catholic lithographs]. The back of the altar is occupied by numerous carafes in baked clay, called *canaris,* which contain the . . . *mystères* [spirits taken from the heads of the dead] gathered in the *hounfor;* in front are bottles of wine, liqueurs and vermouth presented to them in homage; then the plates, the cups for the *mangers-marassas* [feasts for the twin spirit], crucifixes, hand bells, *assons* for directing the dance or calling the *loa;* plates filled with polished stones [celts] inherited from the Indians—"thunder stones," symbols of Damballa, which Saugo [Sobo] the god of lightning hurls from the sky into the enclosure of his favorite *papaloi* [*houngan*]. Beside these miraculous stones are many coins of copper or silver [property of the *loa*]. The *loa* . . . possess coins of Joseph Bonaparte, King of Spain, minted in 1811; of Frederick VII of Denmark, 1859; of Charles IV of Spain, 1783, and of President Boyer, dated year 27 and year 30 of Haitian Independence. On the ground there is placed a coconut-oil lamp; in the corner, the flags of the *hounfor* and the saber of [the] *laplace,* the man who acts as master of ceremonies in the services. In the court, the bases of four sacred trees . . . are surrounded by circles of masonry [low brick walls]. These *reposoirs* are inhabited by the *loa* Legba, Ogoun, Loco and Saugo.[5]

There is little in Aubin's description to suggest that hounfors were much different a half century ago from what they are today. He errs in identifying the "thunder stones" solely with Damballa. But his eye for detail was acute. In 1950 a mambo in the neighborhood of this hounfor described by Aubin affirmed that some of the loa stones and old coins which he mentioned are still to be found among the properties of a hounfor in the Cul-de-Sac Plain. Others were lost in one of the cleric-inspired raids which despoiled cult temples of drums and other paraphernalia about fifteen years ago.

Many services are held outside the hounfor and the peristyle. Some rituals, such as animal sacrifices and "talking to the loa below the water," may take place some distance from the cult buildings. Indeed, various Vodoun ceremonies may be held at waterfalls, at the seashore, in sacred groves, in ordinary homes, in a boat at sea,[6] or under a sacred tree.

The rites of the hounfor are almost without number. They are associated with the supplication or conciliation of virtually countless deities, each of which has his own special service. There are services in multitudinous combinations and permutations for the dead, for twins, for albinos, and for unborn children. There are ceremonies for the elevation of hounsi and for initiation, smoke and fire ordeals, and tests of other kinds. There are *mangé loa* (feasts for the deities) and *mangé morts* (feasts for the dead). There are services for the sick, for the crops, and for the harvest. In one context or another, Vodoun relates to nearly every aspect and phase of life—and its counterpart, death. Since every region, every locality, and, in fact, almost every hounfor has developed its own ritual out of the common materials, it is possible to see hundreds of ceremonies without ever seeing precisely the same one twice. Yet the common elements bind them all together.

One such prime element is the possession, the "mounting" of the human body by one of the deities. Possession is a psychological phenomenon common to the rites of many cults throughout the world. It is known in Asia, Africa, Europe, and America. It is not the unique property of the African and his Haitian descendant. In the United States it is a commonplace not only among certain Negro cults but certain white cults as well. The United States Negro had ample West African inspiration for his seizures in the church and at the baptism. The intellectual meaning of these seizures has changed, as have their outward forms to a measurable extent, but their emotional content has not altered.

In Haiti the possession takes many forms, according to the nature of the deity who has entered the body, and depending on whether the possessed person has learned to "control" that deity. The possessing, or "mounting," of the possessed individual is manifest proof of the loa's existence and his constant proximity. Vodoun is built upon the premise of the existence of loa, and the possession is the instrument of direct contact and of constant proof of the loa's imminence.

Although much of Vodoun is cast in the Dahomean mold, it is no longer what it was originally in Dahomey. Many of the original deities of the Dahomean Earth pantheon, the Sky pantheon, and the Thunder pantheon have survived. Others have been forgotten, but in their place there has grown a vast array of loa, recruited partly from the Yoruba deities and perhaps from deities of other West African tribes. By far the largest group has come into existence in Haiti—loa whose names, at least, probably would go unrecognized in West Africa.

There have been prolific intrusions into Vodoun from the rites of the Catholic Church, though they have not affected the general framework of the system. The original Dahomean supreme being, Nananbuluku, is nearly forgotten; in her place the Christian God is named in many a Vodoun service. Yet, though God is the supreme creator, giver, and taker, it is the loa who must be supplicated and mollified. Most important Vodoun rituals are begun under the supervision of the *prêt' savane,* or "bush priest," who leads off with brief prayers from the Catholic rites. While the Catholic Church itself rejects any direct part in Vodoun, the self-tutored prêt' savane, unordained and unsponsored by the Church, brings elements of its theology into the hounfor. The origins of the prêt' savane are not clear. But there is little doubt that his place in Haitian life became assured during the years of conflict between postrevolutionary governments and the Church of Rome. After the slave revolts of 1791, the priests of the French colony fled from the scene or went into hiding along with the other white colonists. From the date of Haitian independence throughout the following half century, Haiti was "in open schism from the Roman Catholic Church."[7] Some Haitian presidents were friendly toward the Catholic Church; others even had the objective of making Catholicism a state religion with the president at its head. Henry Christophe, for example, made the Catholic Church official but stipulated that ecclesiastical decrees must be approved by the president. Alexandre Pétion's constitution for southern Haiti (the country was divided) also established the Church as official but laid upon it strong restrictions.

Leyburn points out that in 1814 there were in Christophe's kingdom only three priests, one of whom Christophe had named archbishop. During Boyer's administration, 1818–1843, Catholicism was the state religion, but the president was its chief. Leyburn notes:

Every effort of the state failing to provide proper religious leadership, Boyer resigned himself to permitting those who professed to be priests to practice in the republic. There were seventy so-called priests in the country in 1840. Some of them had once been in the holy orders but had been unfrocked: they found in Haiti not only a haven but a fertile field for gain. In addition to these religious renegades came adventurers who knew just enough of ritual and theology to use the priestly garb as a cover for easy graft. . . . They baptized houses, boats, and doorposts, and blessed fetish charms or amulets, all for a fee.[8]

It was not until 1860, after the death of the "Emperor" Soulouque, that Haiti signed a concordat with the Roman Church.

The role of the prêt' savane became defined after the slave revolts of 1791. His cue was taken from the activities of freebooting Europeans who apparently needed neither religious orders nor profound Catholic knowledge for their pseudo-clerical work. And the long period without a responsible priesthood gave the "bush priest" an opportunity to flourish.

The prêt' savane of today has a respected place in the community, though his prestige is not so great as that of the houngan on the one hand or the Catholic priest on the other. His place is guaranteed by his ability to bring to the Vodoun service elements of a competing system which the houngan, operating within the framework of African tradition, does not provide. Acceptance of these Catholic elements as a peripheral part of Vodoun is characteristic of much West African religious thinking, in which new deities and rituals may be added to the old when circumstances require.

The prêt' savane opens many Vodoun services with an *action de grâce,* reads prayers when a death has occurred, participates in marriage rites, and "baptizes" the hounfor, the cult drums, and the sacred rattles—not to mention the loa themselves! But it is the houngan's powers that are paramount. The "bush priest" is in a sense performing a service for the Vodoun priest, whose rituals and administrations are regarded as the effective and vital ones. The prêt' savane is a cultural afterthought.

In certain remote and isolated mountain places the prêt' savane is virtually unknown. But there is no sense of deprivation, for the cult priests —even the poorest and the most rustic—have their own way of dealing with the saints, God, and the forces of nature. An aged houngan of the Morne la Selle region explained it this way:

"In everything that is done, God's permission is asked first. Most houngans in the mountains do not know how to read, and they don't know how to pray. But they know many things. They know where the sun rises, and they address St. Nicholas, who opens the day, and they know the wish of God. In the name of St. Nicholas they raise a glass of water and ask God for the power to do."

In ordinary usage the Haitian refers to the various cults or "nations" as though they were quite separate and mutually exclusive. He speaks of the *service* Pétro, or *rite* Nago, or the *nanchon* Ibo. Yet in practice the cults are usually bound together into two or three major groups.

The "nations" belonging to the Vodoun (or Dahomey) group include the Arada or Dahomé, the Anago, the Mahi, the Amine, and the Ibo. There is ample evidence that the cults of these "nations" were once separate and apart. Even today in isolated regions of Haiti there are cult centers devoted exclusively to Nago deities. Elsewhere, Mahi or Ibo services are held without the intrusion of "foreign" rites and deities. Some cult centers have several hounfors—one for Dahomé, one for Nago, one for Ibo, and so on, with a separate building for the "dead" spirit Gèdé. More often, however, one finds a single hounfor containing separate altars. Of all the "nations" within the Vodoun group, the Ibo perhaps has the most independent status, and in some regions it is tied in with Pétro rather than Vodoun rites.

The Pétro group also includes numerous "nations," some completely absorbed, others more loosely affiliated. Within this group, which for convenience may be called the Congo-Guinée family, are the Pétro, Bumba, Moundongue, Bambarra, Congo Loangue (Loango), and other "nations." In certain regions the Congo cult, like the Ibo, is regarded as separate and apart. Sometimes the Pétro service is kept distinct from the others, though it has drawn so heavily on them for its roster of deities that the distinction is not easily seen. In places such as Port-au-Prince where the cults have deeply infiltrated one another, major differences between the Vodoun and Congo-Guinée rites have disappeared, and altars to both Pétro and Dahomé deities may be found within the same hounfor.

It is not difficult to detect a certain pattern of regional grouping within the Vodoun and Congo-Guinée families. Within the Vodoun family are gathered "nations" from Dahomey, Togoland, and Nigeria, while in the Congo-Guinée cycle are "nations" from Central Africa, miscellaneous "nations" such as the Bambarra, and the Pétro cult which is regarded as "Haitian" rather than "African," but whose rites and loa have been recruited in large measure from other services.

One often hears of Kitta services, or Chango services, or Legba rites. These are not separate cults but simply rituals for specific loa.

3. The Loa: Gods of the Haitian Mountains

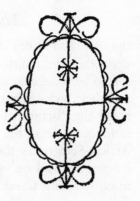

The supernatural world of the common people of Haiti is a vast, rich, and unexplored world. It is peopled with thousands of gods who may at any time come down a rocky mountain trail, or up from the bottom of the sea, or out of the springs where people drink, to enter the hounfor of the Vodoun priest or the humblest of thatched huts. The gods—variously called *loa, mystère, hounaié,* or *vodoun* [1]—may come at strange, unexpected moments to the unlikeliest places. Yet whenever they come they are recognized for what they are. The things they say and do bear the mark of their character and their special powers, and usually there is little disagreement over their identity.

The Haitians tell you that the loa live "in Africa," or on "the island below the sea," or "beneath the water," or in a mythological city called La Ville-aux-Camps. The loa are believed to share this residing place with the spirits of certain categories of the dead. What goes on in the land of the loa is no man's knowledge and every man's conjecture. They say that a few privileged people have been able to go down "below the water" and return.

In the region of Gros Morne there is a legend of a woman named Madame Ste Île who went under the water and returned after seven years. There is another widespread tale of a man near La Bai Moustique who, in full public view, walked into the bay and disappeared, and returned in a few hours bearing a cake in his hands—a gift from the loa below the water. And in the hills near Aux Cayes in the south a story is told about a loa named Général Clermeil, who drove up in a fine carriage and carried off a woman to his place below the water.

On certain occasions the loa come to pass the time among their "children" in Haiti. When a loa comes to the people he enters the body of one or another of them, or he enters many of them at the same time. In cult terminology, these people are his "horses." The loa mounts his horses, as they say, and "rides" them. What the possessed persons do then depends upon the personality and whim of the loa. Generally they take on the special personal characteristics of the loa. Their voices and manners change and their postures and attitudes undergo transfiguration. They may talk about the "island below the water," about community ancestors, about intimate affairs of the community, or about how things are going back in Africa. Sometimes they utter words or phrases recognized as "African language." And on occasion possessed persons talking *langage* are said to be speaking Greek, Arabic, Hebrew, or Spanish. At the moment of first impact, when the loa enter their heads, they stagger, jerk, and tremble, often falling on the ground. Then, soon afterward, their behavior begins to move in a groove of conventionalized activity.

Most commonly the loa arrive during religious rituals or dances. They come by way of the *po'teau mitan,* the center pole which supports the roof of the peristyle. It is around this pole that the sacred vèvès, or flour drawings, are made. At the foot of the pole sacrifices are offered and libations are poured.

Yet possession may occur anywhere and at any time. The sound of a certain drumbeat may be the signal for it, or a sudden fright, or an emotional crisis, or any situation to which possession has been conditioned. The houngan or the mambo may facilitate possession, control it, and terminate it. The cult priest is acutely sensitive to the conditions favorable to possession. He knows how to heighten emotional tension and how to soften it. A competent houngan "plays" his service as though it were a delicate instrument. He takes everything in, issues instructions to his servitors from time to time, orders the drum tempo increased or diminished, knows how to change pace. Sometimes he hovers in the background unobtrusively, encouraging the singing and dancing like a benevolent father. At other times he comes to the center of the activities and takes command. He becomes the focus of all eyes. His slightest action is watched with intensity. He may take the hand of one of the servitors, pirouette him about, and compel the loa to enter. When the servitor is "mounted," the houngan may conduct him through ritual activity. At the right moment the houngan may help the loa to leave.

The spectators who observe possession in others are usually aware of the identity of the loa who has entered. When the ancient loa Damballa Wèdo comes in, his "horse" falls to the ground, wriggles like a snake, and makes what are considered to be snakelike sounds in his throat. For Damballa is the venerable deity identified with the rainbow, which in ancient Dahomean lore was thought to be the great serpent come out from the underworld to drink after a rain. When the loa Ogoun Chango enters, his "horse" may trample in glowing coals, plunge his hands in boiling oil, or play with red-hot iron bars. For Ogoun Chango is a fire-eater—a deity of the forge and of battle. The deity Legba is characterized as a limping old man. A "horse" possessed by Legba may cavort about on a kind of cane-crutch called a Legba stick. Each loa has his distinctive mark. As the Haitians say, "you learn about the loa by watching his horses."

In addition to having homes in Africa or below the water, most loa have special residing places in Haiti, such as stones, caves, trees, waterfalls, or springs. One may come across a boulder or a bamboo grove sacred to a certain loa, and food offerings are likely to be seen there. Many loa are identified with some specific variety of tree and will "inhabit" all such trees throughout the country. Loa Calbassie, for example, lives in the calabash tree, and Loa Général Brisé in the chardette tree. Offerings to these deities are set out underneath the tree or hung in its branches, and services may be held around the trunk.

Loa also live in the old Carib and Arawak celts which are found from time to time. These "loa stones," as they are called, are identified by their forms and their ability to pass certain tests. Some Haitians declare the stones must be able to "whistle," to perspire when blown upon, and to "talk." The loa stones ordinarily are passed on from one generation to another, in the hounfor and in the peasant hut alike. In this way the loa who inhabit them are inherited. Sometimes, but rarely, stones are sold; disposing of a loa stone requires an elaborate ceremony to guarantee that the seller will not be injured by the loa, who is likely to feel "wounded." In such a ceremony the loa is fed and placated and asked to go his way in peace. The loa stones are sometimes called "thunder stones," in the belief that they were hurled to earth by the deities Kebiosu, Sobo, and Chango (all of whom had similar functions among the Arada and Yoruba peoples of West Africa). The stones are cared for by their owners with the greatest reverence.

Loa are acquired by individuals in various ways. Many Haitians hold that every infant is born with a *maît' tête*—a spirit who is "master of the head." In this light, no individual is without a loa, although the deity may never manifest interest in the individual by an act of possession. A man may acquire a loa in the course of his life, although in that event the original maît' tête must be retired from his head. The "inherited" loa are usually not the personal deities but the special protectors of the household or the hounfor and are known as "loa of the house" or "family loa."

Should a man acquire a new loa to replace the old as his maît' tête, he must undergo a ceremony known as *lavé tête*—the "washing of the head." The old loa is retired and sent away, leaving the field clear for the new one. Sometimes a loa who is making life too hard for a devotee will be retired without a replacement. The "washing of the head" must be accompanied by ritual safeguards, and all possible circumstances must be taken into account by the officiating cult priest. There are many stories of people who became mentally deranged as a result of the removal of their loa from their heads.

The maît' tête must also be removed from the head of a person who dies. Should this not be done, the spirit of the deceased will go to reside "below the water" and may cause trouble for the family. This loa is usually transferred to a special jar as a temporary resting place, and later perhaps into the head of another member of the family.

Though the loa is a powerful ruling force in the life of the individual, the human "horse" has controls over his deity too. He may reproach or admonish his loa for bad behavior or for failing to protect him. He may expose the loa's irresponsibility in public through the use of songs in religious rites. And though the loa is frequently encouraged to "enter," steps may be taken to restrain him from possession. This is called *marré loa* —"tying the loa." A woman may "tie" her loa by fixing a hairpin in her hair in a special way. A man may do it by placing his hands in cold water.[2]

Nevertheless, the loa are always lurking in the background. They are a constant and dramatic element in the religious life of the people. They may sometimes be controlled by the houngan, but they are an authority stronger than the priesthood. They give advice, courage, consolation, and status to their followers. They add much to an otherwise hard and ungenerous environment and evoke remembrances of Africa from which the Haitians' ancestors were uprooted. They can also cause concern and anxiety; for the loa are not always benevolent, and they are frequently unpredictable.

Many of the loa are ancient deities, sib-founders and ancestors who loom out of a misty, half-forgotten past. Nananbouclou, Legba, and Ayida Wèdo have been known for many lifetimes in Dahomey. Chango, Ogoun, and Loko were old spirits in Nigeria before the first slave ships sailed from Africa to the New World. Their names and many others in present-day Haiti come from an ancient lore. They recall places, tribes, and old kingdoms from Senegal in northwestern Africa to the heart of the Congo. They are a bond which holds the people of Haiti to Africa. In the mountains people sometimes say, "Haiti is the child of Dahomey," or "Haiti is the child of Guinée." The gods divide their time between their Haitian and their African children.

Yet in some respects the Haitians' concept of their loa is no longer purely African. The African religious patterns have been infiltrated by the lore of the Catholic Church and fused with old folk beliefs of Europe. In Dahomey, which was the wellspring for much of Haiti's culture, there was no supreme deity quite like the one introduced to the slaves by the missionaries. There was a pantheon of gods with Mawu and Lisa at the top. They were children of a common parent, Nananbuluku. None of these deities was strictly comparable to our idea of a supreme being. Nananbuluku survives in Haiti as Nananbouclou or Nananbélécou, one of many loa. Among the neighboring Yoruba the high god was Olorun. Like the Dahomean Mawu and Lisa, Olorun was quite remote from the lives of men. The gods who were invoked and placated were the several hundred *orisha* created by Olorun. The nearby Ashanti people had a simpler pantheon, with the sky god Nyame supreme among them.

In the present Haitian concept of the supernatural, God is at the very apex of the pantheon, though he is distinctly of another order. His power as the supreme source of all things is fully recognized. A Haitian song, associated with Vodoun ritual but of probable recent origin, goes:

C'est Bondieu qui voyé moin, quand li vlé moin l'apprend. [Ex. 37]

It is God who sent me, when he wants me he'll take me.

Another song, from the Guinée service, goes:

Oh, Kitta, oh so'ti nan dleau, li tout mouillé!
Oh, nen point houngan passé Bondieu nan pays-ya! [Ex. 36]

Oh, Kitta comes out of the water, he is dripping wet!
Oh, there is no houngan in this country greater than God!

Although it is recognized, or at least stated, that God is a supreme force, God is not regarded as the entire supernatural force of the world. In many Vodoun services the houngan may invoke, as separate categories of the unseen, the loa, the dead, the *marassas* (twin spirits), and God. Haitians do not have a consistent schematized picture of the supernatural world. God comes first, but (as in West Africa) he is less immediate than the loa. He is identified with destiny; yet within the framework of that destiny man's lot can be bettered or worsened through dealings with the dead, the baka and lou-garos (demons and vampires), and the cult priests.

In many of the folk tales of Haiti, God appears as another character in a cast which may include as protagonists animals, loa, Christian saints, and ordinary men and women. One such tale is about a visit which all the dogs decided to pay to God. They started off through the woods together, but one of them was distracted by the smell of carrion. He left his friends for a brief time, found the carrion, and ate some of it. Then he hurriedly joined his companions again. Together they came to God's house and were admitted to the parlor, where they sat around making polite conversation with God and one another. But after a while God caught the scent of the carrion which was still smeared on the nose of the dog who had eaten it. He sniffed the air several times to test the unpleasant odor. Misjudging it, he concluded that one of the dogs had befouled his parlor, and he demanded to know who had done this impolite thing. The dogs were deeply concerned that one of their party had desecrated God's house. They immediately began to run around smelling each other to determine who the culprit was. But they never found the evidence, because it was on a dog's nose. The dogs still, to this day, are trying to discover who committed a deed that never actually happened.

In some of the tales God competes in the real world with other supernatural and natural forces. One story tells how he was overcome by a Vodoun priest:

A houngan named Bocor Zandolite once held a great ritual service. People came from the whole countryside. It was a long service, scheduled to last for seven weeks. Chickens, goats, and bulls were sacrificed. The finest drummers in the country were drumming. Everyone danced, and the celebration went on day after day, night after night, without stopping. The noise was deafening. God heard it. It kept him from sleeping at night, and in the daytime he could not concentrate on his work. Finally, God decided he would have to put a stop to it. So he called St. John and instructed him to go down and order Bocor Zandolite to bring the service to an end. St. John went down and approached the gate of Bocor Zandolite's hounfor. Bocor Zandolite met him at the gate. He took St. John by the hand. St. John sang:

> Factionnaire ouv'é bayè pou' moin passé!
>
> Guard, open the gate for me to pass!

And Bocor Zandolite replied by singing:

> Wa wa ilé londja londja!
> Bocor Zandolite wa wa ilé londja londja! [Ex. 38]

[This is supposed to represent the houngan talking *langage*.] Then he shook St. John's hands three times and pirouetted him around, first to the left and then to the right. Suddenly St. John staggered and began to talk *langage*. He grasped the center pole of the dance court and twirled round and round it. Then Bocor Zandolite gave him a lighted candle and a glass of water, and St. John spilled a bit of the water on the ground in honor of the loa who had entered his head.

When a week went by and St. John didn't come back, God became angry. The noise of the drumming and singing was getting worse. So he

called St. Patrick and sent him down to stop the ceremony. St. Patrick
approached the hounfor and sang:

> Factionnaire ouv'é bayè pou' moin passé!

And again Bocor Zandolite came to the gate and sang:

> Wa wa ilé londja londja!
> Bocor Zandolite wa wa ilé londja londja!

He took St. Patrick by the hands, pirouetted him around, and a loa came
into St. Patrick's head, too.

Another week went by, and when St. Patrick didn't return, God sent
St. Michael. The same thing happened to St. Michael. God then sent St.
Anthony, and later he sent St. Peter. But when St. Peter didn't return,
God became very angry indeed. He hadn't slept for weeks. So he decided
to go down himself and put an end to the affair. He approached the hounfor singing "Factionnaire ouv'é bayè pou' moin passé!" And Bocor Zandolite replied as he had before. He took God by the hands to greet him.
He shook hands downward three times, then he pirouetted God to the
right and to the left. God suddenly staggered and reeled from one end of
the habitation to the other. The drummers beat a special salute, and the
singers sang loudly and clapped their hands, for God had a loa in his head.

This tale appears to relish the superiority of the loa over God. Yet there
is no sense of sacrilege. Although the Haitian concept of God is that of
a supreme force, and a source of good, the Christian deity also has some
of the attributes of paramount gods in certain West African religious
systems which make him less remote and even, on occasion, somewhat
fallible. He figures in Haitian lore very much like the Ashanti sky god,
Nyankonpon, who has dealings with animals and human beings and is
sometimes outwitted by them. Although Nyankonpon has the power to
dispense favors, justice, and punishment to mortals, he himself lives
within, rather than superior to, a well-established physical system. His
marvelous deeds are only slightly superior to those of other, lesser gods,
or of sorcerers, or of the trickster Anansi. In fact, in one Ashanti tale
Nyankonpon finds himself very much in the same situation as God in
the Haitian tale, being forced to dance to the music of the trickster's drum.

The Christian saints, too, have been incorporated into the Haitian system, and they also have been syncretized with Vodoun elements. They
have become identified with various loa according to their most obvious
characteristics. St. Patrick, because he is always pictured with snakes, has
become one with Damballa and Ayida, who are also symbolized by
snakes. Èzilie Fréda, the female loa characterized by purity, has become

one with the Holy Virgin. St. Jacques has become one with Ogoun, St. George with Linglessou, St. Anthony and St. Christopher with Legba, guardian of the highway, and St. Nicholas with Marassa Trois. In northern Haiti the word *zange* (from the French, *les anges*—the angels) sometimes is used synonymously with loa or mystère. As for the saints, they are sometimes identified with one loa, sometimes with another.

No one in Haiti knows all the loa. Some of them are so ancient as to be nearly forgotten. Others are spontaneous creations or revelations on the part of a possessed person. Some loa names may be the result of a devotee's seizing upon a word or phrase in a religious song and imparting to it the concept of a loa. Sometimes a word in a phrase of *langage* is taken to be a loa's name, and sometimes agglutinated Creole words become the name of a loa.

The possibility of frequent additions to the list of loa is heightened still further by the general illiteracy of the Haitian people and the lack of a stabilizing influence in the written word. The Creole language has marked regional differences. Furthermore, change of consonants or vowels is a commonplace occurrence, so that a single loa's name may have several forms. One may well wonder whether Aza, Adja, and Akadja were not originally a single individual. Nevertheless, in the Haitian scheme they are now different personalities.

There is one more complicating factor in identifying loa or compiling a comprehensive roster—the use of multiple names. In addition to the names by which they are generally known, many of the deities have a variety of nicknames. Some of these nicknames are in Creole, some appear to be of West African provenience. The deity Agwé, for example, is frequently called Coqui-nan-Mer—Coqui-in-the-Sea. A loa may have four, five, or even more such nicknames. Sometimes short forms are used. Damballa may be called Da, Sobo may be called So, Azaka may be called Za. In addition, some deities have "secret" names, which theoretically are known only to the priesthood and the inner circle of servitors. Multiple naming and the reservation of certain names for special occasions appear to have West African precedents.

In the naming of the loa no neat and methodical system is apparent at any point. The "surname," or what may be in some cases a generic designation, may appear first or last. One may hear Ogoun Chango or Chango Ogoun, Général Brisé or Brisé Général, Congo Savane or Savane Congo. (This is characteristic of everyday speech. A former president of Haiti, Nord Alexis, is often called Alexis Nord.) The "surname" can be a description of "tribal" or "national" affiliation, regional provenience, character and temperament, or an indication of function. Thus we find

Boulicha Nago, or Boulicha of the Nagos; Èzilie Wèdo and Èzilie Doba, possibly from Wèdo and Doba in Dahomey; Tijean Pied Chêche (Tijean Dry Feet), a loa of bad character, "dry feet" signifying malevolence; and Legba Grand Chimin, or Legba of the Highway.

Identification of loa is often made difficult by the use of the generic or family title only. The term Nago covers all the loa associated with this "nation" (Nago Piment, Amine Nago, Boulicha Nago, etc.), but in a song or service any one of them is as likely as not to be referred to simply as Nago, with no clue to his exact identity. Each listener takes the name to designate the Nago loa with whom he is most familiar, unless possession occurs and the loa is otherwise identified by the behavior of his "horse."

On the whole, it appears that there was in the beginning a strong awareness of regional origins. There are names among the cult pantheons which indicate Senegal, Dahomey, Nigeria, Congo, and Angola origins. Many loa bear the names of African towns. Among the Ogoun family of loa, for example, are such regional designations as Badagry and Jèkkè, the first being a town in Nigeria and the second in Dahomey. It is clear that a detailed geographical knowledge of certain West African regions would considerably illuminate a study of Haitian loa.

Local shrines, too, doubtless enter into the naming system. Badagry is the name of a town in Nigeria, and it is also a Dahomean word designating the structure in which young men used to be circumcised and initiated into the secrets of warriors. In this particular light, the loa Ogoun Badagry might be regarded as the deity of that particular ritual center.

In discussing the complicated relationship of their loa, Haitians sometimes say: "There are seven of everything. There are seven Marassas, seven Ogouns, seven Èzilies. There are seven brothers and sisters in every family of loa." Or they say something such as: "There is only one Legba, but there are seven. There is only one Ogoun, but he has many moods and names. There is only one Èzilie, but she has seven faces." This concept is also held by the Arara (Arada) cult of Cuba. It is interesting to note the extent to which duplications and new generations of loa have been set up into family households in the most literal sense. Those families are still growing. In the Gèdé family I have counted more than thirty seemingly distinct individuals (see Appendix I). Herskovits mentions a number of others, and still more have been cited by other writers on the subject. When I pointed out to some Haitians that the Gèdé family numbered far more than seven individuals, they were unable to account for the situation. Other Haitians took the vast army of Gèdés as a matter of course. The Ogoun family, too, is large and growing. Twenty-seven Ogouns are listed in the compilation in Appendix I. Still more have been recorded elsewhere.

Another factor that may explain some of the confusion over which rites a loa is attached to is the concept of the *escorte,* a kind of army or association of loa which may include deities of different nations. In discussing the loa Wanilé, for example, one Haitian noted:

"Wanilé is neither Rada nor Dahomé, but Pétro. She is an escorte, and she walks with Dahomé. In the escorte, Dahomé and Pétro walk together. A big loa—a loa with a big name—has many other loa who walk with him. In an escorte there are twenty-one in all. The escorte has a chief, and under the chief there are soldiers—that is, smaller loa who must do what the chief says.

"For example, a man goes to a houngan and gets him to send a strong loa against you to hurt you in some way—to make you sick or lose your crop. Your own loa may be a strong one, but the houngan has sent a still stronger one against you, and so your own loa can't really protect you. So he will go away and send in his place one of his escorte. This smaller loa is not as strong perhaps as the one he is replacing, but he is stronger in that the houngan did not calculate on him. He has certain abilities which he can use to help you. And it isn't suspected that he is your protector. So in this way he is in a better position than your own loa.

"The smaller loa go together in an escorte. Many people may have a certain loa, and he is busy all the time. If someone needs him and he can't go, he will send one of his escorte, the next one below him.

"If you are made sick by a loa, there are so many in his escorte you don't know which one made you sick, so you can't do anything about it. It is difficult sometimes to identify the loa that is hurting you. You really have to dig to find out who he is. You have to give a *mangé.* There is a big ceremony, and you have to be bought back from the loa. But some loa who are persecuting you won't sell you back. They won't go away. Rather than leave you alone they would see you die. Perhaps the person who sent this loa against you sent him to kill. If your own loa can't protect you he will send one of his escorte to do it. *Gainyain connain passé connain* [There is knowledge that surpasses knowledge]. *Si fer pas coupé fer, machoquette pas gainyain travaille* [If iron didn't cut iron, the blacksmith would have no work to do]."

This concept of the escorte, some of whose members may be Rada and some Pétro, helps to explain why certain deities are identified with rites of different "nations." For the Haitian himself it provides a way of accounting for "families" that have grown beyond the ritual number seven. Yet there are some Haitians who declare that every member of an escorte is simply a different manifestation of a single deity.

The loa, like the rites, vary somewhat according to region and to the practices of the individual cult priests. New concepts spring up, and they thrive in one locality while remaining unheard of in another. Yet many new concepts travel from hounfor to hounfor. As in the old days in Dahomey, the Vodoun priests sometimes make journeys to visit other cult centers. At one service near Jacmel, on the south coast, I met a houngan from Dondon in the far north and heard him discuss with the local cult chief the appropriate behavior of a loa who had mounted a servitor. The Dondon houngan declared that in the north the loa conducted himself differently. The Jacmel houngan parried with the remark that a loa's behavior is consistent. He said there were only two possibilities concerning the possession as described by the cult chief from Dondon: either the loa had been mistakenly identified, or another deity had attempted to impersonate him. Such exchanges hasten the spread of developing theology from one area to another. They also raise contradictions which remain forever insoluble.

That confusions and contradictions are not merely of Haitian making is made clear by Herskovits' voluminous study of the pantheons of Dahomey.[3] Each of the great cults—the sky cult, the earth cult, and the thunder cult—has its own explanations of the origins and functions of the deities; and even within one cult there are contradicting explanations. The Haitians have taken over, built upon, and diverged from a Dahomean system that contained its own contradictions. In adding to it the system of the Yoruba, with its parallelisms and similarities, they have made the whole picture more complex than ever.

4. Death Rites

The community of the Haitian is one that extends far beyond his immediate family and his village, for it takes in not only the various loa but multitudinous dead relatives and ancestors. Some Haitians believe that the dead live in close proximity to the loa, in a place called "Under the Water." Others hold that the dead have no special residing place. But it is the view of many that a dead person may eventually become a loa in his own right. How this happens is not entirely clear. Under certain circumstances the spirits of the newly dead do not go quietly on their way but remain behind to annoy and harass the living. They must be buried with suitable ritual and properly placated throughout the years; otherwise their activities and influences will be unpredictable. Many of them, under special conditions, become almost indistinguishable from loa. And a few, in the course of time, become minor deities in the pantheons. The main loa of the Pétro cult, Dan Pétro, formerly was believed by some Haitians to be a houngan of the eighteenth century who had been buried without having his own loa removed from his head. There are African precedents for deified ancestors' becoming deities. Indeed, some of the great *vodouns* and *orisha* of the Dahomean and Yoruban pantheons in West Africa are believed to be deified clan ancestors or great kings.

Whether they achieve the status of loa or not, the spirits of the dead must forever be coped with. This Haitian view of the dead is essentially that held in many parts of West Africa. Speaking of West African belief in general, Maurice Delafosse noted:

After a creature dies, only his spirit remains. It survives with the same character, the same personality, affections and hatreds as during his lifetime, but it can no longer command the vital breath. It becomes all the more powerful on escaping from the confines of its material envelope, since it no longer needs to direct and control the functions of the body, and is not itself regulated by the vital breath. . . . These spirits are all of the same nature. They are invisible but can see and judge everything that happens. They are easily angered and mete out severe punishment to anyone offending them. They are also vain and capricious, can be conciliated by prayers and gifts, and propitiated by sacrifices. This animistic religion . . . includes many variants of the worship of countless spirits of men's ancestors and innumerable spirits of nature, all ranking as gods.[1]

Another observer, speaking of the Bapindi, the Babunda, and other related tribes of the western Congo draws quite similar conclusions:

The people of these tribes recognize a supreme deity, Nzambi, creator of all things. But this supreme spirit is too distant from men to enlist active worship on their part. The basic worship is to the ancestors of the clan. The clan is in effect a community consisting of all the living and the dead descended from a common ancestor. Towards the dead it is necessary to make offerings as a mark of deference when one wishes to consult them on problems. The dead are spoken to through the chief, who uses a special drum for this purpose. The dead have the responsibility of protecting their descendants.[2]

Among the Bantu people of South Africa, also, the worship of ancestors is based upon the belief that when a man dies he continues to influence the lives of his relatives remaining on earth. He is as interested as ever in descendants who remain "outside on the earth," but indifferent to members of other communities unless they bear them some grudge. The characters of people who die are not changed by death. They are as prone to jealousy in death as in life, and as rancorous toward descendants who wound their vanity, flout their wishes, squander their bequests, or infringe the ancient laws and customs of their clans; but they are also as willing as ever to help those of their lineage who treat them with becoming respect and obedience.[3] The affairs of mankind in general do not concern them; they are exclusively interested in their own family and tribe, and without their help and guidance their living descendants cannot hope to flourish. As long as the moral code is strictly followed, they confer blessings and abundance; but if offended by any breach of custom, they can also send drought, cattle plague, tribal or personal disaster, sickness, or death.[4]

This deeply rooted concept of the relationship of the family to its ancestors continues to motivate the Haitian in his observance of services for the dead.

In addition to the ordinary dead with whom the Haitian has to deal, there are the spirits of twins, known as *marassas*. As there are feasts for the ordinary family dead, the mangé morts, so there are feasts for living and dead twins, the mangé marassas. Twins are believed to have special powers, and even when alive they are given more than usual consideration. The spirits of dead twins are especially willful and capricious, and unless properly placated they may cause illness and misfortune. Once each year, on dates fixed by local custom, special services are held for the marassas.

The dead twins are offered food in special earthen or gourd bowls. In any market place where pottery is sold you will find the joined marassa double or triple bowls. The annual rites for the marassas are routine, but once every five years there is a *grande service* for them.

It is not merely the twins of one's immediate family that are served, but twins—that is, the spirit of twins—in general. They are supplicated even when a family knows of no incidence of twins. In part, this precaution is a recognition that there may have been twins among ancestors long dead and forgotten. It is also recognition of a twin spirit as a separate force affecting all people. The twin spirit has been personified in the loa named Marassa. The child born after twins is believed by many Haitians to be even "stronger" and more to be placated than twins themselves. He is known as a *doçu* if a boy, *doça* if a girl. Their patron loa are known as Marassa Doçu and Marassa Doça. The patron loa of triplets is Marassa Trois. Triplets are regarded as a special category of twins. Some Haitians, in fact, believe that the twins are merely a partial manifestation of the group of three, which is completed on the birth of the doçu or doça. In the marassa feast, triplets are served in the triple clover-leaf bowl, as are twins in combination with their doçu or doça. It is also believed by some that the child born before twins is "weak" both in physical vitality and psychic powers, because his strength has been sapped by the marassas who have followed him.

For some Haitians the loa Marassa is the most potent of forces to be placated at the time of death. They hold that he is only incidentally the patron of twins and triplets. His significance is said to lie in the fact that he is the spirit of the first of all human children who died. And as the child precedes the man, Marassa is the first and foremost of all loa. When a service is held for Marassa, he is given foods and beverages that all children love.

Rites for the dead continue endlessly for the living. Before a child is witness to a death in his own family he may observe many rituals for the family ancestors, twins, and the unknown dead. For those who are a part of Vodoun, the cycle is a perpetual one in an endless system of integration and continuity.

Special rites are held to remove the loa from the head of a deceased person. It is believed that the spirit of a person who has not had his loa removed will be restive and perhaps will even cause difficulties for his family and his descendants. And there is also the matter of the loa's welfare. The *maît' tête* is, in a sense, a captive in the head of the person who has died. The head is his home. But should the corpse be taken to the graveyard without the loa's having been removed, the loa would refuse to be buried with the corpse. He wants nothing to do with the domain of the Gèdés. He liberates himself from the corpse at the cemetery and retires "below the water." He is no longer a friend and benefactor of the family. He cannot be inherited by the children of the deceased. Such controls as the deceased once exercised over him are dissipated. He may, in fact, be angered at the treatment he has received and return only to harass the family. Thus, if a family fails to have the maît' tête of one of its members properly removed at death, it may be persecuted afterward by the "spirit" of the dead ancestor and the loa as well.

The rite of dispossessing a deceased person of his loa is called *déssounin,* or *déssouné*. The essence of it is the transference of the maît' tête from the head of the dead person into a special receptacle, an earthen jar called a *govi* or *pot tête*. Sometimes it is transferred to the head of a child in the family, though usually this comes later.

There have been many descriptions of this ritual, and they seem to show that, though the tradition is a constant one, the specific patterns of the services are variable. Different regions, different cult centers, and different houngans conduct the rites in different ways.

Eugene Aubin wrote, for example:

On the day of death, the deceased is placed standing up; the *papaloi* [houngan] conducts the rites which retire the *mystère* [loa] from the body and introduce it into a jar, which is then carefully sealed. On the ninth day, after the feast for the dead, the jar is broken and liberty given to the *loa*.[5]

Melville Herskovits reported:

If the dead person was a Vodun priest or otherwise had strong *connaissance*, steps are taken . . . "to remove the *loa* from his head" so that his soul will not go under the water, for, as has been explained, such souls are held to be powerful spirits which may cause the family much harm if, after a time, an expensive and troublesome ceremony is not performed to bring them out and lodge them in a jar. . . . The *houngan* stands in place and calls the name of the dead. He puts some of the hair of the dead in the jar or in a calabash, into which the *loa* is supposed to go, and, unless another member of the family, nominated to receive the *connaissance* of the dead, is present, the jar or calabash is sealed until these spirits can be "given" to a successor.[6]

As Herskovits understands it, it is the "soul" of the dead person that would go to live "under the water," rather than the loa. This would appear to be a fusion of two separate elements—the wandering, troublesome "spirit" of a dead person and the maît' tête who retires "under the water." Actually, Haitians are not always consistent in their explanations of what happens, or of the difference between loa and souls. On the hounfor altar there may be some govis that contain "souls" or "spirits" and others that contain loa; though the distinction is readily appreciated, Haitians are sometimes hard put to explain the similarity of treatment of these two categories.

Another investigator, Alfred Métraux, has provided a vivid description given by a Haitian of a ceremony of removing the loa. In this instance the corpse was not placed in an upright position as described by Aubin but was laid on a specially prepared bed. Attending the body were the houngan, his hounsi, and a child of the dead man who was to receive the liberated loa.

The child . . . grasps in his hand a black-and-white or a white cock. On the ground in front of the bed they arrange a fine white napkin. On top of it there are syrup, candles . . . , *tafia,* and other things. After they have finished sprinkling water, clapping their hands, singing to the *loa,* they all go around the bed of the dead person. The child, with the cock in his hand, makes the rounds with the *houngan.* They wave the rooster, they wave it back and forth two, three, four, five, six times over the dead person's head. During this time all those present get possessed by the *loa,* sing, clap their hands. The dead person's bed begins to creak. The *houngan* climbs on the bed and grabs the dead person's two arms. . . . He pulls him to a sitting position. The child (into whose head the *loa* is to be transferred) strikes the chicken three times on the head of the dead person. He lets go the chicken, and the chicken flies up and starts to run all around the room, smashing pots and vessels. They grab the chicken and let it go in the air three times, shouting: *Ai bobo loa à!* Immediately the *loa* goes into the head of the dead person's child.[7]

The houngan cited by Métraux is described as pulling the corpse to a sitting position, but more commonly it is believed that the houngan has the power to make the body sit up by itself. A man from Jérémie explained it this way:

"The body is laid out on a mat. The houngan shakes his asson over the dead man, and talks to the loa in the head. He calls the loa's name: 'Changogolo! Changogolo! Changogolo!' He calls, calls, calls. He doesn't call the dead man's name, he calls the maît' tête. 'Changogolo! Changogolo! Get up! Wake up! Sit up!' The corpse sits up. It even talks. Then the houngan says, 'Lie down!' And the corpse lies down. But it is not the dead man who sits up. The dead man is dead. It is the maît' tête who has forced the body to sit up. After this the houngan takes the loa from the head and puts it in a pot tête. Then the body can be buried. And afterward the loa can be put in the head of someone else or freed. Or the houngan may keep the loa in the pot tête and sell it to someone who needs a loa to work for him. If they buried the corpse without a *déssounin,* the loa would resent it and go away below the water."

George Eaton Simpson has written an excellent description of a ceremony for removal of the loa from the head of a deceased houngan.[8] The rites took place in the region of Plaisance in northern Haiti. Such a ceremony, Simpson notes, may be attended by several houngans other than the Vodoun priest who is officially in charge. They "share the obligation and pleasure of conducting this service for their colleague, their former rival, and perhaps their former enemy." In a room of the deceased houngan's house is the body, attended by the family, relatives, close friends, and the officiating houngan and his assistants.

. . . Near the body, which is covered by a sheet, are placed a jug and a new canari (a large earthen jar). The officiating houngan makes the sign of the cross, mumbles a few ritual formulas, and taking a spoon puts some "manger les morts" (special food for the dead) in the canari: plantains, yams, bananas, tairauts, sweet potatoes, corn meal, roasted corn, bread, cakes, rice, millet, meat, chicken, pistachio, chopped coconut, and other kinds of food. He then adds some water and stirs this mixture. . . . The other houngans perform the same rite. The family, friends, and others in the room imitate the acts of the houngans with the green branches which they hold in their hands. In a grave voice and with solemn gestures the officiant then appeals to the *loas* with songs and prayers. He invites them to come to the aid of their faithful servant, to protect him in the other world as they have protected him in this world. Following the songs and prayers the leader pronounces these words:
"Innocent! A good man has left us!
    The mother of the children weeps.
    Weep, console yourselves.
    Boss Accelon, he was here.
    He died.
    Master Pierre Jean-Baptiste, he was here.
    He died.
    General Baptiste, he was here.
    He died.
    Marius who was left,
    He died.
    But Brother Joseph survives,
    We will cry, we will console ourselves." [9]
The weeping and the cries redouble, but the *père-savanne* [prêt' savane] and the houngan carry on. In the other room the *père-savanne* solemnly intones:
    "I have only one soul
    Which must be saved.
    By the eternal flame,
    I must preserve it." [10]

The officiating houngan speaks directly to the dead man: "Boss Marius, here is a canari that your heirs have especially prepared for you so that in the future you will not have any trouble and demand other sacrifices of them. You others, the dead, are always unreasonable. Because you have peace you forget that the times are hard and that on this earth we unfortunate men are crushed by suffering. Leave your family in peace after this service, Boss Marius. Do not torment them, and do not send illnesses to their children or misery to their older people. You were always a good father when you were living. Continue to protect your family after death. If you need other services give abundantly to your heirs in order to obtain satisfaction. Oh, good father, good servant, good parent, good friend! Good-bye! Do not forget us as we shall not forget you." [11]

Then the houngan goes to the canarie, strikes it three times with a piece of palm bark, and chants an invocation to the loa and to God, while members of the family dance where they stand, shaking the green branches they hold. There follows an invocation to twins. After a number of loa have "entered" the service, as manifested by possessions, the houngan undertakes to find out how death came to the deceased man. An assistant brings the sacred divining shells [12] of the dead man, and the officiating houngan throws them on the floor, pours tafia three times, and lights a candle. The shells are then consulted. Three times he goes through the procedure of casting the shells and consulting them. Later he announces that "the death of Boss Marius is not the death of an ordinary man, that he is now resting in La Ville-au-Camp (capital of the loas which is 'under the water'), and that the loas will continue to protect his descendants provided that they show themselves worthy of protection." [13] There is more singing and ritual, and then the canarie is covered. The loa from the head of Marius has found a temporary resting place. A little later in the service "the houngan raises the canari as high as possible, almost as high as his face, as he repeats the last line: 'Where may I find refuge?' With a quick movement the canari is shattered. The food is scattered, the loas are satisfied, and the crowd breaks into disorderly flight. . . ." [14] A few hours later the body of the deceased is buried.

It is obvious that these rituals vary a good deal according to regional practices and according to the importance of the persons for whom they are conducted. Furthermore, there is a good deal of difference of opinion among Haitians as to what actually takes place when the maît' tête is taken from the head of the deceased man.

Although the prêt' savane (bush priest) is subsidiary to the houngan at death rites, his is nevertheless a conspicuous presence. He may begin the services with prayers for the dead, in which the family joins, while the houngan remains in the background. Later, the houngan takes over. In certain regions, however, the prêt' savane is dispensed with altogther, his function being absorbed by the houngan.

As reported by Herskovits, the wake for the dead is one of the most important ceremonies in the death rites. He says:

Wakes are held for all dead, even for very young children if they have been baptized, though if a baby dies before baptism, it is buried without ceremony in a little box in the courtyard of the habitation. . . . The wife and the children either stay with the corpse or are nearby with friends. The one who bathed the corpse remains constantly at its side as members of the family come and go, since the body must never be alone.[15]

But outside the house another kind of activity goes on. There the young people usually gather to sing gay songs, to play games, and to listen to stories. A professional storyteller, or a nonprofessional of repute, is called upon to entertain the children. He may give an entire night to Bouki and Malice stories, or to *contes* with interspersed songs in which the audience participates. Special singing games, stick games, and card games are played. But the drums are silent, both in the dead person's house and in the countryside at large. Rhythms for the game songs are provided by hand-clapping, or by vocal sounds which simulate percussion instruments.

Burial ceremonies vary according to local tradition and the status of the deceased person. Near the little fishing village of Petit Goave in south-western Haiti, I witnessed a funeral cortege which might have been seen almost anywhere in the country. It was led by the widow of the dead man. She rode on a white horse, followed by four men carrying the dead body on a litter made of plain planks. There was no coffin, the body being covered only by its white shroud.[16] Behind the corpse plodded a group of twelve or fifteen peasants, friends and relatives of the dead man. Some of them had just come in from the fields and still carried their machetes in their hands. Others carried short *cocomacaque* sticks, which are believed useful for warding off baka and other demons who lurk along the path of the traveler.

The woman on the horse lamented loudly. When she came to where other peasants stood respectfully at the road's edge, she stopped her horse and faced them, raising her voice to an anguished pitch, calling on them to take note of her bereavement and of the fine virtues of the dead man. Some of the spectators whom she addressed, standing with their hats in hand, nodded and tried to say consoling words, such as "Oui Manman, li grand moune" (Yes, Mama, he was a fine man), or "Quand Bondieu vlé ou li prend" (When God wants you he takes you). A market woman with a load on her head suddenly became possessed by a loa as the cortege passed her. This seemed to increase the anguish of the widow, who lamented with increased vigor.

The four men carrying the corpse sometimes moved in a zigzag course, first to one side of the road, then to the other. When the procession came to a crossroad it stopped momentarily. The houngan, scarcely distinguish-able from the other peasants in blue denim, came forward and stood in the center of the crossroads shaking his tiny hand bell and calling upon Maît' Kalfu (Master of the Crossroads) to grant safe passage. While he invoked the loa, the pallbearers brought the body forward as though to go straight ahead, but then they began to lurch and sway as though an invisible force were pushing them around. They veered as though to take the right turn, and again they lurched and staggered. At last they turned toward the left, and in this direction they found the road clear. The houngan thanked the Master of the Crossroads, the widow took her place at the head of the procession, and it proceeded on its way to the cemetery.

In the services for a dead houngan described by Simpson, the body is placed in a coffin, which is carried to all the places sacred to the loa of the hounfor before being taken to the cemetery. First it is taken to the sacred trees where the loa reside, then to the sacred spring "whose waters have cured many sicknesses which physicians had pronounced incurable . . . The bearers of the coffin circle the spring several times. The coffin is swung [toward] each of the four cardinal points." Afterward the procession continues its way to the burial ground.[17]

But the treatment given to the dead may vary according to the manner in which they died. Leyburn notes, for example, that "a person struck by lightning . . . would have no ceremonies at all, for lightning is an act of God." [18] It may well be that the Haitian rationale for not holding ceremonies for an individual killed by lightning is that God has already held the final ceremony. But in the Haitian mind all deaths are, in the last analysis, acts of God, even though magic, poison, or accident may have played an immediate part. Why, then, should the corpse struck by lightning be treated so differently? The answer would appear to lie in a custom of the Yoruba of dispensing with all burial rites for persons killed by lightning, such persons being considered enemies of the lightning deity Chango. In Dahomey, Herskovits reports, the same attitude prevails in regard to persons killed by lightning:

> If a person is killed by lightning he . . . stands convicted by this fact of some grave crime which has incurred the displeasure of the god of the Thunder Pantheon (Xevioso). A person so killed is never buried by his family, but the body is turned over to the chief priest and cult-members of these deities. It is believed that a man killed in this fashion remains upright until the chief priest questions him and forces him to confess the crimes he had committed to be so punished. No one touches any of the belongings of such a man, not even his money. The house in which he lived is allowed to go to ruin, an *azan* of palm fronds being placed around it to guard against anyone entering it. The moveable property of such a man, his clothes, his stools, and his dishes, are thrown away at the crossroads . . .[19]

The burial of a Haitian who dies of smallpox likewise differs from that of one who dies a "normal" death. The victim of smallpox is buried without a coffin in a segregated part of the cemetery. The reason for this lies beyond the obvious fear of contagion. In his study of Dahomey, Hersko-vits notes:

> . . . Small-pox is believed to be sent as a punishment for grave offenses in the eyes of these [the Sagbata] deities, and it is taken to indicate that either the dead person himself or a member of his family has committed some heinous crime such as the practice of black magic. A person who dies of small-pox may only be buried after permission has been given by the chief priest of the Earth cult.[20]

Thus, in Haiti, though the connections with the past are clouded, it is clear that victims of lightning and smallpox are treated as a special class of criminals or malefactors.

Ordinary malefactors such as malevolent criminals and murderers—until recent years, at least—were not buried in the common graveyard. They, too, were segregated at the periphery of the cemetery or buried at the edge of a trail or road where the traffic would not permit them to rest and where their graves would be under constant surveillance. The roadside grave sometimes was also the fate of a person killed by lightning.

That these special burials are related to the Dahomean and Yoruban concepts of retribution for crimes against the deities is supported by the similarity of treatment accorded victims of lightning and disease and common criminals. In Haiti, Herskovits observes: "Those who die of small-pox or leprosy, suicides, or persons shot as a punishment for crime are not buried in the communal cemetery, but in special sections of the grave-yard," the suicides and criminals being set apart from the others.[21]

Graves found near the seashore, lake shores, or riverbanks frequently are declared to belong to persons who died of drowning.

Approximately nine days after a person's death, the "last prayers" are said, and the soul of the deceased is presumed to have departed from the house. Once more, under the tonnelle outside there are games, storytelling, and singing. On this night, however, there is also drumming and dancing of a special kind. Usually it is the Juba, or Martinique, dance, which is believed to be specially enjoyed by the dead, and it is the older people, rather than the young, who participate. These festivities are believed to give cheer to the deceased and to "encourage" him on his way. On the next night comes the mangé mort, the feast for the family dead, a ritual which continues periodically through the years.

Sometimes in Haiti you may come upon an old tomb or grave before which a dish of specially prepared food has been set. This is part of the mangé mort ritual.

A man may make provision in advance of his death for the rites which follow his burial. He may designate special animals to be killed, leave special funds to defray expenses, or even set a day for the "last prayers"; and it is said that misfortune is likely to overtake his family if his wishes are not carried out. Métraux cites a story of a man who had told his wife that if he should happen to die on a Sunday she should hold "last prayers" for him on a Tuesday. It happened to be a Tuesday when the man died.

They held the burial in the afternoon. As they began the prayers on Wednesday, the last prayer finished on Wednesday week. But as Brother Lédan had always said they should hold his last prayer on a Tuesday, his wife was quite willing to hold it Tuesday. One Tuesday when everyone knew that the last prayer was being held, his wife heard her brother-in-law who told her that wasn't customarily done [that is, shortening the period of prayers]. Then she put off the last prayer.

Thereupon, according to the story, two strangers appeared in the house. They were offered chairs and they sat down. Suddenly, one of the men arose and said that the woman had announced that a last prayer was to be said that day. She said she had put it off. Then the other man got up and said: "Wasn't it today I ordered you to hold the last prayer?" The woman asked, "Who are you?" But both men disappeared. The woman fell unconscious, and died three days later.[22]

The cycle of honoring, encouraging, and placating the spirits of the dead moves continuously. There is no beginning and no end. Although those who have died are no longer seen, they are part of the great community which encompasses those whose names are remembered and those who are forgotten, including ancestors who never left the shores of Africa. Death is merely another aspect of life, and its forces are ever present.

5. Services for the Loa and the Family Ancestors

The Ordeal by Fire: Kanzo

To advance beyond the lowest status in the hounfor, the hounsi must undergo the test of fire. This ritual is known as *kanzo,* meaning "to tie fire." In the drama of the hounfor there are many tests and ordeals. When certain loa enter, the mounted persons will eat broken glass. Other loa will cause their "horses" to rub hot pepper in their eyes. Still others will compel possessed persons to cut themselves with machetes. But these are bravado actions of the deities who have entered into the bodies of the servitors. The kanzo test is a formalized and premeditated ritual, in which it is demonstrated that the power of the cult—and the spirit of the individual—is superior to fire. Once having passed through this rite, the ordinary hounsi becomes a *hounsi kanzo.*

The kanzo ceremony—or, as it is known in some parts of Haiti, the *brulé zin* (the boiling pot)—is performed in diverse ways according to the tradition of the particular hounfor. But common to all is the dipping of the hands into boiling oil.

The common hounsi, the bossale, is prepared gradually for kanzo. In the course of certain rites she undergoes a smoke ordeal. On all fours, her head close to a fire, she must breathe in smoke without choking or coughing. When these and other tests indicate that she is ready, she will be permitted to undergo the rite of the brulé zin.

Near the town of Thomazeau in the Cul-de-Sac Plain I witnessed one of these rituals. It began with a dance, in which only the hounsi of the cult participated. They were all dressed in white. The chief drummer wore a woman's blouse, a kerchief on his head, and on top of that a woman's straw hat. He played alone while the houngan invoked the loa Legba. Then there were songs for Ogoun, and the dancing resumed.

The dance court was larger than average—about forty feet by sixty.

Attached to the ever-present po'teau mitan, or center post, were three oil lamps which threw a flickering light. At the entrance to the dance court a glowing-hot iron bar stood erect in a charcoal fire—the symbol of kanzo and of the loa Ogoun.

When the preliminary dances were over, the hounsi retired to one side of the court, where they sat in two rows facing the center.

Ritual rattle and bell in hand, the houngan took his place by the sacred center post. He was an elderly man with a gray beard. He wore a red kerchief like a turban around his head. He smoked a cigar, and in his free hand he held a bottle of rum. The red kerchief, the rum, and the cigar were all in honor of Ogoun. He moved back and forth across the center of the court, talking casually, even joking and laughing. The drums began again, on a signal from the houngan, and a number of visiting houngans and mambos came forward and began a stately Jenvalo dance. The backs of their hands touching their knees, their backs bent low, they moved slowly counterclockwise around the center post. The mambos outnumbered the houngans four to one. The hounsi sitting on the sidelines sang. The song was for Maîtresse Èzilie. The houngan in charge stood by patiently, deep in thought. His assistant, the laplace, kept time with a small rattle and led the singing.

When the song came to an end, the visiting cult priests and priestesses retired from the dance ground. Again the hounsi danced. Afterward the houngan began to talk *langage,* twirling his bottle of rum about recklessly. He was speaking to a loa. The chief drummer beat out a salute to Ogoun. Then the houngan raised the bottle and placed it to his ear. It gurgled away, some of the liquid trickling down his face. He seemed to be swallowing the rum.

While all the hounsi, with bowed heads, sat on the ground, the houngan recited from the ritual of the Catholic service. Latin words, then Creole words in Latin cadences. After a while the houngan's assistant took over the recitation, and the hounsi answered him responsively.[1] When the prayers were over, the hounsi arose and passed into the hounfor. The drums began a fast Nago rhythm, and the hounsi emerged with brilliant silk flags studded with tiny brass rivets. The houngan's chief assistants—the laplace and the houngénicon—carried military sabers upraised. The dancers circled in single file around the center post, a triumphal military heralding of the deity of war and the forge.

To the accompaniment of a crescendo of drums, the procession suddenly reversed its direction. Watching the upraised saber of the laplace for a signal, the hounsi reversed their direction again.

When the dance drama ended, the hounsi carried the flags back into the hounfor. Then they sat on the ground while the houngan came forward to the center post to make his ritual flour drawing. Holding the flour in his hand, he allowed a little of it to trickle out in a fine white line. He worked rapidly, with half-closed eyes, speaking *langage*. A complicated white geometric pattern grew on the earth around the center post. Among its intricate designs highly stylized phallic forms were discernible. When the houngan had finished the drawing, he wrote the name of the loa whom they were serving: Ogoun Badagry. Then the other houngans and mambos came forward, one at a time, to add to the design. When the vèvè was completed it covered virtually the entire dance court.

The laplace came from the hounfor with a bundle of brilliantly colored beads. He stood by the houngan at the center post. One by one the hounsi came before the houngan, dropped on their knees, and kissed the ground. Around each hounsi's neck the houngan placed a string of beads. He raised her, pirouetted her first to the right, then to the left. The pirouette was to encourage possession by the loa.

From the hounfor the hounsi now brought herbs and vegetables for the sacrifice. Baskets and bottles were set out neatly on the ground, along with bundles of sticks and the iron pots, or *zins*.

The dance was resumed in a single rotating line around the houngan and the ritual offerings. Two hounsi in the center of the circle built fires, one on each side of the court. Over the fires they set the ritual iron pots. They poured oil into the pots and began the preparation of ritual food balls, like dumplings, from the ingredients at hand. One by one they dropped the dumplings into the oil, which was soon boiling.

The drumming, singing, and dancing were sustained at a high tension. A second team of drummers took over without a break in the music. The dancers now were almost exhausted. With a quick motion, the houngan spilled some rum into one of the boiling pots. A blue alcohol flame shot high into the air. Some of the hounsi screamed but continued to dance. Three of them fell to the ground, their limbs jerking uncontrollably. The loa had entered. Two of the "mounted" hounsi arose and continued to dance, staggering and jerking across the dance court. The third had to be lifted and carried into the hounfor.

The man who was to undergo initiation was waiting in the *djévo,* a special room in the hounfor. For the past seven days he had lain on a mat in the djévo, in virtual isolation except for visits from the houngan and the laplace.

Now the kanzo initiate was brought out, completely covered with a white cloth. Only his hands and feet could be seen. With one hand on the shoulder of the laplace, who preceded him, he moved with the dancers in a circle around the two boiling pots. On the seventh circuit of the course, the laplace stopped him at the first pot. The houngan grasped the man's free hand and, bending down, dipped it into the boiling oil. There was no visible indication of pain. They moved to the second pot, and the man's hand was dipped again. They proceeded again to the first pot, where the dipping was repeated, then back again to the second pot. The neophyte's hand entered the boiling oil seven times in all. He made no sound, showed no resistance, no reflexes. Then the hounsi took him back to the hounfor. It was all over. After three days of isolation, they said, he would be kanzo.

The houngan peeled an orange, while everyone crowded close to watch. In it he found a two-gourde note. He peeled another orange and found in it a slip of paper with the name of a woman on it. She came forward, and everyone laughed. She was an old woman, the oldest of the hounsi. The houngan held the two-gourde note between his teeth. The old woman took the other end of the note in her teeth, but she had to kiss the houngan before he would let go.

The ritual of brulé zin, or kanzo, is of unmistakable West African origin. Herskovits has described a ceremony in Dahomey which in many details could easily have taken place in Haiti. The Dahomean rite was in honor of the gods of the Thunder pantheon. Here, too, we find a pot of boiling palm oil, in which are the sacred dumplings: "When the fire had finally subsided and only a faint column of smoke issued from the pot, the initiate came dancing toward it, thrust her hand into the boiling oil, and lifted out a dumpling. . . ."[2]

FAMILY RITES AT LÉOGANE

These services for family ancestors took place in the mountains above Léogane at the ancestral home of my friend Libera Borderau. They were conducted on the grounds of his grandmother's house. The ritual began with dancing. Against the wall of the house sat the three drummers with their Arada drums. Near them, leaning against the wall, were the flags of the family loa. Also near by was a long high table serving as a makeshift altar called the *pé*. In the very center of the table in a clean white dish lay eight loa stones—old Carib artifacts. The stones were identical in shape, all of them perfectly symmetrical, resembling small, pointed cigars. In the *pierre-loas* lived the family deities, and much of the ceremony was built around them. The stones had been bathed and polished in oil for the occasion. Set around the plate of stones were numerous small *criches* (French, *cruches*—clay water jugs), glass bottles, and earthenware jars which also contained loa. On the low bench before the table, seven dishes were set out in a row, and before them four *couis,* the half-gourd bowls used in services to the marassas, the twin spirits.

In the house, at the center of the floor, was a round flat stone about ten inches in diameter and about two inches thick, resembling a millstone. This was the *pierre-manman,* the mother stone responsible for the coming of the other loa stones and who cared for them in the absence of the family. In this stone, they said, was the spirit of the old loa Nananbouclou. On a mat in the corner of the room two children slept.

Outside, on a chair, his back against the wall of the house, the houngan sat, his rattle and bell in hand. He had come several miles to conduct the service. Most of those who danced were his own hounsi. The houngan was "strong" and well known in the region; people said he had worked for high government officials, including the president himself.

After several rounds of Arada dancing in which children as well as adults took part, the drums stopped. The houngan and his laplace moved up to the building which served for the night as the hounfor. It was up a steep slope, about a hundred feet from the dance court. There they prepared for the sacrifice to Chébo Profiel, the honored loa of the evening. Passing in and out among the spectators was a woman who would be possessed by Papa Chébo; since he was the guest of the service, she (or the loa in her head) was free to come and go as she chose, to speak as she pleased, and to do what she wished. Mostly she shook hands with people, a ceremony which continued throughout the night. First she would offer the right hand, then the left; or perhaps both at once, in which case the hands would be shaken downward vigorously three or four times. Someone ignorantly said, "Bon soir, Madame!" and she turned on him to reprimand his insolence. She was not "Madame," she was *l'Autorité,* the Authority.

During the course of the evening the conviction became stronger and stronger in her that she was Chébo Profiel. From the time we first saw her until the end of the evening her personality underwent marked changes. She "became" Papa Chébo.

The houngan sat before a small hole, possibly a foot deep and ten inches in diameter, in front of the hounfor. The fresh earth was piled neatly to the side, and an enameled plate was set on top of it. Around the hole were the various dishes to be offered to Chébo Profiel. The laplace prayed in Latin, a short Catholic service. Then the houngan, shaking his beaded rattle and tinkling his bell, called for Chébo to "enter." He made a small maize-flour drawing around the hole, and then began the feeding of the loa. The plates arranged for the feast contained roasted maize, roasted peanuts, bread, cassava, rice, and other foods. There were bottles of rum, kola (a soft drink), *clairin,* and syrup. The houngan, entreating Chébo to accept, poured a little *clairin* into the hole. The loa seemed to accept, for the *clairin* was quickly absorbed in the ground. The houngan took rice from the plate with his fingers, about the amount he might place in his own mouth, and put it gently into the hole. He was feeding Papa Chébo, literally placing the food in his mouth. After the rice, which was dry, the houngan poured in a little more *clairin* to moisten it. He ordered the laplace to break up the bread, and then he placed a small piece in the hole and washed it down with a little rum. The houngan seemed to understand that Papa Chébo Profiel was hungry, and that he was also an epicure. He allowed him to taste the roasted corn, and then washed it down with a trickle of kola. Then he gave him a taste of the roasted peanuts, and another morsel of bread. Once Chébo got his mouth too full in his zest for the meal, and the assemblage had to wait for him to finish "coughing." Then the houngan gave him a long drink of kola to clear his windpipe. After that the houngan was more careful in the way he fed him—a little cassava, a drink, a little bread. As the houngan fed the loa, some of the spectators reached over and placed small coins in the empty dish by the hole. These too were for Chébo. Finally, Chébo was through eating. The food was gone.

The houngan, shaking his rattle and his bell, blew two sharp notes on his whistle. At the door of the hounfor appeared l'Autorité, the hounsi possessed by Papa Chébo. More than ever she resembled the loa, and less than ever she resembled herself. In one hand she held a saber. Her bodily movements were spasmodic, as though she was being forced to do things to which she was not accustomed. She moved slowly into the circle, her eyes almost closed; she leaned backward, then twisted grotesquely around, jerked this way and that, buffeted by the loa. Suddenly she began to whirl. The houngan called "Tambouyé!" and the drummers beat a slow complicated rhythm, a salute to Chébo. The loa had really "entered" now. There was no mistaking the jerky, irresponsible movements of the hounsi's head and shoulders. She leaned backward as though about to fall, incredibly kept her balance, rolled forward as though she were going to plunge to the ground, and twisted herself upright once more. The saber passed close to the faces of the spectators, even scratched some of them and cut their clothing. Her movements had a definitely masculine character. Chébo Profiel was a man.

She reached over to seize a chicken that was held out to her. Grasping its legs with her free hand, she continued her spinning, twisting, lurching dance. Then she cradled the chicken, rocking it back and forth until it was in a hypnotic trance. She placed it on the ground before a tiny pile of ground maize prepared by the laplace. The chicken, released, sat motionless, making no effort to escape. All watched attentively, the houngan shaking his rattle and bell. Suddenly the chicken cocked its head and, seeming to see the corn for the first time, reached out and pecked at it. This was the loa receiving the sacrifice—a difficult conception if one thinks of the chicken itself as the sacrifice. "Chébo," l'Autorité, snatched the chicken up, danced violently about, the loa in full possession of her body. With a swift movement of the saber, she cut the chicken's throat and caused the first drop of blood to fall into the hole. When the chicken stopped struggling, it was left there, head downward. L'Autorité took up a cock which was given her, cradled him, and set him before the ground maize. When he pecked at it, she picked him up and danced, around and around, jerking, lunging, never quite falling. She took his comb between her teeth, supporting his body gently with her hands, and spun around and around. Then she released him, cut his throat, and placed him in the hole with the chicken.

At the side of the hounfor, waiting, was a goat (called by the ritual name Dogwé). He had a fine silky white coat and a long beard. He was brought in to the place of sacrifice, and l'Autorité dropped to her knees to embrace his neck with her arms. She remained there a moment, her cheek against his, talking to him. Then she arose, a machete in hand instead of a saber, and began to pirouette while three men threw the goat on his side. Then she cut with the machete, and the goat's blood, too, began to run into the hole. For the first time her dance became unquestionably frenzied. She swung strong, full blows of the machete at the goat's neck, finally severing the head. From the hindquarters she cut a piece of red meat and placed it in her mouth.

At a signal from the houngan, three men carried the goat's body away to be dressed and cooked, and a woman came forward to wipe the blood from Papa Chébo's face.

The drums began again, a Dahomé dance, and the people relaxed. Many joined in the dancing while l'Autorité strutted about shaking hands and talking *langage*. She also danced, with gestures and movements wholly masculine. At one point she briefly advanced on another woman, making sexual gestures.

The houngan and his houngénicon retired to the front room of the hut. A new mat had been placed there for the houngénicon. She lay down on it, and the houngan sat in a chair against the wall. This was the beginning of the ceremony of calling *les morts en bas dleau* (the dead below the water).

Meanwhile, before the hounfor, the laplace and a hounsi were building

the *card,* a hogan-like structure made of bent saplings covered with cotton
cloth.

Rain had been threatening all evening, and now it began. Some people
crowded into the hut where the goat was being barbecued. Others came
into the hut where the houngénicon lay; in the back room, with the pé,
Chébo, l'Autorité, strutted and shook hands with the visitors. The straw
roof leaked a little, but no one minded very much. The houngan and his
houngénicon, who had been under a strain, relaxed. The rain would mark
the length of the intermission. Except for the sound of the rain and
"Chébo's" *langage,* there was no noise. No one spoke. Then the houngan,
his eyes closed, began to sing an Ibo song.

> Ibo Lazile oh, éya!
> Grand gout manqué tuyé moin!
> A la yun an six mois m' sous la mer,
> Grand gout manqué tuyé moin!
>
> Ibo Lazile, oh, éya!
> Hunger has not killed me!
> One year and six months I have been under the sea,
> Hunger has not killed me!

The others sang responsively:

> Ibo Lazile, oh, Ibo!
> Ibo grand gout pas tuyé'm, Ibo!
>
> Ibo Lazile, oh, Ibo!
> Ibo, hunger has not killed me, Ibo!

After a while the houngan called "Abobo!"—which was the signal to
conclude. The rain was still coming down, and he called "Abobo!" for
the rain to cease also. But it did not stop, and everyone laughed. He began
another song, also Ibo:

> Ianman Ibo lélé!
> Ianman Ibo lélé!
> Pilet pied'm mandé pardon,
> Ça pardon wa fai pou moin?
> Ça ou gainyan con ça? [Ex. 80]
>
> Ianman Ibo lélé!
> Ianman Ibo lélé!
> Step on my foot and ask my pardon,
> What will the pardon do for me?
> What do you have [what are you doing] like that?

And the others came in, spiritedly:

> Ianman, oh, un hunh!   Ianman, oh, un hunh!
> Ianman, con ça'm dansé Ibo!   Ianman, like this I dance, Ibo!
> Ianman, oh, un hunh!   Ianman, oh, un hunh!

While those in the front room were singing, l'Autorité, in the inner room, was suddenly thrown about violently by her possession. She raced into one wall of the hut, striking her head, flung herself back against the opposite wall, kicking, trembling, calling out strange *langage*. She crashed into the pé, upsetting the dishes, and then fell across the mat where the children were lying half asleep. One of them, a boy of about four, became hysterical. He knew the woman, but he had never seen her like this. His mother carried him to the front room, where she finally quieted his crying. L'Autorité, spent for the moment, lay across the mat. No one touched her. Later, when the singing was resumed, she got to her feet and made the rounds once more, shaking hands again and again. She was now smoking a pipe.

When the houngan heard the rain subsiding, he again called out "Abobo!" as though he were giving the order to cease, and everyone, himself included, laughed again. When it had definitely stopped, someone went out to shake the water from the canopy. The drums were brought out of their shelter, and although the ground was sticky with mud, the dancing was resumed. The houngan asked for a fast Nago dance, and the front room of the hut was once more emptied of everyone except the houngan and his houngénicon.

The laplace and his assistant went up the hill to put the finishing touches to the *card,* the temporary structure in which the houngan was going to receive the loa and the dead. From a small chest of chinaware, the houngénicon set a "table" for the loa on the ground where she sat. The sacrifice had been for a single loa, Chébo; the rest of the service was for all the loa served by the family. The houngan, sitting next to the houngénicon, sounded his rattle and spoke *langage*. He sang quietly, a song which only the houngénicon could hear, watching her intently. A large basket of dishes, bottles, and various other paraphernelia was brought by a hounsi. Candles were lighted and set on the ground. The houngan gave a signal, and the hounsi brought a large square of white cotton cloth, which they stretched tight over the houngénicon like a canopy. The candle flame and the silhouette of the houngénicon could be seen through the cloth, but the details of the service were not visible. Sometimes, the houngan, his bell and rattle in hand, would go under the cloth to assist in the calling of the loa. Then, without warning, things began to happen very rapidly.

One of the hounsi who sat before the door began to quiver and make strange noises in her throat: "Ka, ka, k-k-k-k-k-a!" Her body shook violently, and her head rolled on her shoulders. Almost simultaneously something began to happen under the cloth where the houngénicon was, and the members of the family crowded up to the *card* by the hounfor. The houngénicon lay stiffly, her eyes closed, the white cloth removed. The houngan carried out the large round basket in which lay the bottles and the pierre-loas. The hounsi gathered around it, ten of them, to carry it to the *card*. In the bottles were *les morts en bas dleau* (the spirits of the dead from below the water). Carrying the flags, three hounsi danced, singing, up to the *card*. After them the laplace came, carrying in his left hand a plate of maize flour from which he made vèvès in the line of advance, simple marks symbolizing the crossroads. The drums were beating a special salute to the loa. The ten hounsi carrying the basket danced and sang. As they moved up the hill, they rotated, so that the basket revolved like the hub of a wheel. Their progress was not smooth, however; they jerked forward and backward as they rotated. Arriving before the *card,* first one, then a second, was entered by her loa. They fell, jerked, and stumbled. This was all a very good omen. The houngan called "Abobo!" for them to resist such possession, and the hounsi all sat down on the ground. The houngan placed the basket inside the *card* and entered after it. He called for his little bell, which the laplace passed in to him. The laplace closed the flap down tight, from the outside, and placed the flags against it.

Upon a signal given from within, the hounsi began a song:

> La famille semblé,
> Oh semblé nous!
> La famille semblé,
> Oh nous semblé pou nou pa'lé parole nous là!
> La famille semblé!
>
> The family gathers,
> Oh, we gather!
> The family gathers,
> Oh, we gather to speak our words here!
> The family gathers!

The laplace took his position, his back to the *card,* while inside, because of the candle burning there, the houngan could be seen setting out the contents of the basket. The candle went out, and in the *card* the little bell began to tinkle. The singing stopped. The houngan was beginning to talk to the dead below the water. First he talked *langage.* Then his voice was heard through the constant sound of the tiny bell, supplicating Papa Loko to talk a little bit with his "children." A faint, tremulous voice, that of a tired old grandfather, was heard to answer. Papa Loko was stirring himself out of a long silence. He talked a long while to the houngan. Sometimes they both spoke at once. Faintly he was heard to say that he had come a long way to see his children, and that he was very tired. But as he talked his strength returned to him, and, asking the houngan to wait, he spoke directly to his "children," who sat, respectfully and awed, around the *card*. Here everyone participated. This was why they had come. Benevolently Papa Loko greeted them: "Bonjou, ti moune moin yo, c'est Papa Loko" (Good day, all my children, this is Papa Loko). Together they all answered eagerly: "Bon soir, Papa!" "Bon soir, Grand!" "Bon soir, cher Papa!" "Bon soir, cher Loko!" Papa Loko told them about his journey, and persons long dead whom he had seen below the water, and he passed on the news from the island below the sea. Then he began to address them singly, asking questions, giving news of dead relatives, and showing a vital interest in the problems of his "children." They answered him. "Oui, Papa," and "Non, Papa Loko," and took deeply to heart anything he said, whether praise or criticism:

Bon jour, Télisman!	Good day, Télisman!
Bon soir, Papa!	Good evening, Papa!
Comment nou yé, Télisman?	How are you, Télisman?
Tout bien, Papa Loko!	Everything is fine, Papa Loko!
C'est ou même qui travaille tres dit?	Are you one who works very hard?
Oui, Papa, moin travaille an pile.	Yes, Papa, I work a great deal.
Ou travaille pou' vié maman ou?	You care for your old mother?
Oui, Papa.	Yes, Papa.
Télisman, pitit moin, faut ou planté jardin ou encore. Graine, li pas bon.	Télisman, my child, you will have to plant your garden again. The seeds you planted are no good.
Merci, cher Loko!	Thank you, dear Loko!
Ou poco blié'm, Télisman.	You do not forget me, Télisman.
Non, cher Loko.	No, dear Loko.
Yo dit ou praillé travaille en ville.	They say you are going to work in the city.
Lé'm capab', Papa.	When I can, Papa.
Pas blié moune morne ça yo, Télisman.	Do not forget the people of the hills, Télisman.
Non, cher Loko, m' pas blié yo.	No, dear Loko, I will not forget them.
Papa ou dit'm ba ou bon soir pou'li.	Your father asked me to say good evening to you for him.
Merci, Papa.	Thank you, Papa.
Papa Loko fini pa'lé ou, Télisman.	Papa Loko is through talking to you, Télisman.
Merci, Papa.	Thank you, Papa.
Chongé 'm, Télisman.	Remember me, Télisman.

Papa Loko talked in turn to everyone in the family who was present, and inquired, sometimes suspiciously, after those who were absent. After many minutes, Papa Loko said regretfully that he had to go away, and bade them au revoir. They were all sorry he was leaving, because he was well loved. He spoke a few words with the houngan, and then his voice faded away. Only the tinkling of the little bell remained.

Then, faintly, came the broken voice of an old woman who was crying. The houngan said her children were waiting to see her, and asked her to enter. Moyise had been dead many generations already, but she was still crying over the circumstances of her death, and because she had left her children behind her. The houngan, speaking gently, asked her to try to stop crying because her children were waiting. Little by little she controlled herself. She greeted them all and talked with each member of the family in turn. She showed a special interest in the women and children and was concerned about family problems.

After Moyise went away, Docile. Moyise' daughter, came. She greeted them all and then complained that when she had died she had been buried in a grave near that of a thief; now she wished for her body to be moved. Alixe, on whose place the grave was situated, promised to take care of the matter, and Docile became placated. Her voice faded away. Inside the *card,* the houngan talked *langage* and rang his bell.

After Docile came Joseph and his son Jougleau. Joseph and Jougleau timed their entrance badly and came in together, both talking at once. The houngan tried to straighten out the situation, and for a moment the three of them were conversing simultaneously. Then Jougleau withdrew and returned when his father was through. After Jougleau came still later generations, represented by Ti Perci and her children, Na and Bernicia. Bernicia came crying bitterly about something. The houngan asked her to stop, because he could not bear to hear women crying. Everyone laughed, and Bernicia controlled herself.

Then Damballa Wèdo, the ancient loa, came, speaking with an aged and broken voice. Feebly he sang his song in "African" language:

> Ago! Damballa Wèdo!
> Oh Damballa Wèdo kian kian!
> Oh Damballa Wèdo kian kian!
> Oh ha ha ha Damballa Wèdo kian kian!
> Oh Damballa Wèdo kian kian! [Ex. 39]

Later, Damballa sang again, calling on Legba to act as witness to his words:

> Ago-é Attibon Legba oh é!
> Oh Damballa Wèdo é kélé manyan!
> Oh gainyain jou' ya chongé moin là kélé manyan!
> Oh Damballa Wèdo é kélé manyan!
> Oh Ayida Wèdo é kélé manyan!
> Oh gainyain jou' pou' chongé moin là kélé manyan! [Ex. 40]

> *Ago-é* Attibon Legba *oh é!*
> Oh, Damballa Wèdo *é, kélé manyan!*

Oh, a day will come when they will remember me here, *ķélé manyan!*
Oh, Damballa Wèdo *é, ķélé manyan.*
Oh, Ayida Wèdo *é, ķélé manyan!*
Oh, a day will come for you to remember me here, *ķélé manyan!*

During the evening about twenty loa and ancestors came into the *card* to talk. When the last had finished speaking the hills were already light, and the service was over.

SERVICE FOR ÈZILIE FRÉDA AND ST. JACQUES MAJEUR

This service took place not in the open but under a tonnelle surrounded by four walls, adjoining the hounfor of Alexis Stephan on the west fringes of Port-au-Prince. Separate from the hounfor and dance court was a shrine to the "dead" loa Gèdé Nimbo. The shrine was a small shed open on one side. Within, lighted by flickering oil lamps, was a life-size effigy of Gèdé, a scarecrow-like figure dressed in the loa's traditional attire—black tail coat and trousers, and a tall opera hat. On the otherwise blank face of the figure were smoked glasses with white rims.

The dancing was progressing under the supervision of the houngan's adjutant, the laplace. He wandered among the drummers and dancers, encouraged the singing, and issued orders here and there. No one seemed to take him very seriously. There was a good deal of joking, and the gathering seemed very much like an old-fashioned family reunion. There were perhaps a hundred dancers and spectators—friends, relatives, and devotees of Stephan's hounfor. Everyone was watching with affection an old woman who could not be restrained from dancing. She executed old classical steps and postures with a skill that called for running comment all around her. As each piece came to an end someone would step up to her and say something like: "Woy, Manman, mais ou passé mwé!" (Oh, Mother, you are better than me!). Then they would attempt to get her to sit down again, but she would only shake them off and urge the drummers to get going if they were not too tired.

Eventually, the houngan, Stephan, made a casual entrance through the door of his adjoining hounfor. He held the usual ritual rattle and bell in his hand, and sauntered around to chat with his friends.

Gradually, almost imperceptibly, the dancing became more serious. Soon, only the hounsi, the female servitors, were dancing. The drums played a salute to Legba, the first loa to be called upon in a Vodoun service. For it is Legba who opens all gates and all highways, and who paves the way for communication with other deities. Though he is not the greatest of the loa, he is one of the most ancient. The houngan spilled water on the ground as a libation, and the dancing continued.

Then a well-dressed young man entered, and the drummers swiftly changed to the salute reserved for guests of distinction. The hounsi sang, "Président passe là, l'ap monté au gouvernment!" and waved paper flags and kerchiefs. The young man was a distant relative of Stephan's; he also was a houngan.

After a while Stephan brought from his hounfor a second asson, or ritual rattle, and another small hand bell, both of which he handed to the young man. He was extending the courtesy of his hounfor, sharing his instruments of authority and religious power with his fellow houngan. Then followed an exhibition between the two houngans that was half duel and half ballet. They stood face to face, each of them holding the asson in one hand and the tiny bell in the other. Stephan was "testing" the young houngan for the edification of all present. Each tiny move made by Stephan was duplicated simultaneously by his guest, as though he were a mirrored reflection.

Every posture Stephan made was duplicated instantly by his guest. The assons and the bells were agitated constantly. The rattle in the young man's hand did precisely what Stephan's did. The two men looked into each other's eyes with intensity, as though this bound their movements together and unified them. When Stephan twisted to the left, the other houngan twisted to the right. Every contortion of the young man was an exact replica of Stephan's movements. The two assons rattled out the same rhythms and the same signals; so did the bells. The backdrop for this "test" was provided by the drummers. The faces of the two men broke into a sweat from the intense nervous effort. At last it came to an end. A woman came forward and wiped their faces with a colored kerchief. The "testing" ceremony was over. The visiting houngan had been proved.

Stephan then made a ritual vèvè, or maize-flour ritual drawing on the ground. Afterward there was more singing and dancing by the hounsi. They sang several songs for Èzilie Fréda, the "pure" loa. And Alexis Stephan went into a trance. It was unexpected. The servitors had not prepared for it. In this emergency the visiting houngan took over. He seemed a little anxious. He was unfamiliar with the particular psychological factors at play in this particular hounfor. He was not certain of the character of Stephan's possession. But he took over grimly. The houngénicon, an older woman, stepped forward to help. While the young houngan wielded the asson and bell, the woman issued instructions. Stephan, his head hanging back, his eyes closed, was supported by two of the hounsi. Other servitors hurriedly brought out a white sheet and spread it on the ground. A chair and a table were set upon the sheet, and Stephan was placed in the chair, where he now sat with his head hanging limply on his chest.

Stephan had been mounted by Èzilie Fréda, the deity of whiteness and purity. That was why he was protected from the earth by the white sheet beneath him. While the drums continued to beat, the hounsi placed upon the table a bottle of wine, a clean glass, and a white plate with boiled maize meal, topped by a whole egg. Then they held over Stephan—who had become, for the time being, Èzilie—a second white sheet. The possessed houngan began to bend forward and back with great rapidity, toward the surface of the table and back to an upright position, his arms hanging quietly downward. The hounsi fluttered the covering sheet in such a way that the spectators could not see what was going on beneath it. In less than a minute, Stephan's movements ceased. The sheet was removed. Stephan sat limply, talking *langage*. In the white dish only the broken shells of the egg and a small portion of the meal remained. Some of the wine was gone from the upright bottle. The glass still had a little wine in the bottom. Èzilie had accepted the sacrifice. Not once had Stephan's hands changed from their hanging position or approached the table. The eggshells themselves were clean, but a tiny trickle of liquid yolk ran from the corner of Stephan's mouth. The visiting houngan rattled his asson before Stephan, who arose wearily, with the help of the hounsi, and followed him through the door into the hounfor.

Again there was dancing, and a little while later Stephan emerged from the hounfor in a bizarre military costume of red velvet, wearing black glasses, a blue military cap with a red feather, and a sword. He was almost as weird as the effigy of Gèdé that stood outside. The houngan had now become St. Jacques Majeur, or Ogoun, the loa of war and the forge. His personality had undergone a dramatic change. Strictly speaking, Stephan was not in a trance as he had been a little earlier. He was in control of his movements, which were completely conscious, and yet he was certainly not in a "normal" state of mind. Previously Stephan had been in a state of possession; now, one might say, he was in a state of obsession. He had identified himself with St. Jacques. He strode and swaggered like St. Jacques. His bearing was regal, military, and awesome. His costume should have seemed funny, like similar costumes seen during Mardi Gras days, but instead it was unworldly and impressive.

He carried a rum bottle in his hand, and he moved through the gathering making people drink from it. Those who drank from the bottle were sharing with St. Jacques. Stephan poured more rum into an iron pot on the ground and set it afire. The hounsi kanzo, the servitors of the higher order who had been through the fire ordeal, came forward and washed their hands and arms with the burning rum, so that at times their whole arms were aflame, until they quickly snuffed the fire out. Some of the hounsi brought their children forward and washed their arms in the burning rum also, as a foretaste of the kanzo rites they might one day go through.

There was dancing again for others besides the hounsi. The tension had passed. The ceremony was over, and the rest of the night was simply for pleasure.

GÈDÉ NIMBO, THE "DEAD" LOA

Gèdé Nimbo, also known as Baron Samedi, is one of the most powerful deities of the Haitian pantheon. He guards the cemetery and protects the graves, especially those of children. But Gèdé Nimbo is not simply another loa, he is a personification of death. Like death, he is given to whim. He is an intruder. He forces his way into services being held for other deities, behaves badly, and has to be wheedled to depart. He indulges in ribald humor when the mood strikes him, and the most solemn occasions are likely to be disturbed by his pranks. Gèdé Nimbo can be formidable when aroused, as he can be gentle and forbearing when it suits him.

Gèdé is always dressed in black, usually with a tail coat and top hat. He is always represented in this attire in the shrines where effigies of him are to be found. Elsie Clews Parsons, a number of years ago, reported this Haitian description of Gèdé:

He is a *grande diable*. He makes all kinds of motions to make you laugh, but you must not laugh at him, for if you do he makes you "stop laughing" . . . Anything you touch, he takes and never returns, and you have to give him more and more. He smokes cigarettes, not cigars. He wears a coat and a hat, and carries a stick. He can make himself short or . . . as tall as a mast.[3]

The kind of motions Gèdé makes would in certain other cultures be regarded as obscenities. In Haiti they are merely public violations of social restraints and taboos, things no Haitian would think of doing in public view. But Gèdé, the loa of the graveyard, has special prerogatives. He does not fear criticism. He flouts propriety at will, he embarrasses, provokes, and insults with impunity.

At a Nago ceremony which I witnessed near Port-au-Prince, the stronghold of the Gèdé cult, Gèdé Nimbo entered with such gusto that he virtually made a shambles of the service. The first person to be mounted by the loa was the laplace, the houngan's understudy. He stiffened, twisted, jerked, and thrashed about. As the more violent phase of his possession wore off, he began to make lascivious loin movements, as though copulating with the center post. Afterward, he moved about, shaking hands and greeting various persons with insulting remarks calculated to make others laugh at the indignities. Stopping before a distinguished-looking spectator, Gèdé made a few loin movements in his direction. Grasping another man by the hands, he greeted him vigorously and inquired whether it was his *zozo* (penis) to which his glasses were affixed. As the dance progressed, the possessions came rapidly. The possessed persons, men and women alike, leaped about the tonnelle, mimicking copulation. They broke drinking glasses on the ground, threw themselves upon the drummers, and careened and crashed into spectators and dancers. In the course of the service there were nearly twenty possessions—all of them noteworthy for their portrayal of Gèdé Nimbo as a loa who has contempt for proprieties. For he is the spirit of the cemetery, the one who laughs last and best.

Near the mountain town of Kenskoff I saw another service for Gèdé, which showed a different aspect of the loa of the graveyard. It took place inside the hut of a rural houngan, who was conducting the affair for his own immediate family and a few close friends. The hut itself was small. Its single room had been partitioned into two by hanging a sheet in the middle. On one side of the sheet a young child was lying on a mat next to the carefully stored Arada drums. On the other side the ceremony was taking place. Great bouquets of red flowers were arranged in a corner; above them hung a colored lithograph of the Christ child; below, on the floor, was a crude oil lamp with a floating wick. The floor area was no more than seven feet square, but at least twelve persons were crowded there, and others clustered in the doorway. Ritual flags leaned against the wall, one of red silk with a gold fringe, another of white silk with blue polka dots. A tiny space remained in the center of the floor for the houngan, whose "possession" by Gèdé was the feature of the service.

The houngan was dressed in a black stovepipe hat, a blue blouse with white polka dots, and a black skirt over black trousers. In his hand he carried a walking stick. He smoked a pipe constantly, a variation of the customary cigarette. In the tiny space in the center of the room, the houngan—or, more properly, Gèdé Nimbo—danced. The houngan's personality had changed—his voice, his postures, all his mannerisms. He spoke only through his nose, for that is the way Gèdé talks, as though he had a cleft palate.

He whirled around and around, singing and talking *langage* in turn. His family sang:

> Gèdé-vi yo wè ago-é!
> Gèdé-vi yo wè!
> Papa Gèdé c'est loa!

> It is Gèdé-vi they see, *ago-é!* *
> It is Gèdé-vi they see!
> Papa Gèdé is a *loa!*

---

* *Ago:* exclamatory, signifying "I am here."

He was the center of all eyes. Most of the time he danced alone, gyrating recklessly. Sometimes he danced with his houngénicon. Those who watched clapped hands and uttered sounds imitating drums, for drums were not being used in this service. The houngan carried the inevitable *clochette,* or tiny hand bell.

When newcomers arrived, Gèdé greeted them by shaking both their hands downward, vigorously, three times. Then he wiped their faces with his kerchief, a ceremony which he repeated from time to time. He danced with each of them a kind of Jenvalo step, simple, restrained, and dignified. One of the visitors fell to his knees to converse with him.

The entire evening was built around the houngan's representation of Gèdé. Properly speaking, the houngan was not in a trance. He was in full possession of all his normal faculties and was conscious of the slightest inconveniences and disturbances. Several times the clay bowl of his pipe fell from the reed stem, scattering hot ashes on the ground, and each time he paused to allow the houngénicon to clear them away. Yet he was carried away by his certainty that he was Gèdé. The obvious conviction of those who watched seemed to fortify him in his role. As the evening wore on, he became more and more detached from his normal personality. His psychic condition was not that of one who had been "mounted" by a loa; it was, rather, a continuously progressive ecstasy.

Gèdé is, in fact, more than a loa of the cemetery; he is a personification of death in all its macabre, humorous, and unpredictable aspects. Death is not merely a thing dying; it is an entity, a positive force in nature. Death is Gèdé Nimbo. I believe that when the houngan became Gèdé, all who had crowded into his hut felt themselves to be in the presence of death itself. Death, a dynamic, aggressive force, danced and pirouetted among them, talking the language of the dead and of old Africa.

Gèdé is often stern, austere, and forbidding, but he has other aspects. Haitians take amused pleasure at the terror he can strike into the hearts of the mighty. An old Gèdé song goes:

Papa Gèdé bel ga'çon!	Papa Gèdé is a handsome fellow!
Papa Gèdé bel ga'çon!	Papa Gèdé is a handsome fellow!
L'habillé tout en noi'!	He is dressed all in black
Pou'l monté au palais!	For he is going up to the palace!
L'habillé tout en blanc	When he's dressed all in white
Li semblé yun deputé!	He looks like a deputy!
L'habillé tout en noi'!	When he's dressed all in black
Li semblé yun senateur!	He resembles a senator!

According to tradition, the song had its origin in a march on the capital by some houngans many years ago. The story is very old and no one remembers many of the details. But during the administration of President Louis Borno (1922–1930) there was a reënactment of the original march. There suddenly appeared in the streets of Port-au-Prince a crowd of Gèdé *mystères*—houngans "possessed" by Gèdé Nimbo and attired in Gèdé dress: tall black hats, long black tail coats, smoked glasses, black skirts over their black trousers. They carried flags, waved polka-dot kerchiefs, shook their ceremonial rattles, and paused sometimes to wipe the perspiration from one another's faces. They became the nucleus of a huge, noisy crowd moving up the hill toward the palace. Market women followed instead of going home; street gamins screamed and raced among them. Before they had arrived at the palace grounds they had taken on the semblance of a huge Mardi Gras band. They swerved through the gates of the palace grounds and along the drive, right to the steps of the palace itself. The guards, taken by surprise, waited helplessly for their officers to arrive.

At the palace door, the houngans demanded money from the president. Borno was in a dilemma. He was reputed to be sympathetic to Vodoun ritual but was only surreptitiously so. He feared the houngans, and he feared public opinion. What would the upper class of Port-au-Prince think, the Latin-culture Haitians? With Gèdé's worst manners, the Gèdé mystères cavorted on the palace steps. Finally Borno gave in. He sent the money out to them, and then the crowd of Gèdés marched out of the palace grounds, waving their flags and shaking their rattles.

SERVICE FOR THE HOUNSI BOSSALE

This ritual of calling the loa to speak through the mouth of the Vodoun priest took place in the Bolosse section of Port-au-Prince. The hounfor was situated in a congested slum area of the city, but the grounds around it were spacious. The hounfor itself was small and unpretentious, and except for the adjoining tonnelle would easily have been mistaken for another small wooden house. The houngan was a heavy-set man with a black mustache. Quick to laugh and easy in his movements, he nevertheless commanded solemn respect from the hounsi and the other participants. His soft-spoken voice expressed assurance and authority.

There were a number of possessions in the course of the dancing, all more or less routine. Each time a possession occurred, the houngan came forward with his asson and bell, gave a pitcher of water and a candle to the possessed devotee, and conducted her through a ritual at the foot of the center post.

Later, one of the hounsi came and sat at the houngan's feet. She was not possessed but obviously was in a state of high tension. Other servitors brought from the hounfor a wooden washtub and set it on the ground before the houngan. Staring into the tub, he shook his asson and called upon a certain loa to enter. Then he placed a lighted candle upright in the tub and watched it for a moment. The flame was suddenly snuffed out. The houngan looked concerned. He removed the candle and called for another one. When he placed the new candle in the tub it remained burning. The houngan smiled. The loa had agreed to enter. The houngan and his chief assistant placed the tub upon the head of the waiting hounsi. She trembled violently as though she had received a shock, then leaped to her feet. The loa had mounted her and presumably was sitting in the tub on her head. She began to stagger back and forth across the dance court, while the drums beat a salute. The tub tottered dangerously but did not fall. The possessed hounsi then began to whirl. She stopped, and the tub continued to spin for a few seconds on her head. She twirled again in the opposite direction. Each time she stopped she waited for the tub to stop spinning. The twirling motion was accompanied by a constant jerking and lurching, as though she were about to lose her balance, but she never stumbled or fell. After perhaps five minutes of this violent "riding" by the loa, the houngan approached her with his asson and conducted her into the hounfor, the tub still on her head. Inside the hounfor he removed the tub, sent the loa away, and left the hounsi to rest.

There was more dancing, and after a while the service was transferred to a small temporary cloth-covered structure resembling an American Indian hogan. The hounsi bossale—the servitors whose loa had not been "tamed" or conditioned—lay before the structure on their faces, side by side. There were twelve of them. The other hounsi covered them completely with white sheets. The houngan entered the hogan-like structure (the *card*) with a candle and a bell. He tinkled his bell and began to call upon the loa to speak to the hounsi bossale. Through his mouth, first one spirit and then another made comments. The hounsi under the sheets were tensely quiet, until one of them began to jerk and scream. Several others, as though responding to a trigger, joined in the screaming. Older women came to quiet them. The hysterical reaction of the hounsi bossale was regarded as simply a reflection of their beginners' status. Their loa had not yet been controlled. The ritual continued until the early hours of the morning, the loa and ancient ancestors coming in to speak, one after another.

THE FIRST YAMS AND THE FIRST RICE

Each year, when the yams are harvested there is a great festival known as the *mangé yam*. Of all things grown in Haiti, the yam is perhaps the most significant. It is the most vital of all staples, and it is traditional. The yam itself was transplanted from Africa, where in old times as well as in modern it was a staff of life among those who lived by agriculture. The word "yam" is known throughout large parts of Africa, crossing language lines and forests. It signifies the big root on which the African is so dependent, and it also has the general meaning of "eat." In Senegal it is called *nyami,* while across the width of Africa and in the upper Nile region it is called *nyam.*

In Haiti the yam is a tie with the past and a symbol of fertility. When the yams are plentiful, there is food for the winter months and a sense of well-being. When the yam crop is poor, there is insecurity and even hunger. Whatever occurs, lurking in the background is the shadow of the family ancestors, for it is they who have the power to enhance the crops or blight them. This is the concept around which the mangé yam is built.

The annual harvest feast, on the twenty-fifth of November, is rooted in the need for placating the ancestors, so that the dead will insure the fertility of the fields. Before the feast, no yams may be eaten, for the crop must be "baptized" first. Should this rule be violated the yams will spoil and those who eat them will become sick. The precise form of the mangé yam varies from region to region. Sometimes it is held on the premises of the cult chief for the community at large. More traditionally it is held on the family *habitation,* with a houngan in attendance. It is felt that an important obligation rests upon those who have wandered away from the homestead to return for the occasion. For the fate of the family depends to a large degree upon the successful appeal to the vast host of the ancestral dead, and the solidarity of the living in this effort is regarded as vital. Even if one belongs to a Christian sect which proscribes Vodoun, he is obligated and ready to come, for the welfare of the family is paramount. Catholics, Adventists, and Protestants alike participate. As the Haitians say, it is an affair for all who eat yams, and that means all Haitians.

Yams are washed and prepared for eating during the service. They are cut in small portions, placed in dishes or calabash bowls, and offered to the dead, who have prime rights. All categories of the dead are fed—those who are remembered, those who can be recalled only by name, and those whose names are forgotten. The dead of Haiti are invoked, then the dead of Africa. The marassa dead are fed from separate gourds or bowls, and a special table is set for the ancient dead who move slowly because of their age or infirmities, and who may take a long while to arrive at the mangé. A share of the yams is offered to the family loa. Then the members of the family receive symbolic portions. There is singing, drumming, and dancing, and sometimes ritual baths are taken. Afterward, when the yam feast is ended, the crops may be gathered, stored, and eaten.

In the Artibonite Valley, where much rice is grown, a similar ceremony takes place before the rice is gathered from the fields. In this ceremony it is rice that is shared with the family ancestors, who have first rights, and with close friends who have aided with the planting. This feast is called *mangé diri,* or sometimes *gouté diri,* the tasting of the rice. Small amounts of rice are taken from the fields, cooked with red beans or Congo beans, or perhaps made into dumplings. The farmer's friends and relatives gather while the food is still cooking, and play games such as *wari* and *trois-sept.* The children play *gage* games and sing songs, and sometimes a *maît' conte*—a storyteller—comes to entertain them.

When the food is finally ready, the family ancestors are given their share. The farmer takes a calabash bowl of the rice and walks around the house grounds calling upon his immediate ancestors to accept their share. He drops a little food on the ground for the remembered dead, for the unknown dead who preceded them, for the Haitian dead, and for the dead of Africa. He also drops small portions for the dead twins, the dead albinos, the deformed dead, and the dead who have lost limbs, and for the distressed dead who have been improperly buried, or who may not have received the feasts that were due them. Afterward, he offers food to those who died of drowning, or who were lost at sea and never heard of again.

Each course is shared with the ancestors. The farmer takes a pitcher of water, spilling a little here and a little there until the dead have quenched their thirst. He also gives a little of everything to the family loa. Then the calabashes are set out on a bench or table reserved for the dead, and this food is not disturbed. Food for the marassas is set out separately on the ground in three small *couis,* or gourd dishes.

The family ancestors whose good will has made the harvest possible having been taken care of, the food is now shared among the extended family and the friends who helped in the fields. Later there are prayers to the loa, the saints, and God, led by the houngan or a prêt' savane. To finish the affair, there may be Juba-type dances for the older people, while the children watch or play *gage* games.

Only after this service are the farmer and his family and his *coumbite* (mutual labor group), if he belongs to one, free to go out and harvest the rice.[4]

These feasts of the rice and yam harvests are not of New World origin. Similar harvest festivals for yams or rice are held over a wide area of West Africa. There, as in Haiti, the fundamental concern is with the family ancestors, whose good will must be constantly nourished so that the rains continue to fall, the crops flourish, and human beings remain fertile. Among the Ashanti of Ghana, for example, the yam and rice harvests are celebrated with elaborate rituals for the dead. As in Haiti, great importance is laid on the presence of all living descendants, whose numbers are calculated to influence the ancestors' behavior. And as in Haiti, the first yams and the first rice are offered to the dead, and only after the family ritual does the family divide the crop.[5]

SERVICE FOR THE ASSOTOR DRUM

The *assotor* drum is the largest and most sacred of all Haitian drums. Around it is built an impressive and elaborate service known as the *mangé assotor,* which, according to local traditions and circumstances, may be held as often as every three years or as infrequently as every twenty-one years. The period between mangés always consists of an odd number of years. A houngan from Jérémie declared the service might properly be held every three, five, or seven years. Another cult priest in the Cul-de-Sac Plain said it could be held every seven, seventeen, or twenty-one years. The assotor is known as the *plus grand moune* (the most venerable "man") of the hounfor. However, few cult centers possess an assotor. "Assotor c'est fort bagaille, c'est pas zaffai tout moune" (The assotor is powerful, it isn't everybody's affair), Haitians say. This is what a man from Jérémie tells about it:

"The assotor is the greatest of all things in the hounfor. The Rada drums are only for the Dahomey nation. The Congo drums are for the Congo nation. The assotor is a man of Dahomey, but he is for all nations. It is for all loa—Pétro, Congo, Bumba, Dahomey. The assotor belongs to Dahomey, but when there is a great service the assotor is the host to the loa of every rite, the loa of Haiti and of Africa. When the assotor is played, the loa are awakened everywhere. Loa who have been forgotten by the Creoles (Haitians) will come to the service and mount people, and when the loa have gone, many people don't know what loa has been riding them. Some ancient spirits from far away come only to the assotor service, and when it is over they aren't heard of again.

"The assotor drum is not for small things, it is for great occasions. For some people there are no occasions in their whole lives great enough for an assotor service. When all other things have failed, it is only then that the assotor is called upon.

"If a big houngan should have an assotor drum, he can have only one, and it is the chief of the hounfor. All other drums are its servants. You can make an assotor, but it is not necessarily an assotor. It may look like an assotor and not be an assotor. To be an assotor it must not only have the shape of an assotor but it must be accepted by the loa. There was a houngan near Jérémie who made an assotor and held a great service with it, but it wasn't a genuine assotor and the loa didn't come. The drummer beat the assotor, but none of the loa came. As he played, the stick kept falling out of his hand. This was a bad signal (omen). None of the people got loa in their heads. The houngan was in a great sweat, but nothing happened. Another houngan came after the third day and told him to bring the service to an end. He did that. They threw the false assotor away and no one would touch it.

"To make an assotor, there is first a service. The houngan goes into the woods to find a great tree that is suitable. The trunk must be big enough so that the drum is at least as tall as a man. Most assotors are six feet high or more. The houngan must buy the tree from Maît' Grand Bois, the loa who is Master of the Forest. There is a service under the tree, a goat or a bull is killed, and the houngan places money on the ground for Maît' Grand Bois. Then Maît' Grand Bois mounts his horses. He enters the head of the houngénicon or the laplace. Sometimes he rides the houngan himself. He is very rough with his horses. But if he accepts the money, the houngan has the tree cut down, and he has an assotor drum made. When the drum is finished, a special stick must be made to beat it. Again they go to the woods. They carry the great assotor drum with them. There is singing but no dancing or drumming. They find a tree from which they will cut the drumstick, and there is a service. The houngan must buy the branch from which the drumstick will be made. He offers money to Maît' Grand Bois, the same as before. He spills a little water on the ground for Maît' Grand Bois. He holds a candle in his hand. They sing to Maît' Grand Bois to let them have the stick. Maît' Grand Bois is the master of all the trees, but he is thinking also of the other loa and how they feel about it. On the Island Below the Water he consults with them. If he agrees to give the stick, he makes it known by mounting some of the hounsi, or the houngan, or maybe the man who will be the special assotor drummer. Then they cut down the branch and make the drumstick.

"The assotor drum is not dedicated to Ogoun or Èzilie or any other single loa. If it is baptized, it is given its own name, Assotor. The spirit of the assotor is multiple, for it is the *rappel* for all loa everywhere. The spirit of the assotor is called Assotor, and it is a kind of loa, but it is not one loa but all loa.

"In the assotor service, all loa come. Ogoun, Damballa, Legba, Tijean Pétro, Dan Pétro, Gèdé, Maît' Cimitière, they all come. The big loa come and the little loa, the chiefs and their escortes. Every big loa has an escorte of twenty-one smaller loa. Some of the smaller loa have their own escortes. Damballa comes crawling like a snake. Makanda comes crawling like a snake. Ogoun comes fighting, chewing on nails or anything iron. Badé comes quietly. Pié Cassé comes crawling because of his broken feet. Each loa comes in his own way.

"First there is dancing for the Congo and Pétro loa. There is dancing for the Kanga and Ibo nation. Last of all is Dahomé, for the assotor belongs to the Dahomé nation, and Dahomé is the host.

"The assotor service is the biggest of all services. It last fifteen days. Old people say that once there were services lasting more than twenty days. Every day, animals are killed—bulls, goats, pigs, chickens, turkeys—all according to the loa who are there to be fed. When Moundongue is fed, a dog's ears are clipped in his honor, because Moundongue is fond of dogs. More happens in the assotor mangé than all the rest of the year. Dahomé is host to the other nations, so the Rada service comes last. But the assotor drum is the host even to Dahomé, and it is fed last of all.

"The assotor drum is dressed in the finest of clothing and kerchiefs during the mangé. It is the king of everything.

"When the mangé assotor is ended, when the drum has been fed, there is an immediate Mass held in church for the souls in purgatory. You don't need to have any special reason, but you must hold the Mass for all the dead. You serve coffee, sandwiches, cake, and other refreshments for all the people.

"When there is no mangé going on, the assotor is kept in a special place in the hounfor. Every seven or nine months the houngan has a special *rappel* beaten for it on the Rada drums, and rum is spilled on the ground for it. It is a great responsibility to own an assotor. But it does great things for the houngan who owns it." [6]

SERVICE FOR MAÎT' GRAND BOIS AT ANSE-À-VEAU

Orthodox tradition in the region of Anse-à-Veau places the loa Maît' Grand Bois as the most potent and venerable of deities. He is the supreme mystère, whose good will or eccentric whim determines the fortunes of all men. Somewhat subsidiary to Grand Bois, but served within the same rites, are two other non-Dahomé loa—Moundongue (of Congo origin) and Ibo. Older people of Anse-à-Veau regard this trilogy, along with Femme Grand Bois (the wife of Maît' Grand Bois), as the core of "Guinée" ritual. There is also a second group of deities, consisting primarily of Ogoun Feraille, Èzilie, and Fréda Dahomé; these loa are of the Dahomey family and are regarded as somewhat less important. Should services for any of them be held, they follow rites for the Grand Bois constellation. People in this region hold that there is only one Ibo loa, one Moundongue, one Ogoun, and one Èzilie, each of them with many names or manifestations. Legba, the Dahomean spirit of procreation, the gate, and the crossroads, is not regarded in the same light as the other loa but as a messenger and interceder, and as the crossroads protector. He it is who helps in the placation of the major gods, and who guards people against accident, chance, and evil spirits on the highway.

In traditional form, services for Maît' Grand Bois and Femme Grand Bois are conducted by the family without the aid of a houngan, under the direction of the oldest male member of the family. The rites begin on a Thursday. With a tiny bell in his hand, the elder who directs the service (he is called *grand famille*) calls upon Maît' Grand Bois to come and receive his feast. The procedures are solemn. The grand famille and the family sing. At last Grand Bois enters the head of the old man who is conducting the rites. Then the sacrificial animals are brought forward and killed, and the women take the meat and begin the cooking of the mangé. While the food is cooking, the family sits and waits. Sometimes the grand famille begins a song, in which others join. The cooking takes a long while. Sometime during the night, when the food is ready, it is placed in two baskets—one for Maît' Grand Bois and one for his wife, Femme Grand Bois. Into each basket goes meat, corn meal, rice, bread, cookies, peanut cakes, cassava, and other delicacies. The two baskets are hung by ropes from the roof of the tonnelle, or from the branch of a tree. During the entire night, none of the family eats. Mâit' Grand Bois and his wife partake of the feast as they please. At six o'clock in the morning, the baskets are taken down, and the family is free to eat what the loa have left for them.

When the food is gone, the bones that are left are carried to a nearby stream and washed until they are white and shining. The bones are then placed in a large calabash bowl. Sweet-scented leaves from special trees are placed in the bowl with the bones, and water is added. The mixture becomes a ritual lotion, or "bath." The entire family kneels before the liquid, which they rub on their faces, heads, arms, hands, legs, and feet. When the ritual bathing is over, they sing:

La famille vin' payé sang,	The family comes to pay blood,
La famille vin' payé sang,	The family comes to pay blood,
Cérémonie là c'est fini! [Ex. 41]	The ceremony is finished!

Afterward, each member of the family places a small coin in the calabash dish with the bones and leaves, and the residue is then buried in a deep hole at a crossroads. A heavy post (*borne*) is erected at the site, with markings to indicate the date of the service, and the numbers 1, 2, 3, 4, each representing a year. Every year one of the numbers is checked off, and at the end of four years another service for Maît' Grand Bois and Femme Grand Bois is held.

If it should happen that on the appointed day four years later the family is unable to hold the regular feast for Grand Bois, the grand famille goes to the tree sacred to the loa, with a bottle of *siro'* and other token gifts. He explains the difficulties of the family; he tells the loa that it has been a bad year, that the crops have been poor, and that the family has not been able to accumulate enough money to buy sacrificial animals. He asks Grand Bois for a six-month postponement. The loa agrees to the postponement, making his intentions clear through various signs when the grand famille is possessed. "Grand Bois is a good loa," people say, "but if you fail to meet your obligations to him he will be very stern. If you don't keep your promise to him, he may seize you [i.e., kill you]."

When the rites for Maît' Grand Bois are finished, services for Ogoun and the Dahomé deities may be held, beginning on Friday and running through the week end. The Ogoun service is a festive affair. There is much singing and dancing, and early on Saturday morning the sacrificial bull is dressed and decorated with red and blue kerchiefs. Red and blue ribbons are tied to his horns, and he is led on a grand tour to various places, including Ogoun's tree. The drummers walk behind him, and after them members of the family, some dancing, some singing, and some mounted by the loa Ogoun. The procession passes three times around the cemetery, then heads back toward the family *habitation.* When the participants reach the tree sacred to Legba, they sing to this loa, invoking him to "ouvri bayè pou' moin" (open the gate for me). Finally, when the procession reaches the *habitation,* the sacrificial bull is killed. After Ogoun has been served his mangé, the rites are terminated with an *action de grâce.*

Near Anse-à-Veau there is a dried-up spring. It is said that many years ago during a big service for Maît' Grand Bois a man mounted by this loa rushed to the foot of a large tree and began clawing at the ground. He dug a hole there with his hands, and when it was only a few feet deep, water began to flow. The members of the société later enlarged the hole and lined it with stone. It was discovered that a giant crab was living in this water. One year, a service to Maît' Grand Bois was missed. The crab disappeared from the spring, and soon the water stopped flowing. "Grand Bois gives," the people say, "but if he is not remembered he also takes back."

POSSESSION BY THE LOA PINGA MAZA

On the outskirts of Port-au-Prince there is a hounfor dedicated to the loa Pinga Maza, also known by the name Bakulu Baka. He is a ferocious and fearsome spirit of the Pétro family who is known for his propensity to "eat" people; that is, to destroy them. To do this he employs such means as disease, insanity, and destruction of crops. If a man serves Pinga Maza well, the loa protects him in return; but for those who anger him, Pinga is a menacing and vengeful creature. People often say, "Pinga, c'est djab" (Pinga is a devil).

The Pinga hounfor in Port-au-Prince is called the *Société de la Belle Jeune Fleur*. Its peristyle is simple and is hardly distinguishable from those of other small hounfors. Around the base of the center pole is a three-foot-high wall of masonry, decorated with simple cult symbols. The outer room of the hounfor proper also resembles many another. The familiar pot têtes containing loa stand on a wooden altar, and there are Catholic lithographs on the walls. But the inner room belongs exclusively to Pinga Maza. Here are all the accoutrements and objects sacred to the deity. Everything is red. Pinga's clothing and kerchiefs are red. On the walls are painted esoteric designs—hands, skulls, and crosses —all in red. The bottles, magic bundles, and govis on the altar are decorated with red cloth, ribbons, or paint. In the middle of the earthen floor is embedded a heavy wooden cross. On each end of the crossbeam hangs a large calabash resembling a bulbous hand. And on top of the upright is affixed a human skull. The total impression of this hounfor is that of a bizarre aberration, calculated to intimidate and terrify. The houngan himself is relatively young, literate, and city wise. His personality is smooth and sharp, and he lacks the air of sincerity and easy simplicity which most often characterizes the houngan of the mountains.

In this inner room, before the skull and the cross, there took place a small service for a client, to determine what kind of magic was needed to fend off malevolent actions of an enemy. On the day of the divining session, there hung from the rafters of the tonnelle a long rope, which extended into a deep hole in the earth near the door. Hanging on the rope, down inside the hole, were two gray dolls tightly bound together. Hanging still farther down were a knife, a fork, and other, unidentifiable objects. This cluster of magic paraphernalia was an *expédition* at work; it was an elaborate pouin, which was working against an enemy who lived far away.

Before entering the hounfor, the houngan took a long rope whip from the wall and cracked it seven times before the door. This process, known as *frete cache,* was to "wake up" the loa within. The houngan then entered, followed by the client who was seeking help. They paused briefly in the outer room, where the houngan took up his asson and bell and made a small vèvè on the ground. He spoke briefly in *langage* and then passed on through the door to the inner room. There the houngan took his place before the small altar and the cross surmounted by the skull. Again he spoke *langage* and rattled his asson. He took from the altar a small-necked bottle containing a white alcoholic liquid and a tight-fitting iron cross. The presence of the iron cross inside the bottle was represented as a magical phenomenon. The houngan took a mouthful of the white liquid and sprayed it out in a fine mist over the skull. Twice more he sprayed the mist, in different directions. Then he poured a little of the liquid directly on the skull. The room was filled with the smell of alcohol. The houngan lighted a candle and sat in a low chair facing the altar. He shook his asson rhythmically and spoke *langage* to Pinga Maza. Suddenly Pinga Maza entered the houngan's head. The houngan became violent. He jerked this way and that, making strange noises in his throat. He seized a machete from the altar, waved it around, and struck the flat of it against his head. He continued for a while to beat his head fiercely with the machete. Gradually he became quiet. His assistants placed Pinga's red jacket on him. Now he spoke in the tired voice of an old man. He complained that he was hungry, that he had not eaten for a long while. His assistant handed him a razor blade. He placed it in his mouth, chewed it up, and swallowed it, washing it down with more of the white liquid in the bottle. He asked for more, and they gave him a second blade to eat. He demanded a third, and ate that, too, spitting out small fragments of steel that caught in his teeth.

His assistant told him there was a man present seeking advice about a pouin. The possessed houngan looked around with half-closed eyes. He asked the man his name, and what he wanted. After hearing the client's story, the houngan took out a deck of cards and placed them one at a time, face up, on a winnowing tray. After studying the cards he said: "You are strong, but not strong enough. You already have some protections, but they do not protect you from the dangers coming your way. You have powerful enemies. You must have a new pouin." The man said yes, he wanted a new pouin, but how much would it cost? Pinga replied through the mouth of the houngan: "Twenty-five dollars." The man said: "I will get the money and return." He went out after placing five gourdes on the winnowing tray with the cards. Pinga became drowsy. The houngan's head fell forward on his chest and he slept. The divining session was ended.

THE WATER ROAD

The land where the loa live, the place "below the water," is not thought of as being in the water itself. It is dry and airy, like the countryside of Haiti. But the route to it is through water. When the Haitians say "under the water" they do not mean under the sea. The ocean is regarded as the special domain of Agwé, La Sirène, and a few related deities, but it has nothing to do with most loa. "Under the water" specifically means under the springs, the rivers, and the fresh-water lakes. Fresh water has the greatest of significance in relation to most of the Vodoun deities.

When a loa comes to visit his Haitian children he comes by way of the *chimin dleau* (the water road)—that is to say, by way of the river, the waterfall, or the spring. Because the spring is the primary source of fresh water, it is the most direct means of contact with the land of the loa. Tales are heard everywhere of persons who, drawing water from the spring at night, heard the voices of loa or the sound of singing and drumming coming up from somewhere below. And virtually all the tales about human beings who visited the land of the loa describe them as descending into a river or disappearing into a waterfall.

The loa are accustomed to traveling by the "water road." And in all aspects of the Vodoun service, this "water road" is refreshed and replenished. When the road is dry, contact with the loa is diminished. When it is moist, the loa travel easily.

Thus, the houngan constantly uses water to entice and invite the deities. He holds a glass or pitcher of water at the center pole of his peristyle. He extends it toward the four cardinal points. He spills water at the foot of the center pole. He spills water in the hounfor at the foot of the *pé*, or altar. He sets a pitcher of water at the gateway of his *habitation*. And often, during a service, he pours a pathway of water in the dust from his gateway into his peristyle. Within nearly every hounfor there is at least one *bassin*, or pool, dedicated to the loa who is the *maît' caille*, the master of the house. These pools are carefully filled with water drawn from the springs. They are places of rest and refreshment for the deities whose names or portraits are inscribed on the walls above.

Sometimes rites and services are held at the site of the spring, the houngan and his entourage marching down to it from the hounfor for the occasion. So, too, there are annual pilgrimages to waterfalls such as Saut d'Eau, where the loa mount their "horses" in profusion.

Within the hounfor, during a service, the cult priest and the servitors pour "libations" of water on the earth, so that the loa may be refreshed. And virtually without end, the hounfor is the scene of ritual ceremonies in which the loa is bathed and thus "renewed" in the heads of his servitors.[7]

The importance of water in Vodoun has a fundamentally West African character. Among the Yoruba and the Ashanti and in Dahomey, for example, water rites are a significant aspect of religious ritual. Herskovits notes the frequency of religious pilgrimages to streams in West Africa.

In one instance, at Abeokuta, a bedecked procession of worshipers left a shrine atop a high hill, followed a long path to the riverside over two miles away, and returned before the ceremonies could be carried out at the shrine of the god. On one occasion, in Dahomey, the bed of the sacred stream run dry was "filled" from nearby wells so that this water could be ritually redrawn for use in an especially important ceremony. Among the Ashanti, pilgrimages to Lake Bosumtwe and other sacred bodies of water regularly occur. And it is on such occasions that the spirit of the river or lake or sea manifests itself, by "entering the head" of the devotee and causing him to fling himself, possibly possessed, into the water.[8]

So it is also in Haiti, where possession at the river's edge may cause the devotee to leap into the river. At Saut d'Eau, possessed persons plunge into the waterfall without regard for their safety, being in the care of the loa who have mounted them.

Into this water complex the Christian rite of baptism has been easily absorbed, providing merely a new act of veneration for water and its properties. In the Haitian mind baptism is not far removed from the *lavé tête* ritual, the washing of the head, or the *rafraîchi tête,* the "refreshing" of the head, both of which are acts in propitiation of the loa.[9] So related is the baptismal concept in the Haitian mind, that the term "baptize" is used to describe the lavé tête; it is said that the loa is being "baptized." So also are drums "baptized," not to menton yams, and even the hounfor itself.

Marriage to a Loa

Although the term *hounsi* (spirit wife, or wife of the spirit) is applied to a large class of servitors of the Vodoun temple, only a small number of servitors ever pass through rites which give them a husband-wife or wife-husband relationship with a loa. Reasons for these mystic marriages vary, but usually the rituals take place upon the prescription of a cult priest who interprets the will of the deities concerned. Most of the mystic marriages of which I have heard have taken place in the general area of Port-au-Prince and the Cul-de-Sac Plain. In some other areas of Haiti it appears that no such rites have taken place locally within the memory of the elder inhabitants. One aged man living near Belladère declared: "It [marriage to a loa] is impossible. People serve loa, they do not marry them. A man does not marry his burro. A loa does not marry his horse. People marry people. Loa marry loa. A man may have a compact with a loa. That is not a marriage. Some of the things that are going on down there in the Plain are not right. They are not the old way. In the old days we did things differently. We did not always run to the houngan. The grand famille knew how to talk to the loa. Up here we don't do things the way they do them down below in the city. People marry people. Loa marry loa."

Nevertheless, the practice in the neighborhood of Port-au-Prince and the Cul-de-Sac Plain is for mystic marriages to take place when deemed useful, essential, or unavoidable. Foremost among the loa involved in these rites is Èzilie Wèdo, the "pure" one, the deity of love, sometimes identified with the Virgin Mary. Other loa known to have taken part in mystic marriages are Damballa, Ogoun, Ayida, Agwé, Gèdé Nimbo or one of his brothers, Cousin Zaka, and Général Clermeil. All these loa—significantly, I think—have clearly defined personalities; much is known about their character and behavior, their likes and dislikes.

A man married to Èzilie has special obligations to her for the duration of his life. On certain days (especially Thursday, which is sacred to this deity), the mortal "husband" may not have sexual intercourse, even though he has a human wife.

Circumstances leading to a mystic marriage vary widely, but in each case it is a cult priest who determines whether the rites should be held. Perhaps a person has been afflicted with a series of illnesses or misfortunes. He goes to his houngan, who begins a series of communications with the client's loa or with his own. Sometimes many loa are consulted before the desired information is available. Eventually it is determined that a certain deity, for reasons which may or may not be clear, wishes to have nuptial ties with the client. The illnesses or misfortunes that have been sent are a means of informing or warning the person concerned.

Sometimes the houngan relies on well-established divining methods to ascertain the cause of the difficulties. He may employ the *gembo* (a shell that slides on a string), ashes, or small shells that are thrown on the ground. Or he may rely on possession by a loa to provide the information.

If it is found that a loa is demanding marriage, arrangements are then made. The rites that follow may take place in a hounfor or at the house of the human bride or groom. Both a prêt' savane and a houngan officiate.

The person directly involved, like the loa, usually has something to gain from a mystic marriage. For one thing, he can reasonably expect special future help and consideration from the loa (including the cessation of the illnesses or other misfortunes that have led to the marriage). A man (or woman) united with a loa in "matrimony" is "stronger" (*plus fort*) in his relationship to his environment and to other people. For this reason, the initiative for a mystic marriage does not always come from a loa. An ambitious person may seek such a marriage to strengthen his hand, to provide protection against other deities or human enemies, or to gain wealth or position. One observer, Odette Mennesson Rigaud, expresses the opinion that in such instances the marriage "is no longer a religious union of mystic love, but a magic pact." [10] The implicit element of "pact" is so evident in all mystic marriages, even when the initiative comes from the loa, that the distinction is not easily appreciated. However, persons suspected of "pushing" for a marriage with a loa are regarded as presumptuous or reckless, and often they are believed to have hidden motives. It is felt by many that the benefits of such a union can be only temporary and that catastrophe will ultimately follow.

A human party to marriage with a loa is deeply committed. He is subject to jealousy and anger on the part of his mystic mate. His behavior in the hounfor as in his daily life must be beyond the loa's reproach. He must avoid possession by other loa. And he must fulfill endless obligations. Sometimes the prospect of such binding ties is more than a man (or woman) is ready to face, and through the intercession of a strong houngan the loa may be induced to withdraw his demand for marriage. In that event, a special service is held, in the course of which the person buys his freedom with promises of special gifts and feasts for the deity.

One young man I knew was caught in a special dilemma—the houngan and the loa on one side, the Protestant Church on the other. The man, named Maurice, came from the mountains near Léogane. He was married but had no children. His wife's family, still living in Léogane, was Protestant. Maurice himself was a follower of Vodoun, and nominally a Catholic. When his wife was afflicted with a long series of headaches and earaches, Maurice consulted a houngan of Port-au-Prince. The houngan said that the loa Ayida Wèdo was demanding marriage with Maurice, and that the wife's illnesses were an indication of jealousy.

At the same time, the wife's parents came from Léogane and insisted that the girl's illnesses were brought about by God because Maurice was a follower of Vodoun. They demanded that he sever all his connections with Vodoun and become a Protestant.

After considerable anxiety, Maurice "purged" himself of Vodoun and joined the Protestant Church. Subsequently his wife's illnesses subsided somewhat, but she never bore children. Maurice suspected that the latter misfortune was the result of his spurning his mystic suitor.

The actual ceremonies by which a mystic marriage is performed carry over many of the customs and trappings of ordinary mortal marriages. The prêt' savane reads prayers and officiates until the two parties are deemed wed. The loa is represented by a "stand-in," usually a person possessed by the loa and dressed in appropriate garb. Gold wedding rings are placed upon the fingers of the couple. There are wedding cakes and wedding contracts. Nothing appropriate to an ordinary wedding is omitted.

6. Songs of the Peristyle

The songs that are sung in the peristyle are virtually numberless and have a wide range of themes. In general, they are in the spirit of supplication or placation. Preponderantly they relate in some way to the deities. A loa may be described, invoked, or called upon to perform certain deeds. He may be cajoled, joked with, and even criticized. But it is all a family affair. The servitors and the *fidèles* are the loa's "children," his "horses," his "leaves in the woods." The loa, the spirits of the dead, and the living members of the cult are all members of the same "nation." Whether supplication or admonition, the songs of the peristyle and the hounfor all have an intimate character. The affairs of the loa are the affairs of the société. What concerns one individual concerns all.

The themes of the songs have to do with the drama of the cult ritual, the coming and going of the deities, sickness and death, the welfare of the dead, and the behavior of the living.

The cult service is a dramatic presentation which synchronizes and brings into sharp focus the heritage of religious and folk beliefs. The songs describe and evaluate what is going on. Sometimes they are cryptic and tangent, but to those participating and those watching they are clues. As the action is usually related and progressive, so are the songs. Each song has its own place and its own meaning. One song is not readily interchangeable with another. Each service has its appropriate music. So does each developing phase of the hounfor ritual.

Some of the songs are addressed to the loa; others seem to be the words of the loa themselves. In many of the songs there is an implicit dialogue between one or more loa and the singers. This dialogue is not rendered in a form which is immediately understandable to a stranger. There is a constantly shifting point of view, so that sometimes the words are third-person comments about the loa or the situation, sometimes they are the words of the deity, sometimes words addressed to the deity. The name of the loa may appear anywhere in the song, as both an invocational word and a rhythmic device, with the result that unless one is aware of the song structure he may lose the sense and intent of the words. In these two lines, for example:

> Master Agwé comes from the sea,
> My cannon is loaded.

The first line describes what happens, from the standpoint of a third person; the second line is a statement by the loa Agwé. Or, take this single line:

> Marie Louise oh, we are mixed up!

Here Marie Louise seems to be the person addressed, but in fact it is Marie Louise who is talking. Again:

> I don't see my blood, Master Ogoun!

It is not Ogoun who is addressed; the words are his own.

As in nonreligious songs, there is a pattern stanza which is repeated over and over again. As the song goes on, there may be variations for interest and certain embellishments, but by and large the form remains constant. In religious singing there are relatively few examples of songs which progress from one idea to another. When the theme has been stated, that is the song.

One of the preliminary songs in many ritual services is a greeting to the men and women of the société who are present. It is an *ochan,* or salute of welcome, and comes before the loa themselves are addressed:

Messieurs-dames bonsoir!	Gentlemen and ladies, good evening!
M'apé mandé nou!	I ask you!
Messieurs-dames bonsoir!	Gentlemen and ladies, good evening!
M'apé mandé nou	I ask you
Qui gens nous yé! [Ex. 42]	What people are we?

The answer to the question is implicit, for they are the people of the société, members of the Arada "nation" or Anago "nation," as the case may be.

In almost any service of the Dahomey "nation" the first supplicatory song is addressed to Legba, the keeper of the gate, the guardian of the crossroads, and the "go-between" who intercedes with other loa in the affairs of men. The first appeal to Legba is to open the gate, over which he is master, so that the voices of supplication may be heard and understood. The open gate also provides access for other loa to the service.

Attibon Legba ouvri bayè pou' moin ago!
Ou wè Attibon Legba ouvri bayè pou' moin ouvri bayè!
M'apé rentré quand ma tourné,
Ma salut loa yo!

Attibon Legba, open the gate for me, *ago!*
You see, Attibon Legba, open the gate for me, open the gate!
I will enter when I return,
I salute the loa!

After this appeal, or sometimes while it is being sung, the houngan spills a little water on the earth at the base of the po'teau mitan. It is an inducement for the loa to "enter," for the loa reside "below the water" and their passage into the hounfor is made easier by water. The houngan may spill his water in a long path from the entrance of the peristyle to the po'teau mitan, or extend his pitcher invitingly to the four points of the compass. Then, perhaps, another song is sung to Legba:

Papa Legba nan hounfor moin!
Papa Legba nan hounfor moin!
Papa Legba nan hounfor moin!
Ou même qui porté drapeau,
C'est ou même ka paré soleil pou' loa yo!
Papa Legba, Papa Legba!

Papa Legba is in my hounfor!
Papa Legba is in my hounfor!
Papa Legba is in my hounfor!
You who carry the flag,
It is you who shade the loa from the sun!
Papa Legba, Papa Legba!

As the ritual gets under way, there may be a general song of welcome to all the loa of the cult, such as this one:

Bonjou' oh bonjou' bonjou' bonjou' bonjou'!
Bonjou' oh bonjou' bonjou' bonjou' bonjou'!
Oh bonjou' oh bonjou' loa moin! [Ex. 43]

Good day, oh, good day, good day, good day, good day!
Good day, oh, good day, good day, good day, good day!
Oh, good day, oh, good day my loa!

When the service is well in progress, the songs may describe the qualities of the deities—their character, behavior and needs. If it is Balindjo, for example, the song may advertise that persons with this loa in their heads are immune to poison:

Ogoun Balindjo,
Oh Ogoun oh!

Ogoun Balindjo,
Oh, Ogoun, oh!

Ogoun Balindjo,
Oh Ogoun oh!
C'est pas mangé rangé
Pral tuyé chwal moin! [Ex. 44]

Ogoun Balindjo,
Oh, Ogoun, oh!
There is no poisoned food
That will kill my horse!

Ogoun Fai, known also by the Christian name St. Jacques, is the deity of war, and this song describes his courage and valor:

St. Jacques Majeur a voyé dit'm ga'çon déjà!
St. Jacques oh voyé dit'm ga'çon déjà!
St. Jacques Majeur a voyé dit'm ga'çon la-guè!
St. Jacques oh voyé dit'm ga'çon la-guè! [Ex. 45]

Major St. Jacques sent to tell me he is already a man!
St. Jacques, oh, sent to tell me he is already a man!
Major St. Jacques sent to tell me he is a man of war!
St. Jacques, oh, sent to tell me he is a man of war!

Should the service be to the loa Damballa Wèdo, symbolized as a rainbow and a great serpent, this song might be sung, commenting that he cannot be drowned in the water:

Papa Damballa ou c'est coulève oh!
Pouq'ou pas néyé?
Pouq'ou pas néyé?
Damballa pouq'ou pas néyé nan dleau? [Ex. 46]

Papa Damballa you are a snake, oh!
Why don't you drown?
Why don't you drown?
Damballa, why don't you drown in the water?

Damballa, the rainbow, is in fact the source of the water that bubbles from the earth in springs. He is a patron of the spring, and there he often lives in the form of a water snake. In many a hounfor where Damballa is specially revered there is a *bassin,* or pool, dedicated to him. On the wall behind the pool there is usually a painting of Damballa and Ayida, depicted as great serpents, sometimes with a feathered headdress. The pool is kept filled with fresh water from the spring, and here one or more small snakes—symbols of Damballa and Ayida—reside:

Ala loa marché nan dleau
C'est Damballa!
Ala loa marché nan dleau
C'est Damballa!
Papa Damballa c'est tête à dleau!
Papa Damballa c'est tête à dleau!

There is a loa who lives in the water,
It is Damballa!

> There is a loa who lives in the water,
> It is Damballa!
> Papa Damballa is the spring!
> Papa Damballa is the spring!

Ayida Wèdo, another aspect of Damballa, is also known as a snake and a rainbow. A song describing Ayida's attributes goes:

Ayida c'est arc-en-ciel oh!	Ayida is a rainbow, oh!
Ou ap' vin' fai coulève!	You will come in like a snake!
Ayida c'est arc-en-ciel!	Ayida is a rainbow!
Pas wè n'ap fai coulève? [Ex. 47]	Don't you see I come in as a snake?

Agwé Woyo, one of the major deities of the sea, is believed to be responsible for thunder over the ocean, which is described as the sound of his cannon shooting:

> Maît' Agwé so'ti nan la mer,
> Canon'm chargé-é!
> Maît' Agwé so'ti nan la mer,
> Canon'm chargé!
> Maît' Agwé so'ti nan la mer,
> Canon'm chargé oh!
> Canon'm chargé pou'm tiré Maît' A'Woyo! [Ex. 48]

> Master Agwé comes from the sea,
> My cannon is loaded!
> Master Agwé comes from the sea,
> My cannon is loaded!
> Master Agwé comes from the sea,
> My cannon is loaded, oh!
> My cannon is loaded to fire, Master Agwé Woyo!

The loa Kitta, or Simbi Kitta, of the Guinée pantheon is one of the water deities. He is described as coming out of the water dripping wet:

> Kitta oh so'ti nan dleau li tou' mouillé!
> Oh Kitta oh so'ti nan dleau li tou' mouillé!
> Oh Kitta so'ti nan dleau li tou' mouillé!
> Oh nen point houngan passé Bondieu nan pays-yà! [Ex. 37]

> Kitta, oh, comes out of the water, he is all wet!
> Oh, Kitta, oh, comes out of the water, he is all wet!
> Oh, Kitta comes out of the water, he is all wet!
> Oh, there is no houngan in this country greater than God!

Tijean Pétro of the Pétro "nation" is small, and agile even though he has only one foot. (Some people say that Tijean Petro has no feet at all.) This somewhat malevolent deity hides in the leaves of the coconut palm, and from there he sometimes preys on passers-by, particularly children. Persons mounted by Tijean Pétro may move about as though they have no feet and climb into the nearest palm tree. This song comments on Tijean's ability to climb with his single foot. (Haitians do not "shinny" up trees, but walk up, bracing the soles of the feet against the trunk.)

Tijean ou pas gainyain pieds,   Tijean, you have no feet,
Tijean ou pas gainyain pieds,   Tijean, you have no feet,
Comment ou fai monté cocoyé?   How do you climb the coconut tree?
Lans bayè ro Legba, Jean Pétro,   By using Legba's gate, Jean Pétro,
Lans bayè ro!   By using the gate!

When the loa begin to arrive in the hounfor to participate in the ceremonies, there is usually a song taking note of their coming. Sometimes the words describing the action are the deity's own account of what is happening, as in this song to the loa Sobo:

C'est passé n'ap passé là!
C'est passé ma passé là!
É hounsi bossale é yo lommain nom moin!
Yo lommain nom moin yo lommain nom moin!
Yo rélé hounsi kanzo!
Yo rélé Daromain!
Yo rélé mwé! [Ex. 50]

I am passing through, I am passing through!
I am passing, I am passing here!
É, the hounsi bossale call my name!
They are calling for me, they are calling for me!
The hounsi kanzo are calling!
Dahomey is calling!
They are calling me!

In another rite one might hear this song about the arrival of the deity Simba, from the point of view of the servitors rather than of the loa:

Simba Kitta vini wè moin, oh!
Oh Simba wa vini wè moin là, oh saints yà! [Ex. 51]

Simba Kitta comes to see me, oh!
Oh, Simba will come to see me here, oh saints!

When the deity Boulicha Nago comes in, there is a call for the drums to be played:

Nago 'rivé-é,   Nago arrives,
Boulicha Nago 'rivé-é!   Boulicha Nago arrives!
Nago 'rivé-é,   Nago arrives,
Boulicha Nago 'rivé-é!   Boulicha Nago arrives!
Li lè li temps bata là!   It is time, beat the drums!
Li lè li temps bata là!   It is time, beat the drums!
Nago 'rivé jodi-à oh enhé! [Ex. 52]   Nago comes today, oh, *enhé!*

Sobo, too, demands his drums as he arrives, as well as all the other paraphernalia for his ritual:

Coté yo coté yo?	Where are they, where are they?
Sobo mandé hounsi 'Llada!	Sobo asks for his Allada hounsi!
Coté yo coté yo?	Where are they, where are they?
Coté yo coté yo?	Where are they, where are they?
Sobo mandé tambou' Rada!	Sobo asks for his Arada drums!
Coté yo coté yo?	Where are they, where are they?
Coté yo coté yo?	Where are they, where are they?
Sobo mandé pouin Allada!	Sobo asks for his Allada magic!
Coté yo coté yo? [Ex. 53]	Where are they, where are they?

When more than one loa comes into the service at the same time there is confusion. Each loa is supposed to await his turn, so that the ritual and the dance may be conducted in an orderly way. Sometimes, however, two or more dieties come in at once, throwing the orderly process out of gear. This song takes note of the simultaneous arrival of the loa Adja, Loko, Sobo, Sedje, and others.

> Adja non mélé, oh Adja oh!
> Adja non mélé!
> Non mélé Papa Loko, non mélé jodi-à!
>
> Adja non mélé, oh Adja oh!
> Adja non mélé!
> Non mélé Sedje assez non mélé jodi-à!
>
> Adja non mélé, oh Adja oh!
> Adja non mélé!
> Non mélé kilé oudé Nèg' Sobo non mélé jodi-à! [Ex. 54]
>
> Adja we are mixed, oh, Adja, oh!
> Adja we are mixed!
> We are mixed Papa Loko, we are mixed up today!
>
> Adja we are mixed, oh, Adja, oh!
> Adja we are mixed!
> We are mixed Sedje, enough, we are mixed up today!
>
> Adja we are mixed, oh, Adja, oh!
> Adja we are mixed!
> We are mixed all the time, Nèg' Sobo, we are mixed up today!

When the loa come in en masse this way, some are asked to retire so that the service can proceed smoothly. In a similar instance, the deity Marie Louise is willing to withdraw from the scene but demands that a present or sacrifice be given to her first.

Marie Louise oh nou mélé!	Marie Louise, oh, we are mixed up!
Marie Louise oh nou mélé!	Marie Louise, oh, we are mixed up!
Coté ça ou ba moin pou'm allé?	Where is my gift so that I can go?

Often, when it is time to leave the service, the deity announces through the medium of the song that he has other affairs to attend to elsewhere. Ogoun Achadé, for example, makes a swift departure:

Ogoun volé!	Ogoun flies!
Anago!	Anago!
Ogoun volé Achadé!	Ogoun flies Achadé!
Anago Papa! [Ex. 55]	Anago Papa!

As the deity Général Brisé departs, he tells his servitors that he is "going to God," and that he turns responsibility for their affairs over to them:

Général Brisé pays ya nan main oh!
Ago-é! Ago-é-é!
Général Brisé pays ya nan main oh!
Pays ya nan main
M'pral Bondieu djab oh! [Ex. 56]

General Brisé, the country is in your hands, oh!
Ago-é! Ago-é-é!
General Brisé, the country is in your hands, oh!
The country is in your hands,
I am going to God, oh!

The loa Bumba, in reply to a query, declares that he must go because he has work to do in his fields:

Bumba qui coto prallé?	Bumba, where are you going?
Bumba qui coto prallé?	Bumba, where are you going?
Bumba qui coto prallé?	Bumba, where are you going?
Bumba qui coto prallé?	Bumba, where are you going?
M'planté manga!	I am planting mangas!
Planté patate!	Planting potatoes!
Planté jawmoun!	Planting pumpkins!
Planté banane!	Planting plantains!
Waille Bumba qui coto prallé? [Ex. 57]	*Waille* Bumba, where are you going?

The deities Maît' Bois and Maît' Dleau declare as they depart that they are on their way to Africa, and leave the impression that things are pretty nice over there:

Maît' Dleau qui so'ti nans dleau!	Maît' Dleau who comes out of the water!
Maît' Bois qui so'ti nans bois!	Maît' Bois who comes out of the woods!
Nan Guinée plaisi-à belle oh!	In Africa pleasure is beautiful, oh!
A n'allé wè yo! [Ex. 58]	We are going to see!

As the loa Mambo Ayida of the Guinée pantheon leaves the hounfor to return to Africa, her "children" ask her not to stay there too long. And they ask her to bring back to Haiti with her some good magic for use in the hounfor:

> Mambo Ayida é!
> Pral nan Guinée-à, pinga ou misé-à m'tendé!
> Si ou joind bon ouanga wa po'té!
> Si ou joind bon lotion wa po'té! [Ex. 59]

> Mambo Ayida é!
> Go to Africa, take care not to stay, I am waiting!
> If you find a good ouanga, bring it!
> If you find a good lotion, bring it!

Giving food to the loa is a focal point in religious rituals. Many songs describe the sacrifice, signify that the loa are waiting for their food, or otherwise dramatize this significant activity. In the following song the deity Damballa asks for the goat with which he is to be fed.

> Damballa Wèdo oh c'est sang-é!
> Damballa mandé tête cabrit,
> C'est sang li mandé!
> Damballa Wèdo oh c'est sang-é!
> Damballa mandé tête cabrit,
> C'est sang li mandé!
> Damballa Wèdo oh c'est sang li mandé!
> Oh assez! [Ex. 60]

> Damballa Wèdo, oh, it is blood é!
> Damballa asks for the head of the goat,
> It is blood he asks for!
> Damballa Wèdo, oh, it is blood é!
> Damballa asks for the head of the goat,
> It is blood he asks for!
> Damballa Wèdo, oh, it is blood he asks for!
> Oh, enough!

For Ogoun they sometimes sing:

> Papa Ogoun qui gain' yun mangé
> Tout moune pas mangé li!
> Enhé enhé, oh! [Ex. 61]

> It is Papa Ogoun who has a feast,
> Not everyone may eat it!
> *Enhé enhé,* oh!

But sometimes Ogoun is dissatisfied that there is no feast ready for him, and he complains.

Ogoun é oh moin blessé!   Ogoun *é,* oh, I am hurt!
Ogoun é oh moin blessé!   Ogoun *é,* oh, I am hurt!
A pas m'blessé Ferei,   Now I am hurt, Ferei,
M'pas wè sang moin!   I don't see my blood!
M'pas wè sang'm Maît Ogoun,   I don't see my blood, Master Ogoun,
Moin pas wè sang moin!   I don't see my blood!
M'pas wè sang'm Badagry,   I don't see my blood, Badagry,
Moin pas wè sang moin là! [Ex. 62]   I don't see my blood here!

The loa Moundongue, like Damballa, likes goat meat, and it can be cooked in two ways:

> Yè yè yè!
> Moundongue oh!
> Oh Moundongue oh yè yè yè!
> Moundongue mangé cabrit boulé,
> Moundongue mangé cabrit boucané! [Ex. 63]

> *Yè yè yè!*
> Moundongue, oh!
> Oh, Moundongue, oh, *yè yè yè!*
> Moundongue eats boiled goat,
> Moundongue eats roasted goat!

Or again, the servitors may sing:

> Coto passé na ba'ou mangé, oh Ti Moundongue nà!
> Coto passé na ba'ou mangé, Moundongue nà! [Ex. 64]

> Wherever you are, we give you food, oh, Ti Moundongue there!
> Wherever you are, we give you food, Moundongue there!

The loa Adja also has animal sacrifices and special dishes for his mangé, but sometimes he—and the "horses" he mounts—will eat broken glass:

> Oh Adja mangé bounda dèmijon!
> Adja véco' véco'!
> Adja mangé bounda dèmijon!
> Adja véco' véco'! [Ex. 65]

> Oh, Adja eats the bottom of a bottle!
> Adja, old one, old one!
> Adja eats the bottom of a bottle!
> Adja, old one, old one!

For the loa Ianman Ibo the proper sacrifice is a rooster, and the deity declares:

> Nanchon Ibo m'ta mangé gros coq oh nanchon Ibo!
> Nanchon Ibo m'ta mangé gros coq!
> Nanchon Ibo m'ta mangé gros coq oh nanchon Ibo!
> Waille waille waille! [Ex. 66]

Ibo nation, I am going to eat a large cock, oh, Ibo nation!
Ibo nation, I am going to eat a large cock!
Ibo nation, I am going to eat a large cock, oh, Ibo nation!
Waille waille waille!

The Ibo service is often a strictly family affair rather than a broad community ritual. The family replies to the Ibo loa in the following song.

La famille vin' payé sang,	The family comes to pay blood,
Vin' payé sang!	Comes to pay blood!
La famille vin' payé sang,	The family comes to pay blood,
Ibo Lazile volonté! [Ex. 41]	It is Ibo Lazile's wish!

The loa Nago frankly tells the people that if they want to come to his house (his shrine, or the hounfor) they will have to pay something for the privilege:

Si nou wè coté'm demeuré,	If you see where I live,
Si nou wè coté'm demeuré,	If you see where I live,
Fau'm payé bonbon pou' ça!	You have to give cookies for that!
Anago Nago!	Anago Nago!
Vin' wè coté'm demeuré! [Ex. 67]	Come see where I live!

The "dead" spirit Gèdé Nimbo, the guardian or master of the cemetery, who often engages in bizarre activities which poke fun at the codes of social behavior, is sometimes regarded as a special protector of children. Precisely because he is overlord of all that has to do with the grave, his good will is sought, particularly in behalf of the young; and in many services of the Nago rites his protection is bought by money gifts:

Gèdé main la'gent,
M'apé ba ou la'gent la'gent,
M'apé ba ou la'gent pou' ga'dé zenfants la yo!
M'apé ba ou la'gent pou' ga'dé zenfants la yo!

Gèdé, take the money,
I will give you money, money,
I will give you money to guard the children!
I will give you money to guard the children!

In the course of the ceremonies when, from time to time, the honored loa of the occasion enters into the head of one of the servitors, the houngan will place in the hands of the mounted person a lighted candle and a pitcher of water. The possessed servitor approaches the sacred center post and spills a little water on the ground for the deity. After certain other rituals, the houngan, or one of his assistants, conducts the mounted "horse" into the hounfor to the altar. In the following song, as the possession comes on, there is a call for a lighted candle.

Simbi non wè oh!
Simbi djab non wè!
Oh Simbi non wè oh!
Simbi non wè oh!
Simbi wa lumé chandelle pou' clairé moin! [Ex. 68]

Simbi doesn't see, oh!
Stern Simbi doesn't see!
Oh, Simbi doesn't see, oh!
Simbi doesn't see, oh!
Simbi [says] you will light the candle so I can see!

Some of the songs refer to the dancing of the loa who enter the bodies of the servitors. The deity Loko asks for his hounsi, through whom he will dance:

Coté pitits moin yo,
Mainain'm nan hounfor, m'ap djaillé!
Na pas Loko,
Coté pitits moin yo! [Ex. 69]

Where are my children,
Take me into the hounfor, I will *djaillé!*
Now, Loko,
Where are my children!

Another deity, who is not expressly named, tells his "leaves in the woods"—that is, his hounsi—that he has danced since he was a child:

Fé nan bois hélé moin!	Leaves in the woods call me!
Oh dépi'm pitit m'ap dansé!	Oh, since I was small I have danced!
Fé nan bois hé-é!	Leaves in the woods *hé-é!*
Fé nan bois hélé moin oh!	Leaves in the woods call me, oh!
Oh fé nan bois hélé moin oh!	Oh, leaves in the woods call me, oh!
Dépi'm pitit m'ap dansé!	Since I was small I have danced!
Fé nan bois hélé moin! [Ex. 70]	Leaves in the woods call me!

In the following song the loa Macaya Bumba is called upon by the hounsi to hurry up and get on with his dancing.

Macaya Bumba Bumba!	Macaya Bumba Bumba!
Lèvé dansé!	Get up and dance!
Macaya Bumba!	Macaya Bumba!
Bumba mon cher vini dansé! [Ex. 71]	Bumba my dear, come and dance!

A song for the deity Ianman in the course of the Ibo dancing and ritual goes:

Ibo lélé!
Ibo lélé!
Nanchon Ibo ça ou gainyain con ça Ibo lélé!

Ianman con ça, con ça!
Ianman con ça'm dansé Ibo!
Ianman con ça, con ça!
Ianman con ça'm dansé Ibo!
Ianman con ça, con ça!
Ianman é-wa é-wa é-wa! [Ex. 72]

Ibo *lélé!*
Ibo *lélé!*
Ibo Nation, what are you doing there, Ibo *lélé!*
Ianman, like that, like that!
Ianman, like that I dance the Ibo!
Ianman, like that, like that!
Ianman, like that I dance the Ibo!
Ianman, like that, like that!
Ianman *é-wa é-wa é-wa!*

Another song containing the same zestful appreciation of dancing is for the loa Kitta. The words "my mother isn't dead" and "my father isn't dead" are simply expressions of good fortune and happiness which embellish the command to do the Kitta steps:

Ai ti ga'çon ba'm pas Kitta!
Kitta Congo oh ti ga'çon ba'm pas Kitta!

Manman pas mouri ba'm pas Kitta!
Kitta Congo oh ti ga'çon ba'm pas Kitta!

M'dit pitit ga'çon ba'm pas Kitta!
Kitta Congo oh ti ga'çon ba'm pas Kitta!

Papa pas mouri ba'm pas Kitta!
Kitta Congo oh ti ga'çon ba'm pas Kitta! [Ex. 73]

Ai, little man, give me the Kitta steps!
Kitta Congo, oh, little man, give me the Kitta steps!

My mother is not dead, give me the Kitta steps!
Kitta Congo, oh, little man, give me the Kitta steps!

I say little man, give me the Kitta steps!
Kitta Congo, oh, little man, give me the Kitta steps!

My father is not dead, give me the Kitta steps!
Kitta Congo, oh, little man, give me the Kitta steps! [1]

A song for the loa Bambarra describes the movements of his dance. Bambarra is symbolized by the crab, and the dance posture with "low hips" is regarded as characteristic of the crab's movements:

Bambarra kap proméné, taille bas!
Bambarra allé proméné, taille bas!

Bambarra is walking, low hips!
Bambarra is going to walk, low hips!

Damballa Wèdo, being a snake deity, "threads" or "winds" his way like a serpent, and this song describes a serpentine course taken by the dancers as Damballa (here identified as a Nago man) arrives:

Filé na filé, Damballa Wèdo vini wè moin!
Filé na filé, Nèg' Nago vini wè'm là! [Ex. 74]

Wind, we wind, Damballa Wèdo comes to see me!
Wind, we wind, the Nago man comes to see me here!

After the dancing has been going on for a long while and the pace is fast, there may be a song of banter, such as the following from the Dahomey rites. The dancers sing *laillé, laillé!*, describing a figure of the dance in which the skirts are swirled, and note that they have worn out the drummers. They even offer to carry on their backs those dancers who are ready to fall by the wayside:

Laillé laillé!
Oh laillé laillé oh viéco'!
Tambouyé bouké!
Tambouyé bouké viéco'!
Laillé laillé oh viéco'!
Laillé laillé tambouyé bouké houngan'm!
M'po'té sou corps moin vié sor!
Tambouyé bouké ça!
Laillé laillé! [Ex. 75]

Laillé laillé!
Oh, *laillé laillé*, oh, old people!
The drummers are tired!
The drummers are tired, old people!
Laillé laillé, oh, old people!
Laillé laillé, the drummers are tired, my *houngan!*
I'll carry you on my back, old sister!
The drummers are tired there!
Laillé laillé!

Interspersed among the songs of the hounfor there are sometimes warnings or admonitions. Usually they are tangent and indirect in statement, and may be from the point of view of the loa or of the houngan. In the following pouin song, which accompanies the ritual of making magic, there is a warning to certain people who will feel the effects of the magic. The ceremony includes, among other things, the dropping of lemons, roots, and leaves by the houngan into his sacred basin or pond. The houngan sings:

Trois fé trois citron oh!
Trois fé trois citron oh!
Moin dit rwo, youn jour ou wa besoin moin!
Trois fé trois racine oh!
Moin dit oui, youn jour ou wa besoin moin!
Gainyain bassin moin trois racine tombé ladans,
Quand ou wa' blié fau' ramassé chongé! [Ex. 76]

Three leaves, three lemons, oh!
Three leaves, three lemons, oh!
I say *rwo,* one day you are going to need me!
Three leaves, three roots, oh!
I say yes, one day you are going to need me!
I have my pond into which three roots fall,
When you wish to forget you will have to remember!

In another song the houngan warns against ingratitude on the part of persons for whom special magical services have been carried out:

Ouanga ça oh ouanga chaud!
Ouanga ça ouanga chaud!
Lè pou' payé li pinga ou faché!
Ou mandé'm ouanga là ou content!
Ou mandé'm ouanga là ou content!
Lè pou' payé li pinga ou faché! [Ex. 77]

This ouanga, oh, hot ouanga!
This ouanga, oh, hot ouanga!
When it's time to pay for it don't be angry!
You ask me for the ouanga, you are happy!
You ask me for the ouanga, you are happy!
When it's time to pay for it don't be angry!

Somberly and in metaphor, the deity Kitta Démambré speaks of an unhappy event which occurred in the town of Léogane, and warns those concerned that it must not happen again:

Kitta Démambré, pinga ou fai'm ça 'core oh!
Nan Léogane ti poule-là mouri nan zé!
Nan Léogane ti poule-là mouri nan zé oh!
Kitta Démambré, pinga ou fai'm ça encore oh! [Ex. 78]

Kitta Démambré, take care that you don't do that to me again, oh!
In Léogane the little chicken died in its egg!
In Léogane the little chicken died in its egg!
Kitta Démambré, take care that you don't do that to me again!

An unnamed spirit warns that the moment for placation has come and suggests that calling on him after he has gone from the *pavillon* of the houngan Deréa would be of no use.

M'apé rélé moin en bas pavillon loa moin!
Laissé'm démélé moin en bas pavillon oh Deréa!
Jou'm allé pinga you lommain nom moin! [Ex. 79]

I will call, I am under the loa's canopy!
Let me get straightened out under Deréa's canopy!
The day I am gone take care they do not call my name!

In a lighter vein, to the gayest of music, there is this admonition that a wrong cannot be righted simply by saying "excuse me":

Ibo lélé!
Ibo lélé!
Pilé pied'm ou mandé'm pardon!
Pilé pied'm ou mandé'm pardon!
Ça pardon-là wa fait pou' moin? [Ex. 80]

Ibo *lélé!*
Ibo *lélé!*
You step on my foot and ask my pardon!
You step on my foot and ask my pardon!
The pardon, what good will it do me?

And the deity Ogoun Kénison warns those who do not speak of him with respect that he is not ready to accept such a slight as a light matter.

Ogoun Yèkkè Yèkkè ça Nèg' Kénison é!
Ogoun Yèkkè ça Nèg' Kénison é!
Oh tous les jours c'est pa'lé Ogoun mal!
Ogoun pas conn' betisé! [Ex. 81]

Ogoun Yèkkè Yèkkè there, man of Kénison!
Ogoun Yèkkè there, man of Kénison!
Oh, constantly talking bad about Ogoun!
Ogoun doesn't like joking!

The loa Ogoun Panama, like ordinary mortals, is concerned about people who "come to look and go away to talk."

Ogoun oh m' c'est Nèg' Panama é!
Ogoun oh m' c'est Nèg' Panama é!
Yo vini ga'dé!
Yo vini pa'lé!
Oh Ogoun oh m' c'est Nèg' Panama é! [Ex. 82]

Ogoun, oh, I am the Panama man *é!*
Ogoun, oh, I am the Panama man *é!*
They come to look!
They come to look!
Oh, Ogoun, oh, I am the Panama man *é!*

The loa Aïson complains more vigorously of the bad behavior of human beings:

> Aïson Aïson!
> Dipis temps y'ap pa'lé sou moin!
> Coté ça yo gainyain?
> Bouche à yo paya paya!
> Djaule à yo pènè pènè!
> Coté ça pou' yo pa'don oh? [Ex. 83]

> Aïson, Aïson!
> For a long time they have been talking about me!
> What's wrong with them?
> Their mouths go *paya paya!*
> Their jaws go *pènè pènè!*
> What is the excuse?

Even on routine business the loa are inclined to be petulant, or to protest that they have been mistreated, that their followers gossip about them, or that they are not ardent enough. Here the deity Simbi en des Eaux complains bitterly that she is not loved by her servitors, the "leaves in the woods," and asks a hounsi named Lolo for news to take to spirits of the ancestors who live "below the water":

> Fé nan bois con ça nou yé!
> Nen point raimain pas mandé quitté!
> Fé nan bois con ça nou yé!
> Nen point raimain pas mandé quitté!
> Simbi en des Eaux,
> Qui sorti en bas dleau!
> Gardé ça yo fai moin!
> M'dit Lolo, ba moin nouvelle pou'm ba yo! [Ex. 84]

> Leaves in the woods, that's the way you are!
> There is no love that does not ask to end!
> Leaves in the woods, that's the way you are!
> There is no love that does not ask to end!
> Simbi en des Eaux,
> Who comes from below the water!
> See what they do to me!
> I say, Lolo, give me the news to give them!

But if the loa complain about the behavior of their followers, the servitors also may complain. Songs sung in the hounfor may chide the deities for antisocial deeds, for forgetting their "children," or for carelessness. In the following song the spirit Maît' Grand Chimin is criticized for mounting his "horses" with such fury that they are thrown about violently. The hounsi complain that Maît' Grand Chimin treats them as though they were flour being ground in a mill:

Temp' changé nouvelle allé!
Bonjou' Papa bonjou' Roi Grand Chimin!
M'mandé Papa ça'm fai!
Temp' changé nouvelle allé!
Bonjou' Papa bonjou' Roi Grand Chimin!
M'mandé Papa ça'm fai!
Papa m'pas maïs moulin!
Nou dit na bougit moin!
Papa m'pas maïs moulin!
Nou dit na bougit moin! [Ex. 85]

Times change, the news goes out!
Good day, Papa, good day, Roi Grand Chimin!
I ask you, Papa, what did I do?
Times change, the news goes out!
Good day, Papa, good day, Roi Grand Chimin!
I ask you, Papa, what did I do?
Papa, I am not corn flour!
You say you will grind me!
Papa, I am not corn flour!
You say you will grind me!

When there is sickness within the société there may be songs for the absent ones. Here is a song for an ailing hounsi:

Moin allé wè là, hounsi malade oh!
Moin allé wè ça, hounsi malade oh!
Moin allé wè houngan, hounsi malade oh! [Ex. 86]

I am going to see there, the hounsi is sick, oh!
I am going to see it, the hounsi is sick, oh!
I am going to see, houngan, the hounsi is sick, oh!

Again, the members of the société call upon Ogoun, or St. Jacques, to help one of their number who is sick:

St. Jacques marré chwal li,   St. Jacques ties his horse,
Li pas dit personne oh,   He tells no one, oh,
Véyé li pou' moin!   Take care of him for me!
Li met gainyain verre,   He may have worms,
Li met gainyain maline nan dos,   He may have sores on his back,
St. Jacques oh!   St. Jacques, oh!
Ba li lavie pou' moin! [Ex. 87]   Protect him for me!

Ogoun is the dispenser of rum, and in virtually all Ogoun rituals rum is at some time or another in evidence. Sometimes rum is poured into a hot iron pot and bursts into flame. The iron pot is described as Ogoun's house, which is on fire. But there is no grief, because Ogoun is the master of fire:

Pierre, Pierre Narcisse oh!   Pierre, Pierre Narcisse, oh!
Yago moula-é!   *Yago moula-él*
Caille Ogoun boulé!   Ogoun's house is burning!
Gildive Ogoun bel là!   Ogoun's distillery is beautiful!
Na consolé! [Ex. 88]   We console ourselves!

Some of the ritual songs that have persisted through the years have lost their explicit meaning but continue to survive because of beautiful melodies and perhaps the strange images they evoke. Such a song is this one to the loa Atti Daï, from the Dahomey service:

Atti Daï oh!   Atti Daï, oh!
Yo voyé dit moin   They sent to tell me
Min soleil malade! *   The sun was sick!
Quan'm té rivé   When I arrived
Moin joind soleil mouri!   I found the sun had died!
Quan'm té rivé   When I arrived
Moin joind soleil mouri!   I found the sun had died!
C'est regrettant ça   What grief it was
Pou'm enterré soleil! [Ex.89]   For me to bury the sun!

One of the truly lovely songs of the Dahomey rites, both in melody and in lyrics, is the following one to the deity Èzilie. It shows clear evidence of Catholic ritual influence in both its text and its music. Èzilie Fréda, who seems to be speaking most of the lines, is identified with the Virgin Mary, and the tone of this piece casts her more in her Catholic role than her African. The deity is speaking from Yagaza, a place described as being "on the other side of the water." In form the song is atypical in that it has more than one movement and progresses from one idea to another.

Èzilie Nainain oh!
Èzilie Nainain oh!
Èzilie oh, c'est moin Yagaza!

Èzilie n'ap marché n'ap couté n'ap parlé pou' temps y'ap parlé parole moin!
Èzilie n'ap marché n'ap couté pou' temps y'ap parlé parole mwé!
Èzilie Nainain oh!
Èzilie Fréda oh Nainain oh!
Èzilie Fréda oh, c'est moin Yagaza!

Mesdames nà yo chita nan caille là yo vlé djaillé oh tout temps soleil pas lévé!
Mesdames yo passé ya tombé tè à génoux y'apé plainaint le sort yo!

---

* Some Haitian informants vouched that *soleil* meant "sun." Others felt that this word in the song was really Solé, a diminutive of Attisolé, another name for Atti Dai.

Èzilie Nainain oh!
Èzilie Nainain oh!
Èzilie oh bo' c'est moin Yagaza!

Larouzé fai banda tout temps soleil pas lévé!
Larouzé fai banda tout temps soleil pas lévé!
Èzilie Nainain oh!
Èzilie Nainain oh!
Èzilie Fréda oh, coté moin bo' Yagaza!

Èzilie Fréda Nèg' Sobo Nèg' Grand Chimin Nèg' Balairouzé Cercléquitté abobo ça!
Èzilie Nainain oh!
Èzilie Nainain oh!
Èzilie Fréda coté ou yé? Moin là Yagaza! [Ex. 90]

Grandmother Èzilie, oh!
Grandmother Èzilie, oh!
It is I Èzilie, Yagaza!

Èzilie we are walking, we are listening, we are speaking, they are speaking my
    words now!
Èzilie we are walking, we are listening, they are speaking my words now!
Grandmother Èzilie, oh!
Èzilie Fréda, oh, Grandmother, oh!
Èzilie Fréda, oh, it is I, Yagaza!

The women sitting in the house there, they want to have a good time, oh, until
    the sun comes up!
The women go by, they fall on the earth on their knees, they complain about their
    troubles!
Grandmother Èzilie, oh!
Grandmother Èzilie, oh!
Èzilie, oh, it is I on Yagaza side!

The dew glistens until the sun comes up!
The dew glistens until the sun comes up!
Grandmother Èzilie, oh!
Grandmother Èzilie, oh!
Èzilie Fréda, oh, I am on Yagaza side!

Èzilie Fréda, Nèg' Sobo, Nèg' Grand Chimin, Nèg' Balairouzé, Cercléquitté, finish
    there! *
Grandmother Èzilie, oh!
Grandmother Èzilie, oh!
Èzilie Fréda, where are you? I am on Yagaza side!

---

* These various loa are being called upon here to withdraw and not to intrude upon the scene
while Èzilie is present.

7. In the Mapou Tree: Magic, Demons, and Compacts

It is said by many Haitians that the loa are inclined to shun the mapou tree, for it is the secret rendezvous of countless kinds of demons. On certain nights, they say, you may see a chink of light showing through the trunk of the great mapou, indicating that the demons are in macabre session.

Sometimes it is the baka who meet there to feast and discuss their blood-curdling plans. The baka are described as small and evil creatures, human in form, with red eyes, and legs or arms covered with skin but no flesh. They change into animals at will and may roam the country-side as cats, dogs, or cattle. The baka are notorious sorcerers, and they perform only malevolent acts. They are reputed to "eat people," literally as well as figuratively. Stories are heard of such-and-such a man or child who disappeared and was presumed to have been eaten at a feast in the mapou tree. One man who passed a mapou in the dark of night re-ported that he heard muffled singing coming from within its trunk, ac-companied by the pounding of mortars in which a gruesome feast was being pulverized. But the baka "eat" people also in the sense that they destroy them. It is said sometimes that a person with a withered arm or leg has been "eaten" by a baka. Perhaps he was an innocent victim; possibly he struck a horse or dog which was really a baka; or perhaps he simply brushed against a baka in the market place. Sometimes the baka directs his evil in the most indiscriminate sort of way, "eating" whatever human being he meets. Animals which behave strangely are suspected of being baka in disguise, and they are given wide berth.

A cow once found within an old brick-covered spring was taken to be a baka because no cow could have passed through the small doorway of the spring. It was assumed that she had entered as a small baka and had then changed to her animal form. The spring went unused for days, until some children reported that the baka had vanished. The cow was never seen again, and after a prêt' savane had read prayers over the spring the people again drew water from it.

Baka more often change themselves into gray or red pigs, but one ingenious baka was said to have transformed himself into a bicycle, which was seen traveling alone at night on the road from Port-au-Prince to Léogane.

Some people wear charms against the baka's malevolence; but the most effective weapon is the cocomacaque stick. The cocomacaque, or monkey palm, is a palm tree that grows only a few feet high. It has magical powers to drive off not only baka but other evil beings as well. When the tree is growing in its natural state, it is said, you must never mention its name in its own presence. Should you say within its hearing, for example, "Look at the cocomacaque," it will wilt and fall over, losing all its vital powers. The trunk of this midget palm is a favorite material for fashioning a walking stick or a short baton. A man going on a long journey into strange country may carry a cococmacaque stick with him to brandish at the crossroads where baka lurk, or to drive off strange animals that may be baka in disguise.

In their relationships with human beings, the baka are not always random. Sometimes, for a terrible price, they will undertake to make a man rich or to "eat" his enemies for him.

In some parts of Haiti, baka seemingly have found their way into the ranks of the loa. In the Congo-Guinée pantheon there is a deity called Bakulu Baka, or Babaku Baka. He is a malevolent spirit who "eats" people in the best baka tradition, and he lives, significantly, in the mapou tree, which is shunned by all good loa.

The *engagements,* or compacts, in which baka sometimes figure are usually made with another sort of creature, the *djab,* or devil. A djab is a manlike being but is superhuman, ferocious, and terrible. Some djab are small, some large, some innocent in appearance, some grotesque. They are supernatural sorcerers who deal out riches in exchange for human beings. A frustrated or desperate man may go to a djab and ask for a favor, which will usually be granted for a heart-rending price. Persons who appear to gain wealth suddenly may be suspected of having entered into an *engagement* with a powerful djab.

One story is about a man of Port-au-Prince who, needing a large sum of money, went to a famous djab who lives in a cave known as Trou Fourban. This powerful djab agreed to provide all the money required, but only on condition that the man deliver to him each year one of his children. The man suddenly came into a large fortune. But when the anniversary of his compact arrived, he did not go to Trou Fourban with one of his children as he had agreed. That night his oldest child died. The next year to the day, his second child died. And the third year, the third child died. On the fourth anniversary, the man's wife died. On the fifth, he himself died. The djab of Trou Fourban had collected his debt.

Another great djab lives on the northern mountain called Morne Ronde. A man of Cap Haitien was said to have made a compact with him for wealth. One day there was a great hubbub in front of the man's house. A crowd gathered and stood peering inside his door. What they saw was a rain of money falling down from the rafters. The floor was covered with ten-gourde bills. When the *gendarmerie* came to investigate, they stood at the doorway in awe, watching the money float to the floor. The man finally closed the door. That night he moved away, and no one in Cap Haitien ever saw him again.

The djab are insatiable. For their favors—which range from providing wealth and political position to destroying one's enemies—they always demand more in return than the recipient has counted on. Catholic ritual is called upon in some instances to break the djab's chain of demands.

Some tales are told in which human beings outwit the djab, particularly the lesser ones; but more often than not, the djab have the last laugh. During the big hurricane which hit Haiti in 1954, a huge landslide occurred near the place called Bayè Roche in the La Selle Mountains. An entire village was wiped out, covered by the falling rocks. Throughout this region the disaster was attributed to the action of a djab reputed to live in one of the nearby caves. Many lost cattle were found wandering near Bayè Roche, and they were believed to be people whom the malevolent djab had transformed into animals.

The height of bravado is to demand to be confronted with a big djab face to face. There is a song which goes:

> Conduit'm allé oh!
> Conduit'm allé djab nan Trou Fourban!
> Conduit'm allé! [Ex. 91]

> Take me, oh!
> Take me to the djab in Trou Fourban!
> Take me!

There are still other supernatural creatures in Haitian lore who must be guarded against, such as the *djablesse,* the *revenant,* and the *lutin.* The *djablesse* is a female ghost who must live in the woods for a number of years before she can enter heaven, as a punishment for the crime of having died a virgin. The *lutin* is the spirit of a child who died before baptism.[1] The *revenant* is a spirit of a dead person who feels he has been mistreated, and who returns to the world of the living to plague their families or their enemies.

The *lou-garo* (*loup-garou*) is a being of another kind, a vampire. She is human in form but sheds her skin and assumes animal forms at night when she roams the countryside seeking a victim. Salt is her nemesis. Should her human skin be found and salt sprinkled inside it, she would not be able to put it back on and would be destroyed.

A special form of the lou-garo is the *bizango,* a kind of enormous dog that runs in packs at night seeking people to eat. Also related to the lou-garo is the *démon,* a male creature of amorphous personality and character who can convert himself into an animal at will. There are sociétés of démons which, like those of the baka, meet in the dark of night in their assembly hall inside the mapou tree. Haitians who are conversant with such matters agree that there are many such trees, but that the most notorious of them are Mapou Miteppe in Miragoane, Mapou Simon in Aux Cayes, and Mapou Danpisse at Léogane.

Other fearsome beings such as the *zeaubeaups*—human cannibals— also gather in the mapou to conduct their affairs.

Against all these creatures, and against black magic in general, there are many magical protections, the most common of which is the *garde corps* (protect the body), or simply the *garde*. It is usually obtained from a bocor and consists of a small bag of mysterious ingredients. The owner wears it around his waist or around his neck. Sometimes it is merely a cord with a number of ritually made knots. The garde corps is made to prescription and protects the wearer against specific things such as a lou-garo, poison, or death from a bullet or knife. In describing a garde corps he had prepared for a client, a bocor revealed that it contained dried chicken blood, extract of *wari* bean, and *gris-gris* powder, among "a thousand and one" ingredients. The *gris-gris* powder is made from a dried *gris-gris* bird.[2]

There is another form of protective magic, broader in scope, called the *arrête*. It is used to protect not merely an individual but an entire household, or even a group of households. In addition to warding off supernatural creatures and protecting people against assassins, the arrête is a neutralizing agent against various forms of black magic such as the ouanga and the *makanda*. The arrête bundle or object is hung in the house or in a nearby tree, or it is buried somewhere on the grounds. Sometimes it is nothing more than a pointed stick placed in a certain way before a door or gate, or at one side of the trail leading to the house. A round, polished Indian stone is occasionally used as a *garde habitation*. And old people speak of a very powerful charm known as a *gros arrête* which in former times was placed on the trail to protect entire villages or valleys.

Still another potent defensive charm is the *pouin,* which is the product of ritual magic within the cult temple. A pouin may be an actual bundle containing a formula of special ingredients; more often, it is invisible, consisting of magical forces unleashed into space by the houngan. There are many ceremonies in the hounfor devoted to the projecting of these magical forces. They are called *cérémonie pouin* or *cérémonie magie* and are dramatized by special cult songs and dances. Sometimes the magie ceremony is woven into a more generalized cult ritual. The powers of the pouin are regarded as wider and more potent than those of the arrête. Pouins are said to protect an individual or a group not only against other magic but also against natural phenomena and accident. A pouin may ward off lightning, for example, or protect one from falling trees or from shipwreck or drowning. But it is not solely defensive magic. It may bring success in fishing, or produce a good crop in one's garden, or aid human fertility.

Since the crops and the garden are the substance of life, much attention is given to their protection. An enemy may attack a man or his household through garden magic. He may bury a ouanga in the earth, to bring sickness or ruin. He may poison a tree by performing a special rite at its foot, and its fruits will then carry disease or death to the one who eats them. Or he may make a compact with the earth so that it will dry up and refuse to produce for the one who tills it. Against all these malevolent possibilities, as well as against common thieves, the Haitian peasant has many magical and practical resources. Some people are said to employ zombies as watchmen. These fearsome creatures will capture a trespasser and hold him for the owner of the field.[3] Or perhaps the owner will place special arrêtes in his garden. Occasionally a man will protect his fields by planting *piquettes* in the earth. The *piquette* is a piece of sharpened bamboo or hard wood. Its point is dipped into poison, and it is placed in the ground, sharpened end up. An unwary intruder who steps on a piquette may die of his wound.

To counteract the *maljok,* or evil eye, a man may procure from a bocor a special shirt made of wide strips of red, white, and blue cloth sewed together. This shirt, called a *mayo* or *manyo,* is worn for seven days if the *maljok* is a rather ordinary one. If the evil force is a particularly virulent one, however, the *mayo* will be worn as long as twenty-one days, according to the bocor's prescription. It is also employed to protect an individual against various forms of the ouanga.

Against poisons, the usual protection is the *drogue,* prepared by a bocor or a leaf doctor who specializes in such things. After having drunk a drogue, a man is regarded as immune to poison. Should a man be a "horse" of the loa Ogoun Balindjo, however, no drogue is necessary, for Balindjo's people are regarded as immune even without such precautions.

Foretelling the future and divination take two general forms. In one variety, a bocor or *divineur,* using ritual paraphernalia such as cards, flour, or ashes, takes personal responsibility for the divination. In the other form, the divineur functions only when possessed by a loa, and it is the deity himself who foretells and foresees. An account of this kind of divination is given in chapter 6. "Horses" of the loa Mâit' David when possessed are given packs of cards, for they are reputed to be able to divine the future.

Certain houngans use the instrument known as the *gembo* as a divining device. This is a small shell about the size of a lemon, through which a long cord is passed. When there is no tension on the cord, the shell can easily be slid back and forth. When the cord is taut, the shell will not slide. The houngan holds one end of the cord under his foot, the other end with his hand above it. He starts his divination with the shell at the top and the cord taut. Shaking his asson with the other hand, he talks *langage* and asks questions. To indicate a "yes" answer he relaxes the tension on the cord and the shell slips downward an inch or so. The typical gembo is decorated with beads, old coins, religious medals, snake bones, and a fragment of mirror.

There are several ceremonies for locating a thief or other guilty person. One is called *passage d'alliance.* A ring suspended on a string is held over a person's head. If it moves in a regular pendulous way, the person is innocent; but if it swings in a circle, his guilt is established. Another method is the use of a long stick. The stick is pointed at one man, then another, and when the end vibrates in a circular manner the guilty party has been located. This technique is known as *jugement de baguette.* A third method is the one known as *passé balai.* A man sits in a low chair and small branches and leaves of the *balai* (broom) tree are placed under the chair and fastened to its uprights. A guilty person sitting in this chair will cause the *balai* branches to vibrate and close in on him.

The role of the *docteur fé*—the leaf doctor—straddles the field of magic and pharmacology. Many of his potions are of a mystical and semiritual nature; yet from roots and leaves he brews specific medicines for specific illnesses, such as rheumatism, fevers, malaria, worms, and yaws. Sometimes his cures are effective, sometimes they fail. The leaf doctor is consulted for poisons and their antidotes, though many poisons, such as that in the wari bean, may be gathered and dispensed by anyone.

One of the macabre figures in Haitian folk belief is the *zombie*. In the most general sense, the name designates the bland soul of a person who died without the distinction of having a loa in his head. The soul or spirit has no special will. It cannot affect the living in any way, unlike the lutin, the djablesse, and those who were buried possessed of mystéres. It does not harass enemies or importune its descendants. It is an undynamic, simple, otherworldly spirit, a sort of negative afterimage. It does not need to be placated or feared.

But the word *zombie* has another, more popular meaning, signifying a human being who has "died" and been resurrected from the graveyard by members of the Zeaubeaup Society, by a wicked sorcerer, or by some other person who has realized the "power" to perform this act.

The Haitian countryside is full of tales about fresh graves that have been robbed of their bodies by practitioners of this special form of black magic. By a secret formula these soulless "dead" are revived and given a semblance of life. They lack only the power of will. Without that, they are at the complete command of the sorcerer who has disinterred them. They are presumed to be spirited away and put to work at drudgery in some remote place. Stories are told of plantations in the mountains whose entire labor force is made up of zombies, the animated dead. You can tell a zombie when you see him. His eyes are dull and glazed, he gives no sign of recognition to people he once knew, he moves slowly and ploddingly at his tasks, and he takes orders only from his master. He neither sings nor dances, and he eats and drinks without interest. His facial expression never changes. He is emotionally and mentally dead. Neither the rites of the Church nor those of Vodoun can help him. There is only one formula for breaking the spell. If he eats salt he will either regain full life or die a merciful death. The master therefore takes great care that his zombies never have salt.

Haitians have many explanations of this mystical phenomenon. Some hold that the sorcerer has the unique power to revive the dead. Others believe that the victim is not really dead but has succumbed to a virulent poison which numbs all the senses and stops bodily functions but does not truly kill. Upon disinterment, the victim is given an antidote which restores most physical processes but leaves the mind in an inert state, without will or the power to resist.

The connection between the Haitian zombie and certain soulless beings of West Africa is quite apparent. Herskovits has observed that in Dahomey there are tales of persons thought to be dead who were found wandering in far-off places. These individuals had no memories of their former lives. "They were soulless beings, whose death was not real, but resulted from the machinations of sorcerers who made them appear as dead, and then, when buried, removed them from their graves and sold them into servitude in some far-away land." [4]

According to stories told by some Haitians, in ceremonies for the dead where there is suspicion that the deceased was the victim of this particular kind of poisoning a close relative stabs the body with a knife before burial to assure that it will not become a zombie. In other instances, close guard is kept over the grave for a number of days and nights, so that the body cannot be stolen.

Some members of the elite publicly dismiss the whole business as savage fantasy but privately say something like: "I don't believe in this sort of thing, but how can you explain the case of Marie Zambam in Cap Haitien?" And then they will tell of curious events of which they have firsthand knowledge.

There are numerous legends of persons who died and were buried, only to reappear perhaps years later in some mountain village, or in the big city of Port-au-Prince. An educated man in Port-au-Prince declared that a dead cousin of his reappeared one day in the city ten years after her burial. He tried to speak with her, but she answered only haltingly and gave no sign of recognition. After this one appearance, he said, she was never seen again. Another Haitian from the north told of a graveyard watch in his village to prevent disinterment of the grave of a young girl who had just died. The two watchers dozed fitfully, and suddenly awoke to see a man removing the girl's body. When they jumped to their feet and went after him he escaped into the shadows. But the girl staggered about, fell to the ground, and gave birth to a baby. Both the girl and her newborn child were taken to the village and given salt to eat. Both of them recovered.

One villager from the southern mountains reported that in his travels he came upon a coffee plantation on the sparsely populated mountain called Morne la Selle, and found all the laborers to be zombies. They did not sing as they worked, their movements were slow and cumbersome, and they did not sweat in the hot sun. When he asked for a drink of water, no one replied. While he stood trying to converse, the master of the plantation came with a hard leather whip and angrily ordered him to leave.

When they are not working, it is said, zombies are tied with special ropes made from the leaves of the banana tree. One popular song goes:

Nans Léogane
Yo marré zombie nans paille fig-banane!
Abobo wye-oh!

In Léogane
They tie the zombie with banana straw!
That is all, *wye-oh!*

Some Haitians tell you they know there are zombies because they have seen them. Not too many years ago a visiting writer stoutly declared that she, too, knew there were zombies because she had seen one—in the mental hospital at Pont Beudet. Although her reasoning was not quite airtight, the possibility that mental defectives are sometimes mistaken for zombies is worth considering.

Houngans who "work with two hands" are reputed to be able to gain permanent control over persons by means of a formula known as *tuyé-lèvé* (kill and raise). Either for himself or a client, the houngan gains power over the victim by "killing" him through special magic and then "removing the soul" (*retiré n'âme*). The victim, presumed to be normally dead, is buried by his family; the houngan then retrieves the body and "restores the soul" (*metté n'âme*). With his soul restored, the victim has, in effect, become a slave of the houngan, who can do with him as he wishes. He differs from a zombie in that he has a soul, whereas the zombie has none.

Some Haitians believe that even one who has died a nonmagic death may be raised from the dead. To accomplish this, the houngan or bocor stands over the body, goes through a specified ritual, and calls out the dead person's name: "Albert Moreau! Albert Moreau! Albert Moreau! Lèvé non! Lèvé non! Lèvé non!" ("Get up! Get up! Get up!") Then, it is said, the dead man may awaken.

It is believed that a houngan may also command the souls of dead persons to perform services for him against an enemy. The souls at his disposal for this work are those which he keeps in earthern jars in his hounfor. Should he wish to plague an enemy, he will send one of these souls to the man's house to make him sick, or lazy, or insane. Usually, the man does not know what is happening to him; but if he becomes aware that a dead soul is working on him, he attempts to find out which houngan has sent it. Perhaps the houngan can be bought off. If not, another houngan may provide relief.

While some believe in the reality of the various demons and specters, others only half believe, and many look upon these creatures as imaginary but exciting to talk about.

The zombie finds a favored place in the tales children make up to tell one another, and the traditional song played by children on the earth bow or mosquito drum goes:

Maringouin pinga zombie oh, Bobo Maria!
Maringouin pinga zombie!
Maringouin pinga zombie, pinga zombie, pinga zombie, pinga zombie, pinga zombie!
Maringouin pinga zombie! [Ex. 92]

Mosquito beware the zombie, oh, Bobo Maria!
Mosquito beware the zombie!
Mosquito beware the zombie, beware the zombie, beware the zombie, beware the zombie, beware the zombie!
Mosquito beware the zombie!

Or they may sing with great bravado, to the clapping of hands.

Chaingadaing, nou pral mangé zombie!
Chaingadaing, teau teau!
Chaingadaing, nou pral mangé zombie!
Chaingadaing, colocoto!
Chaingadaing, nou pral mangé zombie!
Chaingadaing, kalainkaintaing! [Ex. 93]

Chaingadaing, we are going to eat a zombie!
Chaingadaing, teau teau!
Chaingadaing, we are going to eat a zombie!
Chaingadaing, colocoto!
Chaingadaing, we are going to eat a zombie!
Chaingadaing, kalainkaintaing!

8. Mardi Gras and Rara: Jugglers, Maypoles, and Kings

From early in January until Easter, each year, the Haitian countryside is infected with a riotous carnival spirit that puts all else in the background. First comes Mardi Gras, beginning early in January and building to a great climax at Shrovetide. And then on Ash Wednesday begins the seven-week festival known as Rara, Lwalwadi, or Chariopié.

Every week end in the Mardi Gras season the country roads and villages are alive with special music, dancing bands, and traditional kinds of masquerading. The little crossroads in the mountains where the *habitants* usually hold their markets are suddenly swarming with drummers, trumpeters, magicians, jugglers, masked dancers, and acrobats. Each band has its own name, its banners and paraphernalia, new topical songs composed for the occasion, and sometimes a dance virtuoso. Each roving band competes for the attention and admiration of the spectators, and its ranks are often swelled by passers-by moving in the same direction who choose to dance their way along the roads rather than walk. Often women and girls on distant market errands will join in the celebration, seemingly unencumbered by the heavy loads they carry on their heads.

The Mardi Gras of the mountains and the plains is a dynamic spring rite of which the urban elite version is only a pale and feeble imitation. There are no pretty floats, no exhibits of female beauty, and no Coca-Cola advertisements. Sometimes the country bands move into Port-au-Prince and join the urban activities.

One by one the spectacles pass by on their uncertain way—to north or south, into the town or out of the town, wherever chance leads them. In addition to the musicians, acrobats, jugglers, and masked dancers, there are baton twirlers, comedians on stilts, and mimes. Each group has its own theme. One may call itself the Zeaubeaups, another the Cochons Gris, another Cochons Rouges—names designating legendary half-demon cannibals who meet in secret in the hollow heart of the mapou tree. Some are dressed in comic ancient military attire, replete with swords, epaulets, medals, and outlandish beards, representing "the Generals." Others, under the name Bande Autophonique, follow a human phonograph—a leader singing through an antique Edison horn.

And there are bands of male *rubaniers,* or Maypole dancers, some of them attired as women, weaving their colored ribbons around portable poles, to the accompaniment of guitars, marimbulas, and cha-chas. Male stick dancers known as *batonni,* dressed in women's clothing, crouch in circles and perform baton-tapping dances to the accompaniment of drumming and singing. Other small bands wander about impersonating characters from folklore or politics in grotesque homemade costumes. One might see, for example, a fanciful bocor driving before him a band of zombies, wielding a whip, and barking out weird raucous commands.

After the cataclysmic grand finale of the Mardi Gras at Shrovetide there is the briefest of lulls, and then the country is in the throes of Rara. The day of the *roi* Lwalwadi (the King of Lwalwadi) has arrived. Hundreds of Rara bands move through the towns and villages, each with its orchestra of bamboo trumpets or conch-shell horns and its "king"—an ornately clad dancer or baton juggler. The Rara bands move from place to place, dance, sing, exhibit their featured performers, and then move on, pressed perhaps by other bands behind them or jostled by another group moving in the opposite direction. When darkness comes, the bands light their way with wooden torches or candelabra of tiny oil lamps. Every week end for seven weeks, in the heat of day and the darkness of night, the mountain trails are alive with these processions.

The Rara festivities reach their climax on Good Friday week end, and by Easter morning they are ended. During these final days there is a last grand display, with troupes coming in from the mountains and the plains to the larger cities and towns. One of the traditional Rara convocation centers in the south is the town of Léogane. On Good Friday week end, Léogane is transformed into a milling, surging, trumpeting mass of celebrating country people.

The songs heard during Rara are full of praise or derision for well-known personalities. Some of them are boldly ribald or licentious. And often the dancing itself is openly sexual in its implications. Haitians humorously refer to this kind of dancing as *enragé* (enraged, crazy).

Early in January, even while the Mardi Gras is in progress, each community gets down to the business of organizing its Rara group. It may be organized in one of several ways. In certain communities there is some continuity over a period of years, the Rara or Chariopié band remaining more or less intact. Normally it has a *maît'* Rara, also called *major* or *président,* who assumes the organizational responsibilities for the group. This means getting new costumes for the participants when required, refurbishing the old costumes and musical instruments, and recruiting special talent—perhaps a new "king." Where the same group continues from year to year, the maît' Rara actually serves as a sort of executive secretary. In some instances, however, the initiative for forming a group is undertaken by the maît' Rara himself. He chooses the costumes and *décor* of the group; he recruits the musicians and the young women and girls who form the singing and dancing chorus; and he chooses the roi Lwalwadi, who will be the group's main feature. He may decide upon the theme around which the group will be built, and may even decide upon the repertoire of songs it will sing. The maît' Rara has specific responsibilities and is obligated to provide his band with refreshments and food.

Expenses of the group are defrayed by collections made in the course of its "exercises." The band will stop before a crowd of spectators, or before a house, and will perform until it receives a gift known as *payé sorti* (pay to go) money. After receiving its payé sorti, the group performs an encore and then moves on. This custom of performing for gifts appears to have been known in colonial days. Eugène Aubin notes that the slaves on the plantations celebrated on New Year's Day with drums and dances.[1] At midnight they appeared before the foreman or owner of the plantation. One of the slaves would recite a speech to him, or perhaps the group would sing a song praising the master's virtues. Then, over the heads of the celebrants, a slave would extend a long bamboo pole with a beribboned basket fastened to the end. The plantation master would place his gift in the basket, after which the group would leave the house.

Some few groups do not have a "king" but are built around musical instruments or other features. However, the "king" is regarded as an old tradition. Aubin reported that the roi Lwalwadi dates from the time of the Emperor Soulouque in the nineteenth century. Soulouque is said to have named the first roi Lwalwadi in the Cul-de-Sac Plain. But there are reasons to suspect that these dancing virtuosi, by whatever name they were called, existed long before Soulouque entered the picture.

The roi Lwalwadi is a dancer of very special talents, and it is said that, though his title is not hereditary, his dances have been handed down within the family from rois of other years. Much care is given to the costume he wears. It is sometimes made of expensive satin or velvet and covered with tiny mirrors or bits of colored glass. The towering headdress of antlers or papier-mâché sculpture unavoidably recalls similar headdresses in West Africa. Each roi has his own style of dance, which is usually accompanied by drums. It may be a belly dance, a dance of delicate balance, or one of complicated footwork and semiacrobatics such as the imitation of a pair of scissors at work. Throughout the dancing the headdress remains majestically erect.

In addition to the roi Lwalwadi and the mâit' Rara (who is constantly in the midst of things, blowing his whistle), there are other traditional Rara personalities: the *major jonc,* who juggles with a metal baton (sometimes two or three of these jugglers work together), and the *jongleur,* a juggler or strong man who performs such feats as dancing while holding a fully set table off the ground with his teeth.

On the southwest peninsula, in the region around Jérémie, there is a splurge of wrestling exhibitions during Rara days. Known as *pingé,* this festival wrestling is done with a background of excited drumming and has a striking resemblance to wrestling traditions in West Africa. Local "champions" will invade a neighboring community, sometimes traveling considerable distances to make a challenge. As in West Africa, some of these wrestlers take their own musicians with them. The musicians often are provided by the village in which the events take place. If a challenge is accepted, the spectators form a large circle, with the wrestlers in the center and the musicians to one side. There may be drums and bamboo flutes, occasionally supplemented by large earthern jars and lengths of bamboo beaten with sticks. The wrestlers are dressed only in shorts. When a man is thrown, the event is over, and another pair of wrestlers takes over. Sometimes a "champion" will take on a series of opponents until he is tired. Afterward he may move on to another community to find new competition, perhaps accompanied by a large group of friends and supporters from his own village. When the Rara season comes to an end, pingé is over for the year. It is one of the few athletic sport activities of the Haitian peasant.

And now and then during Rara a *debois* is seen. The *debois* is a carved wooden marionette with a short handle below. Its arms and legs are moved by pulling a string. It is usually painted, and sometimes it is dressed. One debois observed was provided with a loose dresslike costume; when the string was pulled, a large phallus hinged into view in an erect position. This marionette was an object of endless funmaking among spectators.[2]

Another type of marionette is the "Two Kings," made of papier-mâché and operated with strings. The "Two Kings," sitting in a papier-mâché carriage or on papier-mâché horses, make their appearance during Rara as well as on the Day of the Kings (*Les Rois*).

Among the traditional paraphernalia carried by Rara groups are cocomacaque sticks, cha-cha rattles, metal rattles called *tchancy,* a set of rattles on a tall thin pole (called *joucoujou*), candelabra bearing candles or oil lamps (*lampions*), banners and flags, and such miscellaneous musical instruments as the *grage* scraper, bamboo scraping devices, the *basse* finger drum, *assots* (beating boards), and various kinds of secular drums.

The general tone of Rara is nonreligious. The dancing is free from the decorous restraints which characterize most religious ritual, and some early observers of the festival were shocked by what they saw. Some of them went so far as to attribute Haiti's dense population to the "licentious activities" and reckless abandon of the spring carnival. The Catholic Church and some political administrators have sporadically sought to suppress Rara, along with Vodoun ritual. And even today in Port-au-Prince the foreign visitor often is urged to watch the elite Mardi Gras with its floats and mulatto queens as a substitute.

Although Rara has an over-all tone of secular abandon, it has links with both Catholic and Vodoun ritual. Good Friday is given over in good measure to miming the story of Jesus and Judas. A perambulating band may carry an effigy of Judas hanging from a pole. Another will burn the Judas effigy, or drag it in the dust as the crowd moves along the road. In another group a man playing the part of Judas may crawl on his hands and knees along the trail, while Jesus' avengers pursue him with long, cracking whips.

Tying in with Vodoun ritual, virtually all Rara drums and other paraphernalia are "dedicated" or "rededicated" before Lent in special hounfor services. And on the last day of Rara, usually late in the night, prayers are said, the loa are called upon, and some of the festive paraphernalia is thrown into a fire to be consumed.

9. Land and Work

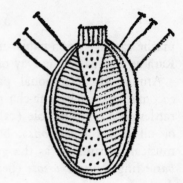

There is a common Haitian saying which goes: "Pitit mangé, travaille youn pile" (A little food, but tremendous work). This is the way the Haitian peasant sees it. There is endless labor in the fields or in the perpetually eroding mountain gardens, on landholdings that are too small to give any promise of a better life. The rains that give life to the crops take away, year by year, the nourishment of the soil. Where forests or lush groves once grew on the hillsides, there are now deep, dry gullies. Where coffee plants, cotton, and yams once grew abundantly, there are now fields of stones. This is the heritage of the peasant farmer of today. Small holdings on the hillsides and in the valleys have become smaller through the years as the population has swelled and the land been subdivided. Three and a half millon people must take their sustenance from that land. More than three hundred persons must share each square mile of soil. But most of Haiti is mountainous and formidable to agriculture. Two-thirds of the land area is untillable by modern standards. There is less than one acre of useful land per person. The best of the land in the alluvial valleys is held by large corporations producing sugar and sisal. Flat, arid stretches elsewhere are semidesert.

In the small gardens the peasants grow maize, *ti mis* (millet), coffee, bananas and plantains, cotton, beans of various kinds, yams, pumpkins, sweet potatoes, and manioc. In the delta areas they grow rice, and along the long coastline thousands of fishermen sail out in crude but sturdy boats to bring back fish fom the sea. Citrus trees, mango trees, and avocado trees grow wild; but they are fewer than in the old days. The Haitian works the soil and manages to subsist, but nature and history have not been kind to him.

Even less kind have been some of the chroniclers of the past, who have sought to disparage the Haitian as a lazy and careless creature who would rather starve than work. An Englishman, James Franklin, wrote in 1828, for example:

Experiments may be tried, laws may be enacted, and encouragement given, but nothing short of coercion and want will impel the Haytian to labour; and I have my doubts as to the practicability of enforcing labour in Hayti until the people have been better instructed, and their characters become changed.

As Franklin summarized it: "Nature is too generous to the Haytian; he never wants, and so never works for hire, as do free labourers in other countries." [1]

The early nineteenth century saw a flood of such bitter comments about the remains of the once rich and flourishing French colony of St. Domingue. The vast productivity of Haiti under French rule had made that colony one of the richest in the New World. The country was dotted with sugar mills, brick-covered wells, and warehouses; and carefully built brick aqueducts, irrigation canals, locks, and dams assured water for the plantations. In 1790, under the slave system, Haiti had exported 163,000,000 pounds of sugar. In 1826, a quarter of a century after the revolution, it was reported to have exported 33,000 pounds.

This falling off in production and exports doubtless had many causes, but one of the most significant was the Haitian's revolt not only against slavery but also against continuing the same kind of work he had performed as a slave. He saw not too much difference between forced, unpaid labor and working for any large landholder at subsistence wages. To the Haitian slave the inspiring battle cry of the French Revolution did not mean that all men would work together on another's man plantation and receive the same wages. It meant that every man would have his own garden to work for himself as he chose; every man would be a full citizen, with land of his own, free to come and go, to plant what he wished, to sell what he could. Despite long years under a colonial slave system, the Haitian still remembered a different way of life in Africa, where mass production for export was not the primary objective of labor.

At the beginning of the nineteenth century the population of Haiti was not much more than half a million—less than one sixth of what it is today. There was plenty of land, and much of it had not yet been wasted by constant tilling and erosion. When the French were driven out, the Haitian peasant re-created an economic world of his own liking. The plantation system which had poured out sugar and coffee and indigo for Europe faded away, and in its place there sprang up an agrarian system which has continued until the present day. In the early years of independence, Emperor Henry Christophe in the north and President Pétion in the south tried to stem the disintegration of the magnificent plantations. Christophe's measures in the region he controlled were sometimes stern, according to legend; but the plantation system and the plantations themselves gradually fell into decay, along with the aqueducts, the warehouses, and the sugar mills. For the Haitian had returned to a tradition of landholding antedating his enslavement.

Europe's loss of the Pearl of the Antilles aroused bitter words from Frenchmen and Englishmen for the better part of the century. They accused the Negro of laziness and lack of ability, repeating endlessly that only as a colony could Haiti ever be of any use to anybody. The London *Times* deplored the Haitian's unwillingness to work for wages, speculating that he had "no desire for property strong enough to induce him to labor with sustained power." In the United States, antiabolitionist enthusiasts cited the Haitian situation as an example of what would happen to the American economy if the slaves were freed.

The Haitian's reluctance to work for wages did not reflect an aversion to owning property, however, as the London *Times* supposed. On the contrary, it was engendered by his desire for property. The land was there and waiting, only needing a house to be built upon it, and to be cleared and tilled. The typical Haitian wanted not dubious, seasonal wage work but a farm of his own. The more ambitious peasant aspired to two farms, or even three, with a homestead and a family on each.

If a man worked hard and made a success of one plot, he could put away money and eventually buy a second. The additional land might be separated by some miles from the original farm. On the new ground the man would build another house and take another wife to take care of it in his absence. Known as *plaçage,* this arrangement had complete community sanction. A man whose energies and good fortune made an extra household possible was expected to make such an arrangement. It was not a new institution bred in the chaos following the Revolution, nor was it, as some missionaries held, an evidence of moral deterioration of the Haitian character. It was simply a persisting concept of West African life.[2] The woman who occupied the second or third household was not a concubine. Like the first wife, she had enhanced prestige in her community. She had authority and responsibility. Her work, her position, and her rewards were not essentially different from those of the first wife.[3] It is true that her marriage was not consecrated by a church or civil ceremony, but, ordinarily, neither was that of the first wife. Contrary to European misconceptions, such unions were true marriages in the sense that they had full sanction of the community.

1. *The Marbial River, a branch of the Gosseline, in southern Haiti. Twenty-eight thousand people, many of them renters or sharecroppers, depend upon agriculture in the Marbial Valley for their livelihood.*

2. Haiti's "Pine Forest," once a dense woodland, is an expanse of mountain terrain denuded of most of its trees and scarred by gullies. The timber was cut primarily for fuel for limekilns.

3. *Country people carrying produce to market. The highways of Haiti's economic life are the mountain trails and the unpaved roads over which the produce of countless small gardens is carried in bundles and baskets.*

4. *A peasant of the Montagnes Noires region, southern Haiti.*

5 and 6. *Cane workers near Croix-des-Bouquets. Only on the large company plantations are oxen and carts used.*

7. *A small coumbite,
northern Haiti.*

8. *Coumbite, southern Haiti. Vaccine players at the right; flag of the société
at the left.*

9. *Calling the coumbite: signaling on a conch-shell trumpet.*

10. *A women's coumbite weeding a cornfield near the town of Plaisance.*

11 and 12. *Market day. On each woman's head is the agricultural produce she will sell in the village or city market. When she returns she will carry a lighter load of things she has purchased, and tied in her handkerchief will be a few small coins.*

13. *Donkey with a load of charcoal. Where the terrain is not too rugged, donkeys or small horses do some of the carrying. The making of charcoal has helped to denude the mountains of their forests.*

15. *Pulverizing grain into meal. The mortar and pestle are standard kitchen fixtures.*

14. *Fishermen of Ville des Matelots, on the Bay of Gonaïves.*

16. *Man with a machete making a wari board. The machete is used for cutting trees, trimming brush, weeding gardens, fashioning wooden objects such as drums and mortars, and many other purposes.*

17. *Winnowing grain with a woven tray.*

18. *Young Haitians in school. After a century and a half of independence, education remains one of Haiti's most acute problems. Only a small percentage of the country's children are in schools.*

19. *Vodoun altar of the hounfor "Caille Agwé" in the Cul-de-Sac Plain. On the wall behind the altar are names of favored loa. On the altar are jars containing loa and souls of dead persons. Painted on its front wall, against which swords and flags are leaning, is the ship of Loa Agwé.*

20. *A Vodoun altar in northern Haiti, scarcely distinguishable from a Catholic shrine. Hounfors range from the simple to the complex, from the poor to the rich, from the primitive to the sophisticated, and from the bizarre to the artistic.*

21. *Altar in the hounfor "Société de la Belle Jeune Fleur" in Port-au-Prince dedicated to the loa Pinga Maza. The cross surmounted by the skull represents the deity. Behind the table, leaning against the cross, is the pestle with which this loa "grinds" his enemies. On the other table are razor blades for Pinga Maza to eat.*

22. *An assortment of stones (Indian artifacts) from the altar of a hounfor in the mountains above Jacmel. All are regarded as thunder stones thrown to earth by the loa Sobo and Kébiosu, or as stones containing the essence of other deities.*

23. *A houngan of southern Haiti divining with the aid of his asson, bell, and (right) gembo.*

24. *A houngan of a small cult center in northern Haiti.*

25. *A prêt' savane. This lay cleric reads the scriptures at appropriate times in the Vodoun rituals.*

26. *Service for the loa Agwé in a boat at sea. In the center, two hounsi hold the société's flags. Between them and the houngan is the bedecked barque d'Agwé, a raftlike miniature vessel which will be set adrift. An organ and a drum are at the lower right.*

27. *Saluting the loa. In the center, with sword, is the laplace, flanked by two hounsi carrying sequin-studded flags. In the background, left, is the houngan with his asson.*

28. *A yam harvest festival. The men are carrying the yams into the peristyle of the hounfor to be cut up and shared with the family ancestors and the loa.*

29. *The* bain de Noël, *or Christmas bath. The men are pulverizing leaves in the mortar, to the accompaniment of singing by the hounsi and drumming. Later, a "lotion" will be made of the powdered leaves, and all will share it.*

30. *A Christmas service near Léogane: ritual "bathing" in fire. The two young women are hounsi possessed by a loa of the Gèdé family, probably Jean Zombie. Their nostrils are stuffed with cotton and their jaws are bound in the manner of corpses, in honor of the deity, who is a "dead" loa. In a state of possession they seem to be impervious to the intense heat.*

31. *An Ibo service in the Cul-de-Sac Plain. Laid out on the mat is a feast for the Ibo loa. The houngan ritually feeds the deities by placing food in the holes at each end of the mat. Designs on the pots are the symbolic patterns found generally in vèvès. The tree in the background, surrounded by a low curbing, is sacred to the loa.*

32. *Maize-flour drawing, or vèvè, for the loa Simbi.*

33. *An ancient assotor drum, believed to have been made early in the nineteenth century. Seen faintly on the painted surface are a guinea hen and a palm tree.*

34. *An assotor drum in full regalia for a service in the Cul-de-Sac Plain.*

35. *A hounsi in the first stage of possession by a loa.*

36. *Possessed by the loa Gèdé Nimbo, two women dance the deity's favorite step, the Banda.*

37. *A small graveyard in the mountains at Furcy. The little alcoves in the tombs are for food offerings on special anniversaries.*

38. *Stone and brick covering of spring on Morne l'Hôpital believed to have been constructed in colonial times. Many persons have testified that here the voices of the loa have been heard bubbling up with the water.*

39. *A wedding scene near Plaisance.*

40. *Saturday night bamboche.*

41. *Vodoun drummers, northern Haiti. The drums are characteristic of that region. The boy at left, although only twelve or thirteen years old, is an accomplished drummer.*

42. *Forged iron "saber" of the loa Damballa, from a hounfor near Léogane. Height, 32 inches.*

43. *Forged iron standard for holding ritual objects, from a hounfor in the region of Léogane. Height, 18 inches.*

44. *Ancient iron figure of the loa Quançon Fer, from a hounfor near Léogane. Height, 12 inches.*

45. *Old iron ritual bell, or ogan, from a hounfor in southern Haiti. Height, 11 inches.*

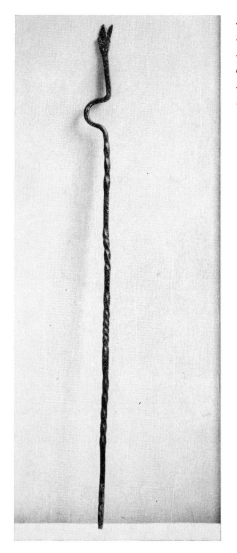

46. *Forged iron rod in the stylized form of a snake, representing the loa Damballa, from southern Haiti. Height, 34 inches.*

47. *Iron sculpture on a Nago altar of a hounfor near Gonaïves, representing a bird sitting on a tree.*

48. *A sculptured iron standard in a hounfor in the Cul-de-Sac Plain.*

49. *Forged snake, representing Damballa, from southern Haiti. Length in coiled form, 9 inches.*

50. *Representation of the loa La Sirène, made by a contemporary blacksmith.*

51. *Representation of the loa St. Jacques by the same blacksmith.*

52 and 53. *Wall paintings representing loa, in a small hounfor on Morne l'Hôpital.*

54. *Inside surface of a calabash bowl used in rituals of the hounfor, painted in black and white. The figure represents the graveyard loa, Baron Samedi, with a pick, shovel, and tombstone. Length, 15 inches.*

55. *An alfor cousin, the traditional peasant knapsack.*

56. *Wari board cut from a mahogany log. Length, 29 inches.*

57. *Old wood carving of an unidentified deity, for a hounfor near Léogane. It is startlingly similar to the African carving shown in no. 58*

58. *A wood carving from the Bambala tribe, western Belgian Congo. (Collection of Segy Gallery.)*

59. *Carvings of more recent date, representing the loa of twins, from a hounfor in southern Haiti. Height, 12 and 14 inches.*

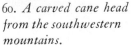

61. *Detail of a wood carving made about 1930 in the region of Port-au-Prince, representing the loa Loko. Work of this kind in mahogany has in the past thirty years deteriorated into neo-"African" carvings made for the tourist trade.*

60. *A carved cane head from the southwestern mountains.*

62. *A cayambouque. Cut from a single calabash, the two parts fit together tightly to form a single container. Some cayambouques are a foot or more tall. Height, 8 inches.*

63. *Terra-cotta figurines from the Cap Haitien region.*

64. *Detail of a dye-painted burlap cloth. Animal and flower figures and geometric designs are used interchangeably.*

65 and 66. *Modern "primitive" paintings by Bourmond Byron. (Collection of Roger Coster.)*

67. *A contemporary "primitive" by M. Stephane.*

68. *A painting by G. Abélard showing a Rara group led by a juggler holding a table in his teeth. (Collection of Marshall Stearns.)*

69. *Rara dancing near Gonaïves. Vaccine players are at the left.*

70. *A Rara group near Port-au-Prince. At the left are the baka drum and a tymbale. One of the four vaccines, center, is made of metal. Behind the musicians are the société's flag and a lampion.*

71. *Rara at Léogane. Behind the dancing majeurs joncs a member of the group holds their banner, which depicts a bird catching a lizard. The costumes are traditional and are believed to date from colonial days.*

72. *A roi Lwalwadi in the Cul-de-Sac Plain.*

73. *Rara stick dancers in Port-au-Prince.*

74. *Chaluska dancers in Port-au-Prince.*

75. *Maypole dancers. Musicians are sitting next to the pole.*

76. *A Rara group near Plaisance. The costumes differ from those in the south. Note the Madras waistcloths, reminiscent of West African dress.*

77. *Playing Théatre*

78. *Playing Balancé Yaya.*

79 and 80. *Playing the tambour maringouin, or
mosquito drum. Beneath the earth bow is a portable
variant. The player plucks the string with one hand
and with the other varies the pitch by pressure on
the end of the bow.*

81. *A miniature brass
casting, an Ashanti gold
weight, in the form of a
spring snare used for
catching small game. The
device can be recognized
as an antecedent of the
Haitian portable
mosquito drum.*

82. *Playing the tikambos, or bamboo stampers.*

83. *Haitian marimbula with keys made of steel springs.*
Height of box, approximately 18 inches, width 24 inches.
The player sits on the box and plays the keys with his
finger tips. Compare with nos. 84 and 85.

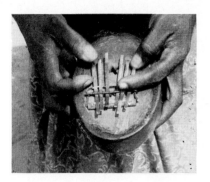

84. *A simple African sansa, or*
likembe, played with the thumbs.
This one is from the Topoke people
in the Congo.

85. *A marimbula from Cuba, still*
small enough to play with the
thumbs in the manner of its
African prototype. The heavy steel
springs are like those on the
Haitian instrument.

86. *The dentlé, or notched scraping stick.*

87. *Sacred calabash rattle from northern Haiti.*

88. *The tchancy, a metal rattle used chiefly for secular music.*

89. *A houngan's asson, showing network of beads and snake bones.*

90. *A ka drum, showing method of lacing and the sliding rope tighteners.*

Like their ancestors in preslavery days, the Haitians had a clear-cut and equitable division of labor between the sexes which was particularly suited to the agrarian life. The pattern of work sharing seems to have been misunderstood by nineteenth-century chroniclers, many of whom complained that the Haitian male napped in the shade while the women performed all the labor. It is quite true that the Haitian peasant woman is a relentless toiler. It may even be, as Sir Harry Johnston declared early in the twentieth century, that "the women are the best part of the Haitian nation." This Englishman wrote glowingly of the Haitian woman's fortitude and energy:

> In the face of all discouragements, with which a bad government clouds their existence the women of Haiti . . . continue to toil, to raise poultry and cattle, till the fields, see to their gardens, make pottery and mats. They cannot stop to reason, but must go on working from three years old to the end of their lives. Such industry (which is almost equally supplemented by that of the peasant husbands) protected should make Haiti one of the richest countries in the world for its size and population.[4]

But as Johnston surmised, the Haitian man, too, treads an unstopping wheel. Although it is the women who are seen crowding the trails and roads on market days, behind the produce they vend is the work of the men. For it is primarily the men who break the ground and plant, cultivate, and harvest the crops. It is the men who cut timber and build the houses, who dig and process lime for plastering the walls, and who thatch the roofs. And the houses do not last forever but must be rebuilt time and again. It is the men who cut and transport wood for fuel, dig red clay from the clay beds for pottery, make the mortars in which the grain is pulverized, build terraces for the gardens, make charcoal, go to sea for fish, and work at the village forge. On the plantations they cut the cane and the sisal. In the city they carry the heavy coffee and sugar bags, load the ships, make bricks, and build roads.

The women, for their part, run the household, care for the children, carry water from the springs, launder at the river's edge, cook, sew, play a supporting role in the field work, carry the crops to market, sell them, and bring back things which the garden does not produce. The woman may be the business manager of the household, and sometimes from the proceeds of special projects she may be able to put aside small savings of her own.

Children slip into their work roles at an early age. Boys and girls as young as three or four may be seen carrying small tins of water on their heads, on their way from the springs, usually in groups with older girls or women. Young girls assume woman's work as soon as they can handle it; lighter work first, heavier work later. Small boys tend cattle and help the men in the fields.

The Haitian *habitant* (the peasant) is poorer and hungrier today than he was fifty years ago, or even twenty years ago. In 1955 I visited a number of peasant families I had known since 1932, and with hardly an exception I found them worse off than they had been before. Their tiny landholdings had shrunk. Some land that had been lush had dried up and eroded. Little groves of trees had disappeared. Clothes had become shabby, and many of the men could no longer afford to wear the inexpensive traditional blue denim costume that was once so common. In the cities there is evidence that some of the elite have improved their life. But in a large part of the countryside the peasants are finding that the old system that served them for a hundred and fifty years can no longer feed them adequately.

One of the adverse forces is the shrinking of landholdings. Once a peasant family may have owned and worked fifty or seventy acres of ground. But it is traditional that on a man's death his land is divided among the heirs. If a man with fifty acres of land has two sons, each son inherits approximately twenty-five acres. On their deaths, the land is again subdivided. But even this is not the whole story. A UNESCO survey of the Marbial Valley region in south Haiti in 1948–1949 reported:

> At the turn of the century there were numerous peasant families who lived in relatively easy circumstances, and who possessed as much as thirty to forty *carreaux* * of land planted with coffee and subsistence crops. The heirs of these lands, when they found themselves in straitened circumstances, would sell some parcels of it in the hope of being able to increase their holdings again later on. In the worst cases they became the tenants of absentee landlords who lived in the cities. Nowadays, not only is the size of holdings very small, sometimes only one-eighth of a *carreau*, but they are also scattered, and most peasants are obliged to go from one place to another to cultivate their various owned, rented, or share-cropped fields.[5]

Haitian law—the civil code—does not recognize the rights of illegitimate children born after a legal marriage. But Haitian custom does. As a result, a Haitian who has a *placée* wife in addition to his "legal" wife may circumvent the law by deeding to her a portion of his gardens during his lifetime, thereby diminishing his holdings.

Furthermore, many landholdings are not clearly defined. There are few accurate surveys, and often the boundaries are vague. Titles to many of the holdings cannot be clearly established, and as a result there are constant lawsuits. To pay the expenses of defending his interests in court, a Haitian may have to sell a strip of his land.

---

* A *carreau* is about three and a third acres.

For many Haitians, the struggle to obtain a piece of ground and to hold onto it is the very heart of the struggle for existence. On Morne l'Hôpital in 1932 I knew a man who owned ten acres of gardens. He had it planted in bananas and plantains, yams, and cotton. He had two cows and a calf and a grove of mango trees and coconut palms. His house was clean, tidy, and by Haitian standards well furnished. Eighteen years later he had less than an acre of land, no trees, no cotton, and no cattle. His family had become impoverished. He had three grown children and virtually no land to leave to them except that on which the house stood. His troubles began with a lawsuit over his land title. He sold his cattle to raise money to pay his court expenses. He lost half of his land as a result of the lawsuit, most of it the part with the good trees. Later, he sold more land to raise "eating money," and then rented it from the new owner. He could not grow enough cash crops to pay the rent and was finally evicted. Today he has not enough ground left on which to grow food for himself and his wife the year round.

The diminution of adequate landholdings has resulted in the disappearances of many of the *lacours* (hamlets) that were a familiar sight a few decades ago. Young people traditionally built their houses near the family homesteads until there were five, six, or a dozen houses in a group. There was a natural family community which shared a common social life and the work of the fields. But as the population increased and the landholdings shrank, young people and old began to move away in search of new land, or work in the cities. Often where the lacour remains it is only as a settlement of landless house renters who work where they may for wages.

Economic refugees from rural areas seek wage work in the cities, returning to their original homes only on special festive days for family reunions. The men find employment as gardeners, servants, construction laborers, and stevedores. Some find work on the sugar and sisal plantations, others in craft industries making straw hats, baskets, shoes, chairs, and mahogany ware for export. The struggle in the big city of Port-au-Prince is for many of them worse than the poverty they left behind. There are the inevitable slums and the constant threat of hunger. It is in the big city that one hears most often the words *moin grand gout* (I am hungry), and least often the words *Bondieu bon* (God is good).

The land hunger increases, and the overflow of the mountain settlements continues to move cityward. In former years there was a trend toward emigration across the eastern border into the Dominican Republic, which has a population density roughly one third or one fourth that of Haiti. This trend was checked, temporarily at least, in 1937 by a massacre in the western part of the Dominican Republic which took the lives of an estimated five thousand to fifteen thousand Haitians. The survivors fled homeward, and many were settled in frontier areas by the government. Even so, today there are believed to be some sixty or seventy thousand Haitians still living east of the border. Large numbers of Haitians, particularly men, migrated to Cuba in the years following World War I, in search of better wages in the cane fields. By 1931 there were more than eighty thousand Haitians in that country.[6] But resentment by local Cuban labor and the onset of the depression combined to force the repatriation of great numbers of them. Thirty thousand Haitians came home from Cuba in the years 1936 and 1937 alone.

Solution of Haiti's problem of overpopulation does not seem imminent. The obvious answers would seem to be birth control, emigration, wiser use of natural resources, and industrialization. Since the country is predominantly Catholic, and since much social value is placed on children, birth control seems unlikely. And as health facilities become more widespread and infant mortality drops, the pressure will become more acute. Emigration seems to offer no hope, since neighboring islands and countries on the mainland give no encouragement. The Haitian may yet learn to conserve his land and to get more out of it, to stock his lakes with fish, and to bring more fish in from the sea. But this will not suffice. Nothing is left but industrialization, and that seems to be a thing of the far-distant future.

Nevertheless, the character of Haitian life remains essentially agrarian. The displaced peasant, whether he is now a hotel "houseboy," a taxi driver, or a cane cutter, dreams of returning to the land some day and growing bananas, coffee, and cotton that will make him independent. In far-off places such as Havana and New York, Haitians work and save money with the expectation that one day they will come home, buy fifteen or twenty acres of ground, build a new house, and live out their lives as decently prosperous *habitants*. The traditions of the agricultural society, along with Vodoun, continue to play a significant role in the life of the people.

One such tradition is the institution of the *coumbite,* a loosely knit coöperative work party of neighbors and friends. The word itself probably comes from the Spanish *convide,* or *convite,* meaning "to invite." A member of the group holds a coumbite by notifying his fellow members that on such-and-such a day his fields will require clearing or hoeing. There are several variants of the work gathering. One, called *carré* or *corvée,* meets at irregular intervals and only on special invitation. There are no regular reciprocal obligations in the *corvée;* the workers are compensated by a "feast" and party given at the end of the day by the host. More usual than the *corvée* is the regular sharing of work on one another's fields—the *ronde,* or "taking turns."

An early morning work gathering is known as a *douvant jou'.* It meets early in the day, sometimes before dawn, continues until ten or eleven in the morning, when the sun becomes hot, and then disperses. An afternoon coumbite is called a *diné-machete* (dinner machete) and lasts from about two in the afternoon until early evening. When the work is finished, the men go to the house of the host, where they have dinner, much in the manner of the American threshing party. An all-day affair is called a grand coumbite.

Essential to all coumbites are musicians and singing leaders. The instruments used are various, according to local custom. In the south they are usually drums, *tymbales,* and bamboo trumpets. In some areas of the north, the *lambi,* or conch-shell trumpet, is favored.

According to the custom in the south, on the day of the coumbite the drummers arise in the false dawn before sunrise and begin a roundabout march to the home of the host. They pass before the huts of all the neighbors who are going to join the party, playing a *rappel* on the drums. By one's and two's the workers come down the trails to join the procession, bringing hoes, machetes, or sickles as required. As the marching group grows larger, there is talking, laughter, and perhaps singing. Most of the men who join the procession are from close by. Others who may have to travel from a distance, perhaps from the next valley, go directly to the house of the host. When the workers arrive there, the women of the house serve coffee. This is the usual breakfast of the Haitian peasant.

Then the drummers play another *rappel,* and the men go down to the field that is to be tilled. There may be ten, twenty, or fifty of them. Some coumbites are even larger. If the group is a small one, the men line up together. The singing leader, called a *samba* or *simidor,* begins a song, the drummers play, the hoes begin to rise and fall in unison, and the workers join in the singing. If the group is large it will divide into two or three squads, each trying to outdo the other. The men stand shoulder to shoulder, moving the hoes up and down together, syncopating their movements by pauses as they sing their responsive parts. Sometimes tafia or rum is portioned out. The squads move forward slowly, inching their way across the field. The samba beats on his hoe blade with a stone to keep time for his song. His job is to "encourage" the men. He may sing old familiar songs or compose new ones, songs with humor and bite in them, ribald songs, and songs of ridicule. They may criticize men who have failed to join the coumbite, or praise the host, or single out various individuals for comment. The songs of the coumbite are a newspaper of the affairs of the people. The news is personalized, editorialized, and replete with comic vignettes.[7]

At noon the drummers signal a halt, and the workers shoulder their hoes, wipe off their machetes, and adjourn to the house for food. If it is a grand coumbite, the men rest for several hours, talking, catching up on sleep, or playing cards or *mayamba*. About three o'clock they go back to the fields to work until evening. Then comes the feast, under the canopy adjoing the house. The host and his wife have killed and cooked one or more goats, depending on the size of the group. The men are served meat, rice, beans, and whatever else has been prepared. Afterward, women join the party, and there is more tafia or rum. Some of the men then drift homeward, but most stay on for dancing. Zesse, Congo, or Juba drums are brought out, and the festivities begin. If another coumbite is not scheduled for the next day, the music and dancing may last well into the night.

Women, too, have coumbites to perform various kinds of large tasks, from field work to winnowing and coffee sorting, though in general the women's work groups lack the festive character of the men's gatherings.

There is a more tightly knit form of coumbite, known as a *société*. In southern Haiti there are the société Congo and the société Martinique; in northern Haiti there is the société Ciyé. These sociétés are clubs built around mutual work needs and recreational activities. The société Congo that appears in the town or city streets during Rara days, with bamboo or conch-shell trumpets, drums, flags, and masks, is usually composed of the men who have joined forces to till the fields. In some instances, it may also conform roughly to membership in a particular hounfor, or cult center. Unlike the ordinary coumbite, the société is not a group which meets only at ground-breaking or harvesting time; it is a permanent organization with regular, sometimes day-to-day, obligations. Week after week it moves from one man's land to another, doing the tasks that have to be done. There is no question of "Can you come?" The group goes first to one man's land, then to another's until all the work has been done. If a member of the société falls sick, so that he cannot work his own field, the société takes over his tasks for him.

Coumbites are held not only for agricultural work but for house-building, and sometimes for the building of a hounfor.

The Haitian coöperative work group has much in common with European and American husking and barn-building parties; but it has many non-European characteristics. The manner of work, even down to specific motor activity, has direct and hardly disputable West African connections. Instead of the short-handled West African hoe, the Haitians use a long-handled one, and they work more erect than stooped. But the rhythmic, synchronized use of the hoe, the singing leader and the musicians who stand to one side to "encourage" the workers, the calling of the workers by drum *rappels,* the special consideration for the sick, and the concept of long-term community endeavor are all of West African beginnings. The coumbite is the legitimate descendant of the Dahomean *dokpwe,* the *kurum* of the Mambila (Cameroons), the *ku* of the Kpelle (Liberia), and other West African coöperative systems.

Although the *dokpwe* of Dahomey is a more formal and intricate institution, permeated with certain abstract and ritual concepts, its social and functional characteristics are not greatly different from those of the Haitian coumbite, in which coöperation is marked. Herskovits notes that working with the Dahomean *dokpwe*

represents recreation rather than labor to the individual member. There is song and dance to drumming and the sound of gongs, on the way and after arrival, and there is feasting and an exhibition of skill. It is an impressive sight to see from forty to a hundred men kneading earth for walls, or laying thatch, or hoeing the earth with unison movements to the accompaniment of conversation and laughter, and the songs of such of their fellows, who, for the moment at rest, have constituted themselves the chorus.

When more than one *dokpwe* is summoned for work on the same project, Herskovits notes,

there is great rivalry among the organizations to see which one will first complete its allotted task. If only one *dokpwe* is present, there is either individual rivalry, or the *dokpwe* may be divided into two groups which compete one against the other. The food which is provided at these times of collective labor is as rich fare as the owner can afford . . .[8]

An underlying factor in the Dahomean *dokpwe* is awareness of itself as "the manpower of Dahomey," and the members regard themselves as exercising their fundamental privilege as Dahomeans. This attitude toward the coumbite continues to prevail in Haiti. Like the hounfor— but even more significantly in terms of routine, workaday life—the coumbite and the société are an expression of social ties and of the pervading interest in the common welfare.

Certain patterns of the coumbite have been carried over into non-agrarian labor in the towns and cities, wherever group work is required. The carrying of coffee and sugar bags in the warehouses, the loading of ships, and the repairing of roads—all are traditionally performed rhythmically, to the accompaniment of drums, *catas,* or horns, while a singing leader composes topical songs in which the laborers join.

The tools which a rural Haitian chooses, and the way he uses them, often are in a West African tradition. He performs a multitude of tasks with his machete, or bush knife: weeding a garden, peeling an orange, cutting down a tree, making a drum or mortar, opening a coconut. It is an all-purpose tool, as it is in Africa. Until a few years ago it was supplemented by the extra-long, heavier, "double machete." The axe and the chisel are known and used too, but the machete is supreme. The hoe is the tool for tilling the soil, even in the flat country, and even though the Haitian has horses and cattle which could pull a plow. Horses are for riding and not for pulling. In carrying loads, the Haitian peasant still prefers the head to the shoulders. If he has a donkey, the donkey will carry for him. An old Haitian proverb goes: "Meçi Bondieu pou' bourrique là, si nous pas gainyain bourrique là faut Haitien po'té tout bagaille" (Thank God for the donkey, if we didn't have the donkey the Haitian would have to carry everything)." Generally speaking, the rough and rocky terrain of Haiti and inadequate secondary roads have done nothing to encourage the use of carts or wagons.

Corn is stored in the trees, as in West Africa, or in granaries built upon stilts, also as in West Africa. The Haitian makes his fire in the African fashion, with several long sticks or poles meeting point-to-point in the heart of the fire. As the ends are consumed, the sticks are pushed toward the center. Grain is pulverized in large wooden mortars, as in West Africa, and winnowed in a woven tray. Fish traps are sometimes woven in the traditional West African manner, and fishermen often set their nets in converging spirals and beat the water with sticks to drive the fish to the center. And on the rivers and lakes are to be seen dugout canoes of a kind familiar on the inland waters of West Africa.

The folklore of the fields contains many themes known to the West African. One old Haitian farmer, discussing the spiritual relationship of the planter to the earth, declared that a man must be strong and potent when he plants, else the crops will be vitiated and sickly. For this reason, he said, a man must not plant seeds the day after he has had sexual intercourse, because he has been temporarily drained of his life-giving powers.[9]

The tale of the hoe that worked by itself in the fields is also widespread. It enters many animal and Bouki stories, and also is known in a form that is familiar in West Africa. In this story, there was once a man who owned a hoe which worked by itself whenever a magical formula was pronounced. It would stop working whenever the magical counterorder was given. The owner of the hoe was happy and prosperous until one day a thief (in one version, the trickster Anansi) stole the hoe and put it to work in his own fields. But the thief knew only the words to command the hoe to begin, not the words to stop it. He could not stop the hoe from working, and it worked its way out of the valley until it came to the country of the white people.[10] The whites knew the words to stop the hoe, and so they gained control of it. It is said by some that the whites fashioned the hoe into a plow.

10. The Arts—
Flour, Wood, and Iron

It is the nonmaterial arts and traditions that have thrived best in Haiti through the years of slavery, political unrest, and poverty. Religious concepts, music, dancing, folk tales, proverbs, and games are found everywhere in profusion. Material arts of the past have fared less well. Today, nothing is left of the old African knowledge of wood carving, metal casting, appliqué work, and weaving. Why such major African arts have died out in Haiti is no mystery. They disappeared simply because there was no place for them under the slave system or in the new Haitian society which followed it.

Under the colonial masters, the demands made on the New World African were for coffee, cotton, and indigo. His creative talents were channeled into carpentry, masonry, and the building of facilities for production. There were no traditional artistic outlets or patrons for the wood carver, and no need for the weaver. Nor, during the years of slavery, was there much leisure for the craftsman to do his work even for the fun of it, should he be so inclined; indeed, this approach to wood carving or any other art would have been little understood or appreciated by most West Africans. A man who made an art object purely and simply to express a creative urge rather than to fill an express need would have been regarded as slightly eccentric. The old West African wood carvings with which we are now familiar were made because they were *required* for some purpose. A figure of a deity was needed in a shrine, a carved protective guard was needed for the household, a grave marker or a ceremonial mask was obligatory.

In Haiti the needs of those who ruled were different. The slave with knowledge of the forge was not put to work making spears, ceremonial axes, and the like; he was assigned the task of making grillwork for houses, hinges and bolts, iron tires for coach wheels, and metal parts for the sugar mills. The anonymous African ironworker did his job well.

And when the revolution came he produced for the Haitian armies knives, gun parts, and wheels to transport cannon. By the tens of thousands he made ingeniously devised metal objects to be thrown on the roads, before the French cavalry troops—objects so shaped that, no matter how they fell, a single sharp point stood erect to cripple the enemy horses. Yet knowledge of the West African uses of iron did not altogether disappear, and during the first century of independence the Haitian blacksmith created many old-style knives, spears, and ritual objects for the cult temple.

Even today, some of this old-style work is to be found in hounfors in the southwestern peninsula. One may see simple or ornate iron standards, made to support ceremonial offerings or candles, strikingly similar to standards in ancestral shrines in Dahomey. There are iron bells, both single and double, made in pure West African style; ornate ritual swords and sabers which are the crests of certain deities; coiled and uncoiled iron serpents representing the gods Damballa and Ayida; and stylized or semirealistic portraits of the deities. Many of these old pieces are nineteenth-century survivals; others have been forged within the past decade.

An over-all impression of Haitian material culture is that artistic decoration is almost entirely absent and that the prime emphasis is on utility. Wooden cooking spoons are efficient in form, but missing from them is the delicate decorative carving often found in West Africa. The long wooden washing bowl, or *gamelle,* and the wooden mortar in which grain is pulverized are likewise clean-cut but stark and plainly utilitarian. Clay bowls, bottles, and storage jars are usually of simple, uniform design, with only accidental variations; there is little use of glazes, and the clay is often heavy and thick. Should there be a wari gameboard in the peasant hut, the chances are that it is roughly made, without legs or carved designs. Dugout canoes are usually crude in appearance, heavy and thick-walled, and irregular in form.

Yet there are many evidences—though one must seek them out—that esthetic impulses are quite alive. The gay peasant straw knapsack, or *alfor,* without which no mountain man makes a journey, has a charm and grace that is not diminished by familiarity and cheapness. Decorated with sisal braid and tassels, and colored with green and magenta dyes, each *alfor* on close inspection appears to be unique. In some communities in the south and southwest, burlap squares also are painted with these traditional dyes. About forty inches across, and made of sugar bags, these paintings swarm with geometric patterns and sometimes with figures of flowers and animals. They are purely decorative, being used for wall hangings much as appliquéd cloths are used in Dahomey. Near Cap Haitien, in the north, ceramic workers make crude clay figurines of roosters, pigs, dogs, cows, and people. The "purpose" of these figurines is obscure, but it is likely that they are intended for use in Vodoun ritual, a number of them having been observed in hounfors in the vicinity of the town of Grande Rivière du Nord. In some mountain villages, canes carved with animal and human heads are commonly seen. Nor is the tradition of carving gourds and calabashes, popular in various regions of West Africa, altogether forgotten. The *cayambouque,* a divided calabash with the top ingeniously cut to fit into the lower part so as to form a sealed container, is sometimes covered with carved geometric designs, usually crude and haphazard but on occasion meticulous. Until recent years the common *cha-cha,* or gourd rattle, was similarly carved.

Most of the visible traditional art is to be found in the environs of the cult temple. The inner walls of many hounfors are covered with ritual designs and symbols and portraits of the deities. On the altar, sometimes, crude wood carvings of deities are seen, along with forged iron objects, carved marassa bowls, and grotesquely shaped drumsticks known as *baguettes guinée.* All the wooden objects are characterized by a plainness that relegates them to the category of purely functional and expendable things. The wood carving of a deity is not an image, it is a representation; it can be sold or otherwise disposed of, even thrown away if infested with beetles, and another object can be used to replace it. The only concern of the cult priest in this matter is that the deity concerned should understand the situation properly and not take offense. Thus there is no strong feeling that the wood carving should be a realistic representation or that it should be "beautiful." One relatively antique wood carving, completely West African in style, was found some years ago in a hounfor near Léogane and is now in the collection of the Musée du Peuple Haitien in Port-au-Prince (see fig. 57).

One of the most flourishing arts of the hounfor is the *vèvè,* or ritual drawing made on the earth in the course of a service. Most commonly these beautiful and ornate designs are made with white meal or flour, and in a few of the cults, primarily the Pétro, lampblack and red brick dust are also used. The vèvè is made by the houngan or the mambo. With sure, practiced movements, the cult priest allows the meal to trickle through his fingertips onto the ground where the rites are taking place, usually in the peristyle of the hounfor itself. The drawings he makes are composed of a multiplicity of cabalistic symbols—heart shapes, stars, interlocked V's, flags, abstract phallic forms, crosses, swords, machetes, circles, mortar shapes, and so on—each with its own specific meaning. Sometimes the vèvè becomes openly pictorial, and there emerges a ship for the loa Agwé, snakes for Damballa and Ayida, a bull for the loa Taureau, a knapsack for the loa Azaka, or even a portrait of a deity, perhaps smoking a pipe or holding a sword.

The vèvè is not a permanent record. It is made as an act of supplication or veneration, and once it is finished it has no further value. In the ensuing ritual and dance, the vèvè is obliterated by the feet that pass across it. At the hands of one houngan, this invocational act results in a crude, even childlike, design. At the hands of another, it produces a drawing of beauty, integration, and highly developed form.

The drum-making craft, too, has offered an unbroken sequence of opportunity for satisfying artistic urges. The drum has a traditional form that cannot be tampered with; its shape is predetermined by its function, by the log from which it is hewn, and by existing standards. And yet, the drum maker has found it an object on which he can devise new decorative motifs, and he may even give it personal uniqueness. Some drums have styles that may be associated with specific regions of the country, others bear the stamp of the individual artist. Paint has been used on Haitian drums for a hundred years or more as a complement to carving. One assotor drum dating from the earliest days of the Republic, and now preserved in a collection owned by the Bureau of Ethnology in Port-au-Prince, is decorated with a medallion showing the Haitian coat of arms, grenadiers, red and yellow snakes, and a sun with a face. This magnificent instrument, apparently the only one of its age and kind to have survived the years, is one of Haiti's art treasures.

The *couis,* or calabash bowl, of the hounfor rites is another object which is decorated with motifs. Abstract designs, ritual symbols, and sometimes human and animal figures are painted on the inner or concave surface of the bowl.

The rural traditional arts of Haiti have had a belated impact on the arts of the city. Within the past fifteen years there have appeared a number of painters, sculptors in wood and ceramics, and ironworkers who constitute an art movement sometimes referred to as the Haitian "renaissance." Many of these artists draw heavily on national lore and legend for inspiration and subject matter. Some of them are men who came only recently from villages or distant farms. Their work adorns many public buildings in Port-au-Prince and is eagerly sought by art collectors. Members of the elite class who once looked with embarrassment on the "primitive" countryside are finding increasing respect for the potentialities of their country cousins.

11. Dancing and Dance Drama

The dances of Haiti, like the loa, are almost beyond counting. Like the loa, too, the dances have personalities of their own, sometimes too subtle for the stranger to detect. If there is one valid generalization, it is that the inspiration for the Haitian dance is primarily African. There have been changes in the course of the more than four hundred years since the first Africans came to the New World. Some of the old dances have disappeared altogether; others have developed new characteristics. New dances came into being with European rather than African form. Some of the most traditional dances have become sparse and lean, stripped of the decorative pageantry of earlier days. There are also the French quadrilles and similar square dances which have survived since colonial days in remote parts of the mountains. But it is the quadrille and not the dance of African origin which is atypical in Haiti's folk culture. Dancing is deeply rooted in almost all the important events of Haitian life. It is one of the few arts that have survived from preslavery days.

Early European travelers in Haiti were greatly taken by the dances they found there. Some observers, like Moreau de Saint-Méry, a Frenchman born in Martinique, have left invaluable documentation of the dances of the late eighteenth century. Saint-Méry described many dances that are still known in modern Haiti, such as the Chica, the Calinda, the Vodoun, and the Pétro. From his accounts one may assume that these dances have not changed much to this day.

But many of the foreign authors and journalists of early days were astoundingly lacking in understanding and quick to bare their prejudices and to pronounce their moral judgments. Like the explorers of our own time who delight in "returning alive" from some jungle land and in commenting upon all the strange, bizarre, dangerous, and wicked things they think they have seen, the explorer of the Dark Island often described the Haitian as a depraved branch of the human species. One such observer, commenting upon the dances of the elite and of the peasant declared:

All the more undisguised is the crude sensuality among the lower classes of the Haitian population. Here every motion is obscene; and I am not at all considering the popular merrymakings or dance festivals secretly held partly in open, partly in forests, which are more like orgies, in which the African savagery, which has outlived centuries, has unbridled expression.[1]

Whatever the Haitian dance is, it is none of these things. The Haitian himself is neither obscene nor unbridled. His dancing, like his everyday life, is governed by social controls. He would be as surprised and offended by a sexual orgy as most Europeans. But he is not burdened with abstract concepts of chastity. Sex impulses are as fundamental and as taken for granted as rain, drought, and sunlight. The Haitian finds no virtue in living according to standards that have no relation to his realities.

The Haitian, like the West African, is undoubtedly a less tormented creature, so far as sex is concerned, than his European and American cousins. Since he is less tormented he can be more frank. And it was an expression of this frankness in certain of the Haitian secular dances that once aroused dismay among foreign chroniclers, and that still stirs the curiosity of tourists.

Yet if you were to witness fifty Haitian dances in their natural setting, you still might not see any direct sex expression. You might see more sex play and display in a dance hall or night club in New York, Chicago, Milwaukee, or Los Angeles. That is not to say that there are no sexual allusions in Haitian dancing. In the ordinary Saturday night *bamboche,* or social dance, there may be a good deal of loin movement and suggestion. In Haitian context, however, it is no more significant than two persons of opposite sexes pressing close together to the music of a dreamy orchestra at the "Roseland." In Haitian religious dancing, sexual motifs may occasionally emerge, but they are integral parts of ritualistic symbolism.

One of the deficiencies of early literature on the dances of Haiti is that it did not differentiate between religious and secular dances. Furthermore, it is evident that writers tended to use a single name, such as Chica or Bamboula, to cover virtually any kind of dance festivity, much as many white Cubans refer today to all sorts of Afro-Cuban cult dances as Bembé. Because the terminology of ill-informed planters was adopted by the chroniclers, we are now able to form only some very general notions of Haitian dancing of the eighteenth century and before. Of all the reporters on the dance, Moreau de Saint-Méry seems to have been aware of differences, though his frequent departures into speculation helped to perpetuate some prevailing misunderstandings and errors. This distinguished observer wrote:

The Negroes of the Gold Coast, warlike, bloody, accustomed to human sacrifice, know only dances as ferocious as themselves, while those from the Congo, Senegalese and other African shepherds or agricultural tribes, love dancing as a relaxation, as a source of sensual pleasure. Brought from all parts of Africa to our Colonies . . . , the Negroes brought here and preserved their taste for the dance, a taste so strong that, however tired out from work the Negro may be, he always finds strength to dance and even to travel a long distance to satisfy this desire.

When the Negroes want to dance, they take two drums, that is, two hollow logs, of unequal length, with one end open, while the other is covered with sheepskin. These drums . . . resound under blows of the wrist and movements of the fingers of a Negro who sits astride of each drum. The larger drum is beaten slowly, the other more rapidly. This monotonous and hollow sound is accompanied by the noise of a certain number of calabashes which have been filled with pebbles . . . Several *banzas,* a sort of large guitar with four strings,[2] join the concert, the tempo of which is regulated by the clapping hands of the Negro women, who form a large circle. They form a sort of chorus, which responds to one or two strident solo voices, which repeat or improvise a song.[3]

As for the dance movements themselves, Saint-Méry wrote:

A male and [a] female dancer, or several dancers divided into equal numbers of each sex, jump into the center of the circle and begin to dance, always two by two. This dance, which varies little, consists of a very simple step in which one foot is put forward after the other, and then drawn back quickly, while striking the toe and the heel on the ground . . . Some turn in place, or around the woman, who turns also and changes places with her partner; that is all which one sees, except for the movement of the arms which the man raises and lowers with the elbows quite close to the body and the hands almost closed. The woman holds two ends of a handkerchief, which she waves . . . One would hardly believe how lively and animated it is, and how much grace it derives from the strictness with which the musical rhythm is followed. The dancers replace one another without respite, and the Negroes are so intoxicated with pleasure that it is necessary to force them to conclude dances of this sort, called *kalendas.*[4]

Saint-Méry then brings forth one of his conclusions, that this dance is obviously the development of a "comparatively uncivilized people," and that it comes from Africa, "where its characteristic features exist everywhere, even among the Hottentots."

Here he missed the point altogether. Although many of the characteristics of this *kalenda* (or Calinda) were African, it had already been intensively hybridized with European dance concepts, such as the pairing off of males and females, who danced as couples. Then, as today, the dances which amazed and shocked the European observer were precisely the ones that had taken over certain European traditions.

Saint-Méry also wrote about some of the religious dances, which he identified by name:

> In Santo Domingo, and especially in the western, French section, there has existed for a long time a kind of dance called the Vaudoux [Vodoun] . . . which is characterized by movements where the upper part of the body, the shoulders and the head seem to move convulsively. This dance is accompanied by the drums, the clapping of hands, and group singing . . .
>
> The Vaudoux is nothing compared to the Don Pedro . . . , another Negro dance, also known in the western part of Santo Domingo since 1768. Don Pedro was the name of a Negro of the Petit-Goave section, of Spanish origin, who by his daring character and certain superstitious practices, had acquired among the Negroes enough influence to be denounced by the government as the instigator of some alarming plots. The dance which bears his name consists, like the Vaudoux, in the shaking of the shoulders and the head, but this shaking is extremely violent, and to increase it still further the Negroes drink, while dancing, brandy in which they have mixed finely ground gunpowder . . .[5] They dance with the most horrible contortions, until finally they fall into a sort of epilepsy . . .[6]

Making allowances for Saint-Méry's imaginative interpretation of many of the things he saw, the Haitian dance of today is not far different from that of the eighteenth century. It is cast in the West African mold, with Dahomean and Yoruban motifs predominating over European and other Western infiltrations. As in Saint-Méry's day, the drummers sit at the edge of the dance court, a leader wielding a gourd rattle leads the singing, and the dancers and spectators constitute the chorus. The dancers usually move around the center of the court in a counterclockwise direction. Their steps and postures vary according to the type of dance being performed. The Jenvalo, for example, is danced with a bent back, hands touching the knees. In the Zépaule dance the dancers are erect, and most of the movements are made with the shoulders. In the Pétro (the Don Pedro described by Saint-Méry) there is a constant, almost agitated movement of the feet. The songs accompanying these cult dances, while presented in African style, may have hybrid or even French melodies, though in the main they are more African than European. The over-all context of the cult dances, as well as most of the secular ones, is West African, with constant interplay between the singers, dancers, and drummers. Sometime the dancers "drive" the drummers, sometimes the drummers "drive" the dancers. Certain beats of the drum are signals for special movements and postures. On hearing special beats or rolls, the dancers may leap vertically into the air, or perform a *laillé* (a swirling motion that causes the skirts to flare out), or a *djaillé* (excitement motions). Increased tension among the dancers may cause the drummers to shift the beat, or to increase tempo. The chorus and leader sing responsively, their parts overlapping in traditional African style. The shoulder movements, foot movements, the way the arms are carried, and the typical posture of feet flat on the ground, bent knees, and swayed back—all are of African derivation.

These postures and movements are broad and direct. There are few of the decorative and "fine" movements that one sees in the dances of Indonesia, Cambodia, and India. Where the Javanese lays stress on the pose of the hands and the delicate movements of the fingers, the Haitian dancer is concerned with the position of the arms and the motions of the shoulders. The Indonesian sense of poised balance or suspended movement is absent. In its place there is an attitude of strong frontal assault against natural forces such as gravity, or direct submission to those forces. There is almost always a feeling of solidity and stability in Haitian posture, and of a proximity between the body and the earth, but the total effect is dynamic. Indonesian dancing seems to express a comprehension of the unseen and the supernatural; Haitian dancing seems to express an intimate understanding of nature.

Dancing touches on virtually every aspect of life in Haiti. It plays a part in the supplication of loa, the placation of the dead, and the making of magic; in the consecration of a hounfor, the installation of a houngan, and the initiation of cult members; in planting, harvesting, and house-building. Catholic Church holidays, Nine Nights, baptisms, the election of a new president, and ordinary social gatherings—all are celebrated, in part, at least, by dancing.

Haitian dancing is participative rather than exhibitionistic. It is to join rather than to watch. There are some dances, however, which require special skills, and a few which are highly individualistic. Several types of dances are described elsewhere in this book. Verbal description cannot do justice to an art such as dancing, of course; but some brief sketches may help to suggest the differences between one Haitian dance and another.

In the Congo Mazonne, for example, men and women pair off and dance face to face, making contact occasionally but only briefly. The arms are stretched forward as though to embrace the partner around the waist, but the actual embrace never materializes. The partners dance sometimes as though they are unaware of each other and are simply part of a larger group; then they approach, move as mirrored reproductions, and separate. Loin movement is free, and there is a restrained sexual intensity, though direct sexual implications are not necessarily present. Sometimes the woman holds the hem of her skirt in her hands, while the man holds his jacket open toward his partner.

The Pétro dance is similar in many respects to other serious cult dances, but it is primarily a complicated and sometimes agitated foot dance. The second of the two drums beats "rest-two-three." On "two" the right foot pushes forward in a thrusting, sliding motion, and on "three" the left moves outward and the right moves in. The position is held on the "rest," though there is no visible pause, because of the speed of the dance. Shoulder movement is only of secondary importance in the Pétro, though the arms are constantly moving gracefuly to balance the foot movements. Women sometimes use a typical Congo pose, with the left hand on the hip and the right hand held poised in the air.

The Jenvalo, the supplication dance of the Dahomey rites, is quite different in both spirit and technique. The dancers, usually older rather than younger people, move in a generally counterclockwise direction around the sacred center post of the dance court. They dance with gracefully bent backs, their hands touching their knees. The shoulders and the upper part of the body move forward and back in a gentle, graceful, undulating movement. The dancers pirouette lightly from time to time, the women holding their long skirts out to the side to make a restrained *laillé*. They sometimes pause to perform a brief cross step with other dancers, but there is no pairing off. They are dancing as individuals—or, more accurately, as a group. There is occasional improvising, inventing, and performing of difficult maneuvers; but the individual dancer moves always with the others in a slowly revolving amorphous circle around the center post. The graceful bending and undulating of the upper body give even to strangers an impression of respectful supplication.

Near the town of Jérémie in southern Haiti some years ago I saw a performance of the Mousondi "battle-dance," an activity of the Congo "nation." The dance was performed by six men, several of them stripped to the waist, the others wearing the traditional blue denim peasant jackets. The leader of the dancers was a bearded man about fifty years old, lean and athletic. On his legs he wore anklets made of seed pods and beer-bottle caps which rattled rhythmically as he moved. On a string around his neck he wore a wooden whistle, which he blew from time to time to accent the beat of the drums and to give signals.

The dancing took place around a bonfire. The music was provided by three musicians, two playing Congo drums and the third beating hard-wood sticks against a board. Each of the dancers carried a stick about thirty inches long. They moved first clockwise, then counterclockwise, then half of them moved in one direction and half in the other, weaving in and out, holding their sticks like sabers. On a signal given by the older man, they leaped into the air and came together in mock combat. First one would strike and the other would parry, then the second would strike and the first would parry, always in time to the beating Congo drums. On another signal all six dancers leaped into the air vertically, twisting into a full turn each time, landing in position to strike and parry.

Spectators standing around the dancers clapped their hands and sang:

> Mousondi na fai la guè!
> Éya éya éya!
> Nous c'est nanchon la guè!
> Ou pas tendé canon'm tiré?

> Mousondi, we will make war!
> *Éya éya éya!*
> We are a nation of war!
> Don't you hear my cannon shooting?

When the dancers and drummers seemed fatigued, they were offered rum to drink. The dancers drank without breaking step or interrupting the battle. The bearded man held the lip of his glass between his teeth, and without using his hands to steady it, tipped his head back and let the rum run into his mouth, all the while stamping his feet and leaping with the others.

I was told later that the Mousondi was from the north, and that the dancers were recent arrivals from Port-de-Paix. But some of the older people declared that in former times the dance was known in the south by the name Calinda.

The Calinda dance, like the Vodoun, the Pétro, and several others, is mentioned frequently in the old literature on Haiti, Trinidad, Martinique, and Guadaloupe. It has been described variously as a funeral dance, an exhibitionistic sexual display, and a stick dance. It was reported by Saint-Méry as a dance in which men and women paired off. Early in the eighteenth century, Père Labat described it as a line dance, with the women on one side and the men on the other. Lafcadio Hearn saw it as a stick dance. And the word Calinda appears sometimes in songs of the Vodoun cult. The name may have lost specific meaning early in the life of the colonies; but it is more likely that early chroniclers used the term inexactly to refer to a multitude of different dances. In Haiti, identification of the Calinda has been further confused by the existence of the Calinda secret society, which had special dances of its own, all called Calinda.

Although confusions and contradictions exist, the testimony of older Haitians is that the Calinda was a stick dance, known also by the name

Mousondi. In present-day Trinidad there is a Calinda dance which closely resembles the Mousondi; Puerto Rico has its Bomba Calindán; and under another name the "battle dance" survives among Negro communities in Surinam. The counterpart of the Calinda in Brazil is the Capoeira, for which musical accompaniment is provided by African-style "belly harps" (musical bows with gourd resonators) called *berimbau*. The tradition lingers on in Haiti in modern mock prize-fighting dances sometimes performed in Rara season.

The stick dance (*Battonie*) of the Haitian carnival season, mentioned in chapter 8, is of more than passing interest for the reason that almost identical dances have been reported from some areas of West Africa. In the Haitian dance (see fig. 73) the baton wielders, all males, for unexplained reasons are attired in women's clothing. A photograph made in 1958 of a baton dance among the Ewe people of Togoland depicts a scene scarcely distinguishable from a Haitian Rara performance, and it is noteworthy that its all-male cast is in women's dress.[7]

In addition, there remain a number of fragments of dances of the past. In religious ritual, on rare occasions, one may see animal dances in which the performers mimic animal movements, holding in their hands long sticks to simulate front legs. This type of dance has been reported frequently in West Africa, particularly in connection with totemic rituals.

There is a dance in the Arada ritual in which the loa Legba is invoked. A hounsi—usually a man—comes onto the dance court wearing a kind of cane-crutch called the *baton* Legba, or Legba stick. The baton is about the length of a cane, with a long, grotesquely twisted "handle" that fits under the crotch of the legs. The dancer wraps one leg around the stick and walks as though he has only one foot. In the dance, he spins around on the stick, leaps, and pirouettes. Identification of the stick as well as the dance with Legba, and its position between the legs, seem clearly to relate it to the phallic sticks used in dances for Legba in Dahomey.

Among the secular exhibitionistic dances of Haiti, there is one in which a man stands on his head and goes through erotic motions to the accompaniment of drums.

In addition to the almost countless dances of African origin or inspiration, there is the ever-popular Meringue, a European-type social dance which is known in many forms. Haitian connoisseurs of this dance believe there are three main forms of the Meringue: the "Meringue de Concert," in which the rhythm is slow and "caressing"; the "dance Meringue," in which the rhythm is quasi-fast and very gay; and the "Meringue Coundjaille," in which the rhythm is very fast. The last form is heard most often during carnival days. In all variations of the Meringue, the dance is performed by couples in ballroom style. Among the elite, it is restrained. Elsewhere it is much more animated, with free and uninhibited pelvic motions similar to those seen at the Saturday night *bamboche*. Although the Haitian regards his Meringue as a national popular dance, Spanish-type music has infiltrated heavily from the Dominican Republic, Cuba, and other islands of the West Indies. Thousands of Haitians returning from contract labor in Cuba have brought with them not only Cuban songs and rhythms but Cuban instruments as well. It has not been a one-way affair, however, for the Arada cults of eastern Cuba have been built substantially around immigrants from Haiti, and in the Cuban mountains you may hear music and see dances of Afro-Haitian origin.

Still other kinds of dances are to be found in remote villages of Haiti—the old folk dances of Europe. The villagers still know and perform the waltz, the polka, the mazurka and the quadrille, usually to the accompaniment of violins or guitars, or possibly an accordion.

But the influences are not all ancient ones. Jazz has infiltrated the Meringue. And some years ago a small boy asked me with some concern whether I had taken proper account of a very important dance called *le black bottom*.

Following is a list of dances known to Haitians today. Some of them are found throughout Haiti, some are known only regionally, and a few are on the verge of extinction.

Dances Connected with Vodoun Ritual

Arada, or *Rada:* One of the main dances of the Vodoun service, named after the Dahomean city and cult center, Allada.

Anago, or *Nago:* Named after the Nagos, a branch of the Yoruba tribe of Nigeria. For deities of Nago origin.

Mahi: Named after the Mahi people of Dahomey.

Déréal: A Mahi dance of northern Haiti.

Parigale: Another Mahi type of dance. Possibly from *pas régal* (royal step).

Jenvalo, or *Yenvalo:* A supplication dance, variously called Jenvalo Doba (*dos bas,* low back), Jenvalo Jénon (*genoux,* knees), and Dobado.

Zépaule: A supplication dance in which the movements are made primarily by the shoulders (*les épaules*). It is sometimes called Jenvalo Zépaule or Jenvalo Débout (standing Jenvalo).

Flavovodoun: Another type of shoulder dance known in the north.

Banda, or *Chica:* A gay and sometimes ribald dance, said to be much favored by the loa Cousin Zaka and the loa Gèdé.

Mazonne Rada: The "Masonic" Rada dance; often danced for the loa Gèdé.

Carabienne or *Crabienne:* A rest dance, interspersed into long-drawn-out Arada rites to break the tension. The name appears to have come from the word "Caribbean."

Magie: A dance accompanying a magic-making ritual.

Pouin: A dance accompanying the making of a pouin.

Calebasse: A dance accompanying the calabash ritual, for the dead.

Dahomé: One of the principal dances of the Vodoun group, named after Dahomey.

Bambocha: Another rest dance, from northern Haiti. Carried over into secular dancing, it has become the commonplace Bomboche.

Bouleverse: From northern Haiti.

Manuba, or *Maniba:* A dance associated with Dahomey rites, accompanied by percussion music played on small drums hung around the neck.

Assotor: A dance accompanying rites for the assotor drum.

DANCES CONNECTED WITH CONGO AND PÉTRO RITUAL

Pétro, or *Dan Pétro:* The principal dance of the Pétro cult.

Kitta Mouillé: The "Wet Kitta," danced for the Simbi family of loa, patrons of rain and the spring. Sometimes called Danse Simbi. On rare occasions the Kitta Mouillé is accepted as Vodoun rather than Pétro.

Kitta Chêche, or *Sêche:* The "Dry Kitta," danced for loa of the Kitta group other than the patrons of the spring. Sometimes identified with Vodoun rites rather than with the Pétro.

Bumba, or *Limba:* Named after Congo tribes.

Moundongue: A dance for the loa Moundongue. Named after a tribe in the northern Congo.

Salongo, or *Kinan:* From southwestern Haiti. Salongo is the name of a tribe in Angola.

Bambarra: Named after the Bambarras of northwestern Africa.

Congo Loangue, or *Congo Franc:* Named after Loango in the Congo.

Congo Mazonne: The "Masonic" Congo dance, known also as Congo Larose and Congo Créole. Some informants believe the dance originated in a hounfor called Société La Rose, from which it derives one of its names.

Pastorel: A Congo rest dance.

Mousondi: A battle dance.

Moutchêtché: A dance of northern Haiti for paying a debt to a loa.

Mayoyo: This dance is nearly extinct.

Mazonne Pétro: The "Masonic" dance of the Pétro rites.

DANCES ON THE PERIPHERY OF THE VODOUN GROUP

Ibo: Named after the Ibo people of Nigeria and used in rites for the Ibo family of loa.

Kanga or *Capläou:* Named after West African tribes.

DANCES OF THE JUBA GROUP

Juba, or *Martinique:* Danced on the occasion of Last Prayers, when the spirit of a newly deceased person has been sent on its way. It is also danced on various coumbite occasions, and sometimes at the special request of a loa or an ancestor.

Baboule, or *Bamboula:* Danced on the occasion of building a new house.
Mascort: Danced by a société after communal work on the land of one of its members.
Ti Coumba: Another société work dance, sometimes closely related to Vodoun ritual. Known in Brazil as Macumba.
Koune, or *Coundjaille:* A dance connected with communal work celebrations.[8]

Rara and Carnival Dances

Rara, also called *Chariopié, Lwalwadi,* and *Vaccine:* The perambulating dances of the Rara festival.
Mascaron, or *Cocoyé:* Danced for the Mardi Gras.
Paillette: Any carnival dance in costume.
Batonnie: A carnival stick dance with West African precedents.
Trèsé Riban: The carnival Maypole dance.
Congo Paillette: The "Straw Congo," or "Costume Congo," the carnival dance of the *société* Congo. It is also known as Ciyé and Congo Mardi Gras.
Rabordage: A Mardi Gras perambulating dance.
Chaluska: A Mardi Gras dance in which the participants are dressed as nineteenth-century generals. Comic mimicry. Also referred to as Charles Oscar.
Zizipan
Roboto
Mayousse

Other Secular and Miscellaneous Dances

Zesse: A *gage* dance of northern Haiti.
Calinda: A mock battle dance. Also a dance of the Calinda "secret society."
Ka: A dance which takes its name from the *ka,* a secular drum.
Bèlè, or *Belair*
Mangouline
Ti Crip: This is regarded by some informants as one of the Pétro dances.
Malfini: "The Hawk," a dance of northern Haiti.
Pinyique: A simple "good time" dance.
Bambilé: A simple "good time" dance.
Bamboche: A "good time" dance. The term is often used to designate any social dance. As a verb, *bamboché* means "to dance" or "to have a good time."

Secular Dances of European Type

Meringue: There are three main types of Meringue—the drawing-room Meringue, the ordinary "ballroom" Meringue, and the Meringue Coundjaille (which is fast and agitated). A development of the last decade or so is the jazz Meringue.
Ti Bobine: This is a sort of square dance, though it is sometimes danced in Meringue style.
Ménwat, or *Mènwat:* The minuet.
Polka
Waltz
Quadrille
Mazurka
Contradanse

12. Songs of Complaint, Recrimination, and Gossip

The use of the song as a weapon of social criticism is an ancient and honored tradition in Haitian life. In West Africa it is common for villagers to air their complaints against, or their praise of, their neighbors, their chiefs, and the Europeans with whom they have dealings, by means of specially composed songs. Usually an ordinary offended person will not approach an official of prestige and denounce him straightforwardly. Such behavior might involve risks, or even violate social decorum. But an acceptable and effective way to make such criticism is through singing. It carries with it the sanction of propriety, custom, and good manners. The songs of criticism seek to air situations that otherwise might remain local or private affairs, and to set in motion public opinion. Thus there are songs which complain about a person's behavior, others that protest against injuries, and still others that expose an individual to ridicule. Often the themes are expressed indirectly by parable, sometimes directly. Among the Negro cultures of America the song of social criticism remains a vital and effective instrument for alleviating a sense of hurt and bringing offending persons before the bar of public opinion. It is found throughout the New World wherever Negroes have settled, from Brazil to the West Indies and the United States. In Surinam there is a formalized presentation of protest and derision songs called *lobi singi,* the function of which is to publicly embarrass and shame someone who has offended.[1] In the United States the song of criticism and complaint has survived strongly in the Negro work songs and blues, and has even infiltrated by this route into the popular "white" music of the country. Countless blues pieces complain of personal mistreatment by husbands, wives, and sweethearts; others, of hardships and injustice. Still others hold up the spotlight of ridicule. The subjects vary from sexual faithlessness to the rigors of prison.

In Haiti this tradition has remained vital and powerful. A work gang may sing that it is being driven too hard, or that it is underpaid. A president may be disparaged, a neighbor who has violated a social propriety may be ridiculed, and one who has committed an indiscretion may be exposed. Such affairs are the property of the community. They are gay or grim editorials on people and institutions. There is no special ceremonial occasion, as in Surinam, when criticism may be voiced. It can happen almost anywhere, at almost any time. Songs of ridicule or complaint may be heard at the ordinary "good time" secular dance, in the Rara festivities, or even in the middle of a Vodoun religious service. If the coumbites working in the fields are not singing songs of praise, the chances are they are singing songs of criticism. Even a lone worker may sing such songs, with the expectation that they will be heard and passed on. One woman I know, who had been abused in the market place of Port-au-Prince, composed a song of recrimination which she sang loudly all along the road to Kenskoff, some twenty miles away.

Even though the songs may be quite personal, referring to situations that affect only an individual or a small group of people, once they are performed in public they are community property. They survive or fade away according to the appeal they have for others. A song which catches on may outlive its protagonists by many decades. Such a song does not lose its moral point, if it has one, or its satirical punch. It can be revived for use on appropriate occasions—usually without change, sometimes with slight modification to give it direct and timely significance.

One of the recurrent themes of protest has to do with faithlessness of friends. This song, couched in bitter metaphor, declares that the only friends to be trusted are those who are not present:

> Zamis près moin quitté ma zamis loin moin yo!
> Zamis près moin quitté ma zamis loin moin!
> Zamis loin moin c'est la'gent sèré!
> Zamis près moin c'est couteau débord, quitté ma zamis loin moin! [Ex. 94]

> Friends close to me, go far away from me, friends!
> Friends close to me, go far away from me, friends!
> Friends far away from me are saved money!
> Friends close to me are a two-edged knife, go far away from me, friends!

A variant of this theme goes:

> Zami cila c'est pas zami pou' moin!
> Zami cila c'est pas zami pou' moin trahison!
> Moin passé caille a li li ba moin chaise moin chita!
> L'al pa'lé mal a moin!

That friend there, he is not a friend for me!
That friend there, he is not a friend for me, treason!
I pass his house, he gives me a chair to sit in!
He goes around speaking bad words about me!

Or again, you may hear:

Nèg' nwè, con ça ou yé, ago-é!
Nèg' nwè, con ça ou yé!
Y'ap mangé avé ou!
Y'ap bwè avé ou!
Y'ap coupé lavie ou débor! [Ex. 95]

Black man, like this you are, *ago-é!*
Black man, like this you are!
He will eat with you,
He will drink with you,
He will cut the life out of you!

A man regards his child's godfather as his closest friend outside the family circle. Should either of the two friends fail to fulfill the high standard of behavior demanded by their tie, the other may express disappointment and recrimination, as in this song:

Compè à moin compè ou malhonnête!
Ou malhonnête compè compè à moin compè ou malhonnête!
Premier pitit moin fai'm ba ou batisé!
Malheur rivé'm nan hounfor ou pas vini wè moin!

My comrade, comrade, you are dishonest!
You are dishonest comrade, my comrade, comrade, you are dishonest!
I gave you my first child to baptize!
When misfortune comes to me in the hounfor, you do not come to see me!

Sometimes even the most domestic of grievances are aired in public through means of song:

Isamise oh!
Ste Hélène oh!
Isamise oh!
Ste Hélène oh!
Trois pairs souflettes mari'm ba moin!
Maladie-à prend moin! [Ex. 96]

Isamise, oh!
St. Hélène, oh!
Isamise, oh!
St. Hélène, oh!
Three pairs of slaps my husband gave me!
This misfortune has taken me!

A protest theme that runs through many a song stems from the feeling of having been slighted or improperly received in the house of another person. The following song airs the complaint of a person who feels he has been treated shabbily. Metaphorically, he says he is used to eating from an earthern bowl but has been served food in a gourd dish, from which only the poorest of people eat.

> Ma 'bitué mangé nan bolle,
> M'pap mangé nan couis ciyé! [Ex. 97]
>
> I'm accustomed to eating from a bowl;
> I'm not going to eat from a cut gourd!

Or again, there is the story of the unwelcome voyager, a person who travels all the way from Jérémie, far out on the southern peninsula, to the distant town of Arcahaye, only to find that he is not wanted there:

> Moin sort' Jérémie!   I come from Jérémie!
> Moin passé Aux Cayes!   I pass through Aux Cayes!
> M'rivé L'Arcahaye, mes amis! I arrive in Arcahaye, my friends!
> C'est moin même yo pas vlé wè yà, It is me they don't wish to see here,
> Moin ya wè!   It is me they see!
> C'est moin même yo pas vlé wè yà, It is me they don't wish to see here,
> Moin ya wè oh!   It is me they see, oh!
> C'est moin même yo pas vlé wè yà, It is me they don't wish to see here,
> Moin ya wè oh!   It is me they see, oh!

A man complains sometimes of the work that has been foisted upon him by an employer, or by a neighbor with whom he exchanges labor:

> M'pas mulette oh moin pas mulette oh!
> Habitant prend moin po'té café!
>
> I'm not a mule, oh, I'm not a mule, oh!
> The farmer takes me to carry coffee!

Even the officials of the hounfor may be publicly reproached in song for acts of injustice. In the following example the houngénicon, the Vodoun priest's assistant, is taken to task. The song probably was first heard in the course of a ceremony at which the houngénicon was present:

> Daromain y wa, houngénicon oh!
> Daromain y wa, 'génicon é!
> Daromain y wa, yo fai mangé raison moin!
> Lè moin vlé pa'lé ou pas vlé moin pa'lé!
> Lè moin vlé chanté ou pas vlé moin chanté là!
> Daromain y wa, yo fai mangé raison moin! [Ex. 98]
>
> Dahomey *y wa*,* houngénicon, oh!
> Dahomey *y wa*, houngénicon, é!
> Dahomey *y wa*, they do me wrong!

---

* The word Dahomey is frequently used as an exclamation.

When I want to talk you do not want me to talk!
When I want to sing you do not want me to sing!
Dahomey *y wa*, they do me wrong! *

Another note of criticism within the hounfor concerns a person who has been putting on airs of importance. The song states that he (or she) in reality has not even qualified for the lowest order within the cult, even though he behaves as though he were the cult chief:

Ou poco hounsi oh!	You are not yet a hounsi, oh!
Ou dit'm ou c'est houngan!	You tell me you are a houngan!
Ou poco hounsi!	You are not yet a hounsi!
Ou dit'm ou c'est houngan c'est ça!	You tell me you are a houngan, it is so!
Oh Paille à Terre!	Oh, Straw on Earth! †
Poussé allé!	Push and go!
Oh Allada malade oh! [Ex. 99]	Oh, Allada is sick, oh! ‡

Poverty is so normal in Haitian life that a man who accumulates wealth in any form becomes conspicuous. Ordinarily he does not welcome this conspicuousness. It makes him a target of gossip and rumors, and of those who might wish to collect debts from him, borrow money, or obtain other favors. He becomes a *gros nèg'*, and finds himself increasingly cut off from the community of ordinary, poor people. Needless to say, Haitians, like other people, dream of striking it rich. Wherever poverty has been acute, whether in Europe, Asia, or America, the folklore is full of tales of finding great treasures. Haiti is no exception. Many Haitian folk tales and folk songs deal with this theme, particularly with obtaining wealth by magical or supernatural means. Sometimes riches are obtained through *engagements,* unholy compacts with devils or demons. In some stories loa facilitate the discovery of treasure, in others a powerful bocor accomplishes it through magical practices. If a man suddenly becomes well-to-do, therefore, rumors may spread in regard to how he came by his wealth. If he is suspected of dealings with devils or with a powerful bocor, his apparent success in his venture makes him a neighbor to be feared. To avoid incurring envy and hostility, people tend to play down their financial successes and pretend they have nothing in life but the clothes they wear, their houses, and their gardens. Spreading word that a poor man has hidden money is regarded as a mean and reprehensible act. Numerous folk songs protest against this injustice:

Désastre tombé nans lacour-wà!
Si m'apé travaille là nans cour-wà,

---

* Literally: They eat my rights.
† An exclamation, the name of a certain ouanga.
‡ Allada, the name of a town in Dahomey, used in the sense of "people of Dahomey." The line means, "Things are in a bad state of affairs."

Yo dit'm gainyain largent séré, oh vrai!
Yo mitté conplotaille oh là sou dos moin!
Oh yo mitté conplotaille oh là sou dos moin!
Fai'm payé largent, évo!
Mandé Bondieu pou' nou wè li, so! [Ex. 100]

Disaster descends on my yard!
If I work in the yard there
They say I have hidden money, in truth!
They plot behind my back!
Oh, they plot behind my back!
Make me pay money, *évo!*
I ask God to see it.

Another theme that runs deeply through Haitian life is the need for a mother. In a society where plaçage is normal and where fathers frequently are transient, the mother has been the stabilizing factor in family life. A *placée* family might see the father only at certain times of the year. If he is a farmer, it will usually be when he comes to work his gardens; then he will move on to other gardens and possibly to another family elsewhere. The loss of a mother, under these conditions, is felt very deeply. Many Haitian songs, in various moods, emphasize the role of the mother in the house. Some of them are gay, like this one, with an undercurrent of sadness:

Oh dèpis manman moin fai moin,	Oh, since my mother made me,
M'pas jamais wè manman moin!	I've never seen my mother!
Waille waille waille waille!	*Waille waille waille waille!* *
Waille waille waille waille!	*Waille waille waille waille!*
M'pas conné manman moin!	I do not know my mother!
Zandolite fai'm!	A *zandolite* made me!
Mabouya fai'm!	A *mabouya* made me!
Zandolite fai'm!	A *zandolite* made me!
Mabouya fai'm! [Ex. 171]	A *mabouya* made me!

The *zandolite* and *mabouya* to which the song refers are small lizards which constantly skitter about on the rocks and in the trees, as though they have no home. The metaphor is clear.

One more song on this subject stresses the importance of having a mother as compared, say, to an unreliable man:

Ma crié,
Oh qua'm perdit manman moin ma rélé!
Ma rélé,
Oh qua'm perdit manman moin crié!
Qua'm perd' un garçon moin join' l'aut' oh!

---

* Exclamation.

Qua'm perd' un garçon moin join' l'aut' oh!
Ma rélé,
Oh qua'm perdit manman moin ma crié! [Ex. 102]

I cried,
Oh, when I lost my mother I cried!
I cried,
Oh, when I lost my mother I cried!
When I lost a man I found another, oh!
When I lost a man I found another, oh!
I cried,
Oh, when I lost my mother I cried!

Protest or complaint songs are sometimes directed against no one in particular but simply call the attention of listeners to the singer's misfortunes. In many such songs the president or one of the deities is mentioned by name. The singer in this way implicitly places responsibility for help. In the following song, one complains of hunger, another theme that runs throughout Haitian folklore and Haitian life.

Rwo! President qui voyé rélé'm!
Moin pas bwè moin pas mangé!
M'pas bwè moin pas mangé!
Oh m'pas bwè moin pas mangé!
President qui voyé rélé'm rwo!
M'pas bwè moin pas mangé! [Ex. 103]

Rwo! * The President sends for me!
I haven't drunk, I haven't eaten!
I haven't drunk, I haven't eaten!
Oh, I haven't drunk, I haven't eaten!
The President sends for me, *rwo!*
I haven't drunk, I haven't eaten!

Here the loa Ogoun Balindjo is called upon to take note of prying, insincere people who come to a person's house, observe what is going on, and go away to gossip:

Ogoun Balindjo
Yo vini ga'dé'm
Pou' y'allé valé oh!
Ogoun Balindjo
Li yé wè bouche pé oh!
Ogoun Balindjo
Pas wè yo vini ga'dé moin? [Ex. 104]

Ogoun Balindjo
They come to look at me

---

* An exclamation.

To go away and talk, oh!
Ogoun Balindjo
The eyes see, the mouth is closed, oh! *
Ogoun Balindjo
Don't you see they come to look at me?

Or again, the loa Ogoun and Loko Attiso are invoked to witness a person's misery, though in this song the cause is not explained:

Ogoun oh ga'dé misè!
Papa Ogoun ou wa ga'dé misè!
Ga'dé misè oh Lok' Attiso ga'dé misè là yé! [Ex. 105]

Ogoun, oh, look at my misery!
Papa Ogoun, you will look at my misery!
Look at my misery, oh, Loko Attiso, look at my misery here!

The impulse to criticism most often stems from personal injuries, but on occasion songs are used as a community affair to exert social pressures on an errant member of the neighborhood:

Frè' Jean-Pierre wa quitté bwè tafia!
Frè' Jean-Pierre ti moune yo touné!

Brother Jean-Pierre, stop drinking tafia! †
Brother Jean-Pierre, the little children are naked!

Although discussions of neighbors' affairs tend to have this moral tone, a vast number of songs are pure gossip and are sung for their ribald or wry humor, as the case may be. In some the objects of ridicule are named; in others the allusions are indirect, so that only those who are familiar with the situation will know the people concerned. Open quarreling often provides amusement and substance for satire. The community can sense petulance, stupidity, and stubbornness through a confusion of charges and countercharges, and is quick to burlesque them. Thus there are public pressures against petty and needless disturbances. The following song refers to a dispute over ownership of an unnamed article.

Moin dit c'est bagaille grand moune! Ciyé!
C'est bagaille grand moune! Ciyé!
Moin dit c'est zaffai grand moune! Ciyé!
C'est bagaille grand moune! Ciyé!
Moin dit n'ap chaché li! Ciyé!
N'ap prend li! Ciyé!
Moin dit c'est bagaille grand moune! Ciyé!
C'est bagaille grand moune! Ciyé! [Ex. 106]

* That is to say, the eyes should see and the mouth should be closed.
† An alcoholic drink.

I say it belongs to the old man! *Ciyé!* *
It's the old man's thing! *Ciyé!*
I say it's the old man's affair! *Ciyé!*
It's the old man's thing! *Ciyé!*
I say I'll look for it! *Ciyé!*
I'm going to take it! *Ciyé!*
I say it belongs to the old man, *Ciyé!*
It's the old man's thing, *Ciyé!*

Another burlesque of a quarrel concerns a mother who has sent her daughter down to the river to do the washing. Some question arises as to whether the girl went down to the river at all, or whether she went elsewhere. There is implicit suggestion that the girl may have been at a rendezvous. The mother and the girl argue back and forth:

Moin voyé Lanmeci nan dleau,	I sent Lanmeci to the water,
Li pas allé!	She didn't go!
Moin voyé Lanmeci nan dleau,	I sent Lanmeci to the water,
Li pas allé!	She didn't go!
Moin voyé Lanmeci nan dleau,	I sent Lanmeci to the water,
Li pas allé!	She didn't go!
Moin voyé Lanmeci nan dleau,	I sent Lanmeci to the water,
Li pas allé!	She didn't go!
Lanmeci coté ou té yé?	Lanmeci, where are you?
Là'm té yé!	I was there!
Là'm té yé!	I was there!
Là'm té yé!	I was there!
Là'm té yé!	I was there!
Là'm! [Ex. 107]	There!

Most of the scandal songs are fragmentary and tangent, though clear in implication, like this one:

C'est pas faute moin!
C'est pas faute moin!
C'est pas faute moin!
C'est pas faute moin!
C'est pas faute moin manman!
C'est pas faute moin!
Gainyain moune t'ap marché dèyè bien!
Rwo woyo!
Gainyain moune t'ap marché dèyè bien!
Gainyain moune nan lacour à,
Prend nouvelle oh, so! [Ex. 108]

It wasn't my fault!
It wasn't my fault!
It wasn't my fault!

---

* Used as an exclamation.

It wasn't my fault!
It wasn't my fault mother!
It wasn't my fault!
There was a man looking for a bargain!
Rwo woyo! *
There was a man looking for a bargain!
There was a man in the yard,
Carry the news, oh, *sol* †

Another scandal song, spiced with ridicule, refers tangently to a specific situation and points a moral:

Coulié li yé waille-o! Coulié li yé waille-o!
Coulié li yé waille-o! Coulié li yé waille-o!
Si ou prend yun femme pas vlé lavé pied
Ou pas besoin mandé qui gen li yé! [Ex. 109]

Now she is there, *waille-o!* Now she is there, *waille-o!* ‡
Now she is there, *waille-o!* Now she is there, *waille-o!*
If you take a woman who doesn't want to wash her feet
You don't have to ask what kind she is!

The practice of washing one's feet before an intimacy enters into numerous gossip songs. In the following one, the woman asks her friend Pierre for water to wash with so that she may take advantage of Joseph's absence in the city:

Ba moin dleau nèg' moin pou' moin lavé pied moin!
Mandé dleau mon chè' Pierre pou' moin lavé pied moin!
Mandé dleau pou' moin lavé pied moin!
Joseph danger pas là, l'allé laville oh!
Joseph danger pas là, l'allé laville oh!

Give me water, my fellow, to wash my feet!
I ask for water, my dear Pierre, to wash my feet!
I ask for water to wash my feet!
Joseph who is dangerous is not here, he has gone to the city!
Joseph who is dangerous is not here, he has gone to the city!

Another bit of gossip with perhaps a more graphic account of the woman's deceit tells what happens in Achélo's house when he isn't home:

Viré do' allé!
Oh viré do' allé!
Achélo viré do' allé!
Viré do' allé!
Oh viré do' allé!

---

* Exclamatory.
† Exclamatory.
‡ Exclamatory.

Achélo viré do' allé!
A la papa viré ga'çon entré nan chamb'!
A la papa viré ga'çon monté caban! [Ex. 110]

Turns his back and goes!
Oh, turns his back and goes!
Achélo turns his back and goes!
Turns his back and goes!
Oh, turns his back and goes!
Achélo turns his back and goes!
When papa turns, a man goes into his room!
When papa turns, a man climbs into his bed!

But a note of sympathy for Achélo creeps into the last stanza:

Viré do' allé!	Turns his back and goes!
Viré do' allé!	Turns his back and goes!
Achélo ou pas nan ronce oh!	Achélo, you are not in the joke, oh!

In the following song, a young man confesses to having despoiled a girl and blemished the family's reputation, but he tells the father and mother not to worry about it.

Bonjou' bonjou' Manman Soso,
Fille ou c'est perdu.
Bonjou' bonjou' Papa Soso,
Ti fille ou c'est perdu.
Pé, ma ba ou l'a'gent.

Good evening, good evening Mother Soso,
Your daughter is ruined.
Good evening, good evening Father Soso,
Your little daughter is ruined.
Don't say a word, I will pay you for it.

An elderly gentleman named Alman fails to come out of his adventure with the same self-assurance, and the community takes full note of the details:

Alman allé bambilé,	Alman went on a spree,
Alman allé bambilé,	Alman went on a spree,
Alman allé bambilé,	Alman went on a spree,
Li retou'né pied cassé!	He came home with a broken foot!
Pas pa'lé parole çila.	Don't say a word about it.
Si ou pa'lé parole çila	If you say anything about it
Gain yun grand moune	There is an old gentleman
Qui va facher!	Who will be angry!

13. Comments on the Mighty: Political Songs

The African-style song of social criticism has found no worthier subjects than the historic political figures of Haiti. There is no doubt that the African slaves used this art form to express their feelings toward the white masters as they had used it to comment upon the behavior of their own chiefs and fellow tribesmen. The worthy leaders were praised in song; the unworthy were castigated and their sins, failures, and social misdemeanors publicized in folk songs. By the beginning of the nineteenth century, slavery had come to an end in Haiti. The deep democratic sense of human dignity had outlasted the colonial masters and emerged tempered and sharp. The songs of criticism became not only comments upon political figures but campaign propaganda as well. They dwelt upon the accomplishments or faults of the candidates for political office. Friendly songs sought out every virtue, and invented others, in the man or woman being praised. Unfriendly songs lashed out and lacerated or poked biting fun at the subject, not even sparing his physical deformities.

Yet the political songs are more than statements of merit or fault. Cumulatively they are a kind of folk history of Haiti. No political aspirant ever went unsung by his peasant army, or unridiculed by his opponent's followers. The songs the people sang about their heroes and their enemies recall events and details that formal history has forgotten or ignored. The memory of the folk song is powerful and long. Some of the recollections go back more than a century.

History books tell us that in December, 1843, Major Charles Hérard aîné Rivière was elected to the office of the presidency, and that a new constitution was drawn up by the Constituent Assembly. The new constitution was an accomplishment of the liberal and democratic forces of the nation. It guaranteed certain civil rights to the people. It provided that judges be elected instead of appointed, abolished life terms for presidents, and emphatically declared the army to be within and under the law.

The new President, finding his office without the prerogatives he had expected it to have, openly complained of the restraints imposed on him by the new constitution. He broke campaign promises he had made to the peasants in the south and stirred up antagonisms on every side. Finally, while he was on a military expedition in the Spanish part of the island, revolution broke out at home. His army was beaten by the Dominicans, too, which completely shattered his morale. He fled by ship to Jamaica, the traditional refuge of outgoing Haitian presidents. In memory of his administration the peasants sang:

> Rivière Président gainyain zyeux vairon!
> Li dit l'ap piyé l'armé Bélanton!
> Piyé lévé trésor!
> Piyé lévé trésor!
> Piyé lévé trésor!
> Yo voyé Lambam depuis Lowinsor!

> La Constitution cé trouva Colombe
> Quand yo voit pays soufri trop misère!
> Li dit yo fait comme Henry!
> Li dit yo fait comme Henry!
> Li dit yo fait comme Henry!
> Pou' fai sang coulé pou' rangé pays!

> Colonel Déro soldat Diplaro
> Marché fanfaron comme un grand fantin!
> Li cré qui li té roi!
> Li cré qui li té roi!
> Li cré qui li té roi!
> 'Pagnol chasse li, li couri con chien qui prend frai charogne!

> President Rivière was cross-eyed!
> He said that he was going to pillage Belanton's army!
> Loot for treasure!
> Loot for treasure!
> Loot for treasure!
> They sent everyone from Lowinsor to Lambam!

> The Constitution was founded by Columbus
> When the country suffered too much misery!
> He said he would do like Henry [Christophe]!
> He said he would do like Henry!
> He said he would do like Henry!
> Make blood run to poison the countryside!

From Colonel Déro to Private Diplaro,
They marched with fanfare, a great army of foot soldiers!
He thought that he was king!
He thought that he was king!
He thought that he was king!
The Spaniards chased him, he ran like a dog after fresh carrion!

Forty-five years later, in 1888, there was a big political rally in Port-au-Prince. The two presidential candidates were General Séide Télémaque and Déus Légitime. Their supporters clashed near the palace, and Télémaque was killed in an exchange of gunfire. Légitime naturally was accused of having murdered his rival, though his supporters would not believe that he had committed such a crime. Evidence for a trial was entirely lacking, and Déus Légitime became president. But feeling ran high, and the followers of Télémaque began to sing:

Écoutez chers amis l'histoire de Légitime!
Assassin de Séide, et lui est président!
Écoutez bien l'histoire, le gens du nord marchaient
Sur Port-au-Prince un fois pou' vengé la mort de Séide!
Allez au diable, bandit Déus!
Échappez vous, ingrat Déus!
Si vous perdre le temps, Déus,
Florvil vous feura fusillé!

Listen my friends to the story of Légitime!
Assassin of Séide, and he is President!
Listen well to the story, the people of the north will march
On Port-au-Prince one day to avenge the death of Séide!
Go to the devil, bandit Déus!
Escape, ingrate Déus!
If you lose time, Déus,
Florvil will have you shot!

Légitime had this possibility clearly in his mind. And the next year, when Florvil Gélin Hippolyte marched from the north with an army of *cacos* (peasant troops who hired out to political aspirants), Légitime hurriedly boarded a steamer in the harbor and sailed for Jamaica. Séide Télémaque was considered avenged, as the army bugles still bear witness. For now when the bugle plays reveille it is supposed to be saying:

Séide Télémaque, Légitime has fled!
Séide Télémaque, Légitime has fled!

The new President, Florvil Hippolyte, died in office in 1896. J. N. Leger, a Haitian historian, tells soberly of Hippolyte's end in the following words.

For some time the President, who was sixty-nine years old, had not been in good health, and disregarding the friendly warning of those who were interested in his welfare he refused to give up his hard work and to take the rest of which he was in sore need. Against the advice of his doctor he decided to undertake a long journey to Jacmel. He started on the 24th of March, 1896, at three o'clock in the morning, but before he even had time to leave Port-au-Prince, he fell from his horse dead in a fit of apoplexy, at a short distance from the executive mansion.[1]

The legend of Hippolyte's death passed on in song is not nearly so dispassionate. It is told that Hippolyte was going out on a drastic punitive trip to Jacmel, where there were rumblings of political opposition and revolution. Among other things, the President was going to seize the powerful Vodoun priest Mérisier, regarded as a powerful force in the opposition. Hippolyte also had sworn to reduce Jacmel to ashes and wipe out the entire population except one male and one female to repopulate the land. As he prepared to leave on his mission, his wife and his son stood by the door to see him off.

Li lévé Mardi bon matin,
Li fai sélé cheval à li.
En montant sa cheval li,
Panama li sorti tombé.

He arose early on Tuesday morning,
He saddled his horse.
As he climbed on his horse,
His hat came off and fell.

L'Hérison rélé "Papa,"
Li dit'l, "Papa à moin,
Panama ou sorti tombé,
Cé déjà youn mauvais signal."

L'Hérison * called out, "Papa!"
He said to him, "Father,
Your hat has come off and fallen.
That is already a bad omen."

Li répond ni, "Pitit à moin,
Moin déjà met' l'armée déhors,
L'armée moin déjà nan portaille.
Y faudra que moin parti."

He replied to him, "My child,
I have already sent the army ahead,
My army is already at the city gate,
I have to go."

Arrivé sou Pont Gentil,
Li tombé sans connaisance.
Yo voyé rélé Doctor Jules,
"Vin sauver Florvil Gélin!"

Arrived at Pont Gentil,
He fell unconscious.
They sent for Dr. Jules,
"Come to save Florvil Gélin."

Doctor Jules tomba à genoux.
Li rélé Manman Ste Anne,
Li rélé St. Augustin,
"Vine sauver Florvil Gélin!"

Dr. Jules fell on his knees.
He called Mother St. Anne,
He called St. Augustin,
"Come to save Florvil Gélin!"

Ste Anne dit, " 'i faut mouri."
St. Augustin 'dit, " 'i faut mouri."
Li rélé St. Jacques Majeur
"Vine sauver Florvil Gélin!"

St. Anne said, "He has to die."
St. Augustin said, "He has to die."
He called St. Jacques Majeur,
"Come to save Florvil Gélin."

---

* Hippolyte's son.

Mérisier rété Jacmel,	Mérisier waited at Jacmel.
Li souqué baksor à li.	He shook his sacred rattle.
Li conné ça qui gainyain.	He knew what was going on.
Tout ti trou déjà bouché!	All the small holes were filled.*

Victoire dit con ça,	Victoire said
Quand Florvil ta va mourit	When Florvil dies
Li tap fai youn belle soirée	She will hold a beautiful party
Avec tout ti gens la yo.	With all the young people.

CHORUS	CHORUS
En allé Dodo!	We are going to dance! †
En allé Dodo!	We are going to dance!
En allé ce soir	We are going this evening
Caille la belle Victoire!	To the house of beautiful Victoire! ‡

The legend of Hippolyte's falling hat is preserved in another folk song called "Panama'm Tombé":

Panama'm tombé,	My hat fell down,
Panama'm tombé,	My hat fell down,
Panama'm tombé; ça qui dèyè	My hat fell down; whoever is behind,
Ramassé li ba moin!	Pick it up for me!

Mérisier, the Vodoun priest whom Hippolyte regarded as an enemy, was not pleased with the rumors and talk about him that was going the rounds in the capital. His displeasure is recorded in a protest song with a familiar theme:

Mérisier yo vini ga'dé moin pou' y'allé pa'lé, wo wa é!
Mérisier yo vini ga'dé ça pou' y'allé pa'lé ça!
Kénan moin yo wè!
Kénan yo séré nan mal!
Mérisier pas là, sonné ochan wa wa é!

Mérisier [says] they come to see me to go away and talk, *wo wa é!*
Mérisier [says] they come to see it and go away to talk about it!
What is mine you see!
What is yours you evilly hide!
Mérisier isn't there, sound the salute, *wa wa é!*

Seven days after Hippolyte's death, General Simon Sam was elected to the presidency. His friends and his enemies had different things to say about him. One song makes a tart comment on Sam's administration.

---

* That is, the affair was finished.
† *Allé dodo* literally means "to go to sleep," but there was a dance called Allé Dodo.
‡ Hippolyte's young wife.

A la youn président,
C'est Tirésius Augustin Simon Sam.
Si tout té con ça,
Haiti ta fini! [Ex. 111]

There was a president,
He was Tirésius Augustin Simon Sam.
If they were all like him,
Haiti would be finished!

In 1902 General Nord Alexis became the chief executive of Haiti. His abilities and accomplishments are still being debated, but he appears to have been a rather lovable old man whom everyone called by the affectionate term Uncle. His administration was fairly stable and prosperous—as prosperity is known in Haiti—and in large measure peaceful. When his election was confirmed, the people were convinced that the nation was in for a period of law and order, and that the constant threat of cacos and brigandage would come to an end. One of the election-year songs goes:

Nous crions vive, c'est pou' l'armé du Nord!
Tintin cila ça va fini!
Nous crions vive, c'est pou' soldats du Nord!
Tintin cila ça va fini!
Tintin cila, tintin cila, tintin cila va fini!
Bassin Vodoun, Bassin Vodoun, Bassin Vodoun c'est pou' nous! [Ex. 112]

We cry long live Nord's army!
The chaos will be ended!
We cry long live Nord's soldiers!
The chaos will be ended!
The chaos, the chaos, the chaos will be ended!
Bassin Vodoun,* Bassin Vodoun, Bassin Vodoun is for us!

One of the serious problems confronting Nord Alexis after his election was that of a disappearing national currency. Haitian paper money was circulating elsewhere in the West Indies and in South America and was becoming increasingly scarce in Haiti itself. Nord Alexis called in all the old currency and issued new, with the happy result that large quantities of money were again seen in the Republic. The common people who made the songs seem to have been very grateful:

Alexis Nord Papa ou bon chef oh!
Ou ba nous moné, ou ba nous papier!
Alexis Nord Papa ou bon chef oh!
Ou ba nous moné, ou ba nous papier!

* Probably a place name.

Nous pas mandé ou anyien!
Nous pas mandé l'a'gent enco'!
Papa Nord ça nous ta mandé oh chef,
C'est bamboche nous mandé ou! [Ex. 113]

Alexis Nord, Papa, you are a good chief, oh!
You gave us money, you gave us paper!
Alexis Nord, Papa, you are a good chief, oh!
You gave us money, you gave us paper!
We don't ask you for anything more!
We don't ask you again for money!
Papa Nord, only one thing we are going to ask you, chief,
It is a big celebration we ask for!

The president's wife, Çéçé, seems to have been very proud of him and very sure of his talents. When the army bugles blow a general assembly call, they are supposed to be saying:

Çéçé té dit Alexis Nord grand moune nan tout corps li!
Çéçé té dit Alexis Nord grand moune nan tout corps li!
Çéçé té dit la quitté pour voir l'heure li vlé!
Çéçé té dit Tonton Nord grand moune nan tout corps li! [Ex. 114]

Çéçé said Alexis Nord is a thoroughly fine man!
Çéçé said Alexis Nord is a thoroughly fine man!
Çéçé said he will quit his office whenever he sees fit!
Çéçé said Uncle Nord is a thoroughly fine man!

Another bugle call, with words attributed to Nord's wife, contains a note of complaint:

Çéçé said *waille!*
Çéçé said that, said that!
Çéçé said if you don't have any money you can't have a woman!
Çéçé said *waille!*
Çéçé said that, said that!
Çéçé said we are working our guts out!
Çéçé said *waille!*
Çéçé said that, said that!
Çéçé said Alexis Nord is president!

Çéçé was not the only one in Haiti who had confidence in Nord's staying power. One popular song of the period goes:

Alexis Nord Papa,
Bondieu qui metté ou là!
Consolidé là yo
Qui vlé ba ou traka!

Alexis Nord, c'un bon Papa!
Ou pas metté ou pas manyien!
Pinga ou manyien, pinga ou manyien!
Pinga ou manyien Alexis Nord! [Ex. 115]

Alexis Nord, Papa,
It is God who put you there!
Take care of those
Who wish to make trouble for you!

Alexis Nord is a good papa!
You didn't put him there, you can't take him away!
Don't try to remove him, don't try to remove him!
Don't try to remove Alexis Nord!

Nord Alexis remained as president until 1909. He was then more than eighty years old, and he planned to turn the government over to General Jean-Gilles, who would carry on the policies of the administration. But Antoine Simon, an assembly delegate from the south, had other plans. He marched on Port-au-Prince with an army of three hundred cacos, who sang:

Tonton oh cher, Antoine pas nen betise oh!
L'apprend l'armée du sud, cher,
L'a fai ou marché zigzag!
Débor débor débor!
Nèg' Nord mandé fusillé!
Débor débor débor!
Nég' Nord mandé corigé!

Dear Uncle, Antoine is not joking!
He brings the army of the south, my friend,
He will make you go zigzag.
Débor débor débor! *
Nord's men are asking for gunfire!
Débor débor débor!
Nord's men are asking for a lesson!

After Nord Alexis had vacated the palace and embarked for Jamaica, Antoine Simon became president. Historians often refer to the period that followed as the "Epoch of Ephemeral Presidents." Simon was not in the palace long before a man named Cincinnatus Leconte was successfully stirring up a new caco movement in the north, and people were singing:

---

* Probably "outflanked."

Antoine Simon pressé oh pou' allé!
Ou pas tendé l'armée Leconte Gonaïves? [Ex. 116]

Antoine Simon, you'd better leave!
Haven't you heard Leconte's army is at Gonaïves?

In August, 1912, Leconte marched on the capital, and Antoine Simon sailed for Jamaica. General Leconte was duly elected to the presidency; but less than a year after he took office a terrific explosion wrecked the palace, killing Leconte, his son, and a number of militia. It was believed by many that this disaster was an act of vengeance by Antoine Simon:

Clairon sonnin, m'mandé ça qui gainyain
C'est Chapuzette qui débordé encore.
Maribaroux min li vini encore,
Ça'l vin' chaché, li vin' mandé revanche.

Nan Ouanaminthe fusil pas té tiré,
Qui raison ça pou' yo té fait pillage?
Bourriques, mulet' jusqu'à feuilles tôle, Chapuzette,
Tout ça passé au prix de trois centimes.

Machetes Leconte pis raide passé jalap,
C'est avec ça Chapuzette bai médicine.
Si ou vlé conné comment bai "vent-main-nez,"
Mandé Oreste avec Antoine Simon.

Antoine Simon té dit avant'l parti,
Li ta va quitté yun bomb nan mitan yo.
Lè l'éclatté, lè-à la va Kingston,
La marré rein'l pou'l ri peuple souvrain.

Aux Cayes du Fond m'tendé Mapou Simon,
Nan Léogane m'tendé Mapou Danpisse.
Lè nou rivé na wè ça qui gainyain,
Couis couvri couis, Antoine viré sou dos.

REFRAIN

Honneur à Chapuzette, St. Juste avec Delphin,
Ducasse et Corvoisier, vive Cincinattus.

The bells ring, I ask what is going on?
It is Chapuzette now who has revolted.
But Maribaroux he comes again,
What he is looking for is revenge.

In Ouanaminthe the guns are quiet,
What was the reason for this pillage?
They have carried off the donkeys, mules, and even the iron roofing,
Everything that was worth more than three centimes.

Leconte's soldiers are stronger than a *jalap*,*
It is with them that Chapuzette gives medicine.
If you want to know how to give the "stomach-hand-nose" †
Ask Oreste and Antoine Simon.

Antoine Simon said before he left
That he would leave a bomb in the middle of the palace.
When it went off he was already in Kingston.
He will pay for laughing at a sovereign people.

In Aux Cayes du Fond, I heard of the Mapou Simon,
In Léogane I heard of the Mapou Danpisse
When we arrive there we'll see what will happen.
Bowl covers bowl, ‡ Antoine will turn over on his back.

REFRAIN

Honor to Chapuzette, St. Juste and Delphin,
Ducasse and Corvoisier, long live Cincinnatus.

Two more presidents—Tancrede Auguste and Michele Oreste—divided the next eighteen months between them. Two caco movements to remove Oreste started simultaneously, one under the leadership of Davilmar Théodore, the other under the Zamor brothers, Charles and Oreste. The Zamor cacos first chased Théodore's army into the mountains and then marched on the capital. Oreste Zamor was elected to the presidency on a reform program, which quickly evaporated into thin air. One song describes the arrival of the President's brother Charles and his "Réform" at the gates of Port-au-Prince, where a crowd of enthusiasts had gathered:

Attention la Réform c'est jeunes jens Port-au-Prince,
C'est jeunes jens Port-au-Prince, la Réform viré dos ba yo.
Yo lèvé Mardi bon matin, l'habillé tout en blanc,
L'habillé tout en blanc pou' y'al entré Charles Zamor.
Al entren Port-au-Prince la Réform débordé,
La Réform débordé, la Réform viré dos ba yo.

Hail the Reform! It is the young men of Port-au-Prince,
The young men of Port-au-Prince, and the Reform turns its back on them.
They arose early Tuesday morning, dressed all in white,
They dressed all in white to meet Charles Zamor.
At the gates of Port-au-Prince the Reform reversed itself,
The Reform reversed itself and turned its back on them.

The Zamors and the reform administration held the palace less than nine months before Davilmar Théodore's cacos were marching on the capital singing the song that other presidents had heard.

---

* A violent purgative.
† That is, upset stomach, hand on the nose.
‡ That is, force replies to force.

Oreste Zamor, pressé pou' embarké!
Oreste Zamor, pressé pou' embarké!
Ou pas tendé l'armée Davilmar rentré pou' Gonaïves?

Oreste Zamor, you'd better embark!
Oreste Zamor, you'd better embark!
Haven't you heard Davilmar's army has entered Gonaïves?

Gonaïves seems to have been the crucial point for invading armies from the north. Whenever revolutionary troops entered this town, the president holding office prepared to leave. True to the tradition, the Zamors sailed for a foreign shore, and Davilmar Théodore became the new executive. Although his tenure was to last only three months, there was much excitement when he entered the capital:

À la théatre, à la bamboche!
Pou' djolle musique à droit à gauche!
La ville embrende ça qui gainyain,
C'est Davilmar kapé rentré!
Davilmar, dur, dur!
Manchete caco pas nen betise!
Papa Da dur, dur!
Manchete Leconte pas nen betise!
Davilmar, dur, dur!

Celebrations and dancing!
Tooting horns to right and left!
The city is in an uproar,
It is Davilmar who is coming in!
Davilmar, hard, hard!
The cacos were nothing to laugh at!
Papa Da is hard, hard!
Leconte's army was nothing to laugh at!
Davilmar is hard, hard!

In 1915 came the United States intervention in Haiti, with the prime objective of freezing out German commercial and political interests. A president named Guillaume Sam had assassinated his political enemies in the prison at Port-au-Prince and had, in turn, been dragged out of the French consulate and killed. The benefits of the American occupation of Haiti are hotly debated to this day, though it is about thirty years since the United States military forces were withdrawn. Some Haitians think the occupation was a good lesson in politics, and that Haiti benefited in many ways. Others continue to look upon it as an overt expression of American diplomacy by force. One of the early assignments of the U.S. Marines in Haiti was the destruction of the roaming bands of cacos, generally regarded as bandit elements. Caco chiefs were imprisoned or killed as outlaws, though much of their activity was directed against the American occupation rather than the civil government. Many of the injustices of the occupation were the result of inadequate understanding of the Haitian people and their way of life. There was much unspoken bitterness against the occupation forces, and in some popular songs the Marines were referred to by the peaceful peasantry as "cacos in khaki." During President Borno's administration the people in the north were singing:

> Grand Prevost ou pas tendé cacos Bayé Bouteille?
> Grand Prevost n'allé wè cacos Bayé Bouteille!
> Ala kilé nen dé nations:
> Americains dévant, cacos deuxieme!

> Grand Prevost, didn't you hear the cacos are at the Bottle Gate?
> Grand Prevost, we are going to see the cacos at the Bottle Gate!
> Now we have two species:
> The Americans are the worst, the cacos come second!

When President Borno's tenure of office came to an end, it was felt in some quarters that Madame Borno was taking the prospective change of residence very hard:

> Madame Borno ça ou gainyain ou apé crié?
> Ou té tou conné palais a parti pou' ou!
> Madame Borno ça ou gainyain ou apé crié?
> Ou té tou conné yun jour pou' oté laissé!

> Madame Borno, what is the matter, why are you crying?
> You always knew one day you would have to leave the palace!
> Madame Borno, what is the matter, why are you crying?
> You always knew one day you'd have to give it up!

In 1930 Sténio Vincent came into office. He was a generally unpopular executive who managed to hold on to the presidency by suppressing the political opposition. When he was elected, the progressives were hopeful, and his supporters were singing: "Sténio Vincent bon garçon." But public sentiment shifted. Times were hard for the Haitian people during the Vincent administration. The darker citizens felt Vincent was "too light" to have their interests at heart. They were violently aroused, too, by his gingerly handling of the massacre of Haitians in the Dominican Republic in 1937. During his administration there were a number of abortive caco demonstrations and an unsuccessful revolt of high-ranking army officers. But in the early days a Meringue piece called "Merci Papa Vincent" was very popular. According to the song, the noteworthy achievement of the President was the law he sponsored to drive the "Syrians" out of the retail trades:

> Nous conné moune qui raimé peuple là,
> C'est Président Vincent!
> Nous conné moune qui raimé peuple li,
> C'est Président Vincent!
> Nous conné moune qui raimé peuple li,
> C'est Président Vincent!
> Nous conné moune qui raimé peuple,
> C'est Président Vincent!
> A nous rélé, merci Papa Vincent!
> A nous rélé, merci Papa Vincent!
> A nous crié, merci Papa Vincent!
>
> Qui moune qui bai commerce en detail là?
> C'est Président Vincent!
> Qui moune qui bai commerce en detail là?
> C'est Président Vincent!
> Qui moune qui bai commerce en detail là?
> C'est Président Vincent!
> A nous rélé, merci Papa Vincent!
> A nous rélé, merci Papa Vincent!
>
> We know the man who loves the people,
> He is President Vincent!
> We know the man who loves the people,
> He is President Vincent!
> We know the man who loves the people,
> He is President Vincent!
> We know the man who loves the people,
> He is President Vincent!
> We call out, thank you, Papa Vincent!
> We call out, thank you, Papa Vincent!
> We call out, thank you, Papa Vincent!
>
> Who is the man who gave us the retail business?
> It is President Vincent!
> Who is the man who gave us the retail business?
> It is President Vincent!
> Who is the man who gave us the retail business?
> It is President Vincent!
> We call out, thank you, Papa Vincent!
> We call out, thank you, Papa Vincent!

This song soon became the "official" musical theme of the President and was heard in the carnival festivities, at salon dances, and at military functions. But as discontent with Vincent grew, less adulatory versions of "Merci Papa Vincent" sprang up in the side streets of Port-au-Prince. One rendition (as translated) went:

> We know the man who loves the people,
> He is Sténio Vincent!
> Who made my wife leave me to go to her family?
> He is Président Vincent!
> Who made my skin show through my worn out pants?
> He is Président Vincent!
> Who is the man who made my house fall down?
> He is Président Vincent!
> Oh, we call out, thank you, Papa Vincent!

So widespread did the burlesques on the original become that the tune itself became suspect. One never knew which versions were running through the minds of the listeners.

In 1950, during the administration of President Estimé, there was a new public works program which provided employment for a good many needy people in the Port-au-Prince area, and a coumbite song of the period went:

> Président Estimé waille, oh!
> Quembé pays yà pas lagué oh!
> C'est Bondieu nans ciel là qui ba moin président!
> C'est Bondieu nans ciel là qui ba moin président cila!
> Quembé pays yà pas lagué oh!
> Port-au-Prince oh tourné Havane oh! [Ex. 117]

> President Estimé *waille,* oh!
> Hold on to the country, don't let go, oh!
> It is God in heaven who gave me this president!
> It is God in heaven who gave me this president!
> Hold on to the country, don't let go, oh!
> Port-au-Prince, oh, is turning into a Havana, oh!

When Estimé was overthrown by a military coup, the melody lingered on, but the name of the protagonist was changed.

No president of Haiti has served his term of office, either for good or bad, without providing the raw materials for a folk song. His heroic deeds, his failures, and his foibles are as likely as not to be perpetuated in the music of the people.

As for the presidency itself, it is held in the highest esteem. A rousing salute song, reminiscent of the Marseillaise, sends every new president-elect on the way to the palace:

> Président passé là,
> L'ap monté au gouvernment!

Président passé là,
L'ap monté au gouvernment! [Ex. 118]

The President passes by,
He is taking over the government!
The President passes by,
He is taking over the government!

It is not only great political events that are perpetuated in songs like these; many are the comments on little people in the government, such as a legislator named Daniel Fignolé. One of Fignolé's deeds, probably apocryphal, which is recorded in folk song has to do with an act of justice in a hospital in Port-au-Prince. According to the song, Fignolé entered the hospital and found the rich patients on beds and the poor patients on mats on the floor. He promptly ordered the rich patients placed on the floor and the poor patients placed on the beds. (A few years later, after serving as president for less than three weeks, Fignolé became a political exile in the United States.)

There is also an old song about a government engineer named Louis Gentil Tippenhauer—or Ti 'Benhauer (Little 'Benhauer), as he was commonly known. Tippenhauer is now an old man, but when he was young he was in charge of the construction of a section of the Haitian narrow-gauge railway. There was an accident in which a smoking locomotive jumped the tracks. Though small in stature, Tippenhauer had a forceful personality. He quickly assembled his workmen, and with chains, ropes, and crowbars they wrestled the locomotive back on the rails. The song commemorating the dramatic event was born at the height of the rescue operation. It is marked with concern for the feelings of Engineer Tippenhauer:

Ti 'Benhauer rélé, "Porté cord pou' marré li!"
Ti 'Benhauer rélé, "Porté chaine pou' enchainé li!"
Si ou marré'l la laguè, devant Bondieu!
Pau' diab', pau' 'Benhauer, machine na deraillé!
Pau' diab', pau' 'Benhauer, machine na deraillé!

Ti 'Benhauer shouts, "Bring a rope to tie it!"
Ti 'Benhauer shouts, "Bring a chain to chain it!"
If you tie it, it unties itself, before God!
Poor devil, poor 'Benhauer, the machine is derailed!
Poor devil, poor 'Benhauer, the machine is derailed!

It is more than half a century since the affair of the derailed locomotive, and the railroad itself is not much longer for this world. But the song is still sung, and mostly by people who have no personal knowledge of the man named Tippenhauer.

14. Songs of Bravado and Boasting

Among the secular songs are many which have boasting, bravado, or challenges as their central theme. Usually this kind of song is playful in tone, though sometimes there may be a serious or even an ominous undercurrent. Often the challenges are directed toward, or concern, djabs and *démons*. Just as often they involve persons of great prestige and power, perhaps the president himself. These songs say, in effect, "Who's afraid of the lou-garo?"—or of the president, or of the demon of such-and-such a mountain, as the case may be. Sometimes the bravado motif is implicit, but as often as not the singer challenges the world to take him before some feared personage, human or supernatural, and see what will happen.

In one such song, the singer boasts that he is ready to be conducted before a fearful and malevolent deity named Jean Zombie. As though to assure the listeners that he is in his right mind, the challenger emphasizes that he has not been drinking anything intoxicating and is perfectly sober:

> Rwo! Jean Zombie oh vini wè moin, conduit'm allé!
> Rwo! Jean Zombie oh vini wè moin, conduit'm allé!
> M'pas bwè tafia pou' nou fait tintin!
> Devant hounfor moin conduit'm allé!
> Jean Zombie oh wie wa conduit'm allé!
> M'pas bwè tafia pou' nou fait tintin! [Ex. 119]

> Rwo! Jean Zombie, oh, comes to see me, take me to him!
> Rwo! Jean Zombie, oh, comes to see me, take me to him!
> I haven't drunk tafia, I am not drunk!
> I am at my hounfor, take me to him!
> Jean Zombie, oh wie wa, take me to him!
> I haven't drunk tafia, I am not drunk!

Another song challenges the community to take the singer to face the president—right into the president's parlor. The fact that the president named in the song has been dead for years does not seem to matter very much:

Mèné'm allé oh parleur!	Take me to the parlor!
Mèné'm allé!	Take me!
Mèné'm allé!	Take me!
Mèné'm allé oh parleur Borno!	Take me to Borno's parlor!
Mèné'm allé oh! [Ex. 120]	Take me, oh!

Sometimes the challenge is directed to a more lowly level of authority, such as the gendarme:

Gendarme, mèné'm nan bureau!
Rwo, gendarme oh! [Ex. 121]

Gendarme, take me to the police station!
Rwo, gendarme, oh!

Haitians are notable for their restraint from physical violence. During holiday celebrations it is not uncommon to see men who have drunk enough tafia to make them act up. Some of them may even be morose and bellicose. But the disturbances of the peace more often than not are verbal. So long as the first blow is not struck, the social pressures against violence operate effectively. But physical assault against an individual—a push, a blow, a slap—is an affront to personal dignity which relieves the victim of the social restraints and gives him the right to bodily revenge. I have seen waterfront rows, fierce and vocal, in which no one but the participants showed much interest. But should one man shove or strike another, the spectators would immediately interfere, for that single physical contact would have removed the barriers to the worst violence. Sometimes at carnival time a man assumes the guise of belligerence. Such a bully may roll up one trouser leg to indicate he is challenging all and sundry to a fight. Usually, passers-by move aside good-naturedly when he approaches. He is not taken seriously; but neither is he challenged, except by another man in the same frame of mind. When two men with rolled trouser legs meet, there may be a verbal encounter, possibly from opposite sides of the street, to the general entertainment of the bystanders. It is usually a serio-comic affair. Some of the folk songs memorialize occasions on which a man has publicly spoiled for a fight, real or imaginary. This song comments briefly on a man named Çalira, who looked for trouble:

Woy woy woy!
Woy woy woy!
Woy woy woy!
Çac bien arrangé corps yo!
Mène en bataille là!

Çalira Çalira ça!
Mène en bataille là!
Ça qui fin arrangé corps yo!
Mène en bataille là! [Ex. 122]

Woy woy woy!
Woy woy woy!
Woy woy woy!
Those who can't fight, take care of yourselves!
Take me into the battle!
Çalira, this Çalira!
Take me into the battle!
Those who are delicate, take care of yourselves!
Take me into the battle!

Another battle cry in song goes:

C'est nou même, c'est nou même!
C'est nou même, c'est nou même!
Pas wè'm déjà gros Nèg' rwo!
Na mainyain djab là!

It is me myself, it is me myself!
It is me myself, it is me myself!
Don't you see I am a big man, rwo?
I will hold that devil!

In the following song an aggrieved man declares he is strong as a bull, and warns his enemy to beware.

Anou mayain tè glissé nou c'est bèf oh!
Anou mayain tè glissé nou c'est bèf oh!

I'll fix you, treacherous fellow,* I am a bull, oh!
I'll fix you, treacherous fellow, I am a bull, oh!

Even a successful game of dice is the subject of bragging:

Passé frai,
Oh passé belle,
Passé un beauté!
Passé frai,
Oh passé belle,
Passé un beauté!
Yr é soir frappé zos,
Non fai trois lasse! [Ex. 123]

More than sweet,
Oh, more than handsome,
More than a beauty!
More than sweet,
Oh, more than handsome,
More than a beauty!
Last night I played dice,
I made three aces!

---

* *Tè glissé,* literally "slippery earth," means a person who is treacherous.

15. Secret-Society Songs

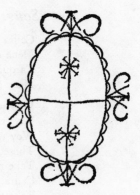

Secret societies were once common in Haiti, as they were in other parts of the New World where West Africans settled in large numbers. The institution of the secret society was strong in various parts of West Africa from which the slaves came. The tradition was particularly notable among the tribes of Nigeria.[1] In the New World it offered to slaves and to freed Negroes an opportunity for social organization and fraternal relationships which otherwise had been pretty well shattered by the nature of slavery and the profuse admixture of cultures. A number of elderly Haitians have suggested that it was the Haitian secret societies rather than the Vodoun and Congo cults which fomented underground resistance and slave revolts against the French in the last years of the eighteenth century.

At this late date it is difficult to reconstruct much of the secret-society picture. Such groups as may have survived until recently did so in vitiated and changed form. They have been supplanted in large measure by the *société*, a kind of mutual-aid association with both economic and recreational functions. It is exclusive, but not irrevocably so, and it is not secret. The société often corresponds roughly with the membership of a hounfor, or cult temple.

Old people still talk about true secret societies, however. There was a Moundongue secret society, separate from the Moundongue cult, whose members were recruited from the survivors of the Moundongue tribe and their descendants. Other secret societies were not based on tribal affiliation but were recruited from the population at large. One such group was the Vinbindingue, also known as the Blinbindingue and the Balbindingue. Its practices were feared. According to tradition, the Vinbindingue was predatory and held cannibalistic rites, as did other groups such as the Moundongue Society, the Cochon Rouge (the Red Pig Society), the Zeaubeaups, the Cochon Gris (the Gray Pig Society), and the Calinda Society. How much of their reputation for cannibalism was deserved is a matter of speculation. Bizarre tales told by the colonists, as well as rumors and legends propagated about the societies by nonmembers who feared them, did result in a body of folklore which portrays these groups as malevolent. The societies themselves, no doubt, often supported such beliefs to increase the awe in which they were held.

In modern Haiti, however, there is no secret or fraternal society of the kind that probably existed in prerevolutionary days. Nor is there anything comparable to the Abakwa, or Carabali, an Ibo secret society that has survived in Cuba.[2]

Curiously enough, the most significant noncult organization in Haiti today is the Masonic order. Yet it has not remained distinct from the cults but has become interwoven with them. Many Vodoun and Congo services have rites or dances that are designated as Mazonne (Masonic). Houngans often feel that affiliation with the Masonic order offers distinction and prestige for the hounfor that the ordinary cult center does not have.

As for the Calinda, the Cochon Rouge, the Cochon Gris, the Zeaubeaup, the Vinbindingue, and the Moundongue societies, they appear to survive in name rather than in fact. The rumors and tales go on, as they do about zombies, devils and lou-garos. It is mostly at carnival time that their names are heard. A Mardi Gras band, appropriately costumed, may herald itself as a Calinda or a Cochon Rouge group. It will sing songs it regards as appropriate to the kind of effect it is trying to achieve. Such groups are not taken seriously. They are merely part of the carnival fun. But to members of older generations they do recall tales about the secret societies that met under the limbs of the mapou tree by torchlight to conduct their nocturnal affairs.

The songs that follow are reputed to belong to the Calinda, Vinbindingue, and Zeaubeaup societies; but they are infected with a frivolous quality which suggests they may have been heard for the first time in the carnival celebration rather than in the dark shadows of the mapou.

One of the legends concerning the Balbindingue, or Vinbindingue, is that of the dancing drum. The theme is a special one, but it is related to other stories about dancing calabashes in the Calbasse ritual and about dancing hoes. This song describes a gathering at such a dance:

> Balbindingue!
> C'est là n'homme mwé yé!
> Cimitière tonnerre!
> Balbindingue!
> C'est yun seul tambour qui dansé!
> Pardon mon père!
> Balbindingue!
> C'est là n'homme mwé yé! [Ex. 124]

Balbindingue!
It is here my men are!
Cemetery thunder!
Balbindingue!
It is a single drum which dances!
Pardon, my father!
Balbindingue!
It is here my men are!

It is told of the Vinbindingue that their members are sometimes required to subject themselves to the ordeal of rubbing hot peppers in their eyes, which results in acute pain and temporary blindness. According to some explanations, this is one of the "tests" of a Vinbindingue man. Red, inflamed eyes are a standard symbol of malevolence. One informant explained that the Vinbindingue members blind themselves so that they cannot see what kind of flesh they are eating:

Jé'm pété m'pas wè ladans ma métté piment!
Jé'm pété m'pas wè ladans ma métté difé! [Ex. 125]

My eyes are blind, I can't see, I've put pepper in them!
My eyes are blind, I can't see, I've put fire in them!

Another Vinbindingue song is a humorously macabre dialogue between the members of the society and a victim. He is asked whether he would prefer to be quartered or eaten whole. Each time they are about to act according to his wishes he changes his mind:

Dévor a déquatier ça ou pitôt? Déquatier!
C'est catcha dévoré ça ou pitôt?
Moin'm assez déquatier!

C'est catcha dévoré ça ou pitôt?
Dévor a déquatier ça ou pitôt?
Moin pitot dévoré!

Dévor a déquatier ça ou pitôt?
Dévor a déquatier ça ou pitôt?
Moin pitot déquatier! [Ex. 126]

Devoured or quartered, which do you prefer? To be quartered!
Cut up or devoured, which do you prefer?
I've been quartered enough!

Cut up or devoured, which do you prefer?
Devoured or quartered, which do you prefer?
I'd sooner be devoured!

Devoured or quartered, which do you prefer?
Devoured or quartered, which do you prefer?
I'd sooner be quartered!

A brief song identifies by name a man who has participated in a Vin-bindingue affair:

> Y'r é soi' Cimila mangé ti moune yo!
> Y'r é soi' Cimila mangé ti moune yo! [Ex. 127]

> Last night Cimila ate little children!
> Last night Cimila ate little children!

A Calinda song speaks more tangently of its business. It refers to doing "washing," a very special kind of washing that requires no bluing:

> Waille waille waille, savonné sans métté 'digo!
> Waille waille waille, savonné sans métté 'digo! [Ex. 128]

> *Waille waille waille,* wash without bluing!
> *Waille waille waille,* wash without bluing!

And a Zeaubeaup song complains that a ouanga (a black-magic bundle) has been swallowed by a snake. It seems to specify that some of the members of the group are zombies, the animated dead:

> L'Arcahaye nous là nous là!
> L'Arcahaye nous là nous là!
> L'Arcahaye, coulève valé ouanga moin!
> Ti ga'çons mes zeaubeaups, waille waille mes zeaubeaups!
> Ti ga'çons mes zeaubeaups, waille waille mes zeaubeaups!
> Ti ga'çons mes zeaubeaups, waille waille mes zombies!

> Arcahaye I was there I was there!
> Arcahaye I was there I was there!
> At Arcahaye a snake swallowed my *ouanga!*
> Young men, my zeaubeaups, *waille waille* my zeaubeaups!
> Young men, my zeaubeaups, *waille waille* my zeaubeaups!
> Young men, my zeaubeaups, *waille waille* my zombies!

16. Folk Tales:
Bouki, Malice, and
Jean Saute

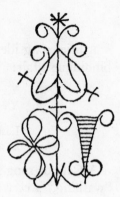

In the folk tales and legends of Haiti there has been a powerful assimilation from many cultures. There are stories of European and African derivation, and countless others that are to be found in one form or another in the Middle East, Asia, and throughout the Americas. The precise origins of many of these stories probably will never be known. Some of them are as ancient as the Panchatantra and have variants in India, Indonesia, Korea, Egypt, West Africa, and northern Europe. It is likely that many tales with this broad distribution came into Haiti by way of Europe, along with the French, Spanish, and English settlers. But numerous stories told in Europe are well known in West and Central Africa too. The folk tales of the world have an astonishing universality. The adventures of the West African hare and spider are closely paralleled in the tales of the American Negro Br'er Rabbit, the hare of Thailand, and the mouse deer of Indonesia.

In Haiti today, as in other islands of the West Indies, there is an endless repertoire of folk stories of many kinds—animal tales; trickster tales; stories about magicians, kings, and princesses; *cantes* fables; and stories that account for the beginnings of things, the behavior of certain animals, and their physical appearance. There are European dragons and devils, and beasts of the African forests. Some of the stories are long and episodic, some are so brief—even curt—that they have lost their original core. They may point out moral or ethical values or, more commonly, strike completely amoral levels in which the humor depends upon acts that in real life would be regarded as cruel. Like the folk songs, the tales are often used to express the democratic equality of the small person with the great. In many instances it is the small man who triumphs over the powerful and rich. In the Bouki-Malice cycle it is usually the little wily trickster who wins over the larger and physically stronger opponents.

None of the Haitian tales are meant to be read, for storytelling is a dramatic art. The narrator interprets his characters as he goes along, providing different voices, singing, giving humorous or tragic emphasis, and changing his facial expressions to convey the temper and mood of the protagonists. He imitates the movements and actions of the animals. In print, his broad gestures and sly intimations are all lost. The Haitian tale is a vehicle for the actor, who plays his theme according to circumstances and the responsiveness of his audience. The storyteller, like the musician, is likely to be found almost anywhere. But there are storytellers of special renown, known as *maît' contes*—who may be called upon to entertain young people at a party or Nine Night gathering. They have seemingly endless repertoires and can go on indefinitely telling tales about Bouki and Malice, or Jean Saute and Jean L'Esprit. In former times, the maît' conte used an instrument such as the *banza* to intersperse his narration with music. Old people recall that trough zithers and other instruments of African design were once employed for this purpose.

Anansi, the spider trickster-hero and buffoon of West Africa, has survived in Haiti as well as elsewhere in the Antilles. In Jamaica and other British islands, Anansi has become Brother Anansi, Sister Nancy, or just plain Nancy. Although he usually figures in tales dealing with other animals, he has more and more come to assume a human form, as he has in Haitian tales. But in Haiti the name Anansi is only rarely heard. Anansi's cleverness and stupidity are now attributed to two characters named Ti Malice and Nonc' Bouki, both of whom are regarded as human beings.

In West Africa the spider hero directed his mischief against the great and strong creatures of the forest, now one, now another. In Haiti, Ti Malice, who has inherited Anansi's wit and guile, pits himself mostly against Bouki, who has inherited Anansi's stubborn nature and his pompous stupidities. Ti Malice (whose first name probably comes from the Spanish *tio*, uncle) has become the slick sharpy of the city, the clever and predatory "operator," the practical joker. Like his spider prototype, Ti Malice has humor as well as cunning, though he is often remorseless. Bouki is full of self-confidence but is slow-witted and an easy prey for Ti Malice. He is thought of as a clumsy peasant of the mountains. He has a constant desire to pit himself against Ti Malice, and a capacity for involving himself in utterly fantastic situations which appeal to the Haitian sense of the ridiculous.

In many respects this team of comedians resembles another pair known in South and Central America—Tío Conejo (Uncle Rabbit) and Tío Coyote; both are pranksters, but the rabbit usually manages to outwit the coyote. Ti Malice and Bouki also figure in the universal tar-baby story, and in many other tales known in the United States in which Br'er Rabbit and Br'er Fox are the protagonists. Many of these tales, like the characters themselves, have West African prototypes, though others seem to have been created out of the workaday substance of Haitian life. They are not, however, essentially children's tales. Some of them involve risqué or ribald escapades.

Among the Haitian tales are numerous themes which stem directly from African lore, such as the hoe that worked by itself in the fields; the single grain of seed corn which, when drawn across the ground, grew an entire field of maize; and the pot that boiled without fire. There are many remnants also of the African tale in which a "tail feather" of an elephant is required for some magic purpose. There is a pursuit which follows the acquisition of the elephant hairs, and the pursued person saves himself with three magical eggs. When he throws one on the ground, a huge river springs up behind him. When he throws down another, a forest appears behind him, and so on.[1] The elephant's tail feather is regarded as a very powerful protective charm in many regions of West Africa. That the memory of it should continue in Haiti so precisely, although there are no elephants, is striking.

Although Haitian folk tales are abundant and are well loved, over the years they have tended to become more and more simple. The episodic European tales of kings and princesses and monsters that have been taken over are, generally, of a naïve kind without moral or intellectual significance. They are interesting for the twists and turns of fate and for momentary laughs.

The tale of Grandmother's Bath is a case in point. In this story, Jean Saute (Stupid John) is left at home to care for Grandmother while Jean L'Esprit (Smart John) goes to market. Jean Saute puts Grandmother in a tub and pours boiling water over her, killing her instantly. He looks at the grimace on her face and concludes that she is enjoying it immensely; so he sticks her pipe in her mouth and pours more water over her. When Jean L'Esprit returns, Jean Saute is very proud of himself. But Jean L'-Esprit discovers that Grandmother is dead. The brothers then pack their belongings to go to the city. There follows a series of strange and bizarre adventures. Jean L'Esprit sends his dull-witted brother back for something he has forgotten; Jean Saute misunderstands and brings the door off the house. Throughout their adventures Jean Saute carries the door with him. When they get to the forest they climb into a tree to sleep for the night, Jean Saute carrying his door along. While they are there, a convocation of devils (*djab*) takes place under the tree. Jean Saute has to urinate, and he does so into the middle of the convocation. The devils shout gleefully that it is wine from heaven and try to catch the water. Eventually the door falls from the tree and frightens them away. The two brothers continue on their way and come to a country where it is always night—a great dragon with seven heads has swallowed the sun.[2] The two brothers kill the dragon, with the help of Jean Saute's stupidity. They cut into the monster and find a silver box, which they open, releasing the sun from captivity. The news goes on ahead. When they arrive at the city, the king, in appreciation, offers them the choice of his daughters. Jean L'Esprit, as might be expected, chooses the youngest and most beautiful. Jean Saute turns them all down and asks to marry the king's cook.

This story seems to be one of the most extended tales in Haitian lore, unless one groups all the Bouki-Malice stories together in a single cycle. However, most European-style tales (Beauty and the Beast and Jack and the Beanstalk, for instance) have suffered considerable deterioration. In the process of adaptation, such tales lost much of the original detail and decorative motif that made them interesting to the European. They became stark and brief, fragmentary anecdotes about kings, devils, and snakes.

With some few exceptions, the African stories have undergone less change: the Singing Tortoise (found later in this chapter) and Anansi's Tug of War, for example. But even in the tales of African origin there has been simplification to the extent that many of them are mere fragments; in some even the central point itself has been lost. The Bouki-Malice tales, counterparts of the Anansi stories of West Africa, have lost the contemplative tone found in the African originals. Moral points of the kind commonly made in African tales have almost entirely disappeared and are to be found only in proverbs. If the good wins over the bad, that is simply an accident of fate; for the bad wins over the good just as frequently. Death and sadism are constant themes. But the prime conflict remains the smart against the stupid, and the small and weak against the large and powerful.

Like kindred tales elsewhere in the West Indies and in the United States, many of the stories have standard beginnings and endings. The storyteller begins by saying "Cric," and his audience replies, "Crac." When he comes to the end he usually uses a variant of:

"I was there and saw it. And Malice gave me a kick and sent me all the way here to tell you about it." Or: "So I have run all the way here to tell it to you." Or: "That's the story, and if you don't believe me, tafia will never kill you." Or: "They gave me a blow, and I have just come to my senses." Or again: "So he kicked me over the house and here I am." These formula endings often provide a dramatic punch for the children who are listening.

The stories that follow are "typical" tales, recorded in various parts of Haiti.

THE PRESIDENT WANTS NO MORE OF ANANSI

Anansi and all his smart ways irritated the President so much that the President told him one day: "Anansi, I'm tired of your foolishness. Don't you ever let me see your face again." So Anansi went away from the palace. And a few days later he saw the President coming down the street, so he quickly stuck his head into the open door of a limekiln.

Everyone on the street took off their hats when the President passed. When he came to the limekiln, he saw Anansi's behind sticking out. He became angry and said, "Qui bounda ça qui pas salué mwé?" (Whose behind is it that doesn't salute me?) Anansi took his head out of the lime- kiln and said, "C'est bounda 'Nansi qui pas salué ou." (It's Anansi's behind which didn't salute you.)

The President said angrily, "Anansi, you don't respect me."

Anansi said: "President, I was just doing what you told me to do. You told me never to let you see my face."

The President said: "Anansi, I've had enough of your foolishness. I don't ever want to see you again, clothed or naked."

So Anansi went away. But the next day when he saw the President coming down the street he took his clothes off and put a fish net over his head. When the President saw him he shouted, "Anansi, didn't I tell you I never wanted to see you again clothed or naked?" And Anansi said, "My President, I respect what you tell me. I'm not clothed and I'm not naked."

This time the President told him, "Anansi, if I ever catch you again on Haitian soil I'll have you shot."

So Anansi boarded a boat and sailed to Jamaica. He bought a pair of heavy shoes and put sand in them. Then he put the shoes on his feet and took another boat back to Haiti. When he arrived at Port-au-Prince he found the President standing on the pier.

"Anansi," the President said sternly, "didn't I tell you that if I ever caught you on Haitian soil again I'd have you shot?"

"You told me that, Papa, and I respected what you said. I went to Jamaica and filled my shoes with sand. So I didn't disobey you because I'm now walking on English soil." [3]

BOUKI AND TI MALICE GO FISHING

Cric! Crac!

Bouki and Ti Malice went into the fishing business together. Ti Malice painted the name St. Jacques on the front of the boat, poured some rum over it and christened it. Bouki took some rum and poured it over the back end of the boat and christened it Papa Pierre. They went out to sea and caught fish. When they came home, Ti Malice counted the fish. "There are eighteen fish," he said. "How shall we divide?"

"I'll take one and you take one until they're gone," Bouki said.

Malice said: "There are so few fish it isn't worth while. You take all the fish today and I'll take all the fish tomorrow."

"Oh no," Bouki said, "I'm not totally stupid. You take all today and I'll take all tomorrow." So Malice took all the fish.

They went out again the next day, and when they came home Malice counted again and said, "There are so few, you take all today and I'll take all tomorrow."

"Oh no," Bouki said, "you're trying to cheat me. You take all today and I'll take all tomorrow." So Malice took all.

The next day they went out again. And when they were returning Ti Malice said, *"Waille,* such a small catch. I'm glad it's your turn to take all today."

Bouki became angry and said, "Are you trying to break my head? I'm no fool. You take the catch today and I'll take it tomorrow."

Every day Ti Malice took the whole catch. Every day Bouki got nothing. Malice got fatter and Bouki got thinner. Every day it was this way, until one day Bouki looked at Malice and saw how fat he was getting. It came to him suddenly that he had been cheated. He shouted at Ti Malice and began to chase him. They ran through the peristyle of the town hounfor, and Ti Malice said "cata-cata," imitating the sound of a drum, and called on Ogoun and Damballa to save him.

They ran through the church, where the priest was holding a service. Malice crossed himself and said a quick prayer, without stopping for a second, and ran out again. They ran, ran, ran, and Bouki was getting closer. Ti Malice came to a limekiln with a hole in it. He tried to crawl through, but he stuck at the hips. No matter how hard he tried, he couldn't get through. Finally Bouki came along. He stopped and looked in all directions. There was no Ti Malice, only the behind facing him from the limekiln.

Bouki put on his best manners, and said, "Behind, have you seen Ti Malice?"

The behind replied, "Take off your hat when you address me."

Bouki took off his hat to Ti Malice's behind. He said politely, "Why are you smiling at me? I only asked if you saw Ti Malice?"

"I smile when I please," the behind said.

"Have you seen Ti Malice?" Bouki said.

"Push me and I'll tell you," the behind said.

Bouki pushed.

"Harder," the behind said.

Bouki pushed harder.

"Harder yet," the behind said.

Bouki gave a big push, and Ti Malice went through the hole into the limekiln. And that was the way he made his escape.[4]

BAPTIZING THE BABIES

Cric! Crac!

Malice and Bouki made a coumbite together. First they were going to cultivate Malice's garden; afterward Bouki's garden. So they took their machetes and started to work cultivating Malice's peas and yams.

Malice said, "Did you hear someone calling me?" Bouki replied, "I didn't hear anything."

They chopped weeds some more, and Ti Malice said, "Someone is calling me." He put down his machete and went over the hill. He went to Bouki's house and took down Bouki's honey gourd. He sat in the shade of Bouki's house and drank as much honey as he could. Then he hung the gourd up and went back to his field, where Bouki was working, working, working.

"Who was it?" Bouki asked. "Oh, those people wanted me to be godfather to their baby." Bouki asked, "What did you name the baby?" Ti Malice said "I named him *Coummencé* (Beginning)."

They chopped more weeds, and Malice said, "Excuse me, someone is calling me again." He put down his machete and went over the hill back to Bouki's house. He took down the honey gourd and sat in the shade and drank as much as he could. Bouki was still in Malice's garden, working, working, working. Malice put the honey gourd back and returned to his garden.

"Some important people wanted me for godfather," Malice said. Bouki asked, "What did you name the baby?" Ti Malice answered, "I called this one *Dé Fois* (Two Times)."

They worked some more, and Malice said, "*Waille,* they are calling me again." He put his machete down and went over the hill to Bouki's house and got the honey gourd down again. He drank, drank, drank until it was all gone. Then he came back.

Bouki had finished weeding Malice's garden. "What did you call this baby?" Bouki asked. "Oh, this one was the last, so I called him *Ai Bobo* (Finish)," Malice said.

Malice's garden was all cultivated. He said to Bouki, "Now we will cultivate your garden." But Bouki was exhausted from doing Malice's work as well as his own. He said, "I'll have to let my own weeds grow. I'm done in."

He went home and took his honey gourd down for a drink, but it was empty. He was so angry he kicked me all the way here to tell you about it.[5]

UNCLE BOUKI GETS WHEE-AI

Uncle Bouki went down to the city to market, to sell some yams, and while he was there he got hungry. He saw an old man squatting by the side of the road, eating something. The old man was enjoying his food tremendously, and Bouki's mouth watered. Bouki tipped his hat and said to the old man, "Where can I get some of whatever you are eating?" But the old man was deaf. He didn't hear a word Bouki said. Bouki asked him then, "What do you call that food?" Just then the old man bit into a hot pepper, and he said loudly, "Whee-ai!" Bouki thanked him and went into the market. He went everywhere asking for five centimes worth of whee-ai. The people only laughed. Nobody had any whee-ai.

He went home thinking about whee-ai. He met Ti Malice on the way. Ti Malice listened to him and said, "I will get you some whee-ai." Malice went down and got some cactus leaves. He put them in a sack. He put some oranges on top of the cactus leaves. He put a pineapple on top. Then a potato. Then he brought the sack to Bouki. Bouki reached in and took out a potato. "That's no whee-ai," he said. He reached in and took out a pineapple. "That no whee-ai," Bouki said. He reached in and took out oranges. "That's no whee-ai," he said. Then he reached way to the bottom and grabbed the cactus leaves. The needles stuck into his hand. He jumped into the air. He shouted, "Whee-ai!"

"That's your whee-ai," Malice said.

BOUKI AND TI BEF

Bouki and Ti Bef (Calf). The calf's mother had died. He was an orphan. Bouki was crossing the fields one day and he saw Ti Bef grazing all by himself. Bouki's mouth watered. He wanted to eat Ti Bef. So he said, "Ti

Bef, I haven't seen you for a long time. Where do you live these days?" But the calf knew Bouki. So he said, "I sleep over there on top of the hill."

That night Bouki took a sack and crept to the top of the hill; but he couldn't find Ti Bef. Ti Bef was sleeping in the woods. Bouki looked all night without finding him, and when he went home his children said, "Where is Ti Bef?" Bouki just slapped them and told them to keep quiet. The next day Bouki saw Ti Bef grazing, and he asked, "Ti Bef, where were you last night? I dropped by and I didn't find you home."

Ti Bef said: "Oh, last night I found a place in the woods. That is where I sleep now."

The next night Bouki searched in the woods, but he didn't find the calf. The next day, he said to Ti Bef, "Oh Ti Bef, I just happened to drop by the woods last night, but I didn't find you home. Where were you?" And the calf replied, "Last night I found a nice place by the spring. That's where I sleep now."

So the next night Bouki took his sack and searched by the spring, but he didn't find Ti Bef. He began to get very angry.

When he saw Ti Bef the next day he said, "Ti Bef, you have been telling me lies. Where do you really live?" Ti Bef said to him, "Nonc' Bouki, I really live in that cave there in the mountain."

The cave belonged to a tiger. That night Bouki took his sack and went up to the cave. He said, "Are you there?" And the tiger replied, "Of course I'm here." So Bouki went into the dark cave, took hold of the tiger, and tried to put him in the sack. But the tiger knocked Bouki down. He tore his clothes off, he bit him, and he mauled him. Bouki ran home. His children wanted to know where Ti Bef was. Bouki said, "Woy, that Ti Bef is a devil! He is so small and weak in the daytime, but at night he's as ferocious as a tiger! So if you happen to meet him anywhere, show him the greatest respect."

I asked Bouki about it myself, and he kicked me from there to here to tell you about it.

JEAN SAUTE MAKES THE KING'S DAUGHTER LAUGH

One day Jean Saute's mother sent him to the city to work as an apprentice with a storekeeper. After Jean had worked with the storekeeper for a month, the man gave him a small goat for his wages. Jean carried the goat home on his head. When the neighbors saw him coming they all had to laugh at Jean's stupidity, and Jean's mother was very embarrassed. "That's no way to do with a goat," she scolded. "You tie it on a cord and put it on the ground."

But the next month the storekeeper paid Jean in money. So Jean tied a string to the money and dragged it on the ground till he got home. Jean's mother was angry. "That's not what you do with money," she said. "You put it in your pocket!"

When Jean got back to the city the king was offering a reward to anyone who could make his daughter laugh. It was said that the king's daughter had never laughed since she was born.

The storekeeper paid Jean off with a donkey the next time. Remembering the scolding his mother had given him, Jean tried to put the donkey in his pocket. Just then the king's daughter passed. When she saw Jean Saute trying to put the donkey in his pocket, she had to laugh. And when the king heard about it he gave Jean Saute the reward.

THE SINGING TORTOISE

A tortoise was crawling along slowly one day when he came to a fine garden where many birds were eating. They were eating the peas and millet of a farmer named Pierre Jean. The turkey, the chicken, the pigeon, the duck, and even the *récinole* [nightingale] were there. They invited the tortoise to eat with them. But he replied: "Oh, no. If the farmer who owns the garden surprises us, you can fly away. But where would I be? He would catch me and beat me."

The birds said, "We will give you wings." And each of the birds took some of its feathers and attached them to the tortoise. So he came and ate with them. But while they were eating, the récinole called out, "Habitant 'rivé! Habitant 'rivé!" (The farmer is coming! The farmer is coming!). And in a panic they all grabbed the feathers they had given the tortoise and flew away. Tortoise crawled, crawled, crawled; but he was too slow. Uncle Pierre Jean caught him. He was going to beat him. But the tortoise began to sing:

> Colico Pierre Jean oh!
> Colico Pierre Jean oh!
> Si'm capab' m'pito volé, enhé!
> C'est regrettant ça, m'pas gainyain zel!

> Colico Pierre Jean, oh!
> Colico Pierre Jean, oh!
> If I could I would fly, *enhé!*
> What a tragedy, I have no wings!

The farmer was amazed to hear a tortoise sing. He liked the tortoise's song, and he asked him to sing again. Tortoise sang his song again. Pierre Jean took the tortoise home and put him in a box. Then he went to

Port-au-Prince and asked the people to make bets with him. He said he would bet them any amount of money he had a tortoise that could sing. Some people bet one gourde, some people bet five gourdes. And then the President came along in his carriage. When he saw the crowd he stopped and said, "Ça nous gainyain icite?" ("What is going on here?")

When he heard about Pierre Jean's singing tortoise, the President said, "This man is a Ti Malice; there aren't any tortoises that sing. I will bet you one hundred thousand gourdes." But Pierre Jean said, "I can't bet that much. I am a poor man." The President said. "Nevertheless, you are a vagabond trying to cheat the people. I will bet you one hundred thousand gourdes. If you lose the bet I will have you shot."

Meanwhile Madame Pierre Jean heard rumors that her husband had a talking tortoise in the house. She searched until she found the tortoise, and she asked him to sing. "I can only sing by the edge of the river," the tortoise said. So she took him to the edge of the river. "My feet must be wet," the tortoise said. So she put him in the water by the bank of the river. And then he crawled into the water quickly and swam away. Madame Pierre Jean heard the crowd coming up to the house from the city. She was frightened. She ran home, and on the way she caught a small lizard. She put the lizard in the box and closed the lid. When the men from the city arrived, Pierre Jean took them to the box. The President said, "Let the singing begin."

Pierre Jean said then, "Sing, tortoise, sing." The lizard replied from inside the box, "Cric!" Pierre Jean said again, "Sing, tortoise sing!" And the lizard replied, "Crac!" The President was angry and said, "You call that singing? Open the box!" They opened the box and found only the small zandolite. The President said, "You are a cheat. Take this man down to the river to have him shot." So they took Pierre Jean down to the river and stood him by a tree to shoot him. And just at that moment the tortoise stuck his head out of the water and sang:

> Colico Pierre Jean oh!
> Colico Pierre Jean oh!
> Si ou capab' ou pito volé enhé!
> C'est regrettant ça, ou pas gainyain zel!
>
> Colico Pierre Jean, oh!
> Colico Pierre Jean, oh!
> If you could you would fly, *enhé!*
> What a tragedy you have no wings!

"Ah, that is my tortoise!" Pierre Jean said. "Listen to him sing!" And the tortoise continued to sing.

Colico Président, oh!
Colico Président, oh!
Nonc' Pierre Jean pa'lé trop enhé!
Sotte pas tuyé Haitien, fai li siè!

Colico President, oh!
Colico President, oh!
Uncle Pierre Jean talks too much, *enhé!*
Stupidity doesn't kill a Haitian, it makes him sweat!

When the President heard that, he turned Pierre Jean loose and paid him the hundred thousand gourdes. But it was the last they saw of the singing tortoise.[6]

FROG, CHIEF OF THE WELL

One time there was a drought, and there was no place for the animals to get water. So God provided a well where all the animals could come to drink, and he put Frog in charge. Frog was to receive the animals who came to quench their thirst. But when the animals came, the frog refused to provide them with water. When the cow came to drink, the frog sang from inside the well:

M'apé mandé ça qui là donc, enhé, ça qui là?
M'apé mandé ça qui là donc, enhé, ça qui là?

I am asking who is there, *enhé,* who is there?
I am asking who is there, *enhé,* who is there?

And the cow sang back:

C'est moin bèf qui nan pi à!

It is I, the cow, at the well!

And the frog replied:

| Moin dit bèf allez donc, | I say, cow, go away, |
| Pi à chêche! [Ex. 177] | The well is dry! |

The cow went away and died from thirst. Then the horse came and asked for water, and the frog conversed in the same way with him as he had with the cow:

M'apé mandé ça qui là donc, enhé, ça qui là?
M'apé mandé ça qui là donc, enhé, ça qui là?
C'est moin ch'wal qui nan pi à!
Moin dit ch'wal nen point dleau,
Pi à chêche!

I am asking who is there, *enhé,* who is there?
I am asking who is there, *enhé,* who is there?
It is I, the horse, at the well!
I say, horse, there is no water,
The well is dry!

The horse went away suffering, and he died of thirst. The other animals came in turn: the donkey, the goat, the dog, the cat, and the birds. The frog turned them all away in the same manner, and they suffered and died of thirst.

So, one day, God said: "What is this? I put Frog in charge of the water. I will have to go and see what is the matter." So he went to the well, and when he got there the frog called out:

M'apé mandé ça qui là, enhé, ça qui là?
M'apé mandé ça qui là, enhé, ça qui là?

And God replied:

C'est moin Papa Bondieu qui nan pi à!

It is I, Father God, who is at the well!

And Frog answered:

Papa Bondieu nen point dleau,
Pi à chêche!

Father God, there is no water,
The well is dry!

So God cut off the frog's tail. From that time on, the frog has had no tail; but you still find him in the well.

UN, DEUX, TROIS, CINQ, SIX

In a small village on the edge of a forest there lived a woman with an only son, a hunchback named Jean. She sent Jean into the forest to gather firewood one day. The boy went a little farther in his search than he had ever gone before, and he came upon a clearing in which a crowd of little *djab* (devil) children were playing games. He stood on the edge of the clearing and watched them. As they danced around in a circle they sang:

Un, deux, trois, cinq, six,
C'est con ça ti djab fai ti mi.

One, two, three, five, six,
That's the way little djab make millet.

One of the djab children saw him and invited him to join in the game. So he joined them, dancing the way they did and singing their song. They were so delighted with him that they took him to the djab village, which lay deeper in the forest. They told their fathers and mothers about how nice Jean was, and how he played djab games with them. The big djab gathered around and asked him to sing the song for them. He sang:

> One, two, three, five, six,
> That's the way little djab make millet.

The djab were so pleased with Jean that they removed the hump from his back and gave him a bag of gold. Jean went home, and when his mother saw he no longer had a hump she was very happy. He told her what had happened, and he gave her the bag of gold.

Next door to the poor woman there lived a rich widow with a spoiled and arrogant boy just Jean's age. His name was Jacques. When the widow heard of the gold Jean had brought home from the djab, she sent Jacques into the forest too. She gave him three empty sacks to fill with treasure, and he went to the clearing where the little djab were playing. They were singing:

> One, two, three, five, six,
> That's the way the little djab make millet.

Without waiting to be invited, he ran forward and said, "What's the matter with you stupid djab, don't you know how to count? The song should go like this:

> Un, deux, trois, QUATRE, cinq, six,
> Djab saute ça yo pas con' fai anyien.

> One, two, three, FOUR, five, six,
> The stupid djab don't know how to do anything.

The djab children stopped their playing. But they took Jacques home to their village and told the big djab, "This boy says we don't know how to do anything." The big djab gathered around and asked the boy to sing for them. Again he sang:

> One, two, three, FOUR, five, six,
> The stupid djab don't know how to do anything.

The big djab frowned and asked him what his empty sacks were for. He told them, "The hunchbacked boy came and you took care of him. I came so you could take care of me."

The djab told Jacques, "We will do something for you, too." And they took the hump they had removed from Jean's back and put it on Jacques' back, and they put rocks in his empty sacks. When he got home, his mother shrieked at the sight of him, but it was too late.

That is why people sometimes warn other people not to be arrogant by saying "Djab saute ça yo pas conné fai anyien."

THE FOUR HUNCHBACKS

Three hunchbacked brothers lived with their father in a village in the deep woods. They were all woodcutters. One day the father, who was an old man, died. When he had been buried and the *gage* had been held for him, the brothers said to each other, "There is no need for us to stay any longer in the woods. Let us go to our brother in the city."

So they dressed in their best clothes and went to the city. They found the shop which their brother owned, and they entered. Their brother, also a hunchback, was not there, but his wife was tending the shop. When they told her who they were, her heart sank. She said to herself, "Now my husband will want to take care of these hillbillies. We'll have to share everything with them!" But she talked nicely as though they were welcome, and she took them to her house and fed them; but she put poison into their food so that they died.

Then she found a man with a boat, and she told him she'd give him twenty-five gourdes if he'd take a body out to sea and dispose of it. So he came to the house, and she showed him one of the bodies. He put it in a sack and carried it down to his boat. He took the body out to sea and threw it overboard. Then he came back for his money. She then showed him the body of the second brother and said, "But you haven't done the work yet. Here is the body just where I left it." The boatman was confused. He was sure he had already done the job. But he put the second body in his sack, lugged it to his boat, and went out to sea with it.

He returned after that to the woman's house, but she said, "What kind of a man are you that wants to be paid before he works?" And she showed him the body of the third brother. The boatman became furious. "So you've come back!" he shouted at the body. "This time you are going out to sea to stay!" And he carted the body down to his boat. This time he sailed far out to sea and disposed of it. "That is the end," the boatman said. "Now I will get my money."

He returned to the woman's house. Night was just falling, and the woman's husband was just returning. When the boatman's eyes fell on him he went into a rage.

"So!" he shouted, "So you're back again! And walking around, too! I'll fix you this time." He leaped upon the woman's husband and killed him, dragged his body down to the sea, and threw it in.

17. Children's World: Gage Songs and Games

On the night of last prayers for a deceased person, and on other party occasions, children while away the hours until bedtime with special songs and games. Sometimes the games are led by an older member of the family. More often, left to their own devices, the children play unsupervised. It is regarded as fitting that the youngest members of the community should be enjoying themselves while the last rites are being held for one who has recently died. This view is held not merely in regard to children; older people, too, engage in gay activities, such as dancing the Juba.

Many children's games are known throughout the country, others have only a regional popularity. The games mentioned here are among those played in southern Haiti, mainly in the neighborhood of the capital, Port-au-Prince.

One favorite is known as Balancé Yaya. The children—as few as four or as many as ten or twelve—crouch on the ground in a circle. Each of them has a stone in his hand, which he strikes rhythmically on the earth as they sing together:

> Jésus, Marie, Joseph oh,
> Rat là mangé pigeon moin.
> Jésus, Marie, Joseph oh,
> Rat là mangé pigeon moin.
> Rat passé, Robinette passé,
> Fai' ti Marie marché, allé là. . . . [Ex. 129]

> Jesus, Mary, Joseph, oh,
> The rat has eaten my pigeon.
> Jesus, Mary, Joseph, oh,
> The rat has eaten my pigeon.
> The rat goes by, Robinette goes by,
> Make little Mary walk, go there. . . .

On the words *allé là,* each of the players slides his stone in front of another person. There is no fixed direction of rotation, and the stone may be passed to the left or to the right, or even across the circle. This passing of stones continues while the players sing:

Balancé Yaya,	Even up, Yaya,
Yaya oh,	Yaya, oh,
Yaya Madame Mango,	Yaya Madame Mango,
Balancé Yaya moin.	Even up, my Yaya.
Moin fai' prière moin,	I say my prayers,
C'est pou' Yaya,	They are for Yaya,
Balancé Yaya	Even up, Yaya,
Yaya oh	Yaya, oh,
Yaya Madame Mango. [Ex. 129]	Yaya Madame Mango.

While this part of the song is being sung, the stones are being passed rapidly this way and that. Players may use only one hand for this purpose, and at some stage one of them finds himself with more stones in front of him than he can dispose of, and he is declared *gage,* or "it." Then the game begins anew.

In another animated game called Théatre, the boys and girls stand in a circle and sing, clapping hands and going through a variety of postures, gestures, and dance steps. It is a sort of "follow the leader" routine. First, one of the group makes rhythmic motions in time to the music, and the other players must do the same thing. The leader may swing his hips, do fancy footwork, posture with his arms, or twist about, and the others in the circle are obliged to imitate him. Then another child gets his turn to set the pace. One of the songs heard with this game is the following, which imitates the voice of the guinea hen:

> Cipan Cimalo!
> C'est ça manman'm té dit moin,
> Cipan Cimalo!
> C'est ça manman'm té dit moin,
> Cipan Cimalo!
> Aie tain tain Cimalo!
> Raing taing taing Cimalo!
> Taink taink taink taink Cimalo!
> Wa taink taink Cimalo!
> (And so on, with variations.) [Ex. 130]

> Cipan Cimalo!
> This is what my mother told me,
> Cipan Cimalo!
> This is what my mother told me,
> Cipan Cimalo!
> Aie tain tain Cimalo!

Raing taing taing Cimalo!
Taink taink taink taink Cimalo!
Wa taink taink Cimalo!

For the game called Délina, two chairs are required as props. They are placed a few feet from each other, facing toward the center. Behind one chair is a boy, behind the other a girl. The other children clap their hands and sing:

Coté'm passé, Délina!	Wherever I pass is Délina!
Coté'm viré, c'est Délina!	Wherever I turn is Délina!
Manman manman, Délina!	Grandmother, Délina!
Papa papa, Délina!	Grandfather, Délina!
Manman manman, Délina!	Grandmother, Délina!
Papa papa, Délina!	Grandfather, Délina!
Coté'm passé, Délina!	Wherever I pass is Délina!
Coté'm viré, c'est Délina!	Wherever I turn is Délina!
Délina jobé oh jobé, Délina!	Délina works, oh, works, Délina!
Jobé pou' la'gent, Délina! [Ex. 131]	Works for money, Délina!

The two children in the center, at a given signal, begin to move, each circling his own chair. The circling continues, the girl pacing her movements in an effort to avoid meeting the boy face to face. The boy times his movements so that he may meet the girl face to face. If and when he accomplishes his purpose he takes his reward—an embrace—and another couple comes forward to repeat the play.

Another game of the courting variety is called Find a Beautiful Woman. A chair is placed in the center of the play area, and a girl is designated to sit there as the "beautiful woman." She has nothing else to do. The others sing:

Chach' yun femme qui belle oh!
Sindé, Sindé Macaya!
Chach' yun femme qui belle, frè'!
Sindé, Sindé Macaya! [Ex. 132]

Look for a woman who is beautiful, oh!
Sindé, Sindé Macaya!
Look for a woman who is beautiful, brother!
Sindé, Sindé Macaya!

Holding a kerchief in his hand, one of the children marches or dances around the chair of the "beautiful woman." After several trips around, he retires and drops the kerchief in the lap of another player, who comes forward and repeats the performance. Anyone who refuses to pay his respects to the "beautiful woman" is "it."

Some games are of the personal "test" or ordeal kind. In one of them the objective is to refrain from laughing. A player stands in the middle of a circle of seated participants, each of whom in turn gives a laugh of some kind—a giggle, a loud laugh, an ironic laugh, a laugh of ridicule, and so on. If the player in the center cannot refrain from laughing with the others, he loses and someone else takes his place in the middle.

Various kinds of blindfold games go by the name Boudè, or Boudé. In one of them, a blindfolded player moves from one seated child to another, feeling them with his hands as he goes, and trying to identify them by touch. When he guesses correctly, the identified person changes places with him, and the game continues.

In a second form of Boudè, it is the person in the center who can see, and the seated players who are blindfolded. The one in the center moves around the inside of the circle with a kerchief in his hand, pressing it against the lap of each blindfolded player as he passes. Somewhere en route he leaves the handkerchief in a lap. It is so light that it is not easily detected. If a blindfolded person guesses correctly that the handkerchief is in his lap he is freed from the circle and comes to the center. If he guesses incorrectly, it a mark against him.

Still another type of game is based on quick and accurate responses. This one is called Uncle Pierre. Each player in the group is given a name specifying a number of sheep. That is, the first player's name may be Ten Sheep; the next one, Fourteen Sheep; the next one, Seven Sheep; the next one, Nineteen Sheep; and so on.

The "master" of the group begins by saying, "Uncle Pierre went to my farm and took Seven Sheep."

The person named Seven Sheep must reply, "Tomantor."

The "master" asks, "How many sheep did he take?"

And Seven Sheep replies, selecting the name of one of the other participants, "Nineteen Sheep."

The one named Nineteen Sheep replies, "Tomantor."

The "master" call out, "How many sheep did he take?"

Nineteen Sheep answers, "Fourteen Sheep."

Fourteen Sheep answers, "Tomantor."

And so on. If a player answers to the wrong number, or if he gives a name for which there isn't a corresponding player, he loses and is *gage*.[1]

18. Musical Instruments

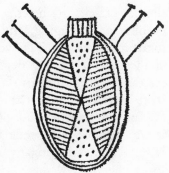

The Haitian people have drawn heavily on both Europe and Africa for their musical inspiration. In music, as in other traditions, the country is bicultural. There is, on the one hand, the music of the so-called *élite*—the literate and educated class which is concentrated in the cities—and on the other hand, the music of the peasants, the plantation laborers, and the lower economic groups of the town. The *élite* music is in the European or Western tradition, while the true folk music of Haiti follows, in the main, in the wake of West African musical culture. The instruments of *élite* music are primarily those of Western Europe. The instruments of the folk music of the country are those which can best interpret the mainstream currents of the West African heritage—instruments of African design and function. European-style instruments have infiltrated into the folk music too, but the over-all pictures is that of a survival of African musical devices to interpret music cast in an African mold. It is the folk-music instruments which call for examination—the instruments that are made in the villages and tiny huts in the mountains, the instruments on which the significant music of Haiti depends.

The materials from which these instruments are made are usually those found upon the land. If a man wishes to make a drum, he cuts down a tree for the purpose. For material for a bamboo trumpet he goes to the bamboo grove. For a flute, he cuts a reed. Metal is used for making African-style bells, rattles, singing horns, and substitutes for bamboo trumpets.

The drum in its many forms is the most common instrument of all. It is used for dances of all kinds, for cult rites, for work music on the road and in the field, and for assembly calls and signals. Not very many years ago the older people in the south of Haiti still spoke of the "talking drums" they had seen as children.

The craft of drum making is a very skilled one, but the tools are simple: chisels, machetes, and fire. The core of the log is removed by burning and gouging, and the outside is shaped with a machete, or sometimes a hachet. The wood is selected and processed carefully. Firing of the core of the log depends a good deal on how dry the wood is, for the wood must burn slowly. It is believed that wood cut at the right stage of growth and at the right phase of the moon is resistant to the ever-present powder-post beetles. Mahogany was once favored because it was durable and beetle resistant, even though it was heavy. But in recent decades mahogany has become scarce, and modern drums are made of lighter woods.

Drums made in the nineteenth century not only conformed to the patterns of certain West African prototypes but were also carved and decorated. Some of these old drums are still to be seen, but there are not many left. An ancient carved assotor drum (previously cited) has fortunately been preserved by the Bureau d'Ethnologie. But between the ravages of the powder-post beetles, age, and the periodic orgies of drum burning by the church and misguided public officials, most of these ancient works of art have long since disappeared. During the American occupation of Haiti—from World War I to 1932—American military personnel also contributed to the mania for drum burning. And as late as 1941 there was a massive, cleric-inspired drive to wipe out these instruments as remnants of *sauvage* elements in Haitian life.

The effect of this war against the drum was only to improve the business of the professional drum maker. Drums had become expendable, hence they were made simpler. The carved decorations disappeared. Paint was substituted, and less attention was given to detail. The important thing was to produce a good functional instrument. But the creative instincts of the drum makers sometimes still take over, and many of the modern drums are beautifully proportioned, with delicate geometric patterns carved around the base, or foot. Among certain categories of drums the painted decorations consist solely of the name of the loa to whom the instruments have been dedicated—St. Jacques perhaps, or Papa Pierre, or Èzilie.

Drums differ in design according to the use for which they are intended. The Arada or Vodoun drums are used primarily in connection with the dances and rituals of the Vodoun cult—the cult built around the gods and rites of Arada and Yoruba theology. They resemble closely drums which are used today in Dahomey, Nigeria, and Togoland. They usually come in sets of three. The largest, the *manman* (also called *hountor* or *hountogri*), may be three to four feet high. The middle-sized drum, or *second* (also called *grondé* or *moyen*), is about two feet

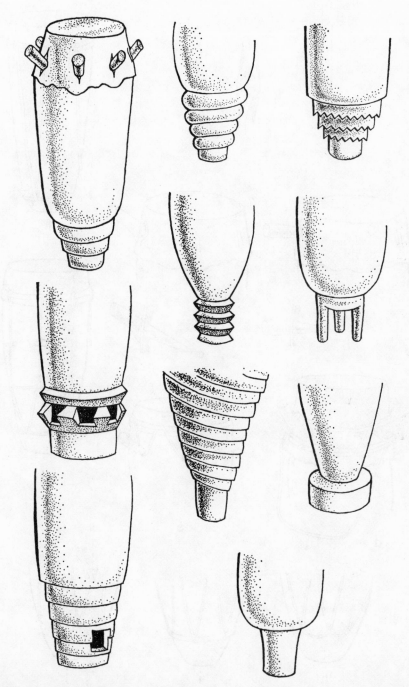

INDIVIDUALITY IN DRUM DESIGNING: Although the Arada or Dahomey-style drum is distinct from those of other "nations" or cults, there is a noteworthy variety of artistic decoration in the carving of the base. Some patterns are found only in certain regions or villages.

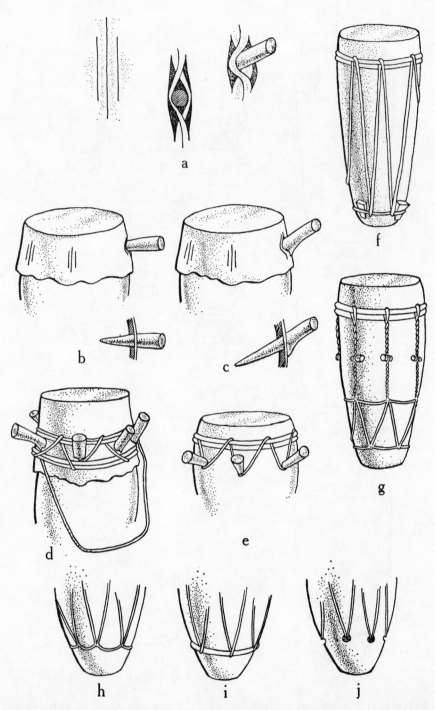

MOUNTING OF DRUMHEADS: To fasten the Arada drumhead to the drum, three slits are made in the skin over the peg hole, forming two short strips (*a*, left); peg or hook is inserted as shown in *a*, center and right. *b*, peg mounting. *c*, hook mounting. *d*, traditional pattern for lacing of cord. *e*, Arada drum showing combination of peg and hoop mounting techniques: the skin is fastened around the lower hoop; the upper hoop, laced to the pegs, holds it in place. Congo and Juba-type mountings are shown in *f* and *g*; in *f*, tension on the cords is provided by hammering down the wedges at the base; in *g*, the tourniquet method is used. *h–j*, three ways of fastening the cords to the base of these drums. In *h*, a cord loop is employed, and in *i*, a wooden hoop. Sometimes holes are provided in the base, through which the cords are laced, as in *j*.

high. The smallest—the *bula,* or *bébé* (sometimes called *dundun*)—is about eighteen or twenty inches high. They are all called sometimes by the Yoruba name *bata,* originally applied to a two-headed instrument.

Arada drumheads are of cowhide, held in place by hardwood pegs set into the bodies of the drums at an angle. The drums are tuned by driving in or loosening the pegs. Even the slitting of the skins where the pegs pass through them is African in pattern. In Cuba the drums of the Arada (there called Arara) cult are made in precisely the same way, though they are used in batteries of four rather than three.

In a variation of the peg type of fastening, the skin is attached to a hoop, which, in turn, is held in place by ropes laced to the pegs. Each drum maker has his own preference as to the angle and size of the pegs, the proportions of the drums, and the wood from which they are made. One drum maker near Léogane claimed to be able to identify the region from which a drum came by examination of the pegs and the carvings around the base.

The small Arada drum, the *bula,* is usually "whipped" with two long thin sticks to provide a sharp and penetrating sound. The middle-sized drum is played with one bare hand and a stick. The stick may be straight or bowed. The bowed drumstick is known as an *agida,* the name used for the same type of stick in Dahomey.[1] On infrequent occasions the *moyen* drum is played with two sticks—one straight and one bowed. The large drum, the *manman,* is played by the most accomplished of the drummers in the orchestra. He plays with one bare hand and one stick, which may be of various forms. It may be straight, have a hook-shaped head, or be mallet-shaped; or it may be the grotesquely twisted stick known as a *baguette Guinée.* All these forms are known in Dahomey and elsewhere in West Africa.

The three Haitian Arada drums, supplemented by an African-style bell known as an *ogan* and small gourd rattles (cha-chas), form the standard orchestra for most dances of the Vodoun cult. The *ogan*—the forged iron bell with an external striker—has all but disappeared in recent years, along with the institution of the village forge. In its place one may see any kind of metallic object, such as a hoe blade, a link of chain, or a length of pipe, all of which are referred to by the old name *ogan.* In Cuba the Arada cult preserves the bell, both in single and double form, under the same name. The word *ogan* probably derives from the Yoruba term for this instrument, *eganran.*

Playing in concert, the three Arada drums produce a range of tones, and the player of the *manman*—the chief of orchestra—adds to the effect by frequently striking his stick against the side of the drum above the pegs. High notes are achieved by striking the drumhead near the rim, and low notes near the center.

The drummers usually sit together on a bench or in chairs at one side of the dance court. The larger and middle drums are slightly tipped to keep their "mouths" open; the *bula* stands squarely on its base and is therefore somewhat muted. The player of the *manman* often drums in a standing position, bracing the instrument by means of a cord around his thigh.

Another drum associated with the Arada rites is the assotor. This drum is usually about six feet high, and may be from two to two and a half feet in diameter. It is played in an upright position, and two or three small "windows" near the base permit the sound to emerge. This big drum is used only for the Assotor service, at which the Dahomey "nation" plays host to the loa of all the various rites. Usually there is only a single drummer, who plays while standing on a bench or raised platform; but on occasion, two or even three drummers play simultaneously on the single drumhead.

It is interesting to note in passing that most of the Vodoun drums have Dahomean names and are of Dahomean design, despite the fact that Yoruban religious motifs have survived. The Yoruban double-headed *bata* drum, used in Nigeria for invocation of the principal deities, appears to have survived in decadent form on the island of La Gonave, where it is known as *pongwé*. Curiously, it is played not like the Yoruban *bata* (one hand on each head) but like another Yoruban instrument, the *dundun,* or pressure drum. The instrument is held under one arm and played only on the forward head. Significantly enough, this drum is said to be used only for Nago (Yoruba) rites. Another drum reserved for Nago services is found in the region of Léogane. It resembles the Arada drum in every respect except that it stands on three carved legs.

Drums associated with the services of the Congo "nation" are distinctly different from those found in Vodoun ritual. No drumsticks are used, and the heads are of goatskin rather than cowhide and are held in place by a system of cords and hoops. The Congo drum seen today stands about three feet high; old people say that within their memory there was a variety of Congo drum as tall as a man. Unlike the Arada drum, the Congo drum usually has no carved or painted decoration. For the "pure" Congo rites, two of these instruments, accompanied by gourd or metal rattles of various kinds, constitutes an orchestra. One typically Congo rattling device, called *mayoyo,* consists of three large gourds containing pebbles, on the top of a long pole.

A variant of the Congo drum is used for Pétro rites. It is similar in construction but stands a little shorter. Two Pétro drums of slightly different sizes and tones, called *baka* and *ti baka,* in combination with one or more rattles, an iron percussion device, and sometimes an assot, make up an orchestra.

The *assot* is a small board which is beaten with sticks. Often these sticks are flat, and sometimes a small wooden bench is substituted for the board.

Dances for which the Congo or Pétro drums are used include Pétro, Kitta, Bumba, Salongo, Bambarra, Moundongue, Congo Loangue, Pastorel, Mousondi, and Moutchétché. The drum for the Congo Loangue dance formerly was somewhat taller and narrower than the present Pétro drum, but the distinction is no longer maintained.

The Juba, or Martinique, drum is similar to the Pétro or Congo but wider and squatter. It is laid on its side for playing, the drummer sitting astride and pressing his heel against the drumhead to mute it or change the pitch. For Juba or related music, a second man, called the *catalier* (the one who *catas*), beats sticks against the body of the instrument behind the drummer.

In the northern part of Haiti one also finds the Zesse drum, used exclusively for the Zesse dance. It is cylindrical, about thirty inches high, and is played in an upright position. A wire is stretched across the goatskin head in the manner of a snare drum. Like all drums with goatskin heads, it is beaten with the naked hands.

A large two-headed drum called the *tymbale* is used as a work drum for labor societies and for processions, and in combination with other drums it sometimes appears in the Juba and secular Congo dances. The heads are mounted on hoops, which are held fast by lacing. The drum is carried by a rope slung over the shoulder or around the neck. Sometimes an assot striking board is affixed to the body of the drum.

A miniature copy of the tymbale is called a *tambourine.* It is used in carnival dances, notably the Mascaron. Carried by a cord which hangs around the neck, it is played with two diminutive sticks. Drumming is primarily a man's prerogative, but during carnival days women or girls may be seen playing the *tambourine.*

In southwestern Haiti, and possibly elsewhere, special drums are used for the Manuba dance. The Manuba drum is about a foot long, cylindrical, and about five inches in diameter, with two drumheads held together with cords. A pair of these drums is joined by a rope about two feet long, which is hung around the neck so that the two drums are in convenient playing position on the chest.

Twin drums which are hung over the knee are known as *marassas—*

the Haitian word for "twins." They are used primarily for secular music of the Cuban type, and may in fact be an importation from Cuba. The marassa is one of the few drums on which a finger technique is used; that is, striking with individual fingers rather than with grouped fingers. Marassas are often played in concert with guitars and marimbas.

The *basse* is the shallow finger drum resembling what in the United States is called the tambourine. Constructed in the pattern of an African prototype, its head is usually fifteen or eighteen inches in diameter and made of goatskin. Small metal disks sometimes are inserted in the frame to act as rattles. The head is kept well coated with resin or beeswax and is tapped and rubbed with the fingers. The *basse* is used only for secular music, except in the rare instances when it is used in Congo services. Some Haitians believe that the name of the instrument comes from the word *Basque*.

It is reported that signal drums were still in use a decade ago in remote sections of the southwestern peninsula. One of these instruments, according to description, is distinguished mainly by its large belly and small mouth; like the Juba drum, it is played on its side. Another style of signal drum has a slit in the side and is played erect, much like an African slit-log drum standing on end.

Another percussion instrument is the bamboo stamping tube, called the *ganbo* or *ti kanmbo*. It is African in origin and probably takes its name from the Loango term for the same device, *dikanmbo*.[2] The stamping tube is simply a length of bamboo, open at one end and closed at the other by a natural joint membrane. The closed end is struck sharply upon the ground, and the tone comes from the open top. The device works like an inverted drum, the closed end functioning like a drumhead. A battery of four or five ganbos may provide the percussion music otherwise played by drums. The musician corresponding to the *bulatier* of the drum orchestra plays two small stamping tubes, one in each hand. The other musicians have one each, thicker and longer than the bulatier's and producing deeper tones. Cupped hands are manipulated over the open ends for varying the sounds. This instrument has survived in various parts of the New World where Africans were settled, particularly other West Indian islands, Brazil, and Venezuela. In Venezuela the stamping tubes are called *quitiplas*.[3] They have recently been reported from various areas of West Africa, including French Equatorial Africa.[4]

The ganbos had a singular burst of popularity in Haiti during the United States military occupation of the country after the first World War, when drums were often seized and destroyed. Drums could not easily be hidden, but the ganbos were simply slipped into the straw roofs and thus put out of sight. Moreover, by some strange process of reasoning, military authorities regarded the bamboos as "harmless," though they were used for the same purposes as the contraband drums.

There are numerous other kinds of simple percussion devices. One such instrument, now less commonly seen than previously, is a length of open bamboo laid in the crotches of two Y-shaped sticks set in the ground. Like other *catas,* the bamboo is beaten with two sticks. Some Haitians believe that in former days such bamboos were played in batteries like a xylophone.

Sometimes a light-weight wooden cylinder, or perhaps a drum denuded of its playing head, is carried by the timekeeper of a coumbite. It, also, is played on the side with sticks.

Wooden mortars for pulverizing grain take on the character of musical instruments when used in combination with voices. When two or more mortars are used, with two men or women wielding the long polelike pestles in each mortar, the rhythmic effects can become fairly complicated.

The *claves* or *palos* (small hardwood sticks) are used primarily in connection with secular dances of a Cuban type, or to accompany such instruments as the guitar and the marimba. One stick is held loosely in the natural fold of the hand, so that it is free to vibrate, and is struck sharply with the second stick. The tone is almost metallic because of the hardness of the wood, usually lignum vitae. The name of the instrument is recognizable as a form of *clavar,* or *clavo,* Spanish for "peg" or "nail." It is thought that wooden shipbuilding pegs provided the name for this device, which has equivalents in West Africa.

Among the folk instruments there are various kinds of horns and trumpets. Cows' horns are played musically in some parts of the southern peninsula, though usually they are used as ritual instruments and signaling devices. Wooden trumpets called *pistons* are carved from the stems of the papaya tree. Conch-shell trumpets, known as *lambis,* are commonly used as signaling devices by fishermen. They are also to be found among the coumbites, in Rara festivities, and occasionally in rituals, where they are usually identified with sea deities. In carnival times the old fashioned phonograph horn makes its appearance as a combined trumpet and voice amplifier.

Probably the most important of the trumpets is the one made of bamboo. It is called a *vaccine,* or *bois bourrique.* Both names have interesting origins. The cow's horn was at one time used for magicomedical purposes. The leaf doctor used it as an "applicator" of powders and potions. A small opening was made in the point of the horn, and the horn itself was filled with the magico-medical preparation, which was called *vaccine*. The point of the horn was applied to parts of the body which needed treatment, and the powers of the potion were thus transmitted to the affected areas. In time, the cow's horn itself came to be known as a *vaccine*. Eventually the horn used for musical purposes took over the name, which was then transferred to the bamboo trumpet. The other name by which the bamboo trumpet is known, *bois bourrique,* means burro wood. But it probably is a corruption of *voix bourrique,* meaning "donkey's voice," an accurate description of the sound it makes.

The vaccine consists of a length of bamboo, with a joint membrane at one end cut into a mouthpiece. Trumpets of different sizes give different tones, and three to five of them together constitute a vaccine orchestra. Vaccines are employed by the coumbites in the fields, and they are heard in the towns and cities primarily during the pre-Easter festivities. In the Rara festivals the vaccine players march together, blowing and tapping their trumpets with sticks, followed by a crowd of dancers. Traditionally, the bamboo trumpet is not employed in religious music, although in recent years it has made its appearance occasionally in Congo-Guinée rites.

There are two kinds of musical scrapers. The one more often seen is the *grage,* a piece of sheet metal perforated in the fashion of our common kitchen grater. It is "played" by scraping a piece of wire or a nail across its rough surface. Found in secular rather than religious settings, the grage is likely to be used in combination with such instruments as the *tambourine,* marimba, claves, and basse. The second form of scraper is the *dentlé,* or *dentli,* a notched stick played with a bamboo scraping blade. The free end of the stick is sometimes braced against a bench or a plank, which acts as a sounding board. Some Haitians reported that in the old days gourds were used as sounding chambers. The scraper in one form or another appears to have both Indian and West African precedents. Its relationship to the washboard as used in Negro folk music in the United States is obvious. The notched gourd called the *guiro,* found in Cuba, Puerto Rico, and other West Indian islands, appears to be present in Haiti only as an imported instrument.

Rattles of various types are used in religious and secular dances, in the invocation of deities, and as accompaniment for solo singing. The most common of the rattles is the simple cha-cha, or *kwa-kwa*. It is a small gourd with a wooden handle, with seeds inside. It is usually played by the singing leader as a device to keep time. Sometimes the long dry seed pods of the cha-cha tree are used as a substitute.

In the Rara season two special rattles are used. One of them is made

of metal and resembles a tin can with a wooden handle. The metal
sometimes is perforated with numerous small holes, and inside are
hoholi seeds, which act as rattlers. This instrument, known as a *tchancy,*
is usually decorated with colorful ribbons when in use. (In northern
Haiti the term *tchancy* is used to designate metal wrist rattles worn
by drummers.) The other Rara rattle, called *joucoujou* or *joucjou,* is
made of three gourds carried on a long pole. One of the gourds is
affixed to the end of the pole, and the others are fastened to the terminals
of a short crossbar, giving the effect of a cross with bulbous ends. Since
many of the Rara processions are dramatizations of the Christ epic,
the instrument could be interpreted as a Christian symbol, though its
conversion into a noisemaker appears to be an African conception. The
joucoujou may be a variant of the small rattle-cross which is used by
the Abakwa secret society in Cuba.[5]

The sacred gourd rattle of the cult priest is called *asson* or *baksor.*
It is pear-shaped and covered with a network of beads which act as
external strikers. It is used by the houngan to summon the spirits of
the dead, to praise or call upon the deities, and to accompany the performance of magic. The asson is of West African derivation, and its
counterparts are to be found among the cults of Martinique, Trinidad,
Cuba, Brazil, Venezuela, and elsewhere where African traditions have
left their mark. The gourds from which the assons are made are grown
in a special grove sacred to the loa.

A large calabash rattle has been reported from several isolated regions
of Haiti, primarily from the north. Some rattles of this kind have been
described as more than twenty inches in height and covered by a network of external strikers, usually wari beans. The calabash rattles are
used in groups of three. They are shaken and thumped against the palm
of the hand, producing both deep and high-pitched sounds. These
oversize rattles are employed without drums and are said to be associated with Arada-Nago rites. They appear to be a survival of the
instrument known among the Yoruba as the *shèkèrè* and are found
in Cuba in both Dahomey and Lucumí (Yoruba) cult centers.

Probably one of the oldest of Haitian folk instruments is the earth
bow, known as the *tambour maringouin,* or mosquito drum. Traditionally the mosquito drum is made in the following way:

A hole is dug in the earth, perhaps a foot or more deep. It is covered
with palm or banana bark, which is pegged firmly all around. A cord
is attached to the center of the bark membrane and drawn taut to a bent
green sapling, one end of which is buried in the ground at a slight angle.
The cord is plucked and snapped with the fingers of one hand, while

its tension is varied by pressure on the bowed stick with the other hand, producing a change of pitch. The covered hole acts as a sound chamber.

In a "portable" model of the mosquito drum a tin pail or can is used for a sounding chamber. The pail is inverted and fastened to a small plank, to which the sapling also is affixed. It is believed by some observers that the instrument has special significance during the pre-Easter holidays (Mardi Gras and Rara),[6] but it may be used at almost any time of the year. The "accompaniment" for the mosquito drum usually consists of some kind of *cata*—sticks beaten upon a board or on the drumhead itself. On occasion, two or three of these instruments are beaten together, and the rough bark membrane may be rasped for additional effects. Most of the songs that go with the mosquito drum are secular. One of the appropriate songs favored by children goes:

> Maringouin dit moin ta zwing oh!
> Maringouin dit moin ta zwing!
> Ta zwing oh!
> Ta zwing! [Ex. 166]

> Mosquito says I will zwing, oh!
> Mosquito says I will zwing!
> Will zwing, oh!
> Will zwing! *

The earth bow has a clear African ancestry. In almost identical form it has been found in the French Sudan, among the Washambala of East Africa, the Bongos in the eastern Congo, the Bafia and Baya in the Cameroons, the Fulbe in the Sahara region, and the Futadjallon people in Nigeria.[7]

The German explorer Georg Schweinfurth might have been describing a Haitian scene when he wrote, some eighty-five years ago, of the Bongos:

Performers may be seen sitting for an hour together with an instrument of this sort: They stick one end of the bow into the ground, and fasten the string over a cavity covered with bark, which opens into an aperture for the escape of the sound. They pass one hand from one part of the bow to another, and with the other they play upon the string with the bamboo twig and produce a variety of humming airs which are really rather pretty. This is a common pastime with the lads who are put in charge of the goats. I have seen them apply themselves very earnestly and with obvious interest to their musical practice, and the ingenious use to which they apply the secrets of the theory of sound.[8]

---

* The hum of the mosquito as it strikes.

Except for the "aperture for the escape of the sound," the Bongo instrument is identical with the Haitian earth bow. The resemblance of the instrument to a spring snare strongly suggests that it may have been developed from some such device for catching game. This possibility is strengthened by the use of the earth bow among certain of the Bambarra hunters of the French Sudan as a game lure, the music played upon it being thought to have magical properties to attract animals to the region of the hunt.[9] A "portable" type of spring snare used among the Ashanti of Ghana is strikingly similar in form to the Haitian "portable" earth bow (see fig. 80).

This instrument has survived not only in Haiti but in the United States as well. The washtub device that is an important part of American Negro folk music is a clear development of the earth bow. The washtub is inverted and a cord is attached to the tin bottom. The other end of the cord is fastened to a stick which is braced against the lip of the bottom side of the tub. The stick and the cord are manipulated precisely like the Haitian and African instruments. There is implicit evidence that the role of the washtub has been taken over in modern jazz orchestras by the double-bass fiddle.

Another device of African provenience is the Haitian *marimba* (also called *malimba, manimba,* and *marimbula*). It consists of a wooden box upon which a series of metal strips is mounted in such a way that they may be plucked with the fingers. In the face of the box, directly behind the keys, there is an aperture to permit the escape of the sound. The number of keys varies from three to seven or more, though some of them may produce duplicate tones. The instrument is usually about the size of a soap box. The musician sits upon it, facing the same way as the keyboard, and plays with his hands between his knees. The marimba is used for carnival music and for dances of the secular types, frequently in combination with a guitar, claves, and a cha-cha. It is a West Indian development of the small African *m'bila* or *sansa,* or "thumb piano." Several examples of the smaller instruments played with the thumbs have been found elsewhere in the West Indies, notably in Cuba,[10] and large forms of the sansa have been reported in recent years in Africa.

Among the instruments more or less restricted to religious service are whistles and small hand bells, which are used for invoking and saluting the loa and the dead. *Canaries* (large clay water vessels) also enter into ritual use. They are sung into, tapped with sticks, and on some occasions are covered with goatskin heads and played like a drum.

Among the noisemakers heard mostly at the time of the Rara festival (usually on Good Friday) are the *von-von,* or bull-roarer—a thin flat piece of wood whirled on the end of a cord—and the *rara,* the common wooden ratchet. Various types of wooden flutes, usually of bamboo, are also used.

In the remoter parts of the mountains you may now and then hear of an instrument known as the *banza.* A century ago, it would appear, the *banza* was a stringed instrument resembling a banjo. The similarity of names is striking, in view of the instrument's early form. Today, however, the word *banza* is applied to the homemade fiddle which is used to accompany the minuet and other old dances of European origin.

A children's instrument seen sometimes in the mountains is constructed of half of a calabash shell, across the opening of which have been stretched a number of cords. This plucked device appears to be a decadent form of the African trough zither.

19. The Music

MUSICAL NOTATIONS BY MIECZYSLAW KOLINSKI OF 186 SONGS AND DRUM RHYTHMS

The 186 examples of Haitian songs, dances, and other tunes presented in this chapter were transcribed by Dr. Mieczyslaw Kolinski from recordings made by the author in Haiti. Both the transcription work and the autography were made possible by grants from the American Philosophical Society. Approximately 400 of the recordings from which the selections were made have been deposited in the Indiana University Archives of Folk and Primitive Music, and copies are in the collection of the Northwestern University Laboratory of Comparative Musicology. Originally they were made with the coöperation and assistance of the Columbia University Archive of Primitive Music.

Examples for transcription were selected to assure that a large number of the song texts appearing elsewhere in the book would be represented. Other examples were chosen so that the musical picture would be rounded out. Included are transcriptions of a variety of drum music for the dances, cult and secular songs, music of bamboo stampers, mosquito-drum tunes, marimbula pieces, concert meringues played on the piano, and various combinations of voices and instruments.

In earlier chapters, extracts of song texts were chosen with the objective of clearly projecting the sense of the words. In a number of instances these extracts do not exactly coincide with the parts chosen by Dr. Kolinski for transcription. Dr. Kolinski found that musical phrasing does not necessarily start at the same point as the word phrasing. Occasionally he chose for musical notation a stanza other than the one from which the words were quoted elsewhere in the book. The song texts in this chapter were prepared by the author.

The titles are arbitrary and are for identification purposes only. Following each title, in parentheses, is the master number of the recording.

Most of the symbols used in the transcriptions are standard ones. To indicate a tone slightly lower than the written note, Dr. Kolinski uses the mark ↓ ; to indicate a tone slightly higher, the mark ↑ . Such variations in pitch may extend to a quarter tone. The symbol ⟨ means that a note is slightly longer than indicated, and the symbol ⟩ indicates a slight shortening.

Example 1: ARADA DRUMS (91-B)

Original pitch. ♩ = 168

Example 2: NAGO DRUMS (91-A)

Original pitch. ♩ = 168

Example 3: MAHI DRUMS (92-B)

Original pitch. ♩. = 168

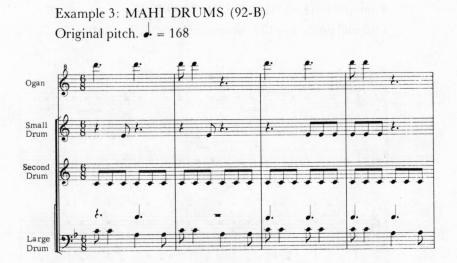

Example 4: JENVALO DRUMS (89-B)

Original pitch. ♩ = 172. Notation: Middle of recording.

Example 5: ZÉPAULE DRUMS (90-A)

Original pitch. ♩ = 156 ◁ 160

Example 6: BANDA DRUMS (305)

Original pitch +8 st. ♩ = 116. Notation: Voice, 2d stanza.
Percussion, middle of tape.

Example 7: CARABIENNE DRUMS (93-A)

Original pitch. ♩ = 168

Example 8: CALEBASSE DRUMS (101-A)

Original pitch. ♩ = 138

Example 9: DAHOMÉ DRUMS (92-A)

Original pitch. ♩ = 160 ⤙ 172

Example 10: PÉTRO DRUMS (94-A)

Original pitch. ♩♪ = 88

Example 11: KITTA MOUILLÉ DRUMS (95-B)

Original pitch. ♩ = 138

Example 12: KITTA CHÊCHE DRUMS (95-A)

Original pitch. ♩ = 208. Notation: From 2d half of record.

Example 13: BUMBA DRUMS (97-A)

Original pitch. ♩ ♪ = 92

Example 14: MOUNDONGUE DRUMS (96-A)

Original pitch. ♪. = 168

Example 15: SOLONGO DRUMS (97-B-2)

Original pitch. ♩ = 152

Example 16: CONGO LOANGUE DRUMS (98-A-1)

Original pitch. ♩ = 208

Example 17: CONGO FRANC DRUMS (23-B-1)

Original pitch. ♩. = 184

Example 18: CONGO LAROSE DRUMS (103-B)

Original pitch. ♩ = 144

Example 19: PASTOREL DRUMS (102-A)

Original pitch. ♩ = 176

Example 20: IBO DRUMS (93-B)

Original pitch. ♩ = 132

Example 21: KANGA DRUMS (94-B)

Original pitch. ♩ = 160

Example 22: JUBA DRUM (98-B)

Original pitch. ♩. = 88

Example 23: BABOULE DRUMS (99-A)

Original pitch. ♩. = 168

Example 24: MASCORT DRUMS (99-B)

Original pitch. ♩ = 168

Example 25: TI COUMBA DRUMS (100-A)
Original pitch. ♩ = 168

Assot

First
Drum

Second
Drum

Example 26: RARA TRUMPETS (35-B-2)
Original pitch – 1st. ♩ = 144

Sticks

Vaccines

1a)   1b)   1c)   1d)

Example 27: MASCARON DRUMS (53-A-1)
Original pitch. ♩. = 164. Notation: Middle of record.

First
Drum

Second
Drum

Third
Drum

Example 28: CONGO PAILLETTE DRUMS (98-A-2)

Original pitch. ♩ = 132

Example 29: CALINDA DRUMS (100-B)

Original pitch. ♩ = 168

Example 30: MAYPOLE MARIMBULA MUSIC (66-A-1)

Original pitch. ♩ = 112

Example 31: CARNIVAL MUSIC (301)
Original pitch – 2 st. ♩ = 126

Example 32: PINYIQUE DRUMS (101-B)
Original pitch. ♩ = 168

Second
Drum

Small
Drum

Large
Drum

etc.

Example 33: BAMBOO STAMPER RHYTHM (66-B-1)
Original pitch. ♩ = 144. Notation: Middle of record.

Example 34: MERINGUE DE CONCERT (PIANO) (244)

Original pitch. ♩ = 120. Notation: Right hand (left hand mostly broken chords in eighth notes).

In the course of this piece various virtuoso scales and arpeggios, running up and down through several octaves, are interspersed without affecting the strict metric scheme.

Example 35: MERINGUE DE CONCERT (PIANO) (245)

Original pitch. ♩ = ±112 rubato. Notation: Right hand (left hand: broken chords, mostly eighth notes).

Example 36: C'EST BONDIEU QUI VOYÉ MOIN (88-B)

Original pitch – 4 st. ♩ = 116

Example 37: KITTA SO'TI NAN DLEAU (74-B)

Original pitch – 5 st. Drum ♩ = 192. Drums similar to 74-A.

Voice ♩ = 112. Second voice in higher octave.

Notation: 3d stanza.

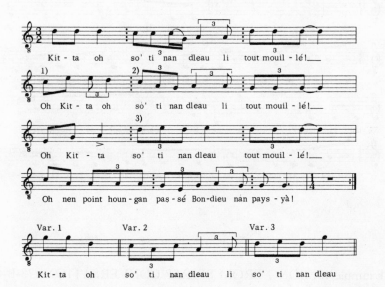

Example 38: BOCOR ZANDOLITE (301)

Original pitch – 10 st. ♩ = ± 132. Notation: 2d stanza.

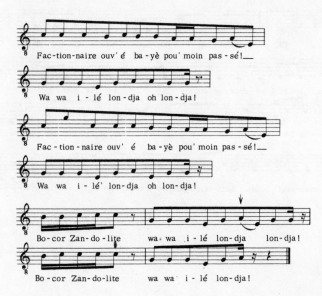

Example 39: SONG FROM SPIRIT CONVERSATION (78-B-1)
Original pitch. ♩ = 92

Example 40: SONG FROM SPIRIT CONVERSATION (78-B-4)
Original pitch. ♩ = 120

Example 41: SONG FROM FAMILY SERVICE (12-B)
Original pitch + 3 st. ♩ = 126 ⟨ 132. Chorus generally in octaves.

Example 42: CULT GREETING SONG (22-B-2)
Original pitch + 1 st. ♩ = 120. Notation: 3d stanza.

Example 43: GREETING THE LOA (2-B-3)

Original pitch – 6 st. ♩ = ± 160

Bon - jou' oh_____ bon - jou' bon - jou' bon - jou' bon - jou'! Bon-

jou' oh_____ bon - jou' bon - jou' bon - jou' bon - jou'_____ oh bon-

jou' oh bon - jou' lo - a moin!_____ Bon - jou' oh bon - jou' lo - a

moin! Oh bon - jou' oh bon - jou' bon - jou' bon - jou' bon - jou'!_____

Ou - i bon - jou' oui bon - jou' Bon - jou' bon - jou' bon - jou' Bon-

jou'!_____ Oui bon - jou' bon - jou' oh bon - jou' lo - a moin! Oui bon-

jou' bon - jou'! Oui bon - jou' lo - a moin! Bon - jou' oh! Oh bon-

jou' bon - jou' bon - jou' ça bon - jou!_____ Oui bon - jou' Pa - pa Lo - ko oui

bon - jou'! Oui bon - jou' Nèg' Da - ro - main oui bon - jou! Oh

bon - jou' mes - sieurs - dames oui bon - jou'! Oui bon - jou bon - jou' bon - jou' bon-

jou'! Pa - pé Gui - non bon - jou'! Bon - jou bon - jou' bon - jou' oh bon-

jou', oh bon - jou', oh bon - jou' lo - a moin! Bon-

jou' oh bon - jou' bon - jou' oh bon - jou' oh! Oh bon-

jou' bon - jou' bon - jou' oh bon - jou', oh!_____

Example 44: SONG TO OGOUN BALINDJO (2-A-2)

Original pitch – 3 st. ♩ = ±132. Man in lower octave.

O - goun Ba - lin - djo,__ Oh   O - goun oh!____   O - goun Ba - lin - djo,__ Oh

O - goun oh! C'est   pas man - gé ran - gé   pral   tu - yé chwal moin!

O - goun Ba - lin - djo   O - goun oh!   O - goun Ba - lin - djo,

O - goun oh! C'est   pas man - gé ran - gé   pral   tu - yé chwal moin!

Example 45: SONG ABOUT ST. JACQUES (64-A-4)

Original pitch – 11 st. ♩ = 144. Sung in octaves.
Rattle in regular quarters. Notation: 3d stanza.

St. Jacques Ma - jeur a vo - yé   dit moin   ga' - çon dé - jà!

St. Jacques   vo - yé   dit moin   ga' - çon la - guè!

(with slight variants)

Example 46: SONG TO DAMBALLA (62-A)

Original pitch – 8 st. ♩ = 152. Notation: 3d stanza.

Drums   etc.

Solo

Chorus   C'est cou - lève oh!____   Pouq' pas né - yé?

Dam - bal - la Wè - do____ c'est cou - lève oh! Pouq' ou pas né - yé?

Pouq' ou pas né - yé? Dam - bal - la   pouq' ou pas né - yé nan dleau?

Example 47: AYIDA IS A RAINBOW (231)

Original pitch. ♩. = 144. Chorus in octaves. Notation after break.

Èh_____ ap' vin' fai cou-lève! A-yi-da c'est arc en ciel! Pas_
_ wè (oh) n'ap fai cou-lève? A-yi-da c'est_ arc en ciel!

Example 48: SONG TO AGWÉ WOYO (44-A-3)

Original pitch – 1 st. Voice ♩ = ±138 rubato. Notation: Voice, 2d stanza.

Drum ♩ = 160.   Drum in the middle of record.

Yé,   Maît' A-gw-é so'-ti nan la mer   Ça-non'm char-gé!
Maît' A-gwé so'-ti nan la mer,   Ça-non'm char - gé   oh!
Ça-non'm char - gé pou'm ti - ré Maît' À'   Wo - yo!

Example 49: I AM A BULL (47-A-2)

Original pitch – 11 st. ♩ = 132 ‹ 144. Notation: 1st to 3d stanzas.

Example 50: YO DIT YO LOMMAIN NOM MOIN (55-B)

Original pitch – 1 st. ♩ = 152 ‹ 160. Notation: Lines 11-17.

Example 51: SIMBA COMES TO SEE ME (111-B-1)

Original pitch −7 st. ♩ = 132. Notation: Stanzas 1-3.

Mortar

Sim - ba   vi - ni   wè moin!___   Oh Sim-ba   vi - ni wè moin, ___ etc.

___   oh Saints ya!   Sim - ba   vi - ni wè moin!___   Oh

Sim - ba   vi - ni wè moin,   oh   Saints ya!

Sim - ba Kit - ta vi - ni wè   moin, (...)   Ah   etc.

Sim - ba   wa vi - ni wè moin___   oh Saints ya!

Example 52: SONG TO BOULICHA NAGO (53-B)

Original pitch – 5 st. ♩ = 126 ⟨ 138. Notation: 2d stanza.

Example 53: SOBO CALLS FOR THE RADA DRUMS (67-A-3)
Original pitch. ♩ = 116. Notation: 1st to 4th stanzas.

Example 54: THE LOA ARE MIXED (2-A-1)
Original pitch – 5 st. ♩ = ± 132

Example 55: SONG TO OGOUN ACHADÉ (3-A-2)

Original pitch. ♩ = 168

Example 56: SONG TO LOA GÉNÉRAL BRISÉ (5-A-1)

Original pitch − 3 st. ♩ = ± 152. Notation: 3d and 4th stanzas.

Chorus in octaves.

Example 57: SONG TO LOA BUMBA (83-A-1)

Original pitch – 4 st. ♪ = 208. Notation: 2d stanza.

(Iron notated from a later section.)

Example 58: SONG TO MAÎT' GRAND BOIS (65-B-2)

Original pitch. ♩ = 144. Drums similar to 65-A-2. Notation: 1st stanza.

Example 59: SONG TO LOA MAMBO AYIDA (234)

Original pitch – 3 st. ♩ = ± 120. Alternately solo and chorus.
Notation: 1st solo.

Mam-bo A - yi da é___ Pral' nan Gui-née-à pin-gaou mi-sé-à m'ten-

dé.___ Mam-'bo A-yi - da oh.   Pral'

nan Gui-neé-a pin-gaou mi-sé-à m'ten-┃ dé Si ou joind bon ouan-ga wa po'-

té. Si ou joind bon lo - tion wa po' - té.___

Example 60: DAMBALLA ASKS FOR FOOD (8-A-2)

Original pitch – 3 st. ♩ = 132. Regular 4/4 meter probably intended.
Notation: 3d stanza.

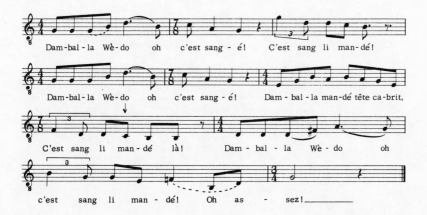

Dam-bal - la Wè-do   oh   c'est sang - é!   C'est sang li man-dé!

Dam-bal - la Wè-do   oh   c'est sang - é!   Dam - bal - la man-dé tête ca-brit,

C'est sang li man - dé là!   Dam - bal - la Wè - do   oh

c'est   sang li man - dé!   Oh as - sez!___

Example 61: SONG ABOUT OGOUN'S FEAST (85-A-2)

Original pitch – 7 st. ♩ = 126 ⤙160. Notation: Beginning of tune.

Ogan
First Drum

É   en - hé   oh!   Pa - pa O-goun qui gain yun man - gé Tout

Ogan
First Drum
Second Drum

moune (...) pas man - gé   Pa-pa O - goun qui gain' yun man - gé Tout___

Ogan
First Drum
Second Drum
Third Drum

_moune pas (..)man-gé li!   En-hé   oh en-hé oh!_____

Example 62: OGOUN ASKS FOR FOOD (54-B-2)
Original pitch – 9 st. ♩ = 152. Notation: 2d stanza.

Example 63: SONG ABOUT MOUNDONGUE'S FEAST (62-B-2)
Original pitch – 6 st. ♩ = 168. Drums similar to 63-A-1.

Moun-dongue   oh _____   Moun-dongue man - gé
cab- rit bou-lé! Moun-dongue oh   yè   yè   yè Moun-dongue
oh _____   yè! Moun-dongue oh   yè   yè   yè
(with variants)

Example 64: SONG ABOUT MOUNDONGUE (63-A-1)
Original pitch – 1 st. ♩ = 168

Co - to pas-sé na ba' ou man - gé oh Moun-dongue nà! Co-
to pas - sé na ba' ou man - gé oh Moun - dongue nà!

oh Ti Moun-dongue nà
oh Ti Moun - dongue nà

Example 65: ADJA EATS GLASS (8-A-3)

Original pitch – 2 st. ♩ = 132. Notation: Last stanza.

A - dja oh! A - dja - sou man - gé boun-da dè - mi - jon!

Vé - co' vé - co'! A - dja man - gé boun - da dè - mi - jon! A - dja

vé - co' vé - co'!

*) Second triplet eighth sometimes omitted.

Example 66: IBO SACRIFICE SONG (76-A)

Original pitch – 7 st. ♩ = 126. Chorus in higher octave. Notation:

3d and 4th stanzas.

Drums similar to 75-B.

(...) I - bo m'ta man - gé gros coq oh nan - chon I - bo

Waille waille waille! Waille waille waille!

Example 67: SONG ABOUT LOA NAGO (53-A-2)

Original pitch – 6 st. ♩ = 152. Notation: 2d stanza.

Example 68: SONG ABOUT SIMBI KITTA (3-B-1)

Original pitch – 5 st. ♩ = ± 144

Example 69: SONG ABOUT LOKO (60-B)

Original pitch – 10 st. Voice ♩ = 144. Drums ♩. = 168. Notation: 6th stanza.

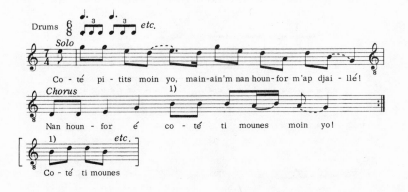

Example 70: LEAVES IN THE WOODS (63-B)

Original pitch – 1 st. ♩ = 184. Notation: 1st and 2d stanzas. Chorus in octaves.

Example 71: SONG TO MACAYA BUMBA (58-A)
Original pitch – 3 st. ♩ = 120 ◁ 152. Notation: 2d time.
Drum notation: Toward end of record. Chorus in octaves.

Ma - ca - ya Bum - ba   Bum - ba!____ lè - vé dan - sé!____
_ Ma - ca - ya Bum - ba 'Ca - ya   lè - vé dan - sé!
Var. 1   Var. 2
-vé dan - sé, Oh! Ma - ca - ya   lè - vé dan - sé!

Example 72: SONG ABOUT THE IBO DANCE (75-B)
Original pitch +2 st. ♩ = 116. Chorus in higher octave.
Notation: Toward beginning of record.

I - bo lé - lé!_____   I - bo lé - lé! Nan-chon I - bo
ça oi gain-yain con ça   I - bo lé - lé!

Example 73: SONG ABOUT THE KITTA DANCE (73-B)
Original pitch – 2 st. ♩ = 200. Main drum in regular eighths.

Kit - ta Con - go oh ti ga' - çon ba'm pas Kit - ta!
M'dit pi - tit ga' - çon p'tit ga' - çon ba'm pas Kit - ta!
*(25 times with
slight variants)*

Example 74: SONG TO DAMBALLA AND NAGO (42-B-2)

Original pitch – 5 st. ♩ = 160 ⪤ 168. Notation: Lines 5-8.

Drum notation: From the middle of record.

Fi - lé na fi - lé Dam - bal - la Wè - do vi - ni wè moin!

Fi - lé na fi - lé Nèg' Na - go vi - ni wè'm là!

Fi - lé na fi - lé Dam - bal - la Wè - do vi - ni wè moin!

Fi - lé na fi - lé Pa - pa____ wa vi - ni wè'm là!

Example 75: SONG ABOUT DANCING (51-A-2)

Original pitch – 6 st. ♩ = 152. Chorus in octaves. Notation: 1st stanza.

La - illé la - illé!____ La - illé la - illé oh vié - co'! La - illé la -

illé oh vié-co'! Tam - bou - yé bou-ké!____ La - illé la - illé oh!__ Tam - bou - yé bou -

ké!____ La - illé la - illé oh vié-co'! Tam - bou - yé bou ké!__ La - illé la -

illé oh la - illé la - illé oh vié-co'!__ La - illé la - illé Da - ro - main! Tam - bou-yé bou-ké la!__

Example 76: THREE LEAVES, THREE ROOTS (29-B-2)

Original pitch +3 st. ♩ = 138. Notation: 1st stanza.

Trois fé trois ci-tron oh!_____ Trois fé trois ra-cine

oh!____ Moin dit rwo, youn jour ou wa be-soin moin! Trois fé trois ra-cine

oh!___ Moin dit oui, youn jour ou wa be-soin moin! Gain'-yain bas - sin moin___

trois ra-cine tom-bé la-dans Quand ou wa 'bli - é___ fau' ra-mas-sé chon - gé!_____

Example 77: SONG OF WARNING (51-B)

Original pitch + 1 st. ♩ = 100. Notation: 1st stanza. (The drum pattern is composed by different instruments.)

Example 78: SONG TO LOA KITTA DÉMAMBRÉ (74-A)

Original pitch – 3 st. Drums: ♩ = 192.

Voice: ♩ = ± 184 (rubato). Second voice in lower octave.

Notation: Voice from 4th stanza.

Drums from toward end of record.

Kit - ta Dé-mam-bré, oh pin - ga ou fai'm ça en-core oh! Kit-

ta Dé - mam - bré, pin - ga ou fai'm ça en-core oh! Kit-

ta Dé-mam-bré, pin - ga on fai'm ça en-core oh! Nan Lé - o-

gane ti pou - le là mou - ri nan zé! Nan Lé - o-

gane ti pou - le là mou - ri zé là! Kit-

ta Dé - mam - bré, oh pin - ga ou fai'm ça en-core é!

Example 79: DERÉA'S PAVILLION (30-B)

Original pitch – 9 st. ♩ = 138 ‹ 152. Notation: 6th and 7th stanzas.

Example 80: STEP ON MY FOOT AND ASK MY PARDON (57-A-1)

Original pitch – 5 st. ♩ = 120. Notation: 2d stanza. Chorus in octaves.

Example 81: FOR OGOUN YÈKKÈ AND OGOUN KÉNISON (54-B-1)

Original pitch – 3 st. ♩ = 152. Notation: 3d stanza.

'goun é Yèk-kè   Nèg' Ké-ni-son é!   O-goun é Yèk-kè

Nèg' Ké-ni-son é!   Tous les jours   n'a-

pé pa'-lé O-goun mal! O-goun   pas conn' be-ti-sé!

Example 82: FOR OGOUN PANAMA (1-B-2)

Original pitch – 3 st. ♩ = ± 116

O-goun   c'est Nèg' Pa-na-ma é!_____ Yo vi-ni ga'-dé!

Yo vi-ni ga'-dé oh!__   Oh O-goun   c'est Nèg' Pa-na-ma

é!____   (Y') O-goun   c'est Nèg' Pa-na-ma é!   O-

goun   c'est Nèg' Pa-na-ma é!   Yo vi-ni ga'-dé!

Yo vi-ni pa'-lé oh!__   Oh O-goun   c'est Nèg' Pa-na-ma é!__

Example 83: FOR AÏSON (65-A-2)

Original pitch –6 st. ♩ = 144. Notation: 2d stanza.

Example 84: FOR SIMBI (61-A)

Original pitch –8 st. ♩ = ±152. Notation: 2d stanza. Chorus in lower octave.

Example 85: SONG FOR MASTER OF THE CROSSROADS (72-A)

Original pitch – 2 st. ♩ =224. Principal drum in regular eighths.

Notation: 1st stanza.

Temp' chan - gé   nou-velle al   - - lé   nou!   Bon-jou' Pa - pa
bon - jou' Maît' Grand Chi - min!   M'man - dé Pa - pa   ça'm fai! (...)
Bon - jou' Pa - pa   bon - jou' Maît' Grand Chi-min!   M'man - dé Pa - pa
ça'm fai!   Pa - pa   m'pas ma - ïs mou - lin!   Nou dit na   bou - git
moin!   Pa - pa m'pas ma - ïs mou - lin! Nou dit na bou-git moin!

Example 86: SONG ABOUT A SICK HOUNSI (66-B-2)

Original pitch – 2 st. ♩ = 152. Percussion similar to 66-B-1.

Notation: 2d stanza.

É   moin al - lé   wè   oh,____   houn - si ma - lade (é)   oh!____
Moin   al - lé   wè   oh,____   houn - si ma - lade (é)   oh!____
M'pral-lé wè oh houn-gan,   houn-si ma-lade (é) jo - di - à!

Example 87: FOR LOA ST. JACQUES (2-B-2)

Original pitch – 6 st. ♩ = ±132

Example 88: PIERRE NARCISSE (64-B-2)

Original pitch – 7 st. ♩ = 138. Notation: 1st stanza. Sung in octaves.

Example 89: FOR ATTI DAÏ (64-B-1)

Original pitch –7 st. ♩ = 138. Sung in octaves. Rattle in regular quarters.
Notation: 1st stanza.

At - ti Da - i oh! Yo vo - yé dit moin Min so - leil ma - lade!

Quan'm té ri - vé___ Moin joind so - leil mou - rit!___

Quan'm té ri - vé___ Moin joind so - leil mou - rit!

C'est re - gret - tant ça Pou'm en - ter - ré so - leil!

Example 90: FOR ÈZILIE (56-A)

Original pitch +2 st. Voice (rubato) ♩ = ±104. Drums ♩ = 144.
Notation: 5th stanza.

Drums ... etc. *(Strict drum rhythm indepen-dent of free voice rhythm)*

La - rou - zé fai ban - da tout temps so - leil pas lé - vé!___

La - rou - zé fai ban - da tout temps so - leil pas lé - vé!___

È - zi - lie Nai - nain oh! È - zi - lie Nain - nain oh!___

___ È - zi - lie Fré - da oh, co - té moin bo' Ya - ga - za!

Example 91: SONG ABOUT TROU FOURBAN (1-B-1)

Original pitch – 4 st. ♩ = ±168

Con - duit'm al - lé___ oh!___ Con - duit'm al - lé djab nan

Trou Four - ban! Con - duit'm al - lé!___ Con - duit'm al - lé con-

duit'm al - lé___ oh!___ Con - duit'm al - lé djab nan

Trou Four - ban! Con - duit'm al - lé oh! Con-

duit'm al - lé djab nan Trou Four - ban! Con - duit'm al - lé!

1) Last Stanza

Con - duit'm al - lé con - duit'm al - lé oh!___ Con-

Example 92: MOSQUITO BEWARE THE ZOMBIE (27-B-1)

Original pitch – 10 st. ♩ = 152. Notation: 1st stanza.

Catas   simile

Ma - rin - gouin pin - ga zom - bie oh, ___ Bo - bo Ma - ri - a! Ma - rin - gouin

pin - ga zom - bie, oh! Bo - bo Ma - ri - a Ma - rin - gouin zom - bie oh, ___

Bo - bo Ma - ri - a! Oh oh oh oh oh oh oh oh oh oh oh oh oh oh Ma - rin - gouin

pin - ga zom - bie Ma - rin - gouin pin - ga zom - bie Ma - rin - gouin pin - ga zom - bie pin - ga zom - bie

pin - ga zom - bie Ma - rin - gouin pin - ga zom - bie

Earth Bow   etc.

(approximately)

Example 93: WE'RE GOING TO EAT A ZOMBIE (14-B-2)

Original pitch – 3 st. ♩ = 132 ⋜ 144. Female chorus in upper octave.

1. Chain-ga-daing, nou pral man-gé zom-bie! Chain-ga-daing, nou pral man-gé zom-bie!

(Sometimes omitted by the Soloist)

2. Chain-ga-daing, nou pral man-gé zom-bie! Chain-ga-daing, nou teau__ teau teau!

(17 more stanzas; then:)

20. Chain-ga-daing, non pral man-gé zom-bie! Tain-ga-daing!__

Example 94: LEAVE ME, FRIENDS (8-A-1)

Original pitch – 4 st. ♩ = 156

Za-mis près moin quit-té ma za-mis loin moin, yo!__

__ Za-mis près moin quit-té ma za-mis loin moin! Za-mis

loin moin__ c'est la-'gent sè-ré! Za-mis près moin__ c'est cou-teau

dé-bord, quit-té ma za-mis loin moin!

(5 times with slight variants)

Example 95: BLACK MAN, LIKE THIS YOU ARE (13-A-3)

Original pitch – 9 st. ♩ = 112. Notation: 2d stanza.

Example 96: THREE PAIRS OF SLAPS (43-B-3)

Original pitch – 3 st. ♩ = 126. Notation: 1st stanza.

Example 97: I'M USED TO EATING FROM A BOWL (108-B-2)
Original pitch −7 st. ♩ = 144. Notation: Stanzas 5-7.

Example 98: TO A HOUNGÉNICON (30-A)
Original pitch +9 st. ♩ = ±104. Drums mainly in eighth triplets ♩ = 160.
Notation: 1st stanza.

Example 99: TO A HOUNSI (50-B-3)

Original pitch – 1 st. ♩ = 168. Notation: 3d stanza.

*(5 times
with variants)*

Example 100: DISASTER FALLS (43-A-3)

Original pitch – 9 st. ♩ = ±126 rubato. Notation: 1st stanza.

Example 101: TALK QUIETLY (47-B-1)

Original pitch – 9 st. ♩ = ±126. Notation: Last stanza.

1st singer

Tout ça (oh) non pa'-lé.   Pi-tit cau-sé nous pa'-lé.

2nd singer

A-na-go   ça nou wè   là?

*(5 times
with variants)*

Example 102: WHEN I LOST MY MOTHER I CRIED (3-A-1)

Original pitch – 6 st. ♩ = ±104

Ma cri-é,   Oh qua'm per-dit man-man moin ma ré-lé!

[*)

[Ma ré-lé,   Oh qua'm per-dit man-man moin ma cri-é!]

Qua'm per-dit un gar-çon   moin join' l'aut' oh!

Qua'm per-dit un gar-çon   moin join l'aut'   oh!____

Ma ré-lé,   Oh qua'm per-dit man-man moin ma cri-é!

*Skipped in 2nd stanza.

(3 times)

Example 103: THE PRESIDENT CALLS ME (111-A-3)

Original pitch – 9 st. ♩ = 132. Notation: 2d stanza.

*Quarter notes occasionally subdivided into two eighths.

Example 104: TO OGOUN BALINDJO (1-A-1)

Original pitch – 1 st. ♩ = ±116. Notation: 2d stanza.

Example 105: TO OGOUN FERAILLE (1-A-2)

Original pitch – 1 st. ♩ = 144

Pa - pa O - goun___ ga' - dé mi - sè! Maît' O - goun___ ga' - dé mi-

sè!   Ga' - dé mi - sè Pa - pa O - goun ga' - dé mi - sè là!   O-

goun___   ga' - dé mi - sè   Pa - pa O - goun nou wè nou wè mi-

sè   Ga' - dé mi - sè O - goun Fe - raille ga' - dé mi - sè jo - di - à!   O-

goun___   ga' - dé mi - sè!___ Pa - pa O - goun ou wa ga' - dé mi - sè!

Example 106: ABOUT AN ARGUMENT (67-B-2)

Original pitch – 6 st. ♩ = 112

Bamboo
Stampers
Ogan
1)

Ci - yé!   C'est ba - gaille grand moune! Ci-

yé!   C'est ba - gaille grand moune!

Var. 1

Ci - yé! Moin dit c'est ba - gaille grand moune! Ci-

Example 107: I SENT LANMECI TO THE WATER (82-A-4)
Original pitch – 8 st. ♩ = 138 ◁ 160. Notation: 3d stanza.
Drum similar to 82-A-3.

Moin vo - yé li nan dleau, Li pas al - lé!

Moin vo - yé Lan - me - ci nan dleau, Li pas al - lé!

Là'm té, co - té ou té yé! Là'm té yé!

Là'm té yé!___ Là'm té yé! Là'm té yé Là'm!

Example 108: IT ISN'T MY FAULT (43-A-1)
Original pitch – 9 st. ♩ = ±126 rubato. Notation: 2d stanza.

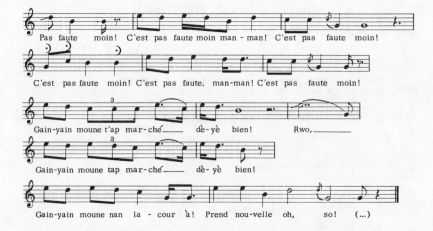

Pas faute moin! C'est pas faute moin man - man! C'est pas faute moin!

C'est pas faute moin! C'est pas faute, man - man! C'est pas faute moin!

Gain - yain moune t'ap mar - ché___ dè - yè bien! Rwo,___

Gain - yain moune tap mar - ché___ dè - yè bien!

Gain - yain moune nan la - cour à! Prend nou - velle oh, so! (...)

Example 109: HOW TO JUDGE WOMEN (104-A-2)

Original pitch −8 st. ♩ = 200. Notation: 1st stanza.

Example 110: SONG ABOUT ACHÉLO (104-B)

Original pitch – 6 st. ♩ = 112. Notation: Percussion introduction and 1st stanza.

Example 111: ABOUT PRESIDENT SAM (37-B-1)

Original pitch – 2 st. ♩ = ±132 rubato.

Notation: 2d and 3d stanzas (stanza 1 = 2, stanzas 4 + 5 = 2 + 3).

Example 112: IN PRAISE OF NORD'S SOLDIERS (37-A-2)

Original pitch – 2 st. ♩ = 112. Notation: 1st stanza.

Example 113: ALEXIS NORD, YOU ARE A GOOD CHIEF (37-A-1)

Original pitch – 2 st. ♩ = ±144. Notation: 3d stanza.

A - le - xis Nord Pa - pa ou bon chef oh! Ou bas nous mo - né,

ou bas nous pa - pier! A - le - xis Nord Pa - pa ou bon chef oh!

Ou bas nous mo - né, Ou bas nous pa - pier! Nous

pas man - dé ou a-nyien! Nous pas man - dé l'a' - gent en - co'! Pa-

pa Nord ça nous té man-dé oh chef, C'est bam-boche nous man - dé ou!

Example 114: ABOUT ÇÉÇÉ NORD (37-B-2)

Original pitch – 7 st. ♩ = 160. Notation: Lines 2-6.

Çé-çé té dit A - le - xis Nord grand moune nan tout corps li!

Çé-çé té dit la quit - té pour voir l'heure li vlé!

Çé-çé té dit Ton-ton Nord grand moune nan tout corps li'l

Çé-çé té dit con ça A - le - xis Nord grand moune nan tout corps l'!

etc.

Çé-çé te dit la lais - sé pour voir l'heure li vlé!

Example 115: IT IS GOD WHO PUT YOU THERE (37-A-3)

Original pitch – 3 st. ♩ = ±108. Notation: 1st and 2d stanzas.

Example 116: ANTOINE SIMON, HURRY AND LEAVE (37-A-4)

Original pitch – 12 st. ♩ = 132. Notation: 1st and 3d stanzas.

stanzas 4, 5, 7, 8 = 1, 2
stanza 6 = 3

Example 117: FOR PRESIDENT ESTIMÉ (204)
Original pitch +4 st. ♩ = 138.
Notation: Last stanza. Chorus mostly in octaves.

Example 118: SALUTE TO THE PRESIDENT (22-B-1)

Original pitch. ♩ = 120. Drum notation: Last stanza.

Pré - si - dent pas - sé là, l'ap mon - té au gou - vern - ment! Pré - si -

dent pas - sé là, l'ap mon - té au gou - vern - ment!

(8 times)

Example 119: ABOUT JEAN ZOMBIE (27-B-2)

Original pitch +7 st. ♩ = 152

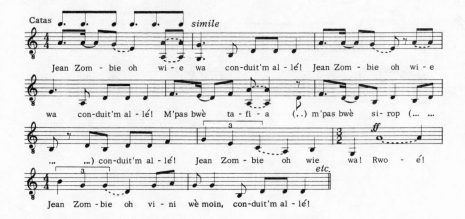

Jean Zom - bie oh wi - e wa con-duit'm al - lé! Jean Zom - bie oh wi - e

wa con-duit'm al - lé! M'pas bwè ta - fi - a (..) m'pas bwè si - rop (... ...

... ...) con-duit'm al - lé! Jean Zom - bie oh wie wa! Rwo - é!

Jean Zom - bie oh vi - ni wè moin, con-duit'm al - lé!

Example 120: TAKE ME TO BORNO'S PARLOR (61-B)

Original pitch –2 st. ♩ = 120.

Notation: 10th stanza (main voice; 2d voice mostly in octaves).

Example 121: TAKE ME TO THE POLICE STATION (68-A-1)

Original pitch – 3 st. ♩ = 168

Example 122: TAKE ME TO THE FIGHT (79-A)

Original pitch – 3 st. ♩ = 132. Notation: 3d stanza.

Example 123: DICE GAME (58-B-2)

Original pitch – 2 st. Voice: ♩ = 92. Marimba and claves: ♩ = 138.
Notation: 4th stanza.

Example 124: VINBINDINGUE SONG (62-B-1)

Original pitch – 3 st. ◁ –2 st. ♩ = 168. Notation: 2d stanza.
Drums similar to 62-A.

Bal - bin-dingue! C'est là n'homme mwé yé! Ci-mi-tière (... ... ...

... ...) qui dan - sé! Par - don mon père!

Bal - bin-dingue! C'est là n'homme mwé yé!

Example 125: PEPPER ORDEAL (49-A-1)

Original pitch – 7 st. ♩ = 152

Jé'm pé - té   m'pas wè la - dans ma mét - té pi - ment!

Jé'm pé - té   m'pas wè la - dans ma mét - té di - fé!

(9 times)

Var. 1   Var. 2a

Var. 2b   Var. 2c

Var. 2d   Var. 3a

Jé'm pé - té moin pas wè la -

Var. 3b   Var. 3c

Var. 4a   Var. 4b   Var. 4c

Example 126: ABOUT A VICTIM (49-A-4)

Original pitch. ♩ = 152. Drums as in Ex. 127. Notation: 2d stanza.

Dé - vor a dé - qua - tier ça ou pi - tôt?___ Dé - vor a dé - qua -

tier ça ou pi - tôt? Dé - qua - tier! Moin pi - tôt dé - qua - tier!

(7 times with slight var.)

Example 127: ABOUT CIMILA (49-A-3)

Original pitch – 1 st. ♩ = 144

Y'r - é - soi' Ci - mi - la man - gé ti mounes yo!___ Y'r - é-

soi' Ci - mi - la man - gé ti mounes yo!___ *(6 times)*

Example 128: WASH WITHOUT BLUING (49-A-2)

Original pitch – 1 st. ♩ = 152

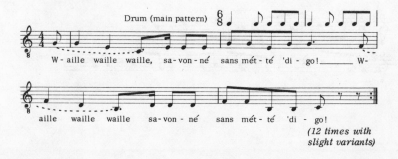

W - aille waille waille, sa - von - né sans mét - té 'di - go!___ W-

aille waille waille sa - von - né sans mét - té 'di - go!

(12 times with slight variants)

Example 129: BALANCÉ YAYA (16-A-3)

Original pitch −6 st. ♩ = 112

Example 130: CIPAN CIMALO (14-B-1)

Original pitch +2 st. ♩ = 126 ◁ 138

With female voices in upper octave

Example 131: DÉLINA (38-A-3)

Original pitch – 2 st. ♩ = 126

Dé-li-na!___ Co-té'm pas-sé c'est Dé-li-na!___ En-hé é en-hé! Co-té'm vi-ré,

Dé-li-na!___ Co-té'm vi-ré c'est Dé-li-na! En-hé oh en-hé! Co-té'm pas-sé,

Dé-li-na!___ Co-té'm vi-ré c'est Dé-li-na!___ Man-man man-man,

Dé-li-na!___ Pa-pa pa-pa, Dé-li-na!___ Man-man man-man,

Dé-li-na!___ Pa-pa pa-pa, Dé-li-na!___ Co-té'm pas-sé c'est

Dé-li-na!__ En-hé oh en-hé! Co-té'm vi-ré, Dé-li-na!__ Co-té'm vi-ré, c'est

Dé-li-na!___ En-hé oh en-hé! Co-té'm pas-sé, Dé-li-na!__ Co-té'm vi-ré, c'est

Dé-li-na!___ Dé-li-na jo-bé oh jo-bé, Dé-li-na! Jo-bé pou' l'a-gent, Dé-li-na!

Jo-bé jo-bé, Dé-li-na! Jo-bé pou' l'a-gent, Dé-li-na! Jo-bé, jo-bé, Dé-li-na!
etc.

Jo-bé pou' l'a-gent, Dé-li-na! Jo-bé jo-bé, Dé-li-na! Jo-bé pou' l'a-gent, Dé-li-na!

Main rhythmic pattern : Sticks / Hand-Clapping   Other notation

Example 132: SINDÉ MACAYA (38-A-2)

Original pitch – 5 st. ♩ = 108 ⤙126. Notation: 2d stanza.

Original pitch of claves: c^4

Example 133: FOR ÈZILIE WÊDO (2-B-1)

Original pitch – 1 st. ♩ = ±132. Notation: 2d stanza.

È - zi - lie Wè - do   a - go___ oh! Cré - ole dit con ça,

nan point Gui - née en - co', n'ap fai ça nou vlé!___

È - zi - lie Wè - do a - go oh!   Créole dit con ça,

nan point Gui - née en - co', n'ap fai ça nou vlé oh! M'a-

po ri - vé corps moin, m'a - po tour - né corps moin

pou'm fai ça nou vlé oh!___ M'a - po ri - vé corps moin, m'a-

pé tour - né corps moin pou'm fai ça nou vlé oh!

(4 times al Fine with slight variants)

vlé!   A - go - é a - go - é!___

Female voice in upper octave

Example 134: PRAYER SONG (2-A-3)

Original pitch – 13 st. ♩ = ± 120

La   qua - ran-taine trois dames, trois vierges   pri - è'   pou' saints yo,

La   pri - è'   pou'   les   saints   mar - ché!

La   qua-ran-taine trois dames, trois vierges   pri - è'   pou' saints yo,

La   pri - è'   pou'   les   saints   mar-ché,___   pri - è'   pou' les saints yo!   Pri-

è'   pou' loa   yo,___   Saint   An - toine,   oh___   n'a - pé   man - dé   par - don!___

Example 135: IN AFRICA THERE ARE LOA (3-B-2)

Original pitch – 1 st. Voice: ♩ = ± 144. Drums in eighth triplets: ♩ = 160

Nan Gui - née   gain-yain   lo - a   oh!___   É - vo   é - vo,   houn - si   kan-

zo!   É -   vo   é - vo   houn - si   kan - zo!   Nan Gui - née   gain-yain loa,

aï - bo - bo!   Nan Gui - née   'a-gain   lo - a   oh!

N.B.   Men in lower octave   (5 times with
                                                                            slight variants)

Example 136: FOR ACHADÉ (4-A-1)

Original pitch – 1 st. ♩ = 160

(4 times with slight variants)

Example 137: BEAT THE DRUM FOR ME (6-A-2)

Original pitch – 6 st. Voice: ♩ = ± 168. Percussion ♩ = 184. Chorus in unison.

Ma - yenne ka pou' moin!___ N'a - pé rè - sul - tè, ma - yenne ka___

pou' moin!___ Ma - yenne ka pou' moin! N'a - pé rè - sul - tè

ma - yenne ka pou' moin! Trois fois pas - sé l'An - ge - lise oh!___ Trois

fois pas - sé l'An - ge - lise oh! N'a - pé ré - sul - tè ma - yenne ka___ pou' moin!

(5 times with slight variants)

Example 138: LIBERIST TOMBÉ (4-A-2)

Original pitch – 3 st. ♩ = ± 132. Notation: 3d and 4th stanzas.

Li - be - rist tom - bé!___ Li - be - rist tom - bé!___ A - dié! M'a

voy' yun qué bèf là oh do - do! Li - be - rist tom - bé ___ é - é!

Li - be - rist tom - bé là yoh! M'a voy' yun qué bèf, en do - do!

Female chorus in higher octave

Example 139: FOR LOKO (13-B-1)

Original pitch − 5 st. ♩ = 132

Example 140: COUSIN, OH (9-B-1)

Original pitch − 4 st. ♩. = ± 80

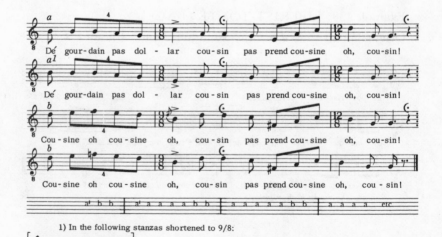

1) In the following stanzas shortened to 9/8:

Example 141: CULT SONG IN LANGAGE (45-B-3)
Original pitch – 3 st. ♩ = 138

Example 142: CALLING DAMBALLA (13-B-2)
Original pitch – 8 st. Voice: ♩. = 80. Rattles: ♩ = 80. Notation: 2d stanza.

N.B. *First measure skipped in 3d to 6th, 9th and 11th stanzas.*

Example 143: ABOUT THE LOA IBO (49-B-1)

Original pitch – 1 st. ♩ = 108 ⤙ 132 (accelerando takes place during the first two stanzas). Notation: Stanzas 2-4.

Example 144: FOR SAMARDI KAMA (49-B-2)

Original pitch – 1 st. ♩ = 132. Chorus in octaves. Notation: Lines 6 and 7.

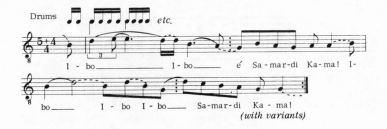

Example 145: FOR MARIANNI (49-B-3)

Original pitch – 1 st. ♩ = 132. Chorus in octaves. Notation: 4th stanza.

Example 146: MAGIC-MAKING SONG IN LANGAGE (45-B-2)

Original pitch – 4 st. ♩ = 132. Notation: 2d stanza.

Example 147: CALLING OSANGE (50-A-2)

Original pitch + 4 st. ♩ = 160 ⤙ 168

Leader
Ré-lé O-sange   ré-lé La - bo-san nan dleau   O-sange
oh ré - lé O - sange   nan dleau!   O - sange
oh,   ré - lé O - sange nan dleau!

(13 times with variants)

Example 148: FOR YABOFÉ LIMBA (55-A-2)

Original pitch − 5 st. ♩ = 138. Notation: 4th stanza.

Drums
Ya - bo - fé mon cher yo pas be - soin moin!____

M'pral-lé wè mi - tan si na djag-wé!____   Ya-bo - fé mon

cher yo pas be - soin mwé!____ M'pral-lé wè mi - tan si na djag-wé!__

Fe - rei pas pé wè'm en-core! M'pral-lé wè mi - tan si ya djag-wé!

Example 149: CULT SONG (51-A-1)

Original pitch −6 st. ♩ = 152. Drums as in preceding song.
Notation: Last stanza.

Mè - né m'al - lé   oh!___   Mè - né m'al - lé   oh!___   Mè - né m'al-

lé   oh! Mè - né m'al - lé   oh! Mè - né m'al - lé   oh! La -caille oh!___

Example 150: SONG TO DAMBALLA (56-B)

Original pitch +2 st. ♩ = 176 ⪦ 184. Notation: 2d stanza.

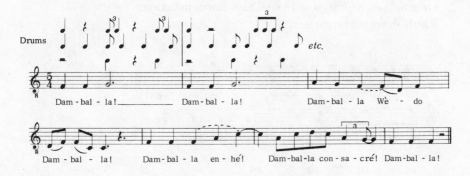

Dam - bal - la!___   Dam - bal - la!   Dam - bal - la Wè - do

Dam - bal - la!   Dam - bal - la en - hé!   Dam-bal-la con - sa - cré! Dam - bal - la!

Example 151: IBO MELODY (57-A-2)

Original pitch −4 st. ♩ = 126. Notation: Toward end of record.
Chorus in octaves. Drums similar to 57-A-1.

I - bo moin yune oh!___

Example 152: ABOUT DAMBALLA (64-A-1)

Original pitch – 8 st. ♪. = 76

Fi - lé   na   fi - lé,   Dam-bal - la Wè - do, c'est cou-lève oh! Fi-lé

na   fi - lé Dam-bal - la   Wè - do   c'est cou-lève oh!

Example 153: LOKO SINDÉ ASKS FOR WIND (64-A-2)

Original pitch – 6 st. ♩ = 144 ⌐152. Chorus in octaves.

Rattle in regular quarters.

A - lo - ko Sin-dé man-dé vent é!   Vent vent vent Lo - ko

Sin - dé man-dé vent é!   Vent vent vent!

Example 154: DON'T YOU SEE I'M INNOCENT (64-B-3)
Original pitch – 7 st. ♩ = ± 144. Second voice in unison. Notation: 1st stanza.

Example 155: SONG FOR MARIANNI MOUNDONGUE (63-A-2)
Original pitch – 5 st. ♩ = 208. Notation: Middle of record. Drums similar to 63-A-1.

Example 156: ABOUT AZUI (65-A-1)

Original pitch −8 st. ♩ = 144. Notation: 3d stanza.

A - zui oh m' c'est cou - lève oh! _____ A - zui Pa - pa
m' c'est cou - lève oh! A - zui oh m' c'est cou - lève oh!
A - zui Pa - pa moin c'est cou - lève oh Pas wè pouin yà ga - té? _____
Ou pas wè pouin yà ga - té? C'est rou-lé n'ap rou-lé'm en bas la boue! M'a sonde as - son!

(with slight variants)

Example 157: FOR AYIDA (230)

Original pitch −1 st. ♩ = 160. Sung alternately as solo and chorus in octaves.
Notation: Solo of 2d stanza.

Ogan
Drums
Ah! C'est moin, c'est moin(... ... ...)
C'est moin! _____ C'est moin oh, c'est moin Man - zè A - yi - da,
c'est moin! _____ Chi - ta 'bord ba - ti - man ya pa'-lé nous mal oh!
C'est moin (...) oh, c'est moin po'-teau plan - té c'est moin. _____

Example 158: AYIDA ISN'T JOKING (232)

Original pitch –2 st. ♩ = ±144. Alternately solo and chorus (in octaves and occasional third parallels). Notation: 1st solo.

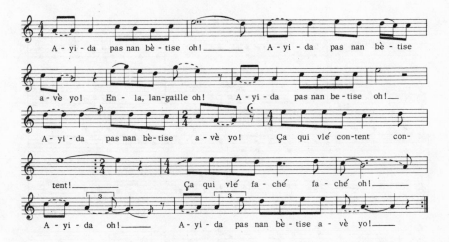

Example 159: VIVE LE ROI (233)

Original pitch –1 st. ♩ = ± 138. Alternately solo and chorus (in octaves). Notation: 1st solo.

Example 160: FOR LEGBA AGUATOR (235)

Original pitch −2 st. ♩. = 120. Alternately solo and chorus.

Notation: Voice, 1st solo. Accompaniment, 1st chorus.

Example 161: COLICO YAYA (FROM A CONTE) (14-B-3)

Original pitch − 4 st. ♩ = 152

Example 162: FROG JUMPS (FROM A CONTE) (36-B-3)

Original pitch. ♩ = 132. Notation: 6th stanza.

Example 163: PIG SAYS WAIN (GAGE SONG) (14-A-3)

Original pitch −2 st. ♩ = 116. Notation: 1st stanza.

Example 164: MAKE BWEMENT GO (GAGE SONG) (16-A-1)

Original pitch −8 st. ♩ = 126. Notation: 2d stanza.

Bwè-ment rwo! A - dieu Bwè-ment fai Bwè-ment

mar-ché! Bwe-ment c'est ça c'est ça Bwè-ment! Fai Bwè-ment mar-ché!

(3 times with slight variants)

Example 165: YOU ARRIVE, RIGAL (16-B-4)

Original pitch −8 st. ♩ = 168. Chorus in upper octave. Notation: 3d stanza.

Ou ri - vé Ri - gal,___ ou en-tré! Ou ri - vé Ri - gal,___

ou ri - vé! A - la ki - lé___ Ri-gal tourné en gros co - chon,

li - ri - vé Jac - mel pou' ra - bou - ré nous!

(In all other stanzas)

Example 166: MOSQUITO SONG (82-A-3)

Original pitch − 8 st. ♩ = 138 ⤙ 168. Notation: Toward beginning of record.

Example 167: CARNIVAL SONG (22-B-3)

Original pitch −7 st. ♩ = 104 ◁ 120. Notation: 2d stanza.

Claves ... simile

Ti ga'-çon rè-té sou ter-race, li frap-pé pié'l da - o dao!____

1. 2. Ti ga'-çon Oh dé-chè-nè bai yo pai-llette oh!

Ti ga'-çon rè-té sou bwe-ton, li frap-pe pié'l da - o dao!____

Dé-chè-ne bai yo pai-llette oh!____ En - ra - gé bai

yo pai-llette oh! Ma-yousse! Cha-ché femme part ou ma-yousse! Ma - you-

5 times D.C.

youss! Part ou Ma-yousse! Cha-ché femme part ou ma-yousse! Ma - you-yousse!

Example 168: MOLTA MALO ("SPANISH" SONG) (58-B-1)

Original pitch −2 st. ♩ = 126. Notation: Toward middle of record.

Claves

Mol - ta ma - lo! É - ya mi ma - lo! Mol - ta ma -

Marimbula

etc.

lo! É - ya mi ma - lo!

Example 169: ANGELIQUE, OH (210)

Original pitch +2 st. ♩ = 132. Rattles in regular eighth notes; guitar in regular sixteenth notes. Accompanying voice of boy in upper octave. Notation: 1st stanza. The chord symbols refer to the guitar.

(with variants)

Example 170: CARNIVAL MELODY (302)

Original pitch −2 st. ♩ = 152. Notation of vocal part: 2d stanza.

(with slight variants)

Example 171: MY MOTHER IS A ZANDOLITE (107-B-1)

Original pitch +1 st. ♩ = 132

Mortar
Dè-pis man-man moin fai moin, m'pas ja-mais wè man-man moin!

Waille waille waille waille! Waille waille waille waille! Moin

pas con-né man-man moin (... ...) Oh!___

farther on:
Zan-do-lite fai'm!___ Ma-bou-ya fai'm!   Zan-do-

Soloist

lite fai'm! Oh ma-bou-ya fai'm!   Zan-do-lite fai'm!

Oh ma-bou-ya fai'm!

Example 172: I'M NOT A MULE (WORK SONG) (47-A-3)
Original pitch – 5 st. ♩ = 144. Notation: Stanzas 1-5.

Oh moin pas mu - lette oh m'pas mu - lette oh!

Ha - bi - tant prend moin po' - té ca - fé!

M'pas mu - lette oh moin pas mu - lette oh!

Ha - bi - tant prend moin pas mu - lette oh!

M'pas mu - lette oh m'pas mu - lette oh!

Ha - bi - tant prend moin pas mu - lette oh!

'lette oh m'pas mu - lette oh

Ha - bi - tant prend moin pas mu - lette oh!

M'pas mu - lette oh m'pas mu - lette oh

Ha - bi - tant prend moin . pas mu - lette oh!

Example 173: COUMBITE SONG (205)

Original pitch +1 st. ♩ = ±116

Soloist

Ya oh___ ya-wé   ya-wé oh___ ya-wé   ya-wé oh

Ya-wé___   Ya-wé   yo oh

Chorus

Ya-wé oh___   ya-wé___   Ya-wé oh___   ya-wé

Ya-wé oh___   ya wé

Soloist

ya-wé. Ya-wé___   ya-wé   ya-wé oh___   ya-wé   ya-

wé___ oh___ ya-wé   ya-wé oh___ ya-wé

etc.

Ya-wé   ya-wé.   *Chorus as above*

Example 174: WHERE SHALL I LAY MY BODY? (34-B-1)

Original pitch +1 st. ♩ = 108

É   La-i-za qui bo' ma mèt-té corps mwé___   Lai-za é!

La-i-za timounes hy-po-crite oh!   É La-i-za (a-é) ma mèt-té

etc.

corps mwé!___   La-i-za qui bo' m'a mèt-té corps mwé!

Example 175: I CUT WOOD AND PICK UP HONEY (16-A-2)

Original pitch – 3 st. ♩ 126 ◄ 138. Chorus in upper octave.

Notation: 2d and 7th stanzas.

Example 176: I MAKE MY PRAYERS (36-B-2)

Original pitch – 1 st. ♩ = 138. Notation: 4th stanza.

Example 177: FROG AT THE WELL (FROM A CONTE) (302)
Original pitch − 4 st. ♩ = 192

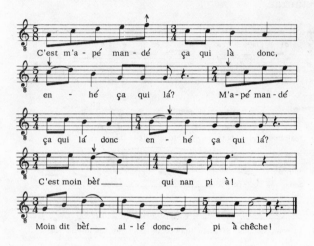

C'est m'a - pé man - dé   ça qui là donc,

en - hé ça qui lá?   M'a - pé man - dé

ça qui lá donc   en - hé ça qui lá?

C'est moin bèf____   qui nan pi à!

Moin dit bèf____ al - lé donc,____   pi à chêche!

Example 178: TO OSAN (50-A-1)
Original pitch − 8 st. ♩ = 152. Notation: 3d stanza.

Drums   *simile*

O - san   oh   Lè - lè   oh!

O - san   oh____   Lè - lè   oh!____   Yo prend as - son loa

ser - vi mé - di - son oh!____ Lais - sé cou - lé!

(with variants)

Example 179: COUNTRYMEN, CALL THE LOA FOR ME (7-B-1)

Original pitch − 8 st. ♩ = 132

Claves

Drums

Voice

Ha-bi - tant ré - lé loa yo pou' moin,   a - go - é

etc.

Ha-bi - tant ré - lé loa yo pou' moin 'tor, ré - lé loa yo

pou' moin 'tor Gè - dé fai moin 'ga - gé!

(12 times)

1a)   1b)

pou' moin!   pou' moin!   a - go - é!

Example 180: THE LOA BOULICHA ARRIVES (34-B-2)
Original pitch – 3 st. ♩. = ± 96

Example 181: HOUNSI, I AM GOING TO SEE (55-A-1)
Original pitch – 3 st. ♩ = 138. Notation: Toward end of record.

Example 182: THEY SIGN MY NAME, BUT NOT MY FEET (48-B-2)

Original pitch – 4 st. ♩ = 160

Moin cri - é hon - neur dé - vant___ so - ba - gui loa moin! Cri - é hon-

neur, per-sonne pas ré-pond moin oh!___

Moin cri - é hon - neur dé - vant___ so - ba - gui loa moin, Cri - é hon-

neur, per-sonne pas ré-pond moin oh! Tout ça qui dit bien yà moin là m'ap cou-

té oh!___ Tout ça qui dit mal nous là m'ap cou-

té yo! Yo si - gné nom mwé 'Lla - da yo pas si - gné pied'm, man - dé___

___ co - té ya wè moin!

*(3 times with
slight variants)*

N. B. First phrase (= first six measures) is left out in 2d stanza.

Example 183: YENVALO MUSIC (303)

Original pitch – 5 st. ♩ = 156. Chorus in octaves. Notation: Middle of record.

Example 184: TIKANBO MUSIC (67-B-1)

Original pitch – 7 st. ♩ = 116

Example 185: DANCE TUNE (401)
Original pitch – 1 st. ♩ = 132⁀144

Example 186: FEMALE DUET (47-B-2)
Original pitch – 8 st. ♩. = ± 104. Notation: 1st stanza.

Appendixes

1. The Pantheons

Most of the loa of Haiti appear to belong to two major cult groupings: the Vodoun (dominated by Dahomé rites and traditions) and the Congo-Guinée (dominated mainly by the Pétro deities). In the Vodoun pantheon one finds deities of Dahomean and Yoruban origin, and others whose names seem to identify them with West African peoples such as the Mahis, the Amines, the Adjas, the Foulas, the Sousous, and the Haoussas. The so-called Congo-Guinée group, in addition to the Pétro escorte, appears to have absorbed many loa from Central Africa. Among the Congo-Guinée loa are such names as Mayombé, Loango, Bumba, Moundongue, Mousondi, Angole, Congo, Baganda, and Solongo, all of them designations of regions or tribes of the Congo area. Also in this pantheon are loa bearing the names Bambarra and Siningal (Senegal), from northwestern Africa.

It is not possible to group the loa in such a way that the system will reflect accurately the tradition and usage in all parts of the country. Had all the old cults or "nations" survived intact, the pantheons might have resembled the following:

Arada or Dahomey loa
Anago or Yoruba loa
Mahi loa
Congo loa (including the Moundongue, the Solongo, the Bumba, etc.)
Ibo loa
Kanga loa
Pétro loa
Etc.

In certain parts of Haiti, in scattered and isolated places, one finds Congo, Ibo, and Nago cults that have resisted absorption; but this pattern does not hold for most of the country. In general, Congo and Pétro tend to "march" together; Anago has become a "nation" within a "nation" in the Dahomé rites; and the Ibo group, though still distinct, is frequently allied with the Dahomé rites or the Guinée rites.

The following list does not pretend to include all the loa known in Haiti. It is doubtful that a complete list could ever be compiled, in view of the continual generation of new deities and the constant cross-fertilization between "nations." The loa are grouped here according to most widespread usage. There are contradictions from which there is no possible escape, and these general groupings will not necessarily correspond to the concepts and practices of any specific locality. It is intended here to give a broad and generalized view.

Under "The Vodoun Pantheon" I have placed constellations of deities of Dahomean and Yoruban origin, along with others that are clearly identified with Vodoun rites. Under "The Congo and Pétro Pantheons" I have listed the Congo-Guinée loa—consisting mainly of deities associated with Central Africa and deities affiliated with the Pétro rites. Ibo and Kanga loa are grouped together, because in many regions of Haiti the two pantheons appear to be interlocked. A separate listing is given for the Simbi family of water deities in view of their ambivalence; they are sometimes found in the Pétro group and sometimes in the Dahomé, according to local practice.

THE VODOUN PANTHEON

DAMBALLA WÈDO, or DAN WÈDO. One of the most venerable of Haitian loa. He is generally recognized as the husband of Ayida Wèdo, though occasionally the two deities are merged in a personality called Damballa-Ayida. The concept of a single identity for Damballa and Ayida conforms to Dahomean belief. In both Haiti and West Africa, Damballa is identified with the rainbow and is symbolized as a snake.[1] In Haiti he is associated also with rainfall, springs, and fertility. He is sometimes described as "white," and the proper food offering to him is a white chicken. Persons possessed by Damballa usually take on stylized characteristics of snakes. Along with many other important loa, he has become identified with characters in Christian religious belief. There are, in fact, "two" Damballa Wèdos. One, identified with Moses, comes in talking; the other, identified with St. Patrick, never talks. Food offerings for the St. Patrick version of Damballa consist of eggs, flour, sugar, and almond syrup. Damballa remains one of the chief gods of the Dahomey cult in Cuba, and he survived into the last century in New Orleans under the name Danny.

AYIDA WÈDO. Generally regarded in Haiti as the wife of Damballa, Ayida is also symbolized by snake and rainbow, and her color, like Damballa's, is "white." In Dahomey and Nigeria, Ayida is known as a male rather than a female spirit and is regarded there as the same divinity as Damballa, or Dji. In Dahomey, Ayida Wèdo was the great serpent who held up the world. According to one myth, the Creator of the World assigned to Ayida the task of holding up the earth to keep it from falling into the sea. The great serpent coiled himself, tail in mouth, and lay below the earth like the carrying pad that women wear to support bundles on their heads. Whenever Ayida Wèdo shifted his position there were earthquakes.[2] When the rainbow appeared after a rain it was said that Ayida had come out from under the earth to drink of the fresh water.

DAMBALLA GRAND CHIMIN (Damballa of the Highway). Another manifestation of Damballa as a protector of those on long journeys.

DAMBALLA VERRE. Another manifestation of Damballa.

DOMICI WÈDO. Considered to be the daughter of Damballa. The ending of her name (*-ci*) suggests that at one time she may have been considered a wife rather than a daughter.

DOKI WÈDO. A member of Damballa's family.

AGÄO WÈDO. A member of Damballa's family. Said to be a "work loa" who aids men with their gardens, especially in time of illness.

ÈZILIE DOBA, or DOGBA, sometimes spelled ERZULIE. One of the "big" loa of the Dahomé pantheon, a symbol of purity, and sometimes identified with the Virgin Mary. Her color is white, and services to her include a ritual sweeping and sprinkling of the earth and a perfuming of the air. Food offerings to her include corn meal and eggs. Male "horses" of Èzilie are sometimes bound to her by mystic marriages, and they are obligated to refrain from sexual intercourse on certain days which belong to her. There are a number of Èzilies, regarded as members of the same family or, in some cult centers, as different manifestations of the same deity. Some Haitians regard Èzilie Doba as the ancestor of the Èzilie family and refer to her as Grand Ézilie. Note that there is a Dahomean town named Dogba at approximately 0° 6′ E., 6° 50′ N.

ÈZILIE FRÉDA, or ÈZILIE DAROMAIN (Dahomé), or ÈZILIE FRÉDA DAROMAIN. Like Èzilie Doba, she is a symbol of purity and is identified with the Virgin Mary. Mystic marriages are performed with her, and her "horses" are obligated to refrain from sexual intercourse on certain days. She is also a giver of wealth.

ÈZILIE WÈDO. A sister or daughter of Èzilie Doba and also related to Damballa.

ÈZILIE MAISOL. A sister of Èzilie Fréda.

ÈZILIE BANDA. A manifestation of Èzilie who is especially fond of the Banda dance.

ÈZILIE JÉROUGE (Red Eyes). A stern and hard Èzilie who is often identified with Pétro rather than Dahomé rites.

AÏSON FRÉDA. A member of the Èzilie escorte, regarded as a market-place protector. In Dahomey, Aïson was a protector of all public gathering places.[3]

AÏSON BELÉKÉTÉ

AÏSON DLEAU BOLO BOSU

MAÎTRESSE MAMBO. A special form of Èzilie as priestess.

MAÎTRESSE ESPAGNOLE, or 'PAGNOLE. A person mounted by this Èzilie talks only Spanish.

SOBO, or SOGBO. A thunder deity who hurls stones to the earth when angered. Some of the stones thrown by Sobo are regarded as the sacred residence of various loa. Sobo (or Sogbo) is a member of the original Thunder pantheon of Dahomey.

SOBO BADÉ, or SOBO BADÈ, or simply BADÉ. A close relative of Sobo, regarded as the protector of the hounfor (*badé*). In Dahomey, Badé is sometimes referred to as the son of the deity Sobo.[4]

AGOMÉ TONNERE, also pronounced ABOMÉ TONNERE. Another thunder loa. Abomé (or Agbomé) is the name of an ancient capital of Dahomey.

BADÈSI. The wife of Sobo Badé.

SO NARCISSE, also called Sogo Narcisse, or simply So. A thunder loa of Dahomean origin. In Dahomey he is regarded as an offspring of Mawu and Lisa, and a member of the Sky pantheon.

KÉBIOSU, or KÉBIOSO. A thunder loa who, like Sobo, hurls stones to the earth. In Dahomey he is known as Xevioso and is thought to be the same deity as So. In Haiti, persons killed by lightning are thought to be enemies of Kébiosu and are given special treatment in burial.

AGWÉ WOYO, known also as COQUI-NAN-MER. He is a loa of the sea; thunder and lightning over the ocean are thought to be Agwé shooting his cannon. He is usually symbolized in pictures by a sailing or steam vessel. His colors are blue and white, and the primary sacrificial animal for him is a male goat. High ceremonies for Agwé are begun in the hounfor and consummated in a sailing boat on the open sea, from which is launched a highly decorated and stylized miniature ship containing food for the deity. This tiny craft is known as the *barque d'Agwé*. Hounfors honoring this spirit usually have a small boat hanging from the rafters. In Dahomey, Agwé is also a sea deity and a member of the Thunder pantheon.

AGWÈTTA WOYO. She is thought to be Agwé Woyo's wife, though in Dahomey she was considered to be his daughter.

AGWÈSU WANDÉOU. Said to be the son of Agwé.

LA SIRÈNE. Another deity of the sea, a latecomer visualized as a mermaid. La Sirène is usually thought of as belonging to a separate family, though she is frequently served along with Agwé. Some sociétés do not recognize her at all.

NANANBOUCLOU, or NANAN BOULOUCOU. A loa of herbs and medicines. In Dahomey this spirit was considered the grandparent of all deities, the progenitor of Mawu and Lisa from whom all demigods are descended.[5] She is still remembered in the Dahomey cults of Cuba.

LISSA or LISHA. Probably the Lisa of Dahomey, child of Nanbouclou.

ATTIBON LEGBA, or LEGBA SÉ. One of the most important of Haitian loa, frequently the first one invoked in any service. He is the guardian of the gateway, the crossroads, and the highway. Cocks and male goats are his favorite foods, as in West Africa. In Dahomean tradition, Legba is the youngest offspring of Mawu and Lisa, the progenitors of all Dahomean deities. He is a divine trickster who is both feared and loved, a force that is capriciously malevolent or benevolent. Today, as in earlier times in Dahomey, the image of Legba, made of clay, stands or sits before the entrance to many villages. Sometimes the image is nothing more than a mound or column of earth symbolizing a phallus. Legba's mischief and tricks are directed against the other deities and human beings. In Haiti, as in Dahomey, Legba is not a personal deity. As Herskovits points out, Legba has no "character" and cannot be relied on. He is the intervener between mankind and the deities. It is in this sense that he "opens the gate," providing a channel of communication between man and loa; and it is for this reason that he is often supplicated first in religious ritual. In Dahomean lore, Legba's mischief is often in the realm of sex. In ritual dances for

Legba in Dahomey, the performers hold a carved phallus between their legs and perform copulating movements. The Haitian Legba is depicted as an aged limping loa, and the carved phallus has become a grotesque crutch-cane that fits into the crotch of the legs. The Dahomean Legba is remembered elsewhere in the New World, notably in Dutch Guiana, Brazil, and Cuba. Until relatively recent times he was known among the Negroes of Louisiana by the name Papa Lebat.[6]

LEGBA GRAND CHIMIN (Legba of the Highway). A special manifestation of Legba who guards the highway.

LEGBA KALFU (Legba of the Crossroads). A special manifestation of Legba who guards the crossroads.

LEGBA MAÎT' 'BITATION (Legba Master of the Household). The Legba who protects the house and its grounds.

LEGBA LAFLEURONDÉ. One of the Legba family.

LEGBA KÉYÉ. One of the Legba family.

LEGBA AGUATOR. Said to be a "Nago" deity.

ATTIBON KÉKÉ. One of the Legba family.

ATTIBON SAMARDI. One of the Legba family.

AZOMBLO KIDÍ. One of the Legba family.

OGOUN FERAILLE, often referred to as MAÎT' OGOUN. The chief and ancestor of a large family of loa whose activities have to do with blacksmithing and war, which are closely related. Ogoun Feraille is a patron of warriors and the forge; his symbol is a piece of forged iron, such as a machete, a hoe blade, a saber, or a piece of iron chain. In West Africa, Ogoun is considered a patron of hunters as well.[7] He was widely known by various peoples in Dahomey and Nigeria. In Dahomey he was considered a child of the divine Mawu and Lisa,[8] and among the Yoruba of Nigeria he was regarded as a brother of Chango and Dada,[9] two spirits who survive in the Haitian pantheon. An altar to Ogoun Feraille, like that of the loa Chango, may consist of a pile of iron scrap, perhaps a broken sugar vat. In Cuba, Ogoun Feraille is a prominent deity in both the Arara (Dahomey) and the Lucumí (Yoruba) cults. Although absorbed exclusively into the Dahomé family of rites in Haiti, Ogoun Feraille and his entire family and escorte are designated as belonging to the Nago "nation." Their color, like that of heated iron, is red. Ogoun Feraille survived until recent times in Louisiana as Joe Feraille.[10]

OGOUN FER (Ogoun Iron). He is sometimes called OGOUN ST. JACQUES, ST. JACQUES MAJEUR, or simply ST. JACQUES, being identified with the saint of that name.

OGOUN MASHOQUETTE (Ogoun Blacksmith).

OGOUN BAKALA. One of the Ogoun brothers.

OGOUN BALTAZA MISHO. One of the Ogoun brothers.

OGOUN JÉNISON, or JÉRISON. One of the Ogoun brothers.

OGOUN BADAGRY, or BATAGRI. Said to be a "grandson" of Maît' Ogoun. He is a "work" loa, as well as an ironworker and a warrior, and helps in the fields, especially in time of sickness. Badagry is the name of a town near the mouth of the Ogoun River in western Nigeria. According to a priest of the Cuban Dahomé cult, the word *batagri* was used to designate the circumcision house in Dahomey. Ogoun Badagry thus may have been associated with that shrine.

CHANGO, or OGOUN CHANGO. A member of the Ogoun family and, like most of his brothers, a warrior and ironworker. Chango's altar is usually a pile of scrap iron, or any iron object, such as a sugar vat. In West Africa, Chango (or Shango) and Ogoun were considered separate deities. In Nigeria, according to Ellis, they were brothers, closely associated with each other. Among the Yoruba, Chango was a thunder-and-lightning god and he is believed to have been one of the early kings of Oyo. The African Chango, like the Haitian, is identified with fire, a corollary of lightning, and persons possessed by him may carry pots of fire on their heads and perform other fire tests.[11]

CHANGO GOLO. Another manifestation of Ogoun Chango.

OGOUN BACHANGO. Possibly the same as Ogoun Chango, or he may be named after the Bachangos, a Congo tribe. A warrior and ironworker.

OGOUN BALIZAI. One of the Ogoun family.

NIMBO NIMBO. One of the Ogoun family.

ARCHARDÉ, ACHARDÉ, CHARDÉ, or CHADÉ. One of the Ogoun escorte, sometimes called OGOUN CHADÉ, or CHADÉ BOCOR.

OGOUN YEMSEN. One of the Ogoun brothers.

OBATALA, or BATALA. A loa of war. Among the Yoruba people of Nigeria, Obatala was a sky deity and protector of the town gates. He was thought to form children in the womb and was therefore believed responsible for albinism and congenital deformities.[12] Obatala and Chango are among the main Lucumí (Yoruba) deities in Cuba.

OGOUN BAYÉ. An aspect of Ogoun who functions as a gateway guardian.

OGOUN BLANC (White Ogoun). He does not drink rum, which is a favorite beverage of his brothers.

OGOUN JEBBA

OGOUN JÈKKA, JÈKKÈ, or YÈKKÈ. A warrior and ironworker. Jèkkè may have been a shrine or regional designation.

OGOUN KÈBÈK

OGOUN KÉNISON

YALODÉ, or OGOUN LODÉ. Brother of Ogoun Badagry and the other Ogouns. Yalodé is clearly of Dahomean origin.[13]

OGOUN PANAMA, or OGOUN PALAMA. Guardian against sunstroke, or spirit responsible for sunstroke. A brother of Ogoun Badagry. He is usually seen wearing a Panama hat.

OGOUN PIERRE NARCISSE

OGOUN JÉROUGE (Ogoun Red Eyes). A malevolent Ogoun brother, red eyes being a mark of bad behavior. Some people feel that he is a member of the Pétro rather than the Vodoun pantheon.

NAGO PIMENT. A member of the Ogoun escorte. He eats hot peppers.

BOULICHA NAGO

GÈDÉ NIMBO, or NIBO, also called BRAVE GÈDÉ. One of the powerful deities of the Vodoun pantheon, particularly in the region of Port-au-Prince, where many hounfors cater extensively to him. Gèdé Nimbo, along with his numerous brothers and his vast escorte, is a "dead" loa, a spirit of the graveyard, a sexual rascal, and a violator of propriety. He is served apart from the other loa, and usually he has a separate altar or shrine outside the central hounfor. Cult centers for Gèdé are often near graveyards, though not necessarily so. Gèdé services abound around the main cemetery of Port-au-Prince. Gèdé Nimbo has various manifestations, but he is usually dressed in a black frock coat, black top hat, and black trousers or a blue, white polka-dotted skirt. He carries a cane and smokes a pipe or a cigarette, according to which manifestation of Gèdé he represents. He talks with a strong nasal accent, which is acquired by anyone mounted by him. Gèdé Nimbo is always asking for money. Persons possessed by him may rub hot peppers on their tongues or in their eyes. In some parts of Haiti, Gèdé is thought to be identical with Baron Samedi. In a Vodoun service, no other loa cares to enter while a Gèdé is present; and Gèdé delights in appearing suddenly, uninvited, and obstructing the orderly progress of a ritual. Although Herskovits points out that Gedeonsu, or Gèdé, is a Dahomean totem,[14] it is worth noticing that in Haiti the Gèdé rites are often regarded as belonging to the Nago "nation."

GÈDÉ NIMBO MAZAKA. A Gèdé brother.

GÈDÉ OUÈSOU. A Gèdé brother.

GÈDÉ L'ORAILLE. A thunder or storm Gèdé. Like the other Gèdés, he is closely associated with death, and he is considered more of a malefactor than most. He is repulsive in appearance, with a dwarflike stature.

GÈDÉ MIVÈVOU. A Gèdé brother.

GÈDÉ NANSOU. A Gèdé brother.

GÈDÉ NOUVAVOU. A Gèdé brother.

GÈDÉ VI. Said to be a son of Gèdé Nimbo, though some Haitians regard this loa as a female, possibly Gèdé Nimbo's wife.

GÈDÉ ZECLAI. A loa of lightning, thought to be responsible for death by lightning, violent death in general, and destruction of cattle and other property by natural forces. He seems to be a Gèdé version of Kébioso or Sobo.

JEAN ZOMBIE. One of the Gèdé brothers, a "dead" spirit.

GÈDÉ TI PISSE (Gèdé Little Flea)

GÈDÉ RACHÉ (Gèdé Tear Off)

GÈDÉ JOYEUSE (Happy Gèdé)

TIWAWÈ GÈDÉ, or GÈDÉ TIWAWÈ PANCHÈ. This Gèdé is one that makes mischief as he enters a hounfor service.

GÈDÉ ZILÉ (Gèdé of the Island)

GÈDÉ YALOVI

GÈDÉ YABOFÉ

CERCLÉQUITTÉ GÈDÉ (The Gèdé Who Mows Down)

JENSIMAN BRITISSE. A loa who works with the Gèdé family, one of Gèdé Nimbo's graveyard assistants. He is described as having a white skin, suggesting that his surname is a corruption of "British."

MARIE GÈDÉ. A sister of the Gèdé brothers.

BALÉROUZÉ. One of the Gèdé brothers. His name means to "sweep and sprinkle," a ritual activity characteristic of certain Vodoun ceremonies.

MANZÈ BRIDGIT, or MANMAN BRIDGIT. The mother of the Gèdé brothers.

MAÎT' SANSAN. One of the Gèdé escorte.

BARON SAMEDI. One of a group of Barons who march with the Gèdés. They are so closely identified that some Haitians feel that Baron Samedi is merely another name for Gèdé Nimbo. Persons possessed in cemeteries are thought to be mounted by Baron Samedi or one of his brothers. Like the Gèdés, the Barons are spoken of as "dead" spirits.

BARON PIQUANT. The loa in charge of grave digging.

AZAGON LACROIX, or BARON LACROIX. Spoken of as "chief" of the cemetery, the one who plants the cross over the grave.

BARON POUCHÈ, or POUSIÈ (Baron Dust)

BARON SAL (Baron Earth, or Dirty Baron)

BARON CHITA. The Baron who sits on the graves.

BARON TIKALÉ

AZAKA MÉDÉ, or ZAKÉ MÉDÉ. Herskovits reports that Azaka Médé is the name of the stream which Dahomeans believe all the dead must cross.[15]

COUSIN ZAKA. The peasant Zaka, special patron of the country farmer and the people of the mountains. He is always portrayed as wearing the blue denim costume of the peasant, carrying the woven peasant knapsack called an *alfor cousin* and a cocomacaque stick, and smoking a clay pipe. Persons possessed by Cousin Zaka are dressed in this way, and they speak in the manner of the mountain man, a style that is heard only in the most remote communities.

MINISE ZAKA, or MINISTRE ZAKA. An aspect of Cousin Zaka. Ministre Zaka is a sort of Minister of Agriculture and a patron of peasant farmers.

SI AZAKA. The wife of Ministre Zaka.

AZAKA TONNERE, or TONNÈ. The Azaka who brings thunder and rain.

AZAKA BAING BAING. One of the Azaka family.

MARASSA. The loa of twins. The Marassa family of deities are in a special category, somewhat apart from other spirits. In an important Vodoun service, for example, there are invocations to the loa in general, to the Marassas, to the family ancestors, and to God.

MARASSA DOÇU. Patron of the first child after twins if it is a boy.

MARASSA DOÇA. Patron of the first child after twins if it is a girl.

MARASSA BLANC. Patron of white twins.

MARASSA TROIS. Patron of triplets.

MARASSA GUINÉE. Patron of twins when one is a boy and one a girl.

MARASSA QUAT'. Patron of quadruplets, or of two consecutive sets of twins.

MARASSA BOIS (Marassa of the Woods). He is considered an "unbaptized" or "untamed" loa, and very savage. He likes sweets and never eats salt.

MARASSA DOGUÉ, or MARASSA CINQ. Patron of consecutive twins and triplets.

MARASSA CAILLE (Marassa of the House). This one eats salt.

LOKO ATTISSO. He is usually pictured as the protector of the hounfor, or cult temple, and as the keeper of the altar (*pé*). In Dahomey, Loko is a deity of the Sky pantheon and a son of the divine Mawu and Lisa.[16] He is still remembered in the Arara (Dahomey) cults of Cuba. He is also called Sindé or Singé.

LOKO ATTISOGUÉ. Said to be Loko Attisso's wife.

LOKO ADÄICO, or DÄICO. A member of Loko Attisso's family.

LOKO DÄIFRÈ. A brother of Loko Adäico (Däico + *frère*).

LOKO DÄINZO

LOKO TOKAMIWÈZO

LOKO DAHOMÉ

LOKO BASSIYÉ

TOR LOKO

AGÄO LOKO BAYÈ. A crossroads protector of the Loko family.
LOKO DÄI PRÉ

DANSI OSOU. Among the Tshi-speaking people of West Africa there was a spirit called Adansi, a malignant giantess.[17]
OSOU JAMAIN
SOUSOU YÈMAIN

ZOMBRA
MAZOMBRA
MAZOMBRA ENPAKA

AMINE. An aged female loa. Sacrifices to her consist of rice, sugar cane, lima beans, and eggs. As in services for the deity Èzilie, perfumes are used during services for her.
AMINE GATIGAL LAFLAMBO. A member of the Amine family. Amine is the name of a tribe of Dahomey.
AMINE NAGO. Another member of the Amine family.

GÉNÉRAL CLERMEIL, or PRÉSIDENT CLERMEIL. He is said to be the "father" and patron of all light children born to dark parents. Stories are sometimes heard of men who wrongly accused their wives of infidelity because of the lightness of their children, and who were finally mounted and punished by Clermeil.
CLERMÉZINE. The light-skinned daughter of the dark Général Clermeil.

The family relationships or escortes of the following deities are not clear. Some of them may belong to one or another of the foregoing groups, or to still uncited families.

ADJA. A female loa associated with the arts of pharmacy. The Yoruba of Nigeria had a spirit named Adja who carried men and women off into the forest to teach them about the medicinal properties of roots and herbs.[18] In Haiti, Adja's mangé consists of cookies and chicken. Persons possessed by her sometimes eat broken glass.
ADJA BOSU, AKADJA BOSU, or KADJA BOSU. This deity is also known in Dahomey.
AGANMAN. A male deity characterized as a *zandolite,* a small lizard capable of changing colors. A person mounted by Aganman sometimes climbs trees or posts. Some Haitians contend that a person possessed by this loa will change color, from dark to light.
AGASU. In Dahomey, according to Herskovits, Agasu is the name of the panther fetish.[19] Dahomeans regard this deity as of special significance to the royal family. He was remembered among Negroes in Louisiana under the name Agoussou.
AGASU YEMAIN. Related to Agasu.
DADAL. Among the Yoruba, Dadal was a brother of Ogoun and Chango, and was a patron of vegetables.[20]
ATTISOLÉ, also known as ST. SOLEIL. Persons mounted as a result of exposure to the sun are thought to be possessed by this loa. The association of Attisolé with the sun may be a syncretism.
AUGISSAUT
AZA. A loa who likes the Juba dance.

AZUI. A snake deity.

BABOULE. A loa who likes the Baboule dance.

CALBASSIE. Loa of the calabash tree.

CHÉBO PROFIÈL. An ancient male deity. Herskovits suggests that he may represent the leopard, *sébo* being the Fon word for that animal. The wildness of the attack on the sacrificial animal by persons possessed by Chébo supports this conjecture. A deity called Dada Segbo is prominent in the Rada Cult of Trinidad.

SIMALO. A male loa who is believed responsible for fine physical proportions and bodily strength in men.

COQUI-NAN-DLEAU. Probably the same as Coqui-Nan-Mer (Agwé).

AKADJA. This loa may well be the King Agadja of Dahomey who was said to be responsible for the coming of *vodu* (loa) into that country. Herskovits tells a legend about a woman named Hwandjile who prevailed upon the king to bring the *vodu* from the kingdom of Adja.[21] Hwandjile herself survives in Haiti under the name

WANILÉ, or HOUANILÉ

LINGLESSOU. A rainbow loa. Persons mounted in sight of a rainbow are thought to be possessed by this deity.

BLINGINSOU. "Marches" with Linglessou.

WANGOL, also called AGOVI WANGOL (King of Angola). This loa appears to be an interpolation from the Congo rites.

ALOVI, or GADALOVI. A masculine, dwarflike spirit who likes to disarrange things and play practical jokes. Persons possessed by Alovi may break up gatherings, discommode spectators and dancers, and generally make a nuisance of themselves. Some Haitians regard this loa as belonging more to the Pétro pantheon than to the Dahomé.

MAÎT' BOIS (Master of the Woods). May be an interpolation of Maît' Grand Bois of the Congo-Guinée pantheon.

MAÎT' DLEAU (Master of the Water). May refer to the loa Simbi.

DAN WÈZO, or WÉZO. A loa known in the Artibonite region. The name is possibly a corruption of Dan Wèdo.

DJA KÉKÉ

ÈVO, or NÈG' ÈVO. The name is that of a tribe on the Calabar coast of West Africa.

FARO PIERRE. Said to be the son of Pierre Basico.

GÉNÉRAL YENBATISSE, or JEAN BAPTISTE. Probably the Christian name of some Dahomé loa.

GRAND LESSAIGNE. An aged, dwarflike loa, guardian and protector of children.

GRAND ALABA, or ALOUBA

GRAND ALOUMANDIA, or MANMAN ALOUMANDIA. Believed to be a loa who was maît' tête of the Emperor Dessalines. Some informants consider this spirit to be a démon or loup-garou rather than a loa.

HOUNTOR. The spirit of the Arada drums. There is a difference of opinion on whether Hountor is a loa in the precise sense or merely a drum spirit. The term is sometimes used to designate the largest drum of the Arada trio.

JEAN BATEAU. A loa well known in the region of Léogane. When he "enters," the possessed persons talk *langage* into a *canarie* (clay water vessel).

MAÎT' DAVID. This loa always talks immaculate French, and persons possessed by him read cards and tell fortunes.

MAÎT' GRAND CHIMIN (Master of the Highway). Probably Legba.

MAKANDA. Believed to be the spirit of the famous houngan Makandal, who lived during the revolutionary period. He is symbolized as a snake which lives in the ground. Some informants think he is a Pétro rather than a Dahomé loa.

MAMBO ÇAÇA

TIJEAN DANTOR (Ancient Tijean)

WHYDAH WALO. Whydah is the name of a seacoast town in Dahomey.

ZO. A fire deity of clear Dahomean origin.[22]

OLICHA

OSAI, or OSANGE. Known also among the Lucumí cults of Cuba. May be any one of the Osanges mentioned by Herskovits.

OSANGE LÉLÉ

OSODJABÈ

PAPA DAHOMÉ

PIERRE BASSICO. This loa is sometimes identified with St. Peter.

PIERRE DAMBALLA, DAMBARRA, or DAMBADA. Sometimes identified with St. Peter.

PIERRE WALO. Related to Whydah Walo.

POULA, or FOULA. This name is probably a tribal designation.

SABATA. Described as a loa of ancient times. Sabata or Sagbata is the so-called small-pox group of deities of Dahomey.

SÄILA. A female deity, thought by some to belong to the Èzilie Fréda family.

SILIBO GWÈTO. In Dahomey, according to Herskovits, Silibo is an ancient sib-founder.

SILIDJA

TAUREAU

TI CRAB. This is a "false name"; this loa keeps his real name a secret.

THE AMBIVALENT SIMBI FAMILY

This group of loa in certain regions has attached itself to the Vodoun pantheon, elsewhere to the Congo-Guinée pantheon; but it has not maintained any kind of independent or semi-independent status. The deity Simbi and his family are of Congo origin.

SIMBA. A male deity, patron of rain and drinking water. Said to be the father of the Simba brothers.

SIMBI DLEAU. The best known of the Simbi family. Like his father, he is the patron of fresh water, is associated with the spring, and usually is symbolized as a snake. The color sacred to him is white. Altars to Simbi Dleau usually are found at the spring or the well. Sometimes ponds are constructed for him within the hounfor.

SIMBI KITTA

SIMBI YENDÉZO, or SIMBI NAN DÉ ZEAUX (Simbi in Two Waters). Symbolized as a water snake who lives in the "upper" waters and the "lower" waters.

GRAND SIMBA. The parent of Simba, and ancestor of the entire family of water loa.

SIMBI TROIS ZILÉ (Simbi of Three Islands)

SIMBI MACAYA

SIMBI GRAND BOIS (Simbi of the Forest)

SIMBI WANGOL

SIMBI YENPAKA

SIMBI LAROUZÉ (The Dew Simbi)

SIMBI DEVANT BONDIEU (Simbi Before God)

SIMBI TROIS FÉ (Simbi Three Leaves—the name of a pouin)

SIMBI TROIS RACINES (Simbi Three Roots—the name of a pouin)

THE IBO AND KANGA PANTHEONS

CAPLÄOU. A Kanga loa. His name appears to be a survival of the Capläou tribe. Some persons feel he is a member of the Pétro group.

IBO FOULA. An Ibo loa. Note that both Ibo and Foula are tribal designations.

IBO MARIANI, or MARIANÉ. An Ibo loa.

IBO HÉQUOIKÉ. An Ibo loa.

IBO JÉROUGE (Ibo Red Eyes). A malevolent spirit. Food offerings to her consist mainly of pigs and cocks.

IBO LAZILE. An Ibo loa. The food offering to this loa is a goat.

IBO LÉLÉ, or IANMAN IBO. An Ibo loa.

KANGA. A Kanga loa. A "hard" or "stern" spirit, thought by some people to be the same as Capläou. Persons mounted by him play with fire and eat hot peppers.

KANGA TROIS. A Kanga loa.

LEGBA IBO. The Ibo form of the Vodoun Legba.

MARDI KAMA, or IBO KAMA. An Ibo loa.

MARIE LOUISE. An Ibo loa.

NÈGÈSSE IBO. An Ibo loa.

IBO SUAMENT. An Ibo loa.

IBO WANÈME. An Ibo loa.

NOMINATION. An Ibo loa.

TOUMENT. An Ibo loa.

BARAK. An Ibo loa.

UN PIED UN MAIN UN JÉ (One Foot, One Hand, One Eye). An Ibo loa.

AKOUPI. An Ibo loa.

DE L'AIR. An Ibo loa.

PAPA ZAO. A Kanga loa.

ZAO LANGÉ. A Kanga loa.

KANGA LANGA. A Kanga loa.

ÇA OU MANGÉ CON ÇA (What Do You Eat Like That). An Ibo loa.

TAKWA, or SAINT AKWA. An Ibo loa. When he comes in he speaks "unknown" languages.

THE CONGO AND PÉTRO PANTHEONS

MAÎT' GRAND BOIS (Master of the Woods). In Congo rites this loa is regarded as one of the most important of deities, holding a place equivalent to that of Damballa in the Dahomé service. When he "comes in" he makes a great din and racket.

FEMME GRAND BOIS. The wife of Maît' Grand Bois.

WANGOL (King of Angola). He also appears in other rites.

YAOMBÉ, or MAYAOMBÉ. This name is a tribal designation, referring to the Mayaombés of the Congo region.

WANGOL DLEAU (Wangol of the Water)

MOUNDONGUE. Often considered to be a "hard" loa. Ritual service to him includes, on special occasions, the cutting off of dogs' ears and tails. He is fond of dogs and is benevolent toward them. The name derives from that of a tribe of the upper Congo region.

TI MOUNDONGUE. Said to be a "son" of Moundongue.

MOUNDONGUE MOUSAILLE. A member of Moundongue's family.

BAIACOU, or BÈLÈCOU. A loa identified with the morning star, also called Baiacou. There is also a town in Dahomey by this name.

GANDA, or BAGANDA, also called Nèg' Ganda. A deity taking the name of the Ganda people of Uganda.

CONGO YAMINGAN. A benevolent loa associated with curing and protecting the sick. Certain curative medicine bundles are called *yamingans*.

MACAYA BUMBA, sometimes called Caya. He takes his name from the Bumba people of the upper Congo River region. The Bumbas are near neighbors of the Moundongues.

MANYO BUMBA. One of the Bumba family.

MARIANI MOUNDONGUE. One of the Moundongue family.

ROI LOANGUE (King of Loango). Refers to the old African kingdom of that name.

NANCHOU. A warrior deity.

AVÉLÉKÉTÉ. Known primarily in northern Haiti.

DAN PÉTRO. A rather malevolent loa, from whom the Pétro cult takes its name. The mangé for Dan Pétro is a pig. Early observers speculated that Dan Pétro was originally a powerful houngan of prerevolutionary days.[23]

AYIDA PÉTRO. A Pétro version of the Vodoun Ayida Wèdo.

BAKULU BAKA, known in some regions by the name Pinga Maza. He is a malevolent spirit who "eats"—i.e., destroys—people. Some informants are inclined to believe that Bakulu and Pinga are separate loa, both of a variety akin to baka or démons.

BAKULU BARAK. Related to Bakulu Baka.

BAMBARRA TAIBA. He is visualized as a sea crab. *Taille bas* in Creole means "low hips" and is used to describe a dance posture. The surname Taiba therefore may describe the movements of this loa as he moves about like a crab.

BOLISI BOLISA

BRISÉ GÉNÉRAL, or GÉNÉRAL BRISÉ. He is enormously large and ferocious in appearance. A special loa of the country people. Although stern, he is fond of children. He is symbolized as an owl; his home is in the chardette tree. His physical description suggests that he may be a deification of the epic folklore character Brise Montaigne, or Break Mountains.

CHANGANAN

CONGO JÉROUGE (Congo Red Eyes). A malevolent male spirit. Loa with red eyes are always of bad character.

CONGO MAPIONNE, or MAPIONGLE. A malevolent spirit.

CONGO SAVANE, or CONGO ZANDOR (Congo of the Plains). Malevolent, fierce, and strong, he is a man-eater; constant reference is made to his mortar in which he grinds people. His ritual color is white; some people believe that his skin is also white. The grinding of a person in a mortar is an African symbolism. A bas-relief in Dahomey reported by Gorer [24] shows King Glele pounding a vanquished king's head in a mortar.

BOSU TROIS CORNES

BOSU YÈMAIN

BOSU SWI YÈMAIN YÈMAIN

DADA ÈZILIE

ÈZILIE BOUCAN

ÈZILIE UN MAIN UN PIED UN JÉ (Èzilie One Hand, One Foot, One Eye)

ÈZILIE BALIANNE

ÈZILIE DANKÉKÉ

ÈZILIE JÉROUGE (Èzilie Red Eyes). A malevolent spirit.[25]

ÈZILIE MAPIONNE, or MAPIONGLE. A malevolent spirit.

ÈZILIE FEMME PÉTRO

ÈZILIE ACOUPI

GRAND ASSONGLO

JEAN PIERRE POUNGUÉ

LIMBA ZÄO. A deity of Congo origin.

DAMBALLA LAFLAMBEAU

MAÎT' PIMBA. Said to be father of Zäo Pimba.

MAMBO AYIDA (Priestess Ayida). A Pétro version of the Vodoun Ayida.

MARINETTE CONGO. A malevolent female loa.

MARINETTE PIED CHÊCHE (Marinette Dry Feet). Sister to Marinette Bras Chêche, and equally malevolent.

OGOUN JÉROUGE (Ogoun Red Eyes). A malevolent spirit. A Pétro form of the Vodoun deity, with a different character.

OGOUN DLEAU (Ogoun of the Water). Brother of Ogoun Jérouge.

OGOUN LAFLAMBEAU. A fire loa. When he comes in he plays with hot coals, hot iron, and flames.

OGOUN PÉTRO. He is malevolent and "eats" men.

PIMBA, or PEMBA

QUANÇON FER (Iron Pants)

KITTA BANDA (Chic Kitta)

KITTA BAYÈ (Kitta of the Gate). A gateway guardian.

KITTA CONGO

KITTA KANGA

KITTA LEGBA. Possibly the same as Kitta Bayè.

RACINE

RIGAL. A brother to Général Brisé. A benevolent loa.

ROI GRAND CHIMIN (King of the Highway). May refer to Legba or to another highway loa.

SILILIRWO BOQUOIMÉ

TAUREAU PÉTRO. A Pétro version of the Vodoun Taureau.

TIJEAN PÉTRO. A malevolent loa who preys on children from the foliage of the coconut palm.

TIJEAN PIED FIN (Tijean No Feet). Brother to Tijean Pétro.

TIJEAN PIED CHÊCHE (Tijean Dry Feet). One of the malevolent Tijean brothers.

TIKITTA DÉMAMBRÉ, or KITTA DÉMAMBRÉ. Thought to be the son of Kitta Bayè.

YABOFÉ LIMBA. A deity of Congo origin.

ZÄO PIMBA

ZAKA TONNERE (Zaka Thunder)

ZAKA GROLI

ZAKA L'ORAILLE (Zaka Storm)

YAKI BOSSAN

GOUNGOUN

MATÉDÉNOSA

SININGAL (Senegal). When this loa enters, the mounted person talks "Arabic."

2. Games

THE GAME OF CAILLE, OR WARI

The African counting game played with beans or stones in a carved wooden tray (known in various parts of Africa as *wari, mungala, adi,* etc.) is still known and played in the southwestern mountains of Haiti, particularly in the region south of the Léogane Plain. In Africa the game has innumerable variants. Most often the carved playing board or tray has two rows of six, seven, or eight holes, or pockets, sometimes with a large pocket at each end for winnings. In Ethiopia the playing board consists of three rows of six pockets each. In the upper Congo region a form of the game uses a board of twenty-eight pockets in four rows. Among wandering herding peoples in East Africa the holes are simply dug in the earth, and for playing pieces stones or dried camel droppings are used. The game not only is widespread throughout Africa but has an ancient tradition in Indonesia, the Philippines, southern and southeastern Asia, and the Arabic Middle East.

In Haiti the game is usually called *caille,* or "house." It is played on a long, sixteen-hole board of the kind used in West Africa. The playing pieces are usually maize kernels, dried peas, or wari beans. Where wari beans are used, the game is sometimes called by that name. This is a curious syncretism. The wari bean itself is so named because of a black marking which looks like a smile, in Creole *wa ri* ("going to laugh"). There are several ways of playing wari in Haiti; all have the common objective of capturing pieces on the opponent's side of the board. This is referred to as entering his "house" and "eating" the occupants, a terminology that is employed elsewhere where the game is known.

One method of playing is as follows. Starting with four pieces in every hole, a player takes up all the pieces from any hole on his own side of the board and redistributes them in a counterclockwise direction, dropping one into each hole as far as they will go. When his last piece is dropped, he picks up the contents of the next hole and continues the re-distribution. Should his last piece eventually fall into an empty pocket, his turn is ended and his opponent begins. However, if his last piece falls into a hole containing one or two pieces, he "eats" those pieces along with the piece which he places there. He continues the play as before, starting with the following hole, monopolizing the play until he ends in an empty hole. The one who takes the most pieces wins. In some Haitian variants of the game, each person's play is limited to the distribution of the contents of a single hole.

THE GAME OF MAYAMBA

This game, like *caille,* appears to be of African origin. It is played with four chips made of shell, baked clay, or broken chinaware. One side of each chip is white, the other usually blue. Any number of players may participate, and, as in dice, all compete against the thrower. *Mayamba* has a strictly gambling incentive. If a player throws two whites and two blues, or four whites, or four blues, he wins. If he throws any odd combination he loses.

3. Proverbs

Jou' fé tombé nans dleau c'est pas jou'l pourri.
The day a leaf falls in the water is not the day it rots. (Don't count your chickens before they're hatched.)

Dèyè morne gainyain morne.
Behind the mountains are mountains. (No matter how powerful someone is, there are others with powers equal to his.)

C'est pas tout chien qui japé ou pou' viré ga'dé.
You don't have to turn around and look at every dog that barks at you. (Don't worry about every complaint or threat that you hear.)

Chien gain' quat' pieds mais'l pas ça fait quat' chimin.
A dog has four feet but he can't travel four roads at once. (Said when someone is making excessive demands.)

Bois plus rwo dit'l wè loin, graine proméné dit'l wè plus loin.
The high tree says he sees far, the walking (traveling) seed says he sees farther. (The small and weak may have more sense than the large and strong.)

Rat mangé cane, zandolite mouri innocent.
The rat eats the sugar cane, the zandolite dies innocent. (One person commits an offense, an innocent person is punished.)

Ça'q ba ou conseil acheté chwal gros vent' saison lapluit mais saison sec li pas aidé ou noui.
A person who gives you advice to buy a horse with a big belly in the rainy season won't help you feed yourself when the dry season comes. (That is, a horse with a big belly is a big eater; there is plenty of grass for him when it rains but not much in the dry season, and a person who gives the foolish advice to buy such a horse isn't likely to be helpful in an emergency.)

Caca pas piquant mais li faut ou marché bwèté.
Excrement isn't sharp but it makes you limp. (That is, it isn't like a thorn, but if you step in it, it throws you off your stride. Said about some unpleasant affair you'd like to ignore but cannot.)

Bocor ba ou pouin mais l'pas dit ou dormi grand chimin.
The bocor gives you a protective charm but he doesn't tell you to sleep in the middle of the highway. (Even if you feel safe, don't take unnecessary risks.)

Jean chaché, Jean trouvé.
Jean seeks, Jean finds. (If you look for trouble you find it.)

Rajé gain' zoreille.
The woods have ears. (Take care not to speak your business loudly.)

Chat chaudé nans dleau chaud li wè dleau frète li peur.
If a cat is burned with hot water, when he sees cold water he is afraid. (Once
  burned twice shy.)

Cochon marron conné souki bois li forté.
A wild pig knows on which tree he should scratch himself. (A person knows how
  to take care of himself.)

Tor' bombé jam' gras.
The bellowing bull is never fat. (Refers to a person who brags but accomplishes
  little.)

Prison pas fait pou' chien.
Prisons weren't built for dogs. (If a person commits a bad act, no one is surprised
  if justice catches up with him.)

Roche nans dleau pas conné douleur roche nans soleil.
A rock in the water doesn't comprehend the suffering of the rock in the sun. (If
  you haven't suffered you can't understand the suffering of others.)

Tambour prèté pas fait bon danse.
A borrowed drum doesn't make a good dance. (A person who lends a drum may
  reclaim it at any moment. If you are dependent on others you are at their mercy.)

Sotte pas tuyé ou, li fait ou swè.
Stupidity doesn't kill you, but it makes you sweat.

Changana changana.
What is mine is mine. (Perhaps what I have isn't as good as someone else's, but
  it belongs to me.)

Zaffair Nèg' pas pitit mais c'est jam' quançon qui jis.
The man's affairs aren't small, it's just that his pants are too tight. (Said of a
  person who may look ludicrous but who nevertheless is well off.)

Bel Français, pas lesprit pou' ça.
Your speaking good French doesn't mean you're smart.

Rayi chien mais dit dent li blanche.
Hate the dog but say his teeth are white. (Give the devil his due. Though you
  despise a person remember that he is not without means to injure you.)

Bef qui gainyain queue pas jambé difé.
A cow with a tail doesn't walk across a fire. (People in glass houses shouldn't throw
  stones.)

Jé wè bouche pé.
The eyes see, the mouth is silent. (Don't talk about everything you observe.)

Bat' chien mais tend' maît' li.
Hit the dog but listen for his master.

Jardin loin gombo dur.
If the garden is far, the okra is hard. (If you can't reach the grapes, they're sour.)

Baton qui bat' chien noi' c'est li qui bat' chien blanc.
The stick that beats the black dog [also] beats the white dog. (A knife cuts both ways, or a misfortune can happen to you, too.)

Bourrique fait pitit pou' dos'l posé.
A donkey has children so that he can rest his back.

Lè ba'b zami ou prend difé metté ba'b ou à latramp.
When your friend's beard catches fire, put your beard to soaking.

Vente gran' gout pas gain' zoreille.
A starving belly doesn't have ears. (That is, it doesn't listen to explanations.)

Mapou tombé, cabrit mangé fé li.
The mapou tree falls, the goat eats its leaves. (When the mighty fall they are helpless even before the weak. This proverb is also used to comment on ingratitude, for the goat eats the leaves that have given him shade.)

Pas quitté bourrique pou' bat' macoute.
Don't leave the donkey to beat the saddle basket. (Don't lose your head and allow the donkey to run away.)

Zozo raide pas gainyain zoreille.
A hard penis has no ears.

Zaffai' mouton pas zaffai' cabrit.
The sheep's affair is none of the goat's business.

Fer coupé fer.
Iron cuts iron. (A person may be strong, but he is not invincible.)

Corde coupé corde.
Cord cuts cord.

Si fer pas coupé fer mashoquet pas gain' travaille.
If iron didn't cut iron, the blacksmith wouldn't have any work. (There's an antidote for everything.)

Apres danse, tambour toujour lourd.
After the dance is over the drum is always heavy.

Jou' fé tombé nans dleau c'est pas jou' li coulé.
The day a leaf falls into the water isn't the day it sinks. (The battle isn't over yet.)

Tambouyé pas capab' dansé.
The drummer can't dance. (Each person has his role. A person can't do too many things at once.)

Dé morne pas capab' rencontré, dé moune capab'.
Two mountains cannot meet, two men can. (That is, agreement is possible among people.)

Pilé pied'm ou mandé pa'don, ça pa'don wa fait pou' moin?
You step on my foot and ask my pardon, what good will the pardon do me? (If you injure me the damage is done and it is too late to apologize.)

Yun seul dwèt pas capab' mangé gombo.

A single finger can't eat okra. (Food is picked up by the fingers. A single finger is inadequate. Used in the sense of "two heads are better than one," or coöperation makes possible what a person cannot do alone.)

Tête caille cap' trompé soleil, main li pas capab' trompé lapluit.

A roof can fool the sun, but it can't fool the rain. (A person may get by in certain situations, but if he has deficiencies they will show up when the real test comes.)

Jou' malheur lait caillé cassé tête ou.

On a bad day clabbered milk breaks your head. (That is, when things are going badly even clabbered milk can hurt if it falls on you.)

Fourmi pas jam' mouri en bas barrique suc'.

The ant never dies under a barrel of sugar.

Gourd couvri gourd, or *couis couvri couis.*

Gourd covers gourd, or bowl covers bowl. (For every force there is an equal or superior force.)

4. Notes on Orthography

The problem of putting the Creole language into writing has confronted Haitian and non-Haitian scholars and writers for some time. During the past decade the problem has been an acute one for education authorities in Haiti. While there developed a consensus that teaching the largely illiterate population would have to be done in Creole and not in French, there remained a controversy about the system of orthography that should be used. One of the first attempts to teach Haitian children in their own language was made by Christian Beaulieu, a Haitian educator who worked out a written method based on traditional French orthography.[1] Subsequently, a simpler system was devised by a clergyman, the Reverend H. Ormond McConnell. Although it had numerous detractors among those who favored French orthography, it was found to be far more suitable for educational purposes. The American linguist Robert A. Hall, Jr., carried out a study, the findings of which supported the McConnell method as "perfectly phonemic and at the same time wholly practicable in that it uses only characters already available in print shops and on typewriters."[2]

Some Creole texts from Haiti and other West Indian islands, taken down by researchers and scholars, have been transcribed in the McConnell orthography, or in a modified one known as the McConnell-Laubach system. It is my opinion that although the system is admirable for teaching purposes, and adequate for recording texts for scholarly needs, it is a disadvantage to a reader who has a French vocabulary at his command but who is not familiar with the McConnell orthography. The extent to which this system can disguise a language is easily seen if it is used, for example, to transcribe Jamaican speech. The effect is identical on French words or words of French origin. The Haitian proverb "Run from the rain, fall into the big river" is written by Hall in the McConnell-Laubach orthography: *Kouri pou-lapli, tôbé nâ-grâ riviè.*[3] A system which permits recognition of the original French words would transcribe the proverb: *Couri pou' lapluit, tombé nan grand riviè.*

In this book, I have in the main used the semi-French forms. Regardless of the status of Creole as a separate language, a great part of its vocabulary is drawn from French, old or modern, and it has seemed unnecessary to disguise the connections of Creole with its antecedents. Nevertheless, I am aware that some of my orthographic choices coincide more with the McConnell-Laubach system than with the Gallic, and some may appear to belong to neither. I hope, however, that my transcribed texts will be easily read.

In most sociological and anthropological reports on Haiti which include texts the transcriptions are based on modified French orthography. Nevertheless, there have been many inconsistencies and contradictions, as there well may be within the covers of this book. One reason may be an inadequate understanding of the Creole language. A second reason can be, and often is, differences of pronunciation in various regions.

But the most significant differences occur in setting down words of non-French or probably non-French origin. One of the more noteworthy of these is *Vodoun*—a very important word without which it would be very difficult to write of Haitian life. Writers and anthropologists have spelled it in the following ways: Melville J. Herskovits—*Vodu* and *Vodun;* George Eaton Simpson—*Vodun* (after an earlier trial of *Vôdoun*); Odette Mennesson Rigaud—*Vodou;* Milo Rigaud—*Voudoo;* Robert A. Hall, Jr.—*Vaudoun;* Selden Rodman—*Vaudou;* Maya Deren—*Voudoun;* Eugène Aubin—*Vaudoux.*

Still other variations are to be found, particularly in the early literature on Haiti. In view of the general lack of agreement on this matter, it is not difficult to defend my own choice of *Vodoun* (French phonetics), which I used in previous writings.

Other important words which have numerous spellings are *hounfor* (*hunfor, humfor, hunfort, humfort, houmphor,* etc.), *hounsi* (*hunsi, hounçi,* etc.), and the names of various loa.

5. Translations of Songs in Chapter 19

Many of the Creole song texts included with the music in chapter 19 are translated and explained in earlier chapters. The following examples are translations of song texts in chapter 19 to which there is no reference elsewhere in the book.

EXAMPLE 133

> Èzilie Wèdo, *ago*, oh!
> The Creoles say like this,
> I am not in Africa any more,
> I shall do as I please!
> The Creoles say like this,
> I am not in Africa any more,
> I shall do as I please, oh!
> I bring myself,
> I take myself away,
> I do what I please, oh!

(Èzilie Wèdo is the name of a loa. She boasts that she comes to Haiti and returns to Africa whenever she wishes. The word *ago* is exclamatory and means something like "I am here.")

EXAMPLE 134

> The Forty Days [Lent], three women, three virgins,
> Prayers for the saints, prayers for the walking saints!
> Prayers for the loa Saint Antoine, oh, we ask your pardon!

EXAMPLE 135

> In Africa are loa, oh!
> *Évo évo*, hounsi kanzo!
> *Évo évo*, hounsi kanzo!
> In Africa are loa, *aïbobo!*

(*Evo évo* is ritual language. Hounsi kanzo are the servitors of the hounfor being addressed by an unidentified loa.)

EXAMPLE 136

> Achadé, oh, oh!
> Achadé, I have no mother here to speak for me!
> Achadé, oh!
> Achadé, I have no mother here to speak for me!
> Oh Achadé, oh!
> Ogoun is bad, oh!
> Achadé Papa!
> Ogoun is bad, oh!
> Etc.

(The song is addressed to the loa Achadé; it complains of the behavior of another loa, Ogoun.)

EXAMPLE 137

> Beat the drum for me!
> I shall . . . , beat the drum for me!
> Etc.
> Three times after the Angelus, oh!
> Three times after the Angelus, oh!

(This appears to be a children's game song. Three "times" after the Angelus would be three hours after six o'clock in the evening.)

EXAMPLE 138

> Liberist fell down!
> Liberist fell down! *Adié!*
> I am sending a whip for his back!
> Etc.

(A children's game song.)

EXAMPLE 139

> Adaïzo!
> *Miyenvalo* Aloko, my Loko, Adaïzo!
> *Miyenvalo* Aloko, my Loko, Adaïzo!
> *Miyenvalo* my Loko, Adaïzo!
> Etc.

(This is a song of supplication to the loa Loko. The word *miyenvalo* signifies supplication.)

EXAMPLE 140

> Ten cents is not a dollar,
> Cousin, don't take cousin, oh, cousin!

Cousin, oh, cousin, oh,
Cousin, don't take cousin, oh, cousin!

(A *gourdain* is one-quarter of a gourde, or the equivalent of five cents in United States money. *Dé gourdain* is ten cents.)

EXAMPLE 141 consists entirely of ritual language.

EXAMPLE 142

Call Damballa, call Domici, call Damballa Wèdo,
Damballa, call Damballa Wèdo, Damballa.

(Damballa and Domici are the names of loa.)

EXAMPLE 143

Ibo, I am a big man, oh!
Ibo, I am a big man, oh!
Ibo, I am the patriarch, oh, I am the patriarch, oh,
I am the chief of my house!

(Ibo is the name of a loa, from whose point of view the song is being sung. Ibo is stating his seniority in his house, or family, for there are other loa related to him. The word *grand* in Creole, as used here, is difficult to translate. It means good or elder, or both. A *grand famille* is the oldest in the extended family, and usually carries the connotation of head or chief.)

EXAMPLE 144

Ibo Ibo é, Samardi Kama!
Etc.

(Samardi Kama is the name of a loa of the Ibo family. The song consists of a repetition of his name, with variations.)

EXAMPLE 145

Ibo Ibo é, Marianni é!
Etc., with variations.

(This is a song to the loa Marianni, of the Ibo family. Except for his name, in various combinations, there are no words.)

EXAMPLE 146 is a song for the making of magic. It is entirely in ritual language.

EXAMPLE 147

Call Osange, call Labosan in the water!
Osange, oh, call Osange in the water!
Osange, oh, call Osange in the water!

(A song for the loa Osange. Literally, the song specifies Osange "in the water," but the sense is "under the water," where the loa reside.

EXAMPLE 148

Yabofé my dear, they don't need me!
I will see [enter through] the center post if they *djagwé!*
Yabofé my dear, they don't need me!
I will see the center post if they *djagwé!*
Ferei doesn't see me any more!
I will see the center post if they *djagwé!*

(Yabofé and Ferei are the names of loa. Even though addressed as "Yabofé my dear," it is Yabofé who is speaking. If one thinks of it as "Dear Yabofé says," the shifting point of view becomes less confusing. The term *djagwé* indicates a kind of tension and excitement which builds up before possessions take place. Yabofé says that if the people *djagwé* he is prepared to enter through the center post.)

EXAMPLE 149

Take me (to go), oh!
To the house, oh!

EXAMPLE 150

Damballa! Damballa!
Damballa Wèdo Damballa!
Damballa, *enhé!*
Sacred Damballa! Damballa!

(The song is an invocation to the loa Damballa. The word *enhé* is exclamatory.)

EXAMPLE 151

Ibo Lélé, oh!

(Ibo Lélé is the name of a loa.)

EXAMPLE 152

We thread our way [like a snake],
Damballa Wèdo is a snake, oh!

(The "threading" is a description of conventionalized dance movements suggesting the crawling of a snake. The loa Damballa is identified as a snake.)

EXAMPLE 153

Loko Sindé asks for wind, é!

Wind, wind, wind, Loko Sindé asks for wind!
Wind, wind, wind!

(The loa Loko Sindé calls for wind to make the sailboat move.)

EXAMPLE 154

Innocent, don't you see I'm innocent!
It is God in heaven who will judge me!
Innocent, don't you see I'm innocent!
It is God in heaven who will judge me!
Ferei's goat here looks for the water road!
The goat of the saints seeks the road to the house!
In Africa everyone is sick, oh!
Papa, I will save them!

EXAMPLE 155

Marianni, oh!
Adié, Moundongue!
Marianni!
To the other side I am passing!
I am leaving here!

(This is a song to the loa Marianni Moundongue. He says he is leaving the hounfor to return to the other side—that is, Africa.)

EXAMPLE 156

Azui, oh, I am a snake, oh!
Azui Papa, I am a snake, oh!
Azui, oh, I am a snake, oh!
Azui Papa, I am a snake, oh!
Don't you see the pouin there is spoiled?
Don't you see the pouin there is spoiled?
It has rolled into the mud!
I sound my asson!

(Azui is a loa characterized as a snake. The second part of the song is topical. It appears that a pouin, or magic bundle, has fallen into the mud and been soiled. The last line represents words of the houngan, who shakes his ritual rattle.)

EXAMPLE 157

Ah! It is I, it is I, it is I!
It is I, oh, it is Mademoiselle Ayida, it is I!
Sitting by the boat there they speak ill of us (me), oh!
It is I, oh, it is I, centerpost, it is I!

(Mademoiselle Ayida is the loa Ayida Wèdo.)

EXAMPLE 158

Ayida isn't joking, oh!
Ayida isn't joking with them!
Enla, [ritual] language, oh!
Ayida isn't joking, oh!
Ayida isn't joking with them!
Those who wish to be satisfied are satisfied!
Those who wish to be angry are angry, oh!
Ayida, oh!
Ayida isn't joking with them!

EXAMPLE 159

Long live the king and dear queen, oh!
Another misfortune, [they] talk behind my back!
Long live the king and dear queen, oh!
Another misfortune, [they] talk behind my back!
Fire, oh, heat!
Fire, oh, heat, oh!
Another misfortune, [they] talk behind my back!

EXAMPLE 160

Legba Aguator é!
Oh what loa are you?
Ago I am a loa!
Legba Aguator é!
Oh what loa are you here?
Quitti quitti yé, oh, I am a Nago loa!
Legba Aguator é! What loa are you!

EXAMPLE 161

Oh, *colico ya ya,* my little banza, *colico!*
In truth, *colico ya ya,* my little banza, *colico!*
Colico ya ya, my little banza, *colico!*
A nou paillé colico ya ya, my little banza, *colico!*

(A children's story song. The italicized parts are not translatable. The banza is a small musical instrument; currently the word is used for a banjo or fiddle, formerly it designated an instrument of African origin.)

EXAMPLE 162

Adié Compère Frog, that is not running!
Frog hops, ti dong, ti dong dong, frog hops!

(A children's song from a story about a race between the frog and the horse.)

EXAMPLE 163

> The pig says wain!
> The pig says wain, hot mama!
> Etc.
> See the pig having fun!
> *Enhé, enhé,* hot mama!

(A children's *gage* song.)

EXAMPLE 164

> Bwèment rwo!
> Adieu, Bwèment, make Bwèment walk!
> Bwèment, that's it, that's it, Bwèment!
> Make Bwèment walk!

(A children's game song.)

EXAMPLE 165

> You arrive, Rigal, you enter!
> You arrive, Rigal, you arrive!
> When Rigal turned into a large pig,
> He came to Jacmel to eat us!

(This song names a specific individual, Rigal, as having turned into a pig, like a member of the Vinbindingue Society, but it is not clear whether it is intended to be taken seriously or is merely banter.)

EXAMPLE 166

> I will zwing, oh!
> The mosquito says I will zwing, oh!
> Etc.

(Zwing is the sound the mosquito makes. The song is usually sung to the accompaniment of the *tambour maringouin,* or mosquito drum.)

EXAMPLE 167

> The small boy stands on the terrace,
> He stamps his feet *dao dao!*
> The small boy stands on the terrace,
> He stamps his feet *dao dao!*
> Oh, [unchained?] gives them *paillette,* oh!
> The small boy stands on the terrace,
> He stamps his feet *dao dao!*
> [Unchained?] gives them *paillette,* oh!
> Furiously gives them *paillette,* oh!
> Mayousse!
> Find your woman, *mayousse!*
> Mayou-yousse!

Your share, mayousse!
Find your woman, *mayousse!*
Mayou-yousse!

(*Paillette* means "all decorated up," "fancy," "in carnival regalia." It is also the name of a dance, as is *mayousse,* used here as an exclamation.)

EXAMPLE 168 was said to be in "Spanish."

EXAMPLE 169

Go to your mother's house,
Go to your mother's house,
Go to your mother's house, my dear,
Do not come and give me an argument!
Go to your mother's house, my dear,
Go to your mother's house, my dear,
Go to your mother's house, my dear,
And do not give me an argument!
Little girl who doesn't know how to wash and iron,
Go home to your mother,
Little girl who doesn't know how to wash and iron,
Go home to your mother!
Angelico, Angelico, go to your mother's house!
Angelico, Angelico, go to your mother's house!

EXAMPLE 172

Oh I'm not a mule,
Oh I'm not a mule, oh!
The farmer takes me to carry his coffee!

(A good-natured protest song of the kind often sung by coumbites.)

EXAMPLE 173 has no text. It is exclamatory throughout.

EXAMPLE 174

É Laiza, where should I go, Laiza é!
Laiza, the children are hypocrites, oh!
Etc.

EXAMPLE 175

Éwa Mambo Susan, I am cutting trees
To take away the honey!

EXAMPLE 176

Adiosa kining kining kining,
Oh I say my prayer to God to send rain!

(The first line is ritual language, but it appears to have been originally a phrase recited by the prêt' savane.)

EXAMPLE 178

> Osan, oh, Lèlè, oh!
> Osan, ah, Lèlè, oh!
> They take the asson of the loa and serve evil, oh!
> Let it sink!

(The song criticizes someone who has become a houngan and has used his powers wrongly. Osan Lèlè is the loa to whom the complaint is being addressed, or he may be the one lodging the complaint.)

EXAMPLE 179

> Farmer, call the loa for me, *ago-é!*
> Farmer, call the loa for me now,
> Call the loa for me now,
> Gèdé has engaged me!

(Gèdé is a loa. *Habitant* signifies "farmer" or "peasant" but could be translated as "countryman.")

EXAMPLE 180

> Boulicha, I arrive,
> See my misfortune!
> I will cut them, I have no knife!
> Boulicha Nago, I will cut them, *maloviê!*

(The loa Boulicha Nago announces his arrival and complains that people have mistreated him. He says he will avenge himself without a knife. *Maloviê* is ritual language.)

EXAMPLE 181

> I am going to see the hounsi bossale, oh,
> I am going to see if they are in accord with me.
> Etc.

EXAMPLE 182

> I cry honor before my loa's altar,
> Cry honor, and no one replies!
> I cry honor before my loa's altar,
> Cry honor, and no one replies!
> All who speak well [of me], I am here, I will listen, oh!
> All who speak evil [of me], I am here, I will listen to them!
> They sign my name, Allada, but they do not sign my feet,
> I ask where will they see me!

Notes

Chapter 1: *The Making of the Haitian (pp. 1-7)*

[1]The name Ganda survives in Haiti as the name of a deity.

[2]Herskovits, in *The Myth of the Negro Past* (p. 47), provides a tabulation of raw data found in the manifests recorded for slaves shipped to Virginia between 1710 and 1769: 20,564 slaves were reported shipped from "Africa," 3,652 from Gambia, 6,777 from "Guinea," 9,224 from Calabar, 3,860 from Angola, and 1,011 from Madagascar. Of those shipped from the island of Madagascar, 473 were listed as coming from Mozambique.

[3]Bartolomé de Las Casas.

Chapter 2: *Man and the Universe: Vodoun (pp. 8-18)*

[1]See Courlander, *Haiti Singing*, p. 7.

[2]Schweinfurth in *The Heart of Africa*, II, 31, says: "In Loango all exorcists and conjurors are called *ganga*." Leo Wiener, in *Africa and the Discovery of America* (Philadelphia: Innes and Sons, 1922), III, 32, reports: "Forms of *ganga* have in Bantu the meaning 'medicine' but also 'magic'—such as Nyika *ganga* and Kongo *nganga*."

[3]Gorer, *Africa Dances*, p. 129; Herskovits, *Dahomey*, II, 208 ff.

[4]From the Fon *houn-so* or *houn-su*. Among the Arada of Dahomey a *houn-su* was regarded as a spiritual wife of the deity. She was a servant of the cult temple, and in some instances a wife of the cult priest.

[5]Translated from the French of Aubin, *En Haiti*, pp. 57-59.

[6]Deren, in her *Divine Horsemen* (pp. 119 ff.), gives an excellent report of a service for Agwé in a boat at sea. Aubin (*op. cit.*, p. 108) seems to have given the first description of this service at sea for the loa Agwé.

[7]Leyburn, *The Haitian People*, p. 119.

[8]*Ibid.*, p. 123. Leyburn advances the theory that Vodoun developed during this period as a result of the vacuum left by the Church. Although the Church did in effect leave the field to the African cults, one must assume that the Arada, Congo, and other cults were already organized and possessed of great vitality before the Haitian revolution. Implicit evidence points to a continuity of cult life from the earliest days of the African on Haitian soil. There are no statistics to reveal the extent of cult membership at the end of the eighteenth century, but the content and form of Vodoun today are so overwhelmingly African that it is difficult to think of Haitian cult activity as the product of a renaissance.

Chapter 3: *The Loa: Gods of the Haitian Mountains (pp. 19-29)*

[1]The term *vodoun*, used in this precise sense, conforms to the original Fon (Dahomean) usage. The term *hounaié*, also of Fon origin, signifies "spirit" and belongs to the same root

as *hounfor, hounsi, houngénicon, hountor,* etc. *Mystère* is of obvious French origin. *Loa* is probably from the Bantu, but it could be from the Yoruba.

[2]Various methods and formulas are employed in "tying" a loa. Sometimes making the sign of the cross is regarded as adequate, or the saying of a prayer. In "The Vodun Service in Northern Haiti" (*American Anthropologist*, XLII, 242–243), George Eaton Simpson reports that the "tying" of a loa sometimes results in a contest between the individual concerned and his houngan. If the houngan wants the *maît' tête* to come in, he must neutralize the ritual barriers the "horse" has put in the way. "One procedure for bringing on possession in a servant who has tried to 'tie' his chief god is for the priest to stand in front of the person whom he suspects, make the sign of the cross, and strike him on the forehead three times with a sacrificial stone. Usually these blows are hard enough to make blood spurt. The servant then begs the pardon of the angry god, and as soon as possible he unties the knots in his handkerchief [the method he has used for 'tying' his loa]."

[3]Herskovits, *Dahomey.*

CHAPTER 4: *Death Rites (pp. 30–40)*

[1]Maurice Delafosse, *L'Ame nègre.* Translation from *Free France*, special issue No. 4, French Press and Information Service, New York, June, 1945.

[2]Leo A. Verwilghen, in booklet describing peoples of the Kwango region, accompanying *Music of the Western Congo*, recordings issued by the Ethnic Folkways Library.

[3]Willoughby, *The Soul of the Bantu*, pp. 88–89.

[4]W. M. Eiselen and I. Schapera, "Religious Beliefs and Practices," in Schapera, *The Bantu-speaking Tribes of South Africa*, p. 250.

[5]Translated from the French of Aubin, *En Haiti*, p. 212.

[6]Herskovits, *Life in a Haitian Valley*, pp. 213–214.

[7]Hall and others, *Haitian Creole*, American Anthropological Association, Memoir No. 54, pp. 188–189.

[8]Simpson, "Four Vodun Ceremonies," *Journal of American Folklore*, April–June, 1946, pp. 155–162.

[9]As translated by Courlander from Simpson's Creole text, *ibid.*, p. 156. The preceding paragraph is from p. 155.

[10]Translated by Courlander from the Creole of Simpson's text.

[11]This and the preceding paragraph are from Simpson, *op. cit.*, p. 156.

[12]These shells, as indicated elsewhere, are part of the paraphernalia of the Vodoun priest and appear to be an inheritance from the priests of the Fa cult of Dahomey. The divining shells are usually thrown on the ground in fours, and the readings depend upon combinations of "heads and tails." The manner of throwing the shells, as well as the number used, corresponds closely with the Haitian secular gambling game *mayamba* (see Appendix 2), though the purpose is obviously different. In some priestly rites in Haiti, ashes rather than the customary shells are used for divining.

[13]Simpson, *op. cit.*, p. 159.

[14]*Ibid.*, p. 161.

[15]Herskovits, *op. cit.*, p. 208.

[16]Herskovits (*ibid.*) notes that persons who die of smallpox, lightning, and certain other phenomena are not buried in coffins. Some of my informants indicated this to be their understanding also, but they said that the dead are buried without coffins for strictly economic reasons as well.

[17]Simpson, *op. cit.*, p. 161.

[18]Leyburn, *The Haitian People*, p. 156.

[19]Herskovits, *Dahomey*, I, 398.

[20]*Ibid.*, pp. 397–398.

[21]Herskovits, *Life in a Haitian Valley*, p. 214.

[22]Hall and others, *op. cit.*, p. 173.

CHAPTER 5: *Services for the Loa and the Family Ancestors (pp. 41–74)*

[1]Note that the houngan and the laplace are performing services normally performed by the *prêt' savane.*

[2]Herskovits, *Dahomey,* II, 165.

[3]Parsons, *Spirit Cult in Hayti.*

[4]Account given by Jean Ravel Pintro.

[5]Informant: Albert Kofi Prempeh, Ghana.

[6]Account given by Voluska Saintvil. A. W. Cardinall notes in his book *Tales Told in Togoland* (p. 69): "Trees are in most cases treated with respect. Before a man dare fell one for a canoe he must and invariably does sacrifice to its spirit and apologizes for the harm he is about to do it."

[7]The rite of *rafraîchi tête* is conducted periodically for a *maît' tête* after the original *lavé tête* ceremony. The purpose is to "refresh" the loa and make him content with his residence in the head of the devotee.

[8]Herskovits, *The Myth of the Negro Past,* p. 233.

[9]It is of interest to note the perseverance of traditional attitudes toward water rites in certain Negro cults in the United States. River baptism often is attended by ecstatic seizures in familiar form.

[10]Odette Mennesson Rigaud, "Notes on Two Marriages with Voudoun Loa," in Appendix A of Deren, *Divine Horsemen,* p. 264.

CHAPTER 6: *Songs of the Peristyle (pp. 75–94)*

[1]This theme is further commented on in chap. 13. Compare with the following excerpt from a Surinam song reported by Herskovits in *Suriname Folk-Lore* (p. 689):

> I have no mother there,
> I have no father there,
> I have no sister there,
> I haven't got anybody there.

CHAPTER 7: *In the Mapou Tree: Magic, Demons, and Compacts (pp. 95–104)*

[1]Simpson, "Haitian Magic," *Social Forces,* October, 1940, p. 97.

[2]Note the coincidence of the term *gris-gris* or *grigri* as used in the United States, where it has the same meaning as *mojo,* or "voodoo" charm.

[3]Simpson, "Haitian Peasant Economy," *Journal of Negro History,* October, 1940, p. 503.

[4]Herskovits, *Dahomey,* II, p. 243.

CHAPTER 8: *Mardi Gras and Rara: Jugglers, Maypoles, and Kings (pp. 105–109)*

[1]Aubin, *En Haiti,* p. 42.

[2]Marionettes of this kind have been observed in both East and West Africa and are well known in the region of Senegal. I saw a phallic marionette, virtually identical with the Haitian version, in the neighborhood of Khartoum, Sudan.

CHAPTER 9: *Land and Work (pp. 110–121)*

[1]Franklin, *The Present State of Hayti,* p. 362.

[2]Herskovits, *Dahomey,* I, 300 ff., describes Dahomean polygamous marriage in its various forms. Although Dahomean plural marriage is complex in terms of gifts, obligations, and

relations between the husband and the wife's family, it is nevertheless commonplace for men who can afford it to have more than one wife.

[3]Simpson, in "Sexual and Familial Institutions in Northern Haiti," *American Anthropologist,* October–December, 1942, p. 656, observes that in northern Haiti there are three distinct types of plaçage. "A *femme-caille* shares her mate's house, while a *maman pitite* is a woman who has born children for a man without living in his house. A *femme plaçée* does not live in her consort's house, and she has given him no children." Although none of these women has any legal rights of inheritance, Simpson notes, "moral claims to a man's property stand in descending order for these three classes of plaçées."

[4]Johnston, *The Negro in the New World.*

[5]UNESCO, *The Haiti Pilot Project,* p. 18.

[6]Simpson, "Haitian Peasant Economy," *Journal of Negro History,* October, 1940, p. 515.

[7]The group work patterns of Haiti show a common ancestry with Negro gang work patterns in the United States. While nothing as formalized as the coumbite persists among American Negroes, similarities are striking. The emphasis on rhythm, the swinging of hammers or picks in unison, the need for a singing leader, the responsive chorus, and the frequent use of some kind of percussion to keep time, all derive from a common concept of the nature of group work.

[8]Herskovits, "Some Aspects of Dahomean Ethnology," *Africa,* Vol. V (July, 1932), pp. 266–296.

[9]Cardinall, *Tales Told in Togoland* (p. 109), observes that among the Krachi people of Togoland "no man may have sexual intercourse with a woman for seven days before he goes hunting."

[10]An Ashanti story told by Rattray in *Akan-Ashanti Folk-Tales* credits the hedgehog with owning the original hoe; according to this version, the hoe escaped across the sea to the country of the white men, who then possessed the secret. Afterward, the white men brought many hoes to Ashanti.

CHAPTER 11: *Dancing and Dance Drama (pp. 126–136)*

[1]Quoted in Courlander, *Haiti Singing,* p. 73.

[2]Actually a banjo-like instrument of African provenience. The similarity of the word *banza* to *banjo* appears to be more than a coincidence.

[3]Saint-Méry, *De la danse,* as translated by Lillian Moore in "Moreau de Saint-Méry and 'Danse,'" *Dance Index,* October, 1946, p. 238.

[4]Moore, *op. cit.,* p. 238.

[5]Brandy or rum with gunpowder is sometimes drunk by persons possessed by the loa Ogoun, deity of war.

[6]Moore, *op. cit.,* p. 238.

[7]United Nations photograph no. 62065.

[8]Students of United States Negro life will recognize the word *coundjaille* as a variant of *coonjine,* a dance known on the lower Mississippi. According to one observer, Dr. Willis James of Spelman College, Atlanta, small Negro boys on the docks used to call to the boat passengers:

> "Throw me a nickel
> Throw me a dime
> If you want to see me
> Do the coonjine."

The term *coonjine* is still used to mean hand-loading of cotton bales on river boats. When this loading was done mainly by hand some years ago, the stevedores worked rhythmically in a line and sang. An old man from Louisiana testified that within his own memory the dockside *coonjine* was accompanied by makeshift drums and other percussion.

CHAPTER 12: *Songs of Complaint, Recrimination, and Gossip*
   (*pp. 137–147*)

[1]See Herskovits and Herskovits, *Suriname Folk-Lore*, pp. 23–32.

CHAPTER 13: *Comments on the Mighty: Political Songs* (*pp. 148–162*)

[1]Léger, *Haiti, Her History and Her Detractors.*

CHAPTER 15: *Secret-Society Songs* (*pp. 166–169*)

[1]Herskovits, *Dahomey*, I, p. 256.
[2]See Courlander, "Abakwa Meeting in Guanabacoa," *Journal of Negro History*, XXIX (1944), 461 ff.

CHAPTER 16: *Folk Tales: Bouki, Malice, and Jean Saute* (*pp. 170–184*)

[1]The theme of throwing magic objects upon the ground to ward off a pursuer is widely known, but the story as told in Africa has special characteristics of its own, such as the elephant hair. In Ashanti tales, the prize is the tail of the queen elephant, which is needed to serve as a coffin.
[2]This part of the tale, at least, dealing with the dragon that swallowed the sun, seems to be known in western Europe. Some reports of the tale of Grandmother's Bath have come from France.
[3]Variants of "The President Wants No More of Anansi" are widely known around the world. The story is told among the Somali of East Africa, with the legendary character Abunuwas, a Persian trickster hero, playing the title role. Anansi plays the same part in West Africa, and other trickster heroes are identified with the same adventure in India and Southeast Asia. The tale has been reported also from the West Indian island of St. Martin ("He Meets the King's Conditions," in Parsons, *Folk-Lore of the Antilles, French and English*, Part II).
[4]The fishing story narrated here, except for the chase, is found in many versions in West Africa. The second part of the tale, the pursuit, has a special Haitian flavor. Bouki chasing Malice through the cult chief's ritual grounds and the church, with Malice trying to make appropriate use of the situation, is a special delight to Haitians. The dialogue between Bouki and Malice's behind is also regarded as very humorous.
[5]Known in virtually all Negro communities in the Americas, the tale of eating the honey (or butter, pork, or lard) seems to have come to the New World by way of Africa, although it is also known in Europe.
[6]The theme of the singing tortoise (or other animal, or an object such as a skull) has appeared in folk tales ranging from West Africa through the Americas to the Far East. This Haitian variant bears a striking resemblance to a tortoise story from the Gold Coast (Ghana). In the Gold Coast variant the tortoise asks the hunter who finds him to keep his singing ability a secret, but the hunter has to tell about his discovery. When the village headman hears about it, he calls for a test. The tortoise refuses to sing, and the hunter is punished. Then the tortoise sings his song, which emphasizes the hunter's bad faith. The philosophical tone of the Haitian tortoise's songs, particularly the last one, is quite similar. The last line of the song is from a Haitian proverb.

CHAPTER 17: *Children's World: Gage Songs and Games* (*pp. 185–188*)

[1]The description of this game is from Paul, "Les Jeux à gage," *Bulletin du Bureau d'Ethnologie*, July, 1947, p. 51.

CHAPTER 18: *Musical Instruments (pp. 189–202)*

[1]Herskovits and Herskovits, *Suriname Folk-Lore*, p. 87. The stick is also known in Surinam.

[2]Informant: Joseph Lengo, Brazzaville.

[3]Library of Congress album, *Folk Music of Venezuela*.

[4]Pamphlet accompanying recordings, *Music of Equatorial Africa* (New York: Ethnic Folkways Library, 1950).

[5]See Courlander, "Musical Instruments of Cuba," *Musical Quarterly*, April, 1942, pp. 233–234.

[6]Comhaire-Sylvain, *Les Contes haitiens*, pp. 97–98.

[7]Curt Sachs, *Geist und Werden der Musikinstrumente* (Berlin, 1929), pp. 60–61.

[8]Schweinfurth, *The Heart of Africa*, I, 287.

[9]Informant: Sobihas Toré, Bamako.

[10]See Courlander, *op. cit.*, p. 239.

APPENDIX 1: *The Pantheons (pp. 335–349)*

[1]Herskovits, *Dahomey*, II, 245 ff.

[2]See Ellis, *The Ewe-speaking Peoples of the Slave Coast of West Africa*, pp. 47–49; and Herskovits, *Dahomey*, II, 245 ff.

[3]Ellis, *op. cit.*, p. 52.

[4]Herskovits, *op. cit.*, pp. 152 ff.

[5]*Ibid.*, pp. 101 ff.

[6]*Ibid.*, pp. 201 ff.

[7]Ellis, *The Yoruba-speaking Peoples of the Slave Coast of West Africa*, p. 67.

[8]Herskovits, *op. cit.*, pp. 105 ff.

[9]Ellis, *The Yoruba-speaking Peoples*, pp. 45, 67 ff.

[10]Library of Congress Recording No. 101.

[11]Ellis, *The Yoruba-speaking Peoples*, p. 47; W. R. Bascom, in Introduction to record album *Drums of the Yoruba of Nigeria* (New York: Ethnic Folkways Library, 1950).

[12]Ellis, *The Yoruba-speaking Peoples*, pp. 38 ff.

[13]Ellis, *The Ewe-speaking Peoples*, pp. 71–74; Herskovits, *op. cit.*, I, 37.

[14]Herskovits, *Life In a Haitian Valley*, p. 267.

[15]*Ibid.*, p. 280.

[16]Herskovits, *Dahomey*, II, 108–109.

[17]Ellis, *The Tshi-speaking Peoples of the Gold Coast of West Africa*, p. 68.

[18]Ellis, *The Yoruba-speaking Peoples*, pp. 79–80.

[19]Herskovits, *Dahomey*, I, 165 ff. Ellis, *The Ewe-speaking Peoples*, p. 83, says that this deity was especially important in the town of Agbome.

[20]Ellis, *The Yoruba-speaking Peoples*, pp. 45, 76.

[21]Herskovits, *Dahomey*, II, 104.

[22]Ellis, *The Ewe-speaking Peoples*, pp. 71–74.

[23]Saint-Méry, *De la dance*, p. 48.

[24]Gorer, *Africa Dances*, p. 188.

[25]Red eyes as a symbol of malevolence appear in the folklore of many Negro cultures. Our own American ballad about the gambler Stackalee states:

"The judge says, 'Stackalee, I would spare your life,
    But I know you're a bad man, I can see it in your red eyes.'"

APPENDIX 4: *Notes on Orthography (pp. 356–357)*

[1]UNESCO, *The Haiti Pilot Project,* p. 39.
[2]*Ibid.*
[3]Hall and others, *Haitian Creole,* p. 199.

Glossary

CREOLE TERMS USED IN TEXT

Abobo or *ai bobo*. A ritual singing phrase meaning "the end."

Agida. A bowed drumstick used on the middle-sized Arada drum.

Ago. An exclamation in Vodoun songs signifying "I am here."

Alfor cousin. A woven straw knapsack, from the Spanish *alforja*.

Arrête. Protective magic.

Asson. The cult priest's ritual rattle with external strikers.

Assot. A board used for striking as a percussion instrument.

Assotor. The largest drum of the Arada rites.

Badji. Altar.

Badjican. Keeper of the altar.

Baguette guinée. A grotesquely twisted drumstick.

Baka. (1) A kind of evil demon. (2) Name of the larger Pétro drum.

Baksor. Another name for the asson.

Bamboche. A "good time" dance.

Bamboché. To dance or have a good time.

Banza. Formerly a stringed instrument resembling a banjo or a trough zither. The name is now used for a fiddle.

Basse. A finger drum resembling our tambourine.

Bassin. A pool, usually referring to a special pool sacred to a deity.

Batonni. Stick dancer.

Bébé. Baby, used to designate the smallest of the Vodoun drums.

Bizango. A form of *loup-garou* seen in the form of a dog.

Bocô, or *bocor*. A cult priest, one who works with magic as well as with the loa and the dead.

Bois bourrique. A bamboo trumpet, also known as *vaccine*.

Bondieu. God.

Bossale. Wild. A *hounsi bossale* is an "untamed" hounsi; a *loa bossale*, an "untamed" loa.

Brulé zin, or *bouillé zin*. "Boiling pot," the name of a ritual in which the hounsi is elevated to the rank of kanzo.

Bula. (1) The smallest drum of the Arada rites, also called *bébé*. (2) A verb meaning to play this drum.

Bulatier. Drummer of the *bula*.

Caco. A bandit, or a mercenary soldier who hires himself out to political adventurers. Sometimes known as a *machete*. Numerous revolutions were accomplished with armies of cacos.

Caille. (1) House. (2) The Haitian version of the game known in West Africa by such names as *wari* and *mungalla*.

Canarie. A clay water vessel.

Canzo. The rank of hounsi whose loa have been "tamed" or controlled.

Capla. Another name for the houngan.

Carré. A type of *coumbite,* or community work group.

Carreau. A measure of land, about three and one-third acres.

Cata. To beat the basic rhythm for a song or dance.

Catalier. The one who *catas.*

Cayambouque. A container with a tight-fitting lid made from a large gourd or calabash.

Cha-cha, tcha-tcha, or *kwa-kwa.* A small gourd rattle used for keeping time for singers and drummers.

Chardette or *chadèk.* Grapefruit, grapefruit tree.

Chimin dleau. "The water road," by which loa come to and depart from the scene of a service.

Clairin. An alcoholic drink.

Claves. Wooden sticks which are beaten together as a percussion instrument.

Clochette. The tiny hand bell of the houngan, used along with his asson.

Cocomacaque. A kind of dwarf palm. Sticks made of this tree are called by the same name, or sometimes *baton cocomacaque.*

Connaissance. "Understanding." Used to indicate a houngan's mastery of his profession.

Corvée. A variety of coumbite, identical with the *carré.*

Couis. A bowl made from a half gourd or calabash.

Coumbite. The community work gathering which shares planting, harvesting, weeding, housebuilding, and other tasks.

Coundjaille. The name of a dance. It signifies "fast" or "agitated."

Criche. An earthen water bottle.

Debois. A marionette seen during carnival days.

Démon. A variety of malevolent demon.

Déssounin or *déssouné.* The rite of dispossessing a loa from the head of a deceased person.

Diné machete. "Machete dinner," a kind of coumbite.

Diri. Rice.

Divineur. One who divines, used for houngans.

Djab. A kind of demon.

Djablesse. A female ghost or demon.

Djaillé or *djaille.* Excitement motions, tension, in the religious dances.

Djévo. An inner room of the hounfor.

Doça. The first child born after twins, if it is a girl.

Docteur fé. Leaf doctor, pharmacologist.

Doçu. The first child born after twins, if it is a boy.

Douvant jou'. An early morning coumbite.

Drogue. A drug or magical potion.

Dundun. A name sometimes given to the smallest Arada drum.

Engagement. A compact with a demon.

Escorte. An association of loa, related or otherwise, who assist each other in their work.

Expedition. Aggressive magic in which a loa or a spirit is sent out by a houngan to work against some person.

Frete cache. Cracking the whip before the Pétro hounfor to "wake up" the loa.

Gage. Games played by children, usually with the objective of making someone "it." Sometimes used as synonymous with Last Prayers or Nine Night, when children play gage games.

Gamelle. A long wooden bowl used for washing clothes or for storing.

Garde corps. A protective charm, often worn by the owner.

Garde habitation. A charm devised to protect a household and its surroundings.

Gembo. A decorated shell devised to slide on a cord, used by houngans for divining.

Govi. An earthen or glass bottle in which loa and spirits are kept in the hounfor.

Grage. A sheet-metal scraping device used in secular music.

Grand famille. The eldest person in the family.

Grand gout. Hunger. *Moin grand gout,* I am hungry.

Grisgris. A bird used for the making of charms, etc.

Grondé. (1) Grumble. (2) Middle-sized Arada drum.

Habitant. A farmer.

Habitation. A farm.

Hounaié. Another name for a loa.

Hounfor. The Vodoun temple or shrine.

Houngan. The Vodoun priest.

Houngénicon. One of the assistants of the houngan.

Hounsi. The servitors of a loa.

Hountogri. Another name for the largest of the three Arada drums.

Hountor. (1) Spirit of the drum. (2) The largest Arada drum.

Joucoujou or *joucjou.* A battery of gourd rattles carried on a pole.

Jugement de baguette. A system of divining a guilty person through the use of a rod.

Kwa-kwa. Another name for the *tcha-tcha,* or common gourd rattle.

Lacour. A group of dwellings inhabited by related families. A hamlet.

Laillé. The swirling of the skirts in a dance.

Lambi. A conch or conch trumpet.

Lampion. The metal candelabra carried by marching bands at carnival time.

Langage. This word usually refers to the "tongues" spoken by the houngan or possessed persons during Vodoun rites. It may mean language in the ordinary sense also.

Laplace. Chief assistant of the houngan.

Lavé tête. A ritual for removing a loa from a person's head.

Loa. The spirit or deity which possesses people during religious rites.

Lou-garo. Loup-garou.

Lutin. The spirit of a child that died before receiving baptism.

Mabouya. A small ground lizard.

Machete. The long all-purpose work knife. See *Caco.*

Magie. Magic.

Maît' conte. A "master" or professional storyteller.

Maît' tête. The loa who resides in one's head.

Major jonc. The baton or machete juggler of the Rara troupe.

Makanda. A specific kind of aggressive magic.

Maljok. Evil eye.

Mambo. Vodoun priestess.

Mambo caille. One of the assistants of the houngan.

Mangé. (1) To eat. (2) A feast.

Mangé assotor. Feast for the assotor drum.

Mangé diri or *gouté diri.* A rice harvest festival.

Mangé loa. A feast for one or more loa.

Mangé marassa. Feast for twins.

Mangé mort. Feast for the dead.

Mangé yam. A yam harvest festival.

Manman. (1) Mother. (2) The largest of the Arada drums.

Marassa. (1) Twins. (2) The spirit of twins.

Marimba, malimba, manimba, marimbula. The modern Haitian version of the African thumb piano.

Marré loa. To "tie" a loa, that is, to prevent him from entering one's head.

Mayamba. A gambling game using four chips for heads and tails combinations.

Mayo or *manyo.* A special shirt worn to counteract the evil eye or some other magic.

Mayoyo. A battery of rattles carried on a tall pole in some Congo services.

Metté n'âme. The process of restoring a soul that has been taken from a body.

Morts en bas dleau. The spirits of the dead "below the water."

Moune. Man, person.

Moyen. The middle-sized Arada drum.

Mwé, moin, or *m'.* I, me.

Mystère. Another name for *loa.*

Nanchon. Nation. Usually refers to a "nation" of deities, such as Anago, Ibo, and Pétro.

Ochan. A musical salute to the loa, or to an important personage present at a service.

Ogan. The metal percussion device that accompanies the Arada drums. Traditionally, a forged iron bell, but it may be a hoe blade or any other piece of resonant iron or steel.

Ouanga. Aggressive magic.

Ouvri bayè pou' moin. "Open the gate for me (us)." Addressed to the loa Legba, to make contact with the other deities possible.

Papaloi. A term sometimes used to designate the Vodoun priest. A corruption of the Yoruba *babalao.*

Passage d'alliance. A method for divining a guilty person by means of a ring suspended on a string.

Passé. (1) Surpass. (2) Pass.

Passé balé. A method for divining a guilty person by the use of a specially prepared chair.

Pavillon. The court of the hounfor.

Payé sorti. The gift that is given to a Rara troupe when it stops to play before a man's house. Literally: "Pay-to-go."

Pé. Altar.

Peristyle. The roofed court of the hounfor.

Pierre-loa. The stone in which a loa is believed to reside.

Pierre-manman. A large, rounded stone regarded as a super loa stone and a protector of the *habitation.*

Pingé. A form of wrestling that is seen at Rara time.

Piquette. A spear or sharpened stick.

Piston. Any instrument resembling a trumpet.

Plaçage. The system of polygamy practiced by some peasants.

Plaçée. A second or third wife of a man under the system of *plaçage.* The first wife may be *plaçée* also.

Po'teau mitan or *po'teau planté.* The center post of the hounfor court, around which most of the rites take place.

Pot tête. Another name for *govi.*

Pouin. A form of protective magic.

Prêt' savane. "Priest of the plains," or "bush priest." This may have been originally *pret' savant,* "learned priest." The functionary who reads or recites Catholic prayers in a Vodoun service.

Rara, or *lara.* The rural Lenten festival. The word *rara* is also used for a wooden noisemaker.

Refraichi tête. A ritual bath for refreshing the loa in one's head.

Reposoir. A small area, sometimes surrounded by a low wall, sacred to a deity.

Retiré n'âme. The act of removing the soul from a body.

Revenant. The troublesome spirit of a dissatisfied dead person.

Roi Lwalwadi. "King of Lwalwadi." Title given to the leader of a Rara troupe.

Ronde. A form of coumbite.

Rubaniers. Maypole dancers.

Samba. The singing leader of a coumbite.

Servi dé main. To serve with two hands. That is, to work with the loa of the Arada and Pétro "nations," or to work with the loa and with aggressive magic at the same time.

Simidor. The singing leader of a coumbite.

Siro'. A sweet drink.

Société. A society. Refers usually to the association gathered around a cult temple, or an agricultural work group.

Tafia. An alcoholic drink.

Taille bas. "Low hips." A dance posture.

Tambour. Drum.

Tambourine. "Mosquito drum." A miniature two-headed drum.

Tambour maringouin. An earth bow, or a portable model of the earth bow.

Tambouyé. Drummer.

Tchancy. A metal rattle used in Rara and in some Congo rites.

Ti baka. (1) Little demon. (2) Name of the small Pétro drum.

Ti kanmbo or *ganbo*. Bamboo stampers, used as a substitute for drums.

Tonnelle. The covering of the hounfor court.

Trois-sept. A card game.

Tuyé-lèvé. Witchcraft in which the practitioner kills someone, then takes him out of the grave, restores him to life, and makes him a servant or slave.

Tymbale. A large cylindrical drum with heads at both ends.

Vaccine. A bamboo trumpet; also known as *bois bourrique*.

Vèvè. The meal or flour drawing made by the houngan on the ground.

Vodoun. (1) Rites and beliefs of the Arada "nation." (2) Rites and beliefs of all the cults except those of non-African origin. (3) A loa.

Von-von. A bull-roarer.

Wari. A large inedible red bean or seed. Also the name of a game in which *wari* beans are used as playing pieces. See *Caille*.

Woy, waille. An exclamation.

Yamingan. A curative medicine bundle.

Zandolite. A small climbing lizard.

Zange. Another name, used regionally, for loa.

Zeaubeaups. According to lore, a society of cannibals.

Zin. The iron pot used in Vodoun ritual. It may, on occasion, be of clay.

Zombie. A creature supposedly disinterred from the grave, dispossessed of its soul, and made to work for a malefactor.

Zozo bef. A leather whip used on horses and burros. Literally "bull penis."

Bibliography and Discography

BIBLIOGRAPHY

AUBIN, EUGÈNE. *En Haiti*. Paris, 1910.

BARKER, W. H., and CECILIA SINCLAIR. *West Africa Folk-Tales*. London: G. G. Harrap & Company, 1917.

BASCOM, WILLIAM R. "The Relationship of Yoruba Folklore to Divining," *Journal of American Folklore*, April–June, 1943.

———. "West Africa and the Complexity of Primitive Cultures," *American Anthropologist*, January–March, 1948.

———. "The Focus of Cuban Santeria," *Southwestern Journal of Anthropology*, Spring, 1950.

———. "The Yoruba in Cuba," *Nigeria*, No. 37, 1951.

CARDINALL, A. W. *Tales Told in Togoland*. London: Oxford University Press, 1931.

COMHAIRE-SYLVAIN, SUZANNE, *Les Contes haitiens*. Wetteren, Belgium, 1936.

COURLANDER, HAROLD. *Haiti Singing*. Chapel Hill: University of North Carolina Press, 1939.

———. "Haiti's Political Folksongs," *Opportunity*, April, 1941.

———. "Musical Instruments of Haiti," *Musical Quarterly*, July, 1941.

———. "Musical Instruments of Cuba," *Musical Quarterly*, April, 1942.

———. "Profane Songs of the Haitian People," *Journal of Negro History*, July, 1942.

———. *Uncle Bouqui of Haiti*. New York: William Morrow & Company, 1942.

———. "Gods of the Haitian Mountains," *Journal of Negro History*, July, 1944.

———. "Abakwa Meeting in Guanabacoa," *Journal of Negro History*, October, 1944.

———. "The Loa of Haiti: New World African Deities," *Miscelanea de estudios dedicados a Fernando Ortíz por sus discipulos, colegas y amigos*. Havana, 1955.

———. Introduction to *Negro Folk Music of Alabama* (record albums). New York: Ethnic Folkways Library, 1956.

DENIS, LORIMER. *Quelques aspects de notre folklore musical*. Port-au-Prince: Bureau d'Ethnologie, 1950.

———. *Le Musée du Bureau d'Ethnologie d'Haiti*. Port-au-Prince: Bureau d'Ethnologie, 1953.

———. "Mariages mystiques dans le vodou," *Bulletin du Bureau d'Ethnologie*, Port-au-Prince, January, 1958.

DENIS, LORIMER, and EMMANUEL C. PAUL. *Essai d'organographie haitienne.* Port-au-Prince: Bureau d'Ethnologie, 1948.

DELAFOSSE, MAURICE. *L'Ame nègre.* Paris, 1922.

DEREN, MAYA. *Divine Horsemen.* New York: Thames and Hudson, 1953.

DORSAINVIL, J. C. *Vodou et névrose.* Port-au-Prince, 1931.

ELLIS, A. B. *The Tshi-speaking Peoples of the Gold Coast of West Africa.* London, 1887.

————. *The Ewe-speaking Peoples of the Slave Coast of West Africa.* London, 1890.

————. *The Yoruba-speaking Peoples of the Slave Coast of West Africa.* London, 1894.

FAINE, JULES. *Philologie creole.* Port-au-Prince, 1936.

FRANKLIN, JAMES. *The Present State of Hayti.* London, 1828.

GORER, GEOFFREY. *Africa Dances.* New York: Alfred A. Knopf, 1935.

HALL, ROBERT A., with the collaboration of Suzanne Comhaire-Sylvain, H. Ormonde McConnell, and Alfred Métraux. *Haitian Creole.* American Anthropological Association, Memoir No. 54, April–June, 1953.

HERSKOVITS, MELVILLE J. "Some Aspects of Dahomean Ethnology," *Africa,* Vol. V, No. 3, July, 1932.

————. *Life in a Haitian Valley.* New York: Alfred A. Knopf, 1937.

————. *Dahomey, an Ancient West African Kingdom.* New York: J. J. Augustin, 1938. 2 vols.

————. *The Myth of the Negro Past.* New York: Harper & Brothers, 1941.

HERSKOVITS, MELVILLE J., and FRANCES S. HERSKOVITS. *Suriname Folk-Lore.* New York: Columbia University Press, 1936.

HERZOG, GEORGE. *Jabo Proverbs from Eastern Liberia.* London: Oxford University Press, 1936.

HONORAT, MICHEL LAMARTINIÈRE. *Les Danses folklorique haitiennes.* Port-au-Prince: Bureau d'Ethnologie, 1955.

HYPPOLITE, MICHELSON PAUL. *A Study of Haitian Life.* Port-au-Prince, 1954.

JOHNSON, SIR HARRY. *The Negro in the New World.* London, 1910.

LÉGER, JACQUES-NICOLAS. *Haiti, Her History and Her Detractors.* New York and Washington, 1907.

LEYBURN, JAMES G. *The Haitian People.* New Haven: Yale University Press, 1941.

LISCANO, JUAN. *Folklore y Cultura.* Caracas: Avila Gráfica (1950).

MAXIMILIEN, LOUIS. *Le Vodou Haitien.* Port-au-Prince, 1945.

MERRIAM, ALAN P., with the assistance of Sara Whinery and B. G. Fred. "Songs of a Rada Community in Trinidad," *Anthropos,* Vol. LI, 1956.

MÉTRAUX, ALFRED. "The Concept of Soul in Haitian Vodu," *Southwestern Journal of Anthropology,* Vol. II. No. 1, 1946.

————. Translated by Hugo Charteris. *Voodoo in Haiti.* New York: Oxford University Press, 1959.

MEYEROWITZ, EVA L. R. *The Sacred State of the Akan.* London: Faber and Faber, 1951.

MOORE, JOSEPH G., and GEORGE E. SIMPSON. "A Comparative Study of Acculturation in Morant Bay and West Kingston, Jamaica," *Zaire,* Nos. 9–10, November–December, 1957.

MOORE, LILLIAN. "Moreau de Saint-Méry and 'Danse,'" *Dance Index,* October, 1946.

ORIOL, JACQUES, LEONCE VIAUD, and MICHEL AUBOURG. *Le Mouvement folklorique en Haiti.* Port-au-Prince, 1952.

ORTIZ, FERNANDO. *Los negros brujos.* Madrid, 1906.

————. *Los cabildos afrocubanos.* Havana, 1916.

——. *Los negros esclavos.* Havana, 1916.

——. *La clave xilofonica de la musica cubana.* Havana, 1935.

——. "La musica sagrada de los negros yoruba en Cuba," *Estudios afrocubanos,* Havana, 1938.

——. *La africanía de la música folklórica de Cuba.* Havana, 1951.

——. *Los bailes y el teatro de los negros en el folklore de Cuba.* Havana, 1951.

——. *Los instrumentos de la música afrocubana.* Havana, 1952 and 1955. 5 vols.

PARSONS, ELSIE CLEWS. *Spirit Cult in Hayti.* Paris, 1928.

——. *Folk-Lore of the Antilles, French and English.* Memoirs of the American Folk-Lore Society, Vol. XXVI, 1936.

PAUL, EMMANUEL C. "Les Jeux à gage," *Bulletin du Bureau d'Ethnologie,* Port-au-Prince, July, 1947.

PRICE-MARS, JEAN. *Ainsi parla l'oncle.* Port-au-Prince, 1928.

RATTRAY, R. S. *Akan-Ashanti Folk-Tales.* Oxford: The Clarendon Press, 1931.

RIGAUD, MILO. *La Tradition voudoo et le voudoo Haitien.* Paris: Éditions Niclaus, 1953.

RIGAUD, ODETTE MENNESSON. "The Feasting of the Gods in Haitian Vodu," *Primitive Man,* XIX, Nos. 1 and 2, January and April, 1946.

——. "Cérémonie en l'honneur de marinette," *Bulletin du Bureau d'Ethnologie,* Port-au-Prince, July, 1947.

——. "Étude sur le culte des marassas en Haiti," *Zaire,* June, 1952.

——. "Vodou Haitien: Quelques notes sur ses réminiscences africaines," *Mémoires de l'Institut Français d'Afrique Noire.* Ifan, Dakar, 1953.

RODMAN, SELDEN. *Haiti: The Black Republic.* New York: The Devin-Adair Company, 1954.

SAINT-MÉRY, MOREAU DE. *Description topographique, physique, civile, politique, et historique de la partie Française de l'Isle de St. Domingue.* Philadelphia, 1797–1798.

——. *De la danse.* Parma, 1801.

SCHAPERA, I. *The Bantu-speaking Tribes of South Africa.* London: George Routledge & Sons, 1946.

SCHWEINFURTH, GEORG. *The Heart of Africa.* New York, 1874. 2 vols.

SIMPSON, GEORGE EATON. "The Vodun Service in Northern Haiti," *American Anthropologist,* April–June, 1940.

——. "Haitian Magic," *Social Forces,* October, 1940.

——. "Haitian Peasant Economy," *Journal of Negro History,* October, 1940.

——. "Sexual and Familial Institutions in Northern Haiti," *American Anthropologist,* October–December, 1942.

——. "The Belief System of Haitian Vodun," *American Anthropologist,* XLII, 1945.

——. "Four Vodun Ceremonies," *Journal of American Folklore,* April–June, 1946.

——. "Acculturation in Northern Haiti," *Journal of American Folklore,* October–December, 1951.

——. "Peasant Children's Games in Northern Haiti," *Folk-Lore,* LXV, September, 1954.

TALBOT, P. AMAURY. *The Peoples of Southern Nigeria.* London, 1926.

UNITED NATIONS, MISSION OF TECHNICAL ASSISTANCE TO HAITI. *Mission to Haiti: Report.* Lake Success, N.Y., 1949.

UNITED NATIONS EDUCATIONAL, SCIENTIFIC AND CULTURAL ORGANIZATION. *The Haiti Pilot Project, Phase One.* Publication No. 796, Paris, 1951.

VICTOR, RENÉ. *Les Voix de nos rues.* Port-au-Prince, 1949.

WILLOUGHBY, W. C. *The Soul of the Bantu.* London: Student Christian Movement, 1928.

DISCOGRAPHY

A Selective Listing of Haitian Music on Records

Voices of Haiti (LP), recorded in Haiti by Maya Deren. Electra. Five examples of ritual songs and dances recorded near Pétionville and Croix des Missions. On the whole, superior material. The first two pieces on the record, which are documentary, are particularly outstanding.

Haiti Dances (78 r.p.m.). Wax. Some of the information provided on the album cover is inaccurate, but the records are worth listening to. Not "documentary," but performed by a good modern folk-dance group.

Drums of Haiti (LP), recorded in Haiti by Harold Courlander. Ethnic Folkways Library. Thirteen examples of drums and other percussion instruments, demonstrating the rhythms of eleven different dances. Contains some of the selections transcribed in this volume.

Folk Music of Haiti (LP), recorded in Haiti by Harold Courlander. Ethnic Folkways Library. Eighteen examples of secular and religious music, work songs, songs of social criticism, carnival music, game songs, and a "spirit conversation" by a cult priest. Contains some of the selections transcribed in this volume.

Songs and Dances of Haiti (LP), recorded in Haiti by Harold Courlander, with the exception of two selections recorded by Marshall Stearns. Ethnic Folkways Library. One side of the record contains cult songs and dances as performed by an authenic but rehearsed group; the other side has a song by a minstrel, a "jazz" Meringue, and two excellent documentary carnival recordings. Contains some of the selections transcribed in this volume.

Calypso and Meringues (LP). Folkways. One side of this disc contains Haitian material, "jazz" Meringues played by village professionals, recorded by Harold Courlander.

Haitian Piano (LP), recorded in Haiti by Harold Courlander. Folkways. Eight examples of old-style salon Meringues, etc., performed by Fabre Duroseau and the Duroseau trio.

Haitian Dances (LP). Eight arrangements of folk tunes, played on the guitar by Frantz Casséus. Folkways.

Haitian Folk Songs (LP), sung by Lolita Cuevas, guitar accompaniment by Frantz Casséus. Folkways. Excellent concert performance of traditional Haitian folk songs.

Index